D0933444

ETHICS AFTER THE HOLOCAUST:

PERSPECTIVES, CRITIQUES, AND RESPONSES

OTHER PARAGON BOOKS ON THE HOLOCAUST

Holocaust: Religious and Philosophical Implications
Edited by John K. Roth and Michael Berenbaum, 1989

Different Voices: Women and the Holocaust
Edited by Carol Rittner and John K. Roth, 1993

Against All Hope: Resistance in the Nazi Concentration Camps 1938-1945
By Herman Langbein, Edited by Harry Zohn, 1994

The Road to Hell: Recollection of the Nazi Death March
Written by Joseph Freeman and Edited by Donald Schwartz, 1998

Courage to Remember: Interviews on the Holocaust
Kinue Tokudome, 1999

ETHICS AFTER THE HOLOCAUST:

PERSPECTIVES, CRITIQUES, AND RESPONSES

John K. Roth, Editor
Leonard Grob
Peter J. Haas
David H. Hirsch
David Patterson
Didier Pollefeyt

PARAGON HOUSE
St. Paul, Minnesota

Published in the United States of America by

Paragon House
2700 University Avenue West
St. Paul, Minnesota 55114

Cover design by Arie Galles

Library of Congress Catalog-in-Publication Data

Ethics after the Holocaust: perspectives, critiques, and responses /
John K. Roth, editor.
    p.   cm.
    Includes bibliographical references and index.
    ISBN 1-55778-771-9 (alk. paper)
    1. Holocaust, Jewish (1939-1945)—Causes.   2. National socialism.
3. Holocaust, Jewish (1939-1945)—Moral and ethical aspects.
4. Levinas, Emmanuel.   5. Heidegger, Martin, 1889-1976—Views on
national socialism.   6. Ethics, Modern—20th century.   I. Roth, John K.
D804.3.E89   1999
940.53'18—DC21   99-10543
                                                                        CIP

10 9 8 7 6 5 4 3 2 1

For current information about all releases from Paragon House,
visit the web site at http://www.paragonhouse.com

To the Memory
of
Harry James Cargas
(1932-1998)

... My companion, my familiar friend, with whom I kept
pleasant company ...

—Psalms 55:13

The Holocaust demands interrogation and calls everything into question. Traditional ideas and acquired values, philosophical systems and social theories—all must be revised in the shadow of Birkenau. Novelists and politicians, poets and moralists, theologians and scholars—all feel compelled to examine their consciences with regard to the Holocaust. Not to do so would mean to live a lie.

—Elie Wiesel

CONTENTS

Introduction

Ethics after Auschwitz

John K. Roth

At six-week intervals in 1943, an Auschwitz truck went to Dessau, Germany. It returned with hermetically-sealed tin canisters of Zyklon B, the commercial name for the bluish hydrogen cyanide pellets that asphyxiated more than a million Jews in that killing center's gas chambers during the Holocaust.

A powerful pesticide developed during World War I, Zyklon B was used to combat contagious diseases by fumigating lice-infested buildings. At first, it mainly served those purposes at Auschwitz, where overcrowding, malnutrition, and poor sanitation made dysentery, typhoid fever, and especially typhus constant threats. By the late summer of 1941, however, much more destructive uses for Zyklon B had been found. Experiments on Soviet prisoners of war confirmed that Zyklon B's vaporizing pellets offered a particularly reliable and efficient way to advance what the Nazis called the "final solution."

Two German companies—the Deutsche Gesellschaft für Schädlingsbekämpfung mbH (abbreviated DEGESCH, the German Vermin-combating Corporation, a subsidiary of I. G. Farben) and Tesch and Stabenow Verlag—profited immensely by supplying Zyklon B to the SS. They even modified it for Auschwitz by removing the special odor that ordinarily warned people about the product's deadly presence.

In 1942, Auschwitz used 8.2 tons of Zyklon B. The tonnage for 1943 was 13.4. Conventional fumigation took relatively little. Most of the Zyklon B was poured into gas chambers packed with Jews. Once exposed to air, the pellets produced lethal gas. Minutes later the human victims were dead.[1]

The four paragraphs you have just read barely scratch the surface of the unprecedented, overwhelming, and uniquely destructive event that is called the Holocaust or the Shoah. But they are more than enough to make us wonder: How could such things happen? Why did they take place? Where were the ethical traditions and teachings that seemingly should have kept such things from occurring? This book does not presume to answer those questions once and for all. No book—indeed nothing that human minds, or perhaps even God's, can provide—would be sufficient to accomplish that task. This book does try, however, to respond to those issues and especially to the third one, which promotes inquiry not only about morality's failures during the Holocaust but also about ethics after Auschwitz.

Books have histories, and this one is no exception. How it came to be accounts for the particular form it takes, a form emphasizing dialogue among six Holocaust scholars who began working together in 1996. Several months before we met for the first time, each of us had responded to the initial call for proposals to participate in the Goldner Holocaust Symposium, which takes place biennially under the leadership of Leonard Grob and Henry Knight at Fairleigh Dickinson University's Wroxton College campus in Oxfordshire, England.

The call for proposals indicated that the 1996 Goldner Symposium would have a practical orientation. Based on Holocaust study, it would encourage participants to address questions such as: How are we to respond in word and deed to a radically transformed world, the post-Holocaust world in which "business as usual" no longer applies? How are we to use our learning from the Shoah to face, responsibly, the genocidal potentials inherent in our own world? The symposium, moreover, would have a limited number of participants—about thirty-five—and it would be designed to stimulate ongoing and sustained collegial work, which would be grounded in small "working groups" where shared concerns could be found. An additional expectation, which this book helps to fulfill, was that the work initiated in the small groups would develop and have some concrete results. Linked by our mutual interest in post-Holocaust ethics, the six contributors to this book formed one of those small "working groups" at Wroxton College in the summer of 1996. Here is a word of introduction about each of us.

Along with his symposium co-director, Henry Knight of Tulsa University, Leonard Grob is a special leader whose gentle spirit and organizational efficiency make a brilliant combination. Without him, neither our group nor this book would exist. Grob is professor of philosophy and coordinator of philosophical studies at Fairleigh Dickinson University. He has written a memoir, "Goodbye Father," published in *Judaism* (Spring 1990), which describes his "roots journey" to Ukraine in 1989. His experience in uncovering the history of the destruction of his father's family during the Holocaust has led him into the field of Holocaust studies. Grob's writings on the Holocaust are supplemented and informed by his special interest in and publications about Martin Buber and Emmanuel Levinas.

Peter J. Haas, another member of our Wroxton "ethics group," is an ordained Reform rabbi and professor of Jewish thought and literature in the religious studies department at Vanderbilt University. Especially interested in the relationship between science and religious ethics in the contemporary world, Haas is the author of *Morality after Auschwitz*, a ground breaking study that explores what he calls the "Nazi ethic." Haas's views on that topic drive much of the discussion found in this book.

Professor emeritus of English and American literature and Judaic studies at Brown University, David H. Hirsch has written extensively on literary topics, including the literature of the Holocaust. His 1991 book, *The Deconstruction of Literature: Criticism after Auschwitz*, is a fine example of his work. With Roslyn Hirsch, he has also translated Holocaust texts from Polish and Yiddish, including Sara Nomberg-Przytyk's *Auschwitz: True Tales from a Grotesque Land* and Gusta Davidson Draenger's *Justina's Narrative.*

David Patterson holds the Bornblum Chair of Excellence in Judaic Studies at The University of Memphis. In addition to his many articles on topics in philosophy, Judaism, education, and Holocaust studies, his Holocaust-related books include *The Shriek of Silence* (1992), *Pilgrimage of a Proselyte: From Auschwitz to Jerusalem* (1993), *When Learned Men Murder* (1996), *Sun Turned to Darkness* (1998), and *Along the Edge of Annihilation* (1999).

Deeply influenced by the great French Jewish thinker, Emmanuel Levinas, whose thought informs a considerable part of this book's discussion, Didier Pollefeyt teaches moral theology and courses on Jewish-Christian relations at the Katholieke Universiteit Leuven, Belgium, where he serves on the theology faculty. Already widely published in Europe and increasingly well-known in English-speaking countries as well, Pollefeyt is the youngest scholar in our Wroxton group and one who is destined to make a lasting, positive mark on post-Holocaust ethics and religious thought.

It has been my privilege to serve as this book's editor, as well as to be a contributing member of the Wroxton "ethics group." Since 1966, I have taught at Claremont McKenna College, where I am the Russell K. Pitzer Professor of Philosophy. Combining interests in American philosophy and religious thought with work on the Holocaust that began in the late 1960s, my Holocaust-related books include *A Consuming Fire* (1979), *Approaches to Auschwitz: The Holocaust and Its Legacy* (1987, with Richard L. Rubenstein), *Holocaust: Religious and Philosophical Implications* (1989, edited with Michael Berenbaum), *Different Voices: Women and the Holocaust* (1993, edited with Carol Rittner), and *Private Needs, Public Selves* (1997).

Our Wroxton discussions in June 1996 committed us to the writing project that led to this book. Knowing that we would meet again during the summer of 1998, we each agreed to write a substantive essay that would set forth fundamental concerns about ethics after Auschwitz. Then we would each respond to one another, a step followed by each writer's reply to the critiques he received. We hope that our readers will find these perspectives, critiques, and responses to be as challenging as they were for us to produce in dialogue with each other.

Before we left the first Goldner Holocaust Symposium in 1996, the six of us realized that our thinking had converged on several basic views. We concurred that they ought to govern the inquiry and writing we planned to do. Thus, our book builds upon and amplifies the following themes:

1. Auschwitz was not only an assault on millions of innocent human beings—Jews first and foremost among them—but also an assault on goodness itself. This assault took place in the heart of a civilization that was Christian and modern. Germany, one of the

most advanced nations of Europe, was among the leaders of that civilization. Therefore, we must speak of post-Holocaust ethics.

2. After Auschwitz, the most difficult questions for ethicists include: How do ordinary people come to do extraordinary evil? What, if anything, can ethics do to check such evil? Or put otherwise, how did human beings who had previously lived unexceptional and inoffensive lives end up watching, condoning, or inflicting continuous acts of intense cruelty and unprecedented genocidal destruction against the aged, women, children, and generally helpless people who engaged in no acts of provocation and committed no crimes, as *crime* is defined by advanced societies?

3. After Auschwitz, the simple reaffirmation of pre-Holocaust ethics will not do anymore, because the Western religious, philosophical, and ethical traditions have shown themselves to be problematic. Far from preventing the Holocaust, they may have been seriously implicated in that catastrophe.

4. The Holocaust is not so much the end of ethics as it is the proof that ethics can be misused and even perverted into pseudo-ethics. Auschwitz shows the vulnerability of ethics—not only then but also now; not only in the Nazis' hands but also in ours.

5. Ethics after Auschwitz must be characterized by openness to the Other. Any ethical system that thinks it has the solution to every problem has the potential to be genocidal. Ethics must no longer be a closed system but a way of living (thinking, feeling, doing) in openness to the vulnerability of others, especially the defenseless.

6. Ethics needs the support of politics, lest it be ineffectual. Politics also needs ethics, lest it waste human life.

7. The ethical study of the Holocaust should not only be a particular discipline, but also it should penetrate the heart of every other discipline—from education to science, from medicine to theology, from the arts to philosophy, from politics and law to everyday life.

Since six of us have contributed to this book, a large number of people—too many to mention by name—deserve our thanks for helping to make its writing and publication possible. Support from family members and encouragement from all the members of the Goldner Holocaust Symposium have been as generous as they are important. We particularly thank Hank Knight, the symposium's co-director, for his attention to detail, his unflagging enthusiasm, and his music. We are also immensely grateful to Arie A. Galles, another member of the Goldner Symposium, who is the son of Holocaust survivors and a distinguished artist who explores Holocaust-related themes. Much interested in what this book has to say, he generously provided the art and design for its cover. Working with wartime aerial reconnaissance photographs that show Nazi concentration and death camps, Galles has created *Fourteen Stations*, a suite of large-format charcoal drawings. He calls *Fourteen Stations* his "Kaddish for all Shoah victims." Fittingly, *Auschwitz-Birkenau*, his Station #1, surrounds and binds the pages of this book, whose contents are defined as much by the topography that Galles has sketched as by the words that the six essayists have written.

Our appreciation also goes to Dr. Nicholas D. J. Baldwin, director of Wroxton College, whose hospitality and humor always make the college a delightful place to work. At Paragon House, Gordon Anderson and Laureen Enright provided the editorial guidance we needed. Most of all, we are indebted to Pastora Goldner, the remarkable woman who makes it possible for the Wroxton group to meet and meet again. Her vision guides us. Her generosity sustains us. Her courageous example inspires us. Finally, this book is dedicated to the memory of Harry James Cargas. Although he was not a member of the Goldner Symposium, his friendship and pioneering work in Holocaust studies encouraged our reflection and writing. As we mourn his death, we also express respect and thanks for his magnificent life.

Note

[1]This brief discussion about Zyklon B is informed by Peter Hayes, *Industry and Ideology: I. G. Farben in the Nazi Era* (Cambridge: Cambridge University Press, 1993), 361-63, and Raul Hilberg, *The Destruction of the European Jews*, 3 vols., revised and definitive edition (New York: Holmes and Meier, 1985), 3:885-92.

CHAPTER ONE

Emmanuel Levinas and the Primacy of Ethics in Post-Holocaust Philosophy

Leonard Grob

The silence of Western philosophy with regard to the events of 1933-1945 is deafeningly loud. The discipline that, ideally, reflects on the nature of all that is—including the nature of human nature—has largely failed to speak out regarding the Holocaust, which was an attack on the very concept of humanity. In the wake of what has been called a transformational event, philosophers have most often gone about their business, "business as usual." Aside from the German Jewish thinker Hannah Arendt, no major philosopher, past or present, has taken it upon himself or herself to make the Holocaust a central element of an ethical analysis. How are we to explain this phenomenon?

I attempt here to sketch the beginnings of such an explanation. I claim that it is no accident that academic philosophy has shied away from a confrontation with the Holocaust. Drawing on the work of the contemporary French Jewish thinker, Emmanuel Levinas, I contend that ethical thinking has always occupied a secondary or derivative place in the history of Western thought. For Levinas, philosophy in the West is fundamentally ontology, the endeavor to grasp the nature of Being itself. For Levinas, ontology is the enterprise of illuminating the world in its totality; the essential task of the philosopher is to *possess* the world through knowing it.

In this fundamental thrust *to explain all that is*, traditional philosophy has embraced the "I" as the fundamental reference point for the comprehension of the totality. Throughout the history of Western thought, the solitary subject is seen to appropriate whatever exists by giving it its meaning: "In the last analysis," Levinas claims, "*everything* is at my disposal, even the stars if I but reckon them...."[1] In this mode of philosophizing, the self is "regal," "unconditioned," "sovereign," desirous of incorporating within itself the whole of what-can-be-thought.

If "everything is at my disposal," how am I to relate to the other person who, like me, should exist as a sovereign being in his or her own right? Would not such an equally "regal" being warrant the designation of a full partner in the task of comprehending the world? Is she or he not my co-subject? For Levinas, philosophy-as-ontology has never been able to answer these questions in the affirmative. In this tradition, the other person, like any other existent, must be able-to-be-encompassed within the categorizations of my mind. As the *object* of my knowing, the other can never meet me as a *co-subject*. The other is always, on principle, "for-me," and thus can never be free of the meanings I inevitably ascribe to him or her. The other person is, for example, kind, dull, beautiful, my enemy, my ally, a mere acquaintance. For Levinas, philosophy has always had an "allergy" to an other-as-truly-Other,[2] one who would remain truly independent of my spheres of meaning.

Philosophy can never see the Other as untouched by the objectifying forces of my consciousness and thus as a being to whom I can have properly *ethical* obligations. If others are constituted as part of my meaning-giving system, how can it be that I have a duty to act in one fashion or another toward them? If the Other is merely part of my sphere of comprehension, the notion of obligation—a key term in most ethical systems—loses its essential meaning. Philosophy-as-ontology can never articulate an ethics in any fundamental sense of that word. It thus cannot offer a radical ethical critique of the events of the Holocaust, as it cannot offer a radical ethical critique of *any* appropriative acts on my part directed toward others. If ethics is merely a derivative branch of philosophy-as-ontology—if it is not freed from the taint of egoist ambition—any so-called "ethical" critique of the events of the Holocaust can never be critical enough.

Yet more needs to be said. Philosophical thinking, as we have seen, is linked to the activity of grasping, of seizing. Such thinking, in Levinas's words, is an "activity...independent...of any finality exterior to it, an activity which is disinterested....[Knowledge] expresses the principle...of the future technological and industrial order."[3] For Levinas, philosophical activity paves the way for instrumentalist thinking, a thinking devoid of all consideration of the *end* to which it might be employed. As has been well documented by scholars of the Holocaust, instrumentalist thought has played a crucial role in generating genocidal behaviors during the Holocaust.[4] In other words, *the Western philosophic tradition, when confronted by the Holocaust, has not merely been found wanting of a radical ethical analysis; in its totalizing intent, it has also provided the fertile ground upon which a holocaust can more easily take shape.* Unless or until philosophy radically rethinks its vocation, it will neither prove able to respond to the Nazi Holocaust, nor will it prove to be a force to combat the threat of potential holocausts in the future.

What, then, is an alternative model of philosophizing? What might a philosophy which can learn lessons from the Holocaust—a post-Holocaust philosophy—look like? And, since I am speaking, ultimately, not only about a refashioning of one academic discipline, but rather about the recasting of fundamental modes of thought *across* the disciplines, how might this renewal of philosophy enter our curricula at many levels of our educational system?

I argue here that a renewed vision of ethics must occupy a central space within philosophy, and, indeed, across the curriculum. A traditional ego-centered philosophy must be replaced by philosophy which grants primacy to the primordial encounter of an "I" with a "Thou," of humans who acknowledge the sacredness of one another's personhood. Only then can philosophers be said to have stood in the shadows of the Holocaust—and learned. Only then can academic philosophers renounce "business as usual" and begin the work of *tikkun olam*, the repair of the post-Holocaust world. Only then can we begin to rethink, radically, how we are to rear and school our young.

A post-Holocaust philosophy would most certainly be required to critique the totalizing aims of the self articulated in traditional ontology. Within an historical frame of reference in which philosophy has been conceived of as an "egology," it will be no easy task to rethink what Levinas calls the "imperialist" vocation of the self. If we look to the grand systems of traditional philosophy, we see, as has been suggested above, that within this tradition to know is to comprehend, that is, to take together or unify all that is within a conceptual order. Such an order reflects the ideal of the adequacy of the thinker to that which is thought. As we have seen, to know is to account for the presence-to-me of all that is, and thus to remove from being its alien character. Indeed, the very word "universe" refers to that unification of beings which renders the world intelligible *as* world.

Utilizing the mediating force of the concept in order to unify the multiplicity of beings within the vision of the sovereign subject, philosophy attempts to reduce the "Other" to what Levinas calls the "same." In classical thought, for example, the "I" employs the mediating force of the concept to reduce what appears to be alien to my all-enveloping sphere of comprehension. That which appears to be independent of me is subsumed under such categories as, for example, substance or cause. In the modern period of Western thought, Immanuel Kant lends his weight to a similar pursuit of this ideal: "Men of the new science," he contends, "learned that reason…must not allow itself to be kept, as it were, in nature's leading strings, but must itself show the way…constraining nature to give answers to questions of reason's own determining."[5] From the immortal soul of Plato, the Nous of Aristotle, and the Hegelian self-consciousness, all the way to the twentieth century Sartrean ideal of the self-as-absolute, Western ontology has paid homage to an image of a *subject sufficient unto itself*.

Given this notion of the philosophical enterprise, how is it thinkable to arrive at a notion of philosophizing in which the self undergoes fundamental ethical critique? On the surface, it appears that self-criticism of a sort is not foreign to philosophers. At the same time as philosophy in the West has embarked on its essentially ontological quest, many in this same tradition have taken upon themselves the task of self-criticism. Philosophers, following the lead of Socrates, have often spoken with humility of the daunting task of knowing the whole. Indeed, genuine philosophical dialogue through

the centuries rests on the notion that no one philosopher has succeeded in achieving the "wisdom" which the philosopher—faithful
to the etymology of the word "philosophy"—is said to "love." Is this
not the critique of an appropriative self for which we are searching?

For Levinas, what is troubling is the fact that it is merely my
ability to know the whole which is challenged in this activity of self-
criticism. Left unexamined by those philosophers who have philoso-
phized with alleged humility is what has always been, and still is, the
ideal of Western thought: the adequacy, *in principle*, of the knower
to the known. Those who have acknowledged our limitations as thinkers have advanced a critique which, for Levinas, is not critical enough.
Such a critique rests on an ideal of adequacy which remains itself
unexamined. Men and women of science, for example, freely admit
that they do not indeed understand all that is to be understood. These
same theorists, however, believe that what lies outside the purview
of their conceptual schemas of the present day remains, *in principle*,
accessible to the powers of the mind of the future. The idea of a self-
sufficient-unto-itself remains impervious to critique.

Levinas's quarrel with philosophy, then, is no quarrel with any
one philosophical theory as opposed to any other, but rather with
the enterprise of theorizing itself. Any totalizing philosophy is doomed
on principle to miss the one encounter which can teach it the necessity of undergoing a radical critique. Awareness of ignorance cannot affect this teaching. As I have indicated, it constitutes a mere
reminder that I have not yet attained a goal which is itself beyond
critique. If my egoist powers are to be challenged in a primordial
sense, the challenge must be directed not toward the degree of *adequacy* of my powers, but rather toward the *arbitrary* character of my
egoist ambition. If we are to speak at all in quantitative terms, I can
say that I am subject to a critique, not of having *too little* power, but
too much! What is submitted to criticism here is not my being as
limited, but rather my being as *unworthy* of whatever powers it has. I
must be taught not what I *cannot* do, but what, in an ethical sense, I
must not do. It is not my success or failure to know that is now at
issue, but rather my right to appropriate the world. Without this teaching, ethics, in any fundamental sense, cannot be born.

Now who is that being who can thus contest me? As we have

seen, this being cannot be the other as usually understood within traditional philosophical discourse. The being who can teach me what it means to be ethical would have to challenge my hegemony as meaning-giver, as appropriator of my world. Such a challenge appears to be offered by Jean-Paul Sartre's other, that other who, by merely "Looking" at me delivers me over to an awareness that *he or she is now subject.*[6] He or she is now the reference point for all meaning. Sartre reminds us that while I am proceeding to fit the other into my conceptual schemas, I can at any moment undergo a primordial encounter of a wholly different kind. Sartre calls the awareness which arises simultaneously with this encounter my "original fall": things lose what was formerly their unique point of reference to me, as they, and I myself, are appropriated by the Look of the other. The experience of the Look of the Sartrean other recalls me to the fact that my powers as subject are now subjected to the powers of another. I am no longer in control of my world.

And yet the Sartrean other, powerful as she or he may be, is not yet the Other who can offer that radical critique of my being of which a post-Holocaust ethics is in search. For what I learn in my encounter with this other is simply that the other and I are both subject to the rule of an overarching philosophical schema within which the concept of a meaning-giving "I" remains supreme. The other and I are simply seen, within this schema, to take turns exercising power. The Sartrean other is my twin, my alter-ego. Though temporarily subdued and thus compelled to acknowledge the limitations of my being, my egoist existence remains fundamentally uncontested, and thus, in ethical terms, an existence unjustified in the assumption of its powers. In recalling to me that I am no longer the master of every situation, *mastery* itself is not called into question. This other, then, is incapable of calling me to account for my existence as a subject. He or she cannot offer a radical challenge to my endeavor-to-know. He or she cannot inaugurate an ethical plane of existence.

To achieve this goal, my Other must be other than an alter-ego. He or she cannot come from the same plane of being I customarily inhabit, a plane upon which the other is subject, on principle, to my appropriative powers. For a *radical* critique of my selfhood to be offered, a rupture in being must occur, since, *within being,* all is the "same." All is, in principle, subject to my appropriative acts. The truly-Other must have changed levels of existence, must inhabit a different realm from that of being itself. He or she must come from what Levinas calls an "exterior" realm, a realm "outside of being."

The ethical plane thus constituted does not consist of any set of rules or principles. It is not something substantive, something given, but rather that which is *enacted* in the course of my face-to-face encounter with a subject who comes to me as fundamentally exterior to myself. The Other and I meet at a distance; an endistancing occurs which is continually renewed and never to-be-eclipsed.[7] I finally encounter a being who, *in principle*, escapes my powers.

The production of this distance, however, does not mean that I remain endistanced from the Other in any ordinary sense of that word. The distance manifested in the encounter with the Other is that of an authentic contestation. As we have seen, what is contested is not the *extent* of my power; I have already experienced that kind of contestation in my encounter with the Sartrean other. Rather, what is contested is my complacency, my desire for self-sufficiency, the arbitrariness of my exercise of power. The Other is thus my "judge" and "master," higher than I am, calling me to responsibility for my thoughts and actions. He or she *requires* me to respond, to be responsible. I am required, in the course of this meeting, to justify my existence.

How does the Other effect this summons to responsibility? Not by the simple use of force against force. Unlike the Sartrean alter ego who shames with a Look akin to my own, the "face" (as Levinas terms the Other) shames me with a power unlike any power I have heretofore known. This is not my alter ego: the face-to-face relationship is fundamentally *asymmetrical*. The Other who can render a radical critique of my being cannot be that other who combats my power with his or her own, but rather one who quits the field of combat altogether. What resists me, paradoxically, is nonresistance, what Levinas calls "ethical resistance."

The encounter with the face of the Other is at one and the same moment a contestation *and an appeal*: the Other disarms me without the force of arms. The face appeals to me without any of the conventional means of the exercise of power. In this sense, the same face that a moment ago seemed to be "higher" than I now appears to be "lower." In Levinas's terms, borrowed from the Bible, the Other is the "poor one," the "widow," the "orphan," soliciting my (what are now) "ethical" responses without the use of any of the conventional modes of force. The Other is dependent on my response to an appeal made not to my power, but to that which is beyond the powers of being: what Levinas calls my "power for power."

This face-to-face encounter is thus no cognitive event. As we have seen, I cannot *know* the Other as Other without diminishing his or her otherness. I can, however, *encounter* that Other in what Levinas terms an *ethical* event. Indeed, it is only with the rending of the ontological schema that ethics first becomes possible. Prior to my meeting with the Other, there is no ethics as such. Within the totality of being, I am limited in my egoist ambition only by a lack of power. The Other who meets me face-to-face challenges my *very right* to exercise power. In so doing, ethics is born. Cognition no longer represents the highest activity of which a human is capable; it is replaced by "revelation" of the Other as an ethical event in which, for the first time, I come to realize the arbitrariness of my egoist ambitions. The *thematizing* of the cognitive subject is replaced by nothing short of an act of *witness* on the part of a being who now becomes an ethical subject.

The Other who contests me is an Other truly independent of my appropriative powers and thus one to whom I can have, for the first time, ethical obligations. As Levinas puts it, this Other is the first being whom I can wish to murder. Before the totality is rent by the manifestation of the face, there can be no will to act *immorally*, as there can be no will to act *morally*, in any ultimate sense of that word. If one begins with the "imperial I" appropriating its world, ethics as such can never be founded. The other with whom I interact is simply a datum, an aspect of my universe. Morality makes its first appearance when I confront the Other who is truly Other.

Although the Other appears to me now, on principle, as someone I could wish to kill, he or she *in fact* summons me to respond with nonviolence: I am called to willingly renounce my power to act immorally. What I hear from the Other, Levinas claims, are the words "Thou shalt not kill." Harkening to this injunction constitutes my inaugural act as an ethical being. In Levinas's words, "Morality begins when freedom, instead of being justified by itself, feels itself to be arbitrary and violent."[8] Addressing the face of the Other I become ethical.

In a turnabout from what has been the norm in the history of Western thought, ethics now is seen, by Levinas, to constitute the essence of philosophy. Ethics is now "first philosophy," a position usurped until now by the ontological enterprise. The meeting with the Other-who-is-truly-Other is a primordial event: "Since the Other looks at me," Levinas exclaims, "I am responsible for him, without even having taken on responsibilities in his regard."[9] In encountering the Other, I assume responsibility for him. "Responsibility," Levinas proclaims, "is the essential, primary and fundamental structure of subjectivity.... Responsibility in fact is not a simple attribute of subjectivity, as if the latter already existed in itself, before the ethical relationship."[10] In other words, my *structure as a human being*, in any significant sense of that word, is to be responsible to the Other. My personhood is not to be identified with that of the solitary ego appropriating its world; it is rather a personhood fundamentally oriented toward the Other.

Ethics, for Levinas, is thus not to be identified with any ethical or even meta-ethical position. Levinas speaks neither as deontologist nor consequentialist. He does not attempt to articulate any list of rights or obligations, or even the principles on which the latter would be based. All ethical theories, he implies, are secondary to, or derivative from, a primordial or founding moment: the encounter with the face of the Other. It is this moment-of-all-moments which institutes the very possibility of the "ethical" systems so hotly debated within the history of Western thought. Before there can be any ethical positioning—before there can be discussions of virtue, happiness, duties—there is the meeting with the Other. Ethics is no set of directives; rather, in Levinas's words, "Already *of itself* ethics is an 'optics,'"[11] a way of seeing which precedes—and founds—all that has heretofore been identified as ethical philosophy.

The import of this notion of the primacy of ethics for a rethinking of philosophy in the post-Holocaust age cannot be emphasized strongly enough. For Levinas, philosophy-as-ontology reveals being as nothing short of "war":

> The visage of being that shows itself in war is fixed in the
> concept of totality which dominates Western philosophy. In-
> dividuals are reduced to being bearers of forces that command
> them unbeknown to themselves. The meaning of individuals
> (invisible outside of this totality) is derived from the totality.[12]

Individuals within the "being" constructed by philosophers are merely
creatures of the schematizing mind. Such a concept of philosophy
is ill-equipped to address the great ethical issues which arise in the
study of the Holocaust. Indeed, for Levinas, "War is not only one of
the ordeals—the greatest—of which morality lives; it renders morality derisory."[13] Within the terms of warfare, lying, stealing—even killing—lose whatever ethical import they might have. I simply engage
in these acts as "necessary" within the universe created by war.

If the being studied by traditional philosophy is conceived of as
war, morality loses its core meaning. Not only is no fundamental
ethical critique of the events of the Holocaust possible within the
terms of philosophy-as-ontology, but, as I have noted above, it can
be argued that the mode of appropriative thinking of philosophers
in our Western tradition has contributed to the creation of a climate
in which genocide can flourish. If, in ontological terms, individual
beings are said to have their meaning solely within the totality in
which they find themselves, *totalizing thinking may well become totalitarian*. Jews and other victims of Nazi oppression were dehu-
manized precisely by being viewed in terms of racial categories applied to them *as a whole*. If philosophy is a mere egology, as Levinas
claims, the totalizing cognitive subject can, at the far end of a continuum, be seen to pass over into the autocratic "I" of the leaders of
the Third Reich.

In contrast to that appropriative thinking which can lead to the
brutal dehumanization of the kind present in war, the face-to-face
relationship is a pacific one. It is a relationship which establishes a
peace which is no mere truce, no temporary cessation of inevitable
hostilities. For traditional philosophy, knowledge is power, a power
capable of harnessing technology to evil ends. The absolute end of

philosophy is its goal of achieving total mastery of being; it is thus not at all illogical to foresee a progression from conceptual to physical mastery of one's world. Once the locus of an "absolute" is placed in the powers of the "I," the other person cannot fail to become merely another datum in a world whose meaning derives itself entirely from me. Often I may treat her or him in terms of what in the West has been called "goodness." Yet such goodness, for Levinas, is accidental, the product of a determination on my part that it is in my self-interest to act in a given manner in a given situation. The fundamental reference point remains the "I." Goodness thus established, I argue, along with Levinas, is a goodness which is simply not good enough!

What does all this mean for the creation of a post-Holocaust philosophy? A philosophy which has witnessed the human evil manifested during the Holocaust cannot but turn back upon itself and reexamine its roots. Such a philosophy must call into question the unquestioned hegemony of the self in the Western tradition, a hegemony which exists on a continuum with bald assertions of supremacy leveled by the warmonger. Such a philosophy cannot be satisfied with a critique which calls into question the *degree or extent* of my powers; rather, a teaching of a radically different order is required. What is to be taught to the philosopher is no preconceived "wisdom," but rather a teaching which transcends what has heretofore been understood as knowledge. The face institutes that primordial moment of Truth which resides in my ability to acknowledge, in true humility, the arbitrariness of my egoist existence. The Other teaches me, in other words, not the finitude of my existence, but rather the infinite extent to which the powers of such an existence must be examined. The Other teaches me to be critical of self, opening me, as we have seen, to an ethical plane of existence.

The teaching of the Other thus has no content which would have preceded the moment of this very encounter. *The teaching in which philosophy is born, and in which it is perpetually renewed, is that teaching in which I receive "only" the desire to be taught!* Philosophy in its primordial moment has no content. It is nothing but the continual process of freeing itself of presumption, a constant undoing of, in Levinas's words, "the inevitable dogmatism that gathers up and gauges an exposition in pursuit of its theme."[14] Faced with the dogma of racial supremacy propounded by perpetrators during the Holocaust, the philosopher must embrace, more than ever, that discipline which at bottom teaches the capacity to be taught.

Without that transformative teaching, philosophy can become a tool in the hands of those who make war. No longer nourished at its core by the acknowledgment of the Other as "master" and "poor one," philosophy dries up, becomes the mere wielding of tools of force on behalf of fixed notions. Ultimately, the urge to philosophize as an appropriative activity runs the risk of degenerating into the acts of those who engage not only in verbal warfare, but in physical warfare, and possibly genocide as well. A line stretches from the endeavor to *master* all-that-is via the concept to the ever-tempting enterprise of mastery via bodily acts. Students of the Holocaust do not need to be reminded of the movement from exhortation to harangue to acts of political demagoguery—all the way to the use of physical force in defense of static ideas-become-ideology. Either we justify our existence in dialogue before the face of the Other, or we may well become vulnerable to the endeavor of imposing a fixed truth on others by means of verbal or even physical force.

How do these ideas of a radically-transformed mode of thinking play themselves out in the educational arena? Philosophical reflection, like all activity of the mind, must be carried out before the face of the Other. That is to say, reflection must, at its core, be ethical: it must never forget that the Other is inviolable. Ethics, we recall, is an optics. The way we must "see" in philosophy—indeed, in all modes of thought—is to obey the injunction: "Thou shalt not kill," where "killing" refers to any form of the violation of another. If, as Levinas enjoins us to remember, the "ethical relationship...subtends discourse,"[15] all that we teach must be taught in reverence for the sacredness of the Other.

More concretely, Levinas gives us (implicit) guidance for how we are to behave, as teachers and parent-figures in our homes and classrooms. Without the image of the face before me, not just philosophy but all teachings which I endeavor to transmit "dry up" and are transformed, eventually, into mere doctrine. To teach another in the Levinasian sense, means never to *impose* thoughts, but rather to *offer* them to another. Philosophy is nothing other, at root, than an offering to my Other. Dialogue, the meeting of what Martin Buber calls an I and a Thou, becomes the sole medium by means of which I say what it is I have to say—and hear what it is that the Other has to say to me. Such dialogue is not a mere "means" to arrive at philosophical truth; it is, rather, the fundamental *enactment* of philosophical truth-as-process. There is no way to dialogue; dialogue is the way.

Without dialogue, classroom "discourse" becomes, at best, the attempt by the mightier of intellect to impress their static "truths" on the weaker. And, as I have just argued, what began as a diatribe can easily end as a thrust of the sword. The genuine teacher, then, invites dialogue in the course of acknowledging his or her "presumption to know." In this sense, teachers model "teachability" for their students. Always teaching with the face of the Other before me, I am rendered unable, in ethical terms, to impose any static truth upon my student or my child.

Philosophy in the post-Holocaust world need not speak *explicitly* of the face of the Other, because, *implicitly*, it is a work addressed to that very face. Guided by this "face" as the absolute, the end of all ends, the teacher of philosophy—or, by extension any teacher or parent—can adopt only that content and pedagogy which ultimately honor the value of the personhood of the Other. In the shadows cast by the Holocaust, all the ways we teach and learn must radically be called into question As that discipline which, perhaps more than others, has modeled the enterprise of an egoist appropriation of the world, philosophy has a special obligation to take upon itself the task of rethinking its fundamental aims. In its movement from warlike to peaceful means and ends, philosophy after the Holocaust must model a mode of thinking which will help prevent new genocidal acts. Post-Holocaust philosophy must recall that it is neither (as has traditionally been said) theory nor practice. In its primordial sense, philosophy is an offering. With Levinas, we must recall that ethics is first philosophy.

Notes

[1] Emmanuel Levinas, *Totality and Infinity: An Essay on Exteriority*, trans., Alphonso Lingis (Pittsburgh: Duquesne University Press, 1969), 37. Emphasis is mine.

[2] Following Levinas, I have adopted the convention of capitalizing "other" when what is meant is that being who stands outside the totality of being, incapable of being appropriated by the powers of my ego.

[3] Emmanuel Levinas, "Ethics as First Philosophy," in *The Levinas Reader*, ed. Sean Hand (Oxford: Basil Blackwell, 1989), 76-77.

[4] See, for example, A. Rosenberg and P. Marcus, "The Holocaust as a Test Philosophy," in *Echoes From the Holocaust: Philosophical Reflections on a Dark Time*, ed. Alan Rosenberg and Gerald Myers (Philadelphia: Temple University Press, 1988), 211.

[5] Immanuel Kant, *Critique of Pure Reason*, trans. Norman Kemp Smith, 2d ed. (New York: The Modern Library, 1965), 20.

[6] For Sartre's discussion of the Look of the other, see *Being and Nothingness*, trans. Hazel Barnes (New York: Pocket Books, 1956), Part Three: *Being-for-Others*, Chapter One, IV.

[7] Levinas refers to this endistancing as "infinity." Such a notion of infinity is not to be understood as a substantive, something relative to my powers as subject. Rather, infinity is produced, enacted in the course of my face-to-face encounter with a subject who comes to me as fundamentally exterior to myself.

[8] Levinas, *Totality and Infinity*, 84.

[9] Emmanuel Levinas, *Ethics and Infinity: Conversations with Philippe Nemo*, trans. Richard A. Cohen (Pittsburgh: Duquesne University Press, 1985), 96.

[10] Ibid., 96.

[11] Levinas, *Totality and Infinity*, 29.

[12] Ibid., 21-22.

[13] Ibid., 21.

[14] Ibid., 29.

[15] Ibid., 195.

Critiques

Critique by Peter Haas

Leonard Grob gives us a stirring call to rethink not only how we conceptualize the doing of ethics, but also how we teach ethics in the classroom. The stimulus for this radical reshaping of the Western philosophical tradition as regards ethics is the Holocaust. The Holocaust tells us that something has gone fundamentally wrong in the Western way of conceiving good and evil. In particular, as Grob relates to us through his reading of Levinas, the problem centers around the focus of Western philosophy on "being" and thus on the assumption that the individual can grasp that being, at least in principle. So, in the end, Western morality is based, in this view, on a move toward control and dominance. Whatever it is that is out there is to be the subject of my understanding and so brought within my horizon of control.

There is no doubt that the Holocaust suggests that something is deeply wrong in the deep mentality of our inherited modern society. That at least one of the urgent claims of this insight is that we have to rethink the doing and teaching of ethics is also, I am willing to concede, beyond question. Up for grabs, it seems to me, is to identify what that problem in Western thinking is.

It has become a sort of accepted truism of twentieth-century philosophy that the central problem of all of the Western philosophical tradition is its "essentialism" or its fixation on ontology, that is, on what *is*. The basic dichotomy was posited already by the Greeks: things either are, and so can be the subject of knowledge; or they are not, and so are not only not knowable but not really worthy of being known. For the Greeks, the problem was becoming, things apparently moving in and out of being. The basic solution that went on to inform the subsequent Western philosophical tradition with all its permutations is that all the phenomena of this world are in fact participating in "being" but to a less than complete extent, and hence

the constant change we experience, presumably toward more perfection.

One basic assumption in doing philosophy along these lines is
that the philosopher can in some significant way stand over against
this structure and, in a sort of independent self-sufficiency, comprehend what in fact is going on. This sets up the basic tension within
which Levinas's critique, and so Grob's use of it, is located. According to this critique, the Western tradition rests on the assertion that
there is an ultimate way of being, a full perfection, which is (in principle) knowable even though nothing in the world, whether subject
or object, is in fact already in that state of perfection. Thus the philosopher can acknowledge the limits or contingency of actual comprehension while still maintaining that perfect comprehension is
nonetheless in principle possible. It is in the effort to achieve this
perfect comprehension that the inclination towards power and control enter.

With this basic scheme in mind, I have two questions about
Grob's application of Levinas's critique to the post-Shoah situation.
The first has to do with whether Western philosophy really requires
that the ultimate is in principle knowable, and the second has to do
with whether the object of our knowledge is really distinct from the
subject, that is, whether or not the mind claiming to do the knowing
is really self-sufficient.

As to the knowableness, and so the controllability of the Ultimate, I think there is a long history of ambivalence in the Western
tradition. It may well be that the classical philosophers thought that
true knowledge was really attainable. After the appropriation of classical philosophy by Christianity, however, this sort of hubris became
in principle impossible. The Ultimate of classical philosophy—
whether called the Good, the Truth, the Just—became identified
with God, and God, by definition, is unknowable, is in fact the Unknowable. There was still an ultimate Truth but it was now certainly
understood to be unaccessible to mere human minds. To be sure,
there were some who could approach this Truth more closely than
others—prophets, for example. But even they could only grasp it in
part, and often could not really communicate their own insight to
others. It was in this space, the gap between what we as humans

could possibly *in principle* know, and what was really true or really real, that faith lay. There is a long tradition in Western thinking that stresses not human power and control, but the need for humility and awe in face of the ultimately unknowable divine mystery. It may be that what we need in the post-Shoah world is not a reversal of the Western philosophical tradition as Levinas seems to be calling for, but rather a retrieval of this strain of our intellectual heritage. In short, it is not that Western philosophy is inherently and necessarily "imperialistic," it is rather that for some reason the thinking behind the Holocaust suppressed certain aspects of the Western religio-philosophical tradition in favor of others. I will return to this thought in a moment.

My other question has to do with the supposed self-sufficiency of the subject. As the preceding indicates, I have serious questions as to whether this sense of self-sufficiency was really as established in all of Western philosophy as Grob's description of Levinas's critique asserts. In fact, there is a deep and abiding conviction in Western religious thinking that none of us is self-sufficient in any real sense, that our very day-to-day existence, or very ability to perceive, is nothing other than an ongoing miracle of God. Or to put it in different terms, what I know, I know by the grace of God. Now to be sure, by the nineteenth century this pietistic realization and acknowledgment of the ongoing grace of God had fallen out of philosophical favor. The living, active and mysterious God of the pre-modern West gave way to an Ultimate Reality that was less mysterious and more logical or mechanical. It is maybe at this juncture that the notion of human self-sufficiency arises. In the wake of Newton and Kant there was a marked growth in confidence that the human mind could really grasp the secrets of nature and could consequently really control and exploit nature. But at the same time there was a countervailing move, a move toward the contingency and imperfection of all human knowledge. The perpetrators of the Holocaust, after all, were as much the heirs of Hegel, Kierkegaard, Nietzsche, and for that matter quantum mechanics, as they were of Newton and Kant.

In short, it seems to me that Levinas's critique of the Western philosophical as presented here is unbalanced. It does, correctly I am willing to concede, point to some of the elements of Western thought that could support the Holocaust, but in doing so it ignores opposing views that were held with equal vigor within the same intellectual tradition. The task maybe is not to redo or overturn the Western philosophical tradition, but rather to identify the very tensions that have always been present within the Western philosophical tradition.

My hunch is that what the Holocaust represents is the ascendancy of those parts of the Western tradition which assert, as Levinas claims, the self-sufficiency of the knower and the principled knowability of the Truth. This turn in the intellectual history of the West, I want to claim, is tied strongly into the scientific and especially technological progress manifest in the West in the nineteenth and early twentieth century. These, I maintain, ratified on the one hand the suppression of the sacred and mysterious while on the other endorsing the notion that humans not only could understand and control reality, but had a right to do so. It was the hubris of the nineteenth-century engineers that provided the foundation for the Holocaust, and so it is this hubris that must be addressed. On this Grob and I are in fundamental agreement. Where we disagree, maybe, is in my confidence that this hubris has been, and still can be, addressed by and within the received Western philosophical tradition.

I close by pointing out that much of the language Grob uses to describe Levinas's "alternative" to the received Western tradition is strikingly reminiscent of traditional language in the West about God. God has always been the truly-Other, who comes from an "exterior realm," an "outside of being" who always challenges our self-sufficiency and complacency. In fact, I think it is not coincidental that after critiquing the tendency of the West to establish objects of knowledge, all of which have capital letters—the Good, the Truth, the Just—Levinas posits his own: the Other. In the end Levinas is not outside the history of Western intellectual discourse, but very much inside it. This suggests that what is needed is a true openness to the other (not Other) voices that are out there, not the imposition of one Other for a different Other.

Critique by David Hirsch

As Leonard Grob points out, the silence of philosophers about the events of 1939 to 1945 has been deafening. I take Grob's word for it that "in the wake of what has been called nothing short of a transformational event, philosophers have most often gone about their…'business as usual'." Not all philosophers, of course, and not always, and the silence of some philosophers, like Martin Heidegger, for example, may be more significant than the silence of others. But to the extent that most academic philosophers have gone about "business as usual" it must be because philosophers in general have not perceived the Holocaust as "a transformational event." The Holocaust, as Grob suggests, occupies a very tiny niche in mainstream academic philosophy. To my knowledge, Holocaust courses are being taught increasingly in history departments, literature departments, sociology departments, but very rarely in philosophy departments.

Grob attributes the myopia of academic philosophers to their preoccupation with ontology. Grob cites Emmanuel Levinas to support this view: "for Levinas, philosophy in the West is fundamentally ontology, the endeavor to grasp the nature of Being itself." It is this preoccupation with ontology, Grob explains, that has blinded academic philosophers to the Holocaust and the ethical issues it raises.

Why is it that mainstream academic philosophers do not seem to perceive that the Holocaust was "nothing short of a transformational event"? It may be that from the perspective of "Being as such," the planned and systematic murder of millions of blameless people is hardly worth thinking about. It may be that some philosophers believe that nothing was really transformed after the Holocaust, least of all human behavior; human beings seem to behave after the Holocaust no less viciously or violently than they did before. Not a day seems to go by without acts of violence that might well be designated unimaginable. As I write, the American national consciousness is still reeling in shock after the mass killing of children by other children that took place in the mid-sized city of Jonesboro, Arkansas.

If the Holocaust is viewed as "a genocide" among genocides, then it merges into the natural flow of history, and does not appear to be "a transformational event." In a collection of essays on comparative genocides, two of the genocides discussed preceded the Holocaust, and ten more took place after. In spite of the Nuremberg trials and the Eichmann trial, and in spite of such new designations as, "war crimes" and "crimes against humanity," coined to signal a sense of the international community's revulsion at inhuman German behavior in the ghettos and extermination camps; in spite of all this, genocides and crimes against humanity still take place. If "transformational event" is intended to designate a set of occurrences that changed the way human beings think and act in this world, then the Holocaust has not been transformational, even to the extent of putting an end to antisemitism; as we know, there are still hate groups and neo-Nazis whose only quarrel with the old Nazis is that they didn't get the job done.

I take Grob to be saying that if philosophers overcome their obsession with ontology, they will be able to devote their philosophical exertions to following the path of ethics set forth by Emmanuel Levinas. When philosophers stop trying to gain a mastery over Being, Grob feels, then they can start concentrating on the encounter between the I and the Other. I also take Grob to be implying, if he is not actually saying it explicitly, that once philosophers concentrate their energies on the philosophy of ethics, philosophy itself may then take its place in bringing about the conditions that would prevent a future Holocaust, or future genocides.

I am not certain that even if academic philosophers were to put the study of ethics above their concern with ontology, this would translate into a significant change in the behavior of a significant number of human beings. By its nature, philosophy—with its sophisticated and often esoteric vocabulary, its involved and convoluted arguments, its long difficult tradition, from the pre-Socratics to Heidegger—is not designed, or intended, to impact on the behavior of ordinary people. For example, let us consider one of Grob's explications of a text by Levinas. Grob writes, "I cannot *know* the Other as Other without diminishing his or her otherness. I can, however *encounter* that Other in what Levinas terms an *ethical* event....Within the totality of being, I am limited in my egoist ambition only by a lack of power. The Other who meets me face to face challenges my *very right* to exercise power. In so doing, ethics is born."

Is Grob providing a model of human behavior, here, or is he providing, rather, a philosophical description, a set of expressions that will encompass the full range of the ways in which all human beings should, in an ideal world, relate to all other human beings? Grob's translation of Levinas asserts the desirability of having human beings relate to each other ethically, but it does not, in my opinion, indicate why they should behave this way, or what would induce them to behave that way, or why they do not always behave that way in the world as we know it. In other words, an ethics should address itself to people as we know them in the world. But Grob's formulation does not do this; it does not address itself to the needs, fears, lusts, passions, phobias, irrationalities that drive individuals to behave unethically. If every "I" were content to "encounter" every "Other," that is, if every self were willing, always, and in every "encounter with an Other," to agree to let himself or herself be limited, to have his or her selfhood contained, by "the face of the Other," then ethical behavior would burst into bloom everywhere, it would become commonplace, and human conflict would eventually wither and become nothing more than a distant memory. Can this description of ethical behavior that Grob attributes to Levinas be said to constitute an imminent reality, or must it always remain nothing more than an expression of desire?

Grob states that "A traditional ego-centered philosophy must be replaced by a philosophy which grants primacy to the primordial encounter of an 'I' with a 'Thou,' of humans who acknowledge the sacredness of one another's personhood." I must admit that I am surprised by this statement, and am not sure what Grob intends by the phrase, "sacredness of one another's personhood." Is "sacredness" a philosophical category that Grob arrives at by means of pure reason? Does "sacredness" belong to the realm of philosophy at all? It seems to me that we already possess a scheme of thought, or a set of beliefs, that calls for "humans [to] acknowledge the sacredness of one another's personhood," and that is biblical religion, or biblical faith. I shall be referring, here, only to Judaism and Christianity, since those are the two faiths of which I am least ignorant. Surely, both Jews and Christians are obliged to recognize "the sacredness of another's personhood" on the basis of their faith alone, without the aid of philosophy. In fact, philosophy is more likely to diminish the notion of the sacredness of the Other than reinforce it.

It seems to me that what Grob does here, in the name of Levinas, is to ask philosophy to perform what has hitherto been, in Western culture, the task of religion, specifically the task of biblical religion. In his essay, "Heidegger and Theology," Hans Jonas demonstrates the way in which Philo's allegorization of biblical religion substitutes "sight, [the] Platonic supposition that the truest relation to being is intuition, beholding" for "hearing," the biblical notion that "the word of God is primarily call and command, and commands are not looked at but heard—and obeyed or disobeyed."[1]

How would we reconcile Jonas's characterization of biblical faith as "primarily a call and command" to be "obeyed or disobeyed," with Levinas's assertion, cited by Grob, that "Already of itself ethics is an 'optics'…"? From what source is such a philosophy of encounter, and an "ethics that is an 'optics'" derived? Is it the end result of pure reason, of logical thinking? Is the primacy of the encounter between an Ego and an Other, with its emphasis on seeing a face, one more instance of what Jonas has identified as the Philonic tendency to convert biblical religion into Platonic philosophy? The kind of thinking Jonas attributes to Martin Heidegger is similar to the kind of thinking Grob attributes to Levinas. Heidegger, Jonas notes, speaks as a philosopher, but bolsters his appeal to Christians by appropriating the language of scripture. Heidegger, Jonas writes, "came to adopt the Judeo-Christian vocabulary,…the vocabulary of guilt and conscience and call and voice and hearing and response and mission and shepherd and revelation and thanksgiving." Is the "acknowledge[ment of] the sacredness of one another's personhood" that Grob finds in the writings of Levinas a dictate of philosophy, of pure thinking, or of faith, that is, of obedience to the biblical commandment?

Would the Holocaust not have been rendered impossible if all Christians had done nothing more than obey the commandments they had, in theory, already accepted as Christians: "Thou shalt not kill….Thou shalt not steal….Thou shalt not covet thy neighbor's house,…nor any thing that is thy neighbor's"? Levinas himself seems to be somewhat equivocal about this. Levinas addressed the question of ethics and the Holocaust quite directly in a highly acclaimed and widely circulated essay, "To Love the Torah More Than God."

Since this Levinas essay bears directly on the Holocaust, it is surprising that Grob does not include it in his discussion. In the essay, Levinas explicates a short story by Zvi Kolitz, "Yossel Rakover's Appeal to God," a fictional account of the Warsaw ghetto uprising, narrated by a fictional Hasidic Jew. Levinas endorses the story enthusiastically, commenting that the tale "is both beautiful and true, true as only a fiction can be."[2] The story, which Levinas embraces in all its parts, does, however, present some ethical problems that Levinas ignores. For one thing, the Hasidic narrator calls upon *el n'kamot adonai* (Lord, God of vengeance, Psalms 94:1), and Levinas, by endorsing the truth of the entire story, seems to support the narrator's delight in a vengeful God.

In the concluding paragraph of the story, the Hasidic narrator declares, "Praised be forever the God of the dead, the God of vengeance, of truth and of law...."[3] Levinas specifically approves the narrator's invocation of a vengeful God. He cites an earlier passage in the story about the vengeful God, introducing the passage with the words, "it is the internal evidence of morality supplied by the Torah. This is a difficult path, both in spirit and in truth, and it cannot be prefigured. Simone Weil, you have never understood the Torah! 'Our God is the God of vengeance,' says Yossel ben Yossel" (the name mistakenly given to the narrator in the version Levinas read).[4]

The theme of the story that particularly impresses Levinas is the narrator's declaration, "I love Him, but I love His Torah more.... His Torah means a way of life" (370). Levinas reiterates the point made by the narrator: "God," Levinas writes, "is real and concrete, not by means of incarnation, but by means of the Law" (145). Here, Levinas seems to echo Jonas's view that man knows God by His voice, as heard in His commandments, which man either obeys or disobeys. Levinas characterizes Jewish faith as "A complete and austere humanism, coupled to a difficult adoration!" (145) What does Levinas mean by "a difficult adoration," if not that obeying all God's commandments requires us to do some things we do not want to do, and to abstain from doing things we would like to do? We may recall the opening words of Father Mapple's Sermon in *Moby-Dick*, "…All the things that God would have us do are hard for us to do—remember that—and hence, He oftener commands us than endeavors to persuade. And if we obey God, we must disobey ourselves; and it is in this disobeying ourselves, wherein the hardness of obeying God consists"(*Moby-Dick*, chapter 9). How is the ethic characterized by "the Other who meets me face to face" (Grob) related to the ethic of the hardness of obeying the call of the commandments handed down from Sinai?

It seems to me that Grob softens Levinas's message. Grob conceives an ethics of "opening to the Other," which if adhered to, will prevent us from "imposing a fixed truth on others by means of verbal, or even physical force." But for the Levinas of "To Love the Torah…," the starting point of ethics is acceptance of the Torah, by which, of course, he means not only the Bible, but the whole Torah, including the God of vengeance, *el n'kamot adonai*. The story that Levinas commends without reserve, "Yossel Rakover's Appeal to God," is an extremely violent tale that celebrates the Warsaw ghetto resistance movement and the ghetto uprising, which, historically (as opposed to Kolitz's fictional "truth"), was organized and carried out by Bundist, Communist, and Zionist youth groups, and not by Hasidic Jews. These groups were motivated in large part by the human desire to avenge their murdered relatives. What is perhaps most surprising in Levinas's endorsement of the moral of this tale is that he sees no problem in Kolitz's use of a Hasidic Jew as the instrument of revenge.

Violence dominates the conclusion of Levinas's commentary on "Yossel Rakover": "To love the Torah more than God—this means precisely: to find a personal God against whom it is possible to revolt, that is to say, one for whom one can die." I don't understand exactly what Levinas is calling for here, but it sounds like something quite distant from the serene universal mutual acceptance of the Other envisioned by Grob.

Notes

[1]Hans Jonas, *The Phenomenon of Life* (New York: Harper and Row, 1966), 231.

[2]Emmanuel Levinas, "Loving the Torah more than God," in *Difficult Freedom: Essays on Judaism* (Baltimore: Johns Hopkins University Press, 1990), 142.

[3]Zvi Kolitz, "Yossel Rakover's Appeal to God," a new translation from the original text, with an Afterword, by Jeffrey V. Mallow and Jozef van Beeck, in *Cross Currents* (Fall, 1994): 362-377 and especially 373.

[4]Levinas, "Loving the Torah...," 144.

Critique by David Patterson

Leonard Grob's essay "Emmanuel Levinas and the Primacy of Ethics in Post-Holocaust Philosophy" is a passionate, intelligent beginning toward a needed examination of the bankruptcy of the ontological thinking that distinguishes much of Western philosophy. Such an examination is especially needful in the aftermath of the Shoah, since, as Grob rightly argues, the Western philosophical tradition has "provided the fertile ground upon which a holocaust can more easily take shape." As viewed by this tradition, knowledge implies power and possession, which are categories that cannot accommodate an ethical way of life. Indeed, when applied to the relationship to the other human being, possession ultimately means murder—a point thoroughly demonstrated by the Nazi SS. That is why "the murder camp was not an accidental by-product of the Nazi empire," as Emil Fackenheim has correctly noted. "It was its pure essence."[1]

Since the Nazis operated in a manner consistent with an accent on the power of the "I," the "good" that they sought—a "goodness which is simply not good enough," as Grob points out—cannot be construed as an ethical good. Power in this case is the exercise of an unlimited freedom, but ethics begins where freedom comes under constraint. Here too Grob proves to be insightful, noting as he does Levinas's comment on the violent and arbitrary nature of freedom. To be sure, Levinas argues that we are not free to choose the Good because the Good has chosen us prior to all our choosing.[2] That is why the Good, ethically understood, challenges our freedom and our power: it opens up a reality other than the reality of power, not by force, as Grob correctly argues, but through a certain revelation, the revelation of the holy. Where do we encounter this revelation? In the face of the Other. Through the revelation that arises in the face of the Other, moreover, we encounter the Other in a dimension of height. Thus, contrary to philosophy's ontological outlook, I am not a being among beings; that is, I do not exist alongside the Other, where the Other occupies a position that is either lower than or level with my own. Rather, I look *up* to the Other. And Grob is astutely sensitive to this important point.

Despite all his courage, care and insight, however, Grob stops short of the needful steps that Levinas would have us take. Subsequently, he remains in the grips of the ontological tradition that he tries to overcome. The most glaring indication of his entrapment in this philosophical quicksand is the fact that, in sharp contrast to Levinas, he omits from his thinking precisely what the ontological tradition would omit from the world: God and the Jews. Referring as he does to "Jews and other victims of Nazi oppression," Grob seems to suggest that the Jews were accidental targets of annihilation, that it could just as well and just as easily have been any other group, as if the Jews as such bore no particular metaphysical significance. The Nazis oppressed many groups, but they were not interested in oppressing the Jews—they wanted to exterminate the Jews *and the teachings of Judaism* that the Jews represent. For in the Western world the teachings of Judaism form the origin of any ethical and metaphysical thinking that might be opposed to the power and possession that characterize the ontological outlook.

Leveling the Jews into the same category as all the other victims, Grob slips into the ontological leveling from which he tries to escape. While he has indeed extricated himself from the concern for power, possession, and freedom that characterizes ontological philosophy, Grob remains under the influence of ontological leveling. That is why he situates the Other, for instance, on a different "plane" but stops short of invoking the dimension of height—the realm of the Most High—that is so essential to Levinas and so necessary to ethical meaning.[3] Grob rightly insists on "the sacredness of one another's personhood"; he correctly calls into question "my being as *unworthy* of whatever powers it has." But he makes no comment on the ground in which the sanctity of a person is rooted or on the One before I stand as unworthy. What Levinas teaches us, however, is that our ethical concern with the Other is a "going towards God" and that there is no movement towards God that does not include an ethical treatment of the Other.[4] The sanctity of the Other lies in the opening to God that is revealed through the Other; indeed, that opening is the "divine image" itself. And my being is unworthy of whatever power it has only inasmuch as I stand before the divine image.

Hence, if the face "shames me," as Grob says, it does not shame me merely "with a power unlike any power I have heretofore known"; it shames me with a responsibility that can never be met. It can never be met because it is the infinite responsibility revealed to me through the face of the Other as the glory of the Infinite One,[5] as when a father gazes upon the face of his newborn babe. Grob maintains, again quite rightly, that "morality makes its first appearance when I confront the Other who is truly Other"; but he balks at taking the step that Levinas takes when the latter declares that this "truly Other," this "otherwise than being," is the glory of God.[6] Grob's hesitation leads him to use Jewish categories such as *tikkun olam* while leaving behind the teaching and the tradition in which such a category is situated; it leads him to invoke the "poor one" (or the "stranger"), the "widow," and the "orphan" referred to in the Torah while leaving out the most important part of the reference to them (see chapters 14, 16, 24 and 26 in Deuteronomy), namely that we are *commanded from on high* to attend to the care of those who have nowhere to turn.

Grob, in fact, has a healthy suspicion of following commandments. He notes, for instance, that the ethical plane "does not consist of any set of rules or principles" but rather is enacted in the encounter with the Other. While it may be the case that ethics does not consist of rules or principles, it is certainly the case that ethics arises from commandments, or rather from *mitzvot*. While the word *mitzvah* means "commandment," a *mitzvah* is understood to be both a summons to do good and the good deed itself. Here too Levinas insists on the interconnection between the ethical relation and the relation to God. According to Levinas, ethics comprises the vision of God. "The attributes of God," he argues, "are given not in the indicative, but in the imperative. The knowledge of God comes to us like a commandment, like a *Mitzvah*. To know God is to know what must be done [for the Other]."[7] And, I would add, to know what must be done for the Other is to receive a commandment through which I may come to know God. As Grob himself correctly points out, "I must be taught not what I *cannot* do, but what, in an ethical sense, I *must* not do." But if this is to happen, then surely rules, principles, laws, or at least commandments—*mitzvot*—must come into play at some point.

In an admirable effort to make way for a philosophy that will be inconsistent with "new genocidal acts," Grob turns to Levinas, as many of us do, to determine how ethics may be established as first philosophy. But inasmuch as he insists on the autonomy of human authority and avoids any consideration of the Holy One who is revealed in the mode of divine commandment, he retains some of the trappings of the philosophy that he would displace. If Levinas teaches us anything about post-Holocaust philosophy, it is this: philosophy cannot operate in a manner inconsistent with murder unless it recovers the divine image in which the human being is created—the very thing that was targeted for murder in the Shoah. And in order to do that, philosophy must recover the Jews and the Judaism that were slated for annihilation.

Notes

[1]Emil L. Fackenheim, *The Jewish Return into History* (New York: Schocken, 1978), 246.

[2]See Emmanuel Levinas, *Nine Talmudic Readings*, trans. Annette Aronowicz (Bloomington: Indiana University Press, 1990), 135.

[3] See, for example, Emmanuel Levinas, *Collected Philosophical Papers*, trans. Alphonso Lingis (Dordrecht: Martinus Nijhoff, 1987), 100.

[4]See, for example, Emmanuel Levinas and Richard Kearney, "Dialogue with Emmanuel Levinas," in *Face to Face with Levinas*, ed. Richard A. Cohen (Albany: SUNY Press, 1986), 23.

[5]For Levinas's discussion of this point, see Emmanuel Levinas, "Signature," *Research in Phenomenology*, 8 (1978): 185-89.

[6]Emmanuel Levinas, *Ethics and Infinity*, trans. Richard A. Cohen (Pittsburgh: Duquesne University Press, 1985), p. 109.

[7] Emmanuel Levinas, *Difficult Freedom: Essays on Judaism*, trans. Sean Hand (Baltimore: Johns Hopkins University Press, 1990), 17.

Critique by Didier Pollefeyt

In *Textes pour Emmanuel Levinas*, the well-known French philosopher Maurice Blanchot writes: "How to philosophize, how to write in the memory of Auschwitz, of those who say to us, sometimes in notes buried near the crematoria: realize what has happened, don't forget and at the same time you will never understand. This is the thinking that runs through the whole philosophy of Emmanuel Levinas, that underpins it, and that he presents to us, without saying, beyond and preceding every obligation."[1] In his contribution to this volume, Leonard Grob illustrates how Levinas's ethical theory influences his philosophical response to the challenge of the Holocaust.

Even though the Holocaust was a personal tragedy for Levinas—with the exception of his wife and daughter, his entire family was killed in the Nazi camps—his writings remain very reticent about these facts. Nevertheless, his philosophy can rightly be read as an implicit, yet very potent, response to Nazism. For Levinas, as Grob explains, the Holocaust is the most violent expression of Western philosophy (as "ontology") that tried to reduce every other to sameness and that attempted to eliminate every irreducible and inconvenient particularity. Grob clarifies how the Holocaust was not merely an anomaly but the revelation of a fundamental possibility intrinsic to Western thought as "ontology." In Nazism, the rational, enlightened understanding of the world produced a situation in which the other became captured in a strangling and murderous physical grip. In Nazism, it has become all too clear how the "will to know" is ultimately a deadly "will to power," how intellectual grasping can lead to the violence of physical grasping. In this sense, the Western philosophical tradition can be understood as a prelude to the Holocaust. All philosophical thinking is conceptual and seizes reality in and through its concepts. Western thinking is a thinking about the universal. Every particularity is thought away, every mystery's secret is stripped away, every intangible seized. Grob joins Levinas to show how Auschwitz represents the last step in this evolution: the step from intellectual understanding to the violence of physical grasping. The *universe concentrationnaire* can be considered as the completely realized grasp of reality. It is no accident that it was precisely

Jews, Gypsies, mentally ill, homosexuals, artists, and other *Entartete* who were finally stripped of their "irritant strangeness" by the Nazis. Indeed, they were the others who were not fit for integration into the Nazi totality. Hitler's politics displayed the deadly limits of the "egological" thinking and acting of the modern world. In this way, Auschwitz can be viewed as the ultimate, awesome, radical effort to realize the Western ontological tradition. Everything that escaped and/or criticized the Nazi totality was denied, suppressed and finally even extinguished.

Grob further shows how Levinas's philosophy is not only a critique of Auschwitz, but also a search for ways of "new thinking" after Auschwitz, perhaps the only credible way of doing philosophy in post-Holocaust times. For Levinas, this philosophy—first and foremost—must be ethical. In the terrorized face of the other, there is a force that radically resists every form of power and violence. This force, stronger than manslaughter, is not a physical power, but the breaking open of the totality by the infinity of human transcendence. In its constant resistance against intellectual and physical violence, the infinite thwarts the exercise of brute power: "You shall not kill!" In the face of the vulnerable other is revealed a resistance that is no resistance: ethical resistance. Grob convincingly argues how philosophy after Auschwitz can only correct itself by respecting this ethical alterity. At this point, he comes close to my own concept of ethics after Auschwitz (see my contribution in this volume), which centers around an openness for the vulnerability of the other. Every person, every philosophy, and every political system after Auschwitz should be questioned ethically in this way: Is it open for alterity, for the vulnerability of the weakest, for growth, discussion, questioning, hesitation, falsification, new challenges, for transcendent experiences?

My first critical comment on Grob's interpretation starts with his presentation of the notions "the other" (*l'autre*) and "the same" (*le même*) in Levinas's thought. He writes that "philosophy attempts to reduce the 'other' to what Levinas calls the 'same'." In my reading of Levinas, however, these two concepts do not stand in such a strong (moral) opposition. In Grob's view, sameness has only negative associations, while otherness has only positive associations. This leads him to a rather pessimistic view of individuality and autonomy, which

are almost exclusively characterized as "imperialistic" and "egoistic." In Levinas's thought, however, I also see a more original, positive appreciation of the "egocentric" dynamic of becoming an autonomous subject. In his early work *De l'existence à l'existant*, Levinas
speaks of the miracle of the *"hypostasis."*[2] In Levinas's thought, hypostasis is the dynamic of becoming-a-subject by the appropriation-
of-being. This hypostasis is originally evaluated positively, because it
is a human victory over what Levinas calls the "there is" (*il y a* or
"being-without-being"). The *il y a* is the primordial catastrophic situation which threatens to take every concrete being by surprise with
its anonymous, all-absorbing presence. It concerns nothing more
than pure and brutal being with its inhuman neutrality. There is
neither this nor that; but there is likewise no nothing.[3] It is simply
this threatening, formless being that awakens in people an exodus-
dynamic, an irrepressible longing for liberation from such a fundamental catastrophe.

It is important to recall that Levinas began writing *De l'existence
à l'existant* during World War II, while being a Nazi prisoner of war.[4]
I interpret Levinas's notion of the *il y a* as the philosophical articula-
tion of his own experience of Nazism.[5] Under Nazism, the Jewish
people were exposed to this *il y a* in the most explicit way. The work
of Elie Wiesel is helpful in describing this *il y a*. Wiesel relates how
the Jewish victims were delivered to the concentration and extermination camps. Packed into stifling train cars, they were deprived of
light and sanitation. There was only the sweltering heat of being
beside and against each other, without ventilation or food. There
was only the dark chaos where one is no longer human but (still)
cannot withdraw from existence.[6] Once in the Nazi camps, the Jews
were stripped of all that made one a person and reduced to a state
lower than that of objects.[7] Here began a life of total de-
subjectivization, of complete reduction to gray uniformity: bald-
shaven, disinfected, reduced to numbers without names.

The actual, concrete meaning of the *il y a*, the Levinasian notion of being, is that everything is dissolved and loses its personal
contours. It is precisely in this sense that we can speak about the *il y
a*-tic dimension of the Holocaust. Similarly, Emil Fackenheim has
described a new manner of "person"-hood that originated during

the Holocaust: Hitlerism created the *Muselmänner*. I would consider the *Muselmänner* to be persons on the way back to the *il y a*: everyone likened unto each other, existing yet without thinking, without reactions, without soul, inescapably submitted to a comfortless anonymity and brutal being. These people deteriorated to "living death"; they became wandering corpses whose only task was to await death upon command.[8]

The *il y a* is thus the oppressive fullness of being that swallows humans and renders them no-body, abandoning them to total desolation and indifference. All distinctions disappear: between men and women, adults and children, learned and illiterate, families and relatives, life and death. Everything is placed under one denominator. To be *Muselmänner* is to simmer in the *il y a*, to be eaten up by the absolute disconsolateness of simply being: always that numbing sameness, with neither workdays nor holidays, with neither yesterday nor tomorrow. There is only the desperate now from which there is no escape. This condition entails the total loss of power over one's own subjectivity; one is entirely subjected to the nothingness of being, without any possibility of resistance. Even suicide loses its meaning as the ultimate act of freedom, for when people are subsumed by being, they can no longer commit suicide since suicide presupposes a meaningful subject. In the Holocaust, suicide (like martyrdom) lost its symbolic power and terminated itself in the chaos of the catastrophe. In such a manner, Nazism delivered people to a "fatal immortality."

It is in this context that hypostasis should be seen first of all in a positive way. A point suddenly emerges when one tears loose from the *il y a*, and one contracts within oneself. It is remarkable how the traumatic experience of Hitlerism forms for Levinas the very vivid background of this concept. In an interview with François Poirié, Levinas relates how the experience of hypostasis came his way during his imprisonment under Nazism. His group of Jewish prisoners (they had to do forced labor in the forest and fight against the *il y a*-tic forces of nature) had taken care of a little dog, which greeted the commando every evening with its barking.[9] To be called no longer by that general, damning name *Juden*, but to be recognized as self-possessed (human) beings within being, is for Levinas the joy of hy-

postasis. When the *Wehrmacht* understood how the little dog contributed to that recognition, the poor animal was mercilessly slaughtered.

For Levinas, "egocentrism" in itself is not negative (in the sense
of "egoism"). It is rather the precondition for breaking through the
totality, since there must first be an independent being that is separated from totality. This is also clear in his notion of creation, which
presupposes a radical form of separation between God and humanity. Hypostasis as *être pour soi* is the refusal of the depersonalizing,
numinous powers of "fascist" being. It is an atheistic, "manly" deed,
the first instance of human freedom; it occurs not by withdrawing
from oneself (*Dasein*), but by establishing oneself as the origin (*archè*)
against all anarchy. This outlook can also explain Levinas's aversion
to sacred ("Nazistic") divinities. In the enthusiasm of religious ec-
stasy, characteristic of the *Gott mit uns*, the subject is destroyed and
one is brought into a fascination of the divine, a non-biblical, anonymous, fascist, *il y a*-tic power.

The philosophy of Levinas is therefore not simply a philosophy
of the other. "I" can also disappear in the otherness of neutral being.
The strength of Levinas's ethics is that he focuses on heteronomy,
but without a total disregard for autonomy. This is crucial in his
answer to Nazism, which can also be seen as a radical negation of
human autonomy, of victims as well as perpetrators.[10] Grob contends that "if one begins with the 'imperial I' appropriating its world,
ethics as such can never be founded." I would rather argue that for
Levinas ethics may never *end* with the "imperial I" but only with the
other.

The ambiguity of hypostasis becomes clear only in a second
movement. Being someone compels the person to be oriented towards reality in a reductionistic and self-interested manner. The ultimate cruelty of fascism is the fundamental revelation and glorification of this degenerate *Wille zur Macht* (will to power) that revolves
around itself. Here, we reach the core of Grob's convincing description of Nazism: It reduces all others to sameness; it is a politics without ethics, which will eventually destroy all that does not comply
with it. It is that attempt of being which radically universalizes itself
and eliminates every non-conforming "other."

But even in my ethical responsibility, which is my response to the face of the other, I need neither *deny* nor *suppress* my "I." My own self-unfolding is—within my responsibility—my one and only investment. What is crucial is that my (originally self-interested) energy must not be eclipsed but transformed and re-directed towards availability for the other. The face of the other is therefore not an obstacle for the development of my "I," but, on the contrary, it claims my "I" completely, it promotes my "I" to the unique possibility to give a concrete answer to the questions raised by the face of the other.

My second critical reflection on Grob's analysis concerns his description of this ethical relation with the other in Levinas's thought. Grob uses the Buberian dialogue between the I and the Thou to explain how Levinas's theory can work in educational settings: "To teach another in the Levinasian sense, means never to impose thoughts, but rather to offer them to another....Dialogue, the meeting of what Martin Buber calls an I and a Thou, becomes the sole medium by means of which I say what it is I have to say." There is, however, also an important difference between the theories of Levinas and Buber.[11] For Levinas, the dialogue of I and Thou implies the danger of interchangeability between both partners of the dialogue. As Grob rightly points out, Levinas's theory centers around the non-reciprocity or asymmetry between the I and the other. Indeed, it makes a difference with whom we start, with me or with the other, because in the ethical relation the other already comes first. In and through his or her radical alterity, the other announces himself or herself, or better, the other penetrates my existence *without asking,* and calls my whole hypostasis into question, not only factually but in principle. Moreover, the other is not only coming from else-where—in the sense that the other is unpredictable, and that he or she can never be created or anticipated by me—but the other also comes "from height." The other does not appear to me as my equal but as my superior—to be sure not on the basis of his or her power or egocentric dominance, but because the other shows himself or herself to me in the epiphany of the face, an ethical experience expressed in the prohibition "Thou shalt not kill."

This analysis does not mean that Levinas thinks that Buber has failed to give attention to the ethical dimension of the I-Thou relation. Rather, Levinas gives a much greater weight and more radical meaning to the ethical. It is not simply one dimension of the I-Thou relation, as a kind of supplementary value that could have just as well not been there, but the fundamental structure, the very ground-ing condition of the I-Thou relation itself. I think that Grob's de-scription is a "too Buberian" reading of Levinas. For example, Grob contends that "in encountering the Other I assume responsibility for him." For Levinas, however, there is not first of all an I-Thou relation in a kind of voluntary, friendly mutuality, upon which an ethical dimension of responsibility is later added, thanks to the ac-tive choice of the I.[12] On the contrary, the I-Thou relation, or to say it in a more Levinasian way, the I-other relation is ethical from the beginning; there is no relation with the other which is not at the same time already ethical. Accordingly, this ethical dimension is not something I choose in a kind of noble gesture towards the other. In Grob's description, the dialogue between I and Thou is seen to be rather activistic: "Philosophy is nothing other, at root, than *an offer-ing to my Other.*" For me, however, Levinasian ethics does not stem from a kind of ethical generosity, but it is the outcome of being-put-into responsibility by the other, despite myself. This ethics is not a kind of altruism, a spontaneous goodness, an easy choice that makes me happy, but the overcoming of my racistic, self-enclosed tenden-cies, which are inherent and intrinsic to my egocentric hypostasis. The other places me in a situation of passivity; I become the "hos-tage" of the other. This relationship is not really a question of choice. I can say "no" to the face, but I have to say "yes." Consequently, the encounter with the other is not primarily an experience of enthusi-asm or exaltation, but of disillusionment. Indeed, it begins with trauma, vulnerability, an exposing of myself to the other. As opposed to an encounter of reciprocity, the ethical encounter takes place in the form of an obsession, a summons, a persecution, and an impris-onment by the other.

In concluding my response to Grob, I have two comments on Levinas's philosophy as a hermeneutical tool for dealing with the Holocaust. First, Grob joins Levinas to warn us that "totalizing think-ing may well become totalitarian." Nevertheless, Grob fails to make clear *how* totalizing thinking in fact becomes totalizing acting. There

is not only continuity but also discontinuity between modern Western thinking and the Holocaust. There is a great difference between
theories with a violent potential and actual evil practices, because
between both always stands the face of the other. How could the
Jewish face be neutralized, while the Germans remained ethical
towards their fellow "Aryans"? To answer this question, we need to
include the thoughts of historians, psychologists and sociologists.

Second, in an important way Levinas's thought leads towards a
reduction of the Jewish religion to an *ethical* religion. Religion is
threatened in that its concerns can become exclusively a matter of
ethics, that is, doing what is good. But what if the person fails, if
courage falls short, and one falls into sin? An ethical God can only
judge. Here the danger and terror of ethics arises. The paradox is
that Nazism could also be interpreted along these lines, as becomes
clear in the thought of Peter Haas. Nazism seems to be founded on
a definite, ruthless (indeed perverted) "ethical" code. Nazism was in
all possible respects merciless. Whoever did not comply with its "ethical" demands inevitably "deserved" to be eliminated. Of course,
Levinas's ethics and Nazi ethics are fundamentally different (see my
contribution to this volume), precisely because Levinas's ethics is
centered on openness and Nazi ethics on closedness. But at the same
time, Levinas's ethics should also be questioned as to its possibility
of becoming fanatic in confrontation with evildoers. We must therefore also put forth the question: "What comes after ethics?" The
Judaeo-Christian tradition is also a tradition of mercy. Ethics can
hereby be saved from its mercilessness. A person's existence can never
be completely reduced to one moment. One is always more than
what one has done. For ethics after Auschwitz, however, one of the
most pressing questions is whether there are situations where humanity has done such great violence that we find ourselves in the
ethical impossibility of forgiveness. In the case of genocide one can
without the least doubt speak of *l'impardonable*.[13] If not, a forgiveness that is too easily granted leads once again to a trivialization of
ethics. The philosophy of Levinas, in other words, should be an oc-
casion that initiates reflection on the relationship between ethics
and forgiveness.

Notes

[1] M. Blanchot, J. Delhomme, and J. Derrida, eds. *Textes pour Emmanuel Levinas* (Paris: Place, 1980), 18.

[2] Emmanuel Levinas, *De l'existence à l'existant* (Paris: Fontaine, 1947), 115-145.

[3] See Emmanuel Levinas, *Ethique et Infini. Dialogues avec Philippe Nemo* (Paris: Fayard, 1982), 45-51, and Roger Burggraeve, *From Self-development to Solidarity: An Ethical Reading of Human Desire in Its Sociopolitical Relevance According to Emmanuel Levinas* (Leuven: Peeters, 1985).

[4] See François Poirié, *Emmanuel Levinas: Qui êtes-vous?* (Lyon: La Manifacture, 1986), 121, and Emmanuel Levinas, *Transcendance et Intelligibilité, suivi d'un entretien* (Genève: Labor et Fides, 1984), 55-56.

[5] Didier Pollefeyt, "The Trauma of the Holocaust as a Central Challenge of Levinas's Ethical and Theological Thought," in *The Holocaust: Remembering for the Future II*, ed. Marcia L. Littell, E. Geldbach, and G. J. Colijn, eds., (Stamford: CT: Vista InterMedia Corporation, 1996).

[6] See Elie Wiesel, *De Nacht. Met een voorwoord van François Mauriac.* Translated from the French by Nini Brunt (Hilversum: Gooi & Sticht, 1986), 29ff.

[7] Emmanuel Levinas, *Difficile liberté: Essais sur le judaïsme* (Paris: Albin Michel, 1984), 25.

[8] Emil Fackenheim, *To Mend the World: Foundations of Future Jewish Thought* (New York: Schocken Books, 1982), 215.

[9] Poirié, *Emmanuel Levinas*, 74: "Dans ce coin d'Allemagne ou, en traversant le village, nous étions regardés par les habitants comme *Juden*, ce chien nous prenant évidemment pour des hommes."

[10] Levinas, *De l'existence à l'existant*, 141: "L'hypostase...signifie la suspension de l'*il y a* anonyme, l'apparition d'un domaine privé, d'un nom. Sur le fond de l'*il y a* surgit un étant....Il exerce une maîtrise sur la fatalité de l'être devenu son atribut."

[11] R. Burggraeve and D. Pollefeyt, *Ethiek als intimiteit met God?: Christelijke ethiek in gesprek met joodse denkers* (Kampen: Kok, 1998), 45-47.

[12] In Emmanuel Levinas, *Noms propres* (Montpellier: Fata Morgana, 1976), 32 and 47, Levinas calls Buber's theory of dialogue an "angelical spiritualism" (*spiritualism angélique*).

[13] Vladimir Jankélévitch, *L'impréscriptible: Pardonner? Dans l'honneur et la dignité* (Paris: Seuil, 1986).

Critique by John Roth

Leonard Grob focuses key philosophical challenges. They are as fundamental as they are difficult. His challenges have those qualities because the gentleness that dwells in the heart of Grob's thought dissents so dramatically from the genocidal cruelty that his post-Holocaust vision of philosophy and ethics profoundly opposes. Specifically, Grob's much-needed gentleness contrasts with a disposition that fueled the Holocaust's consuming fire. Its name is *arrogance*.

Having studied the Holocaust for more than a quarter of a century, I am increasingly struck by the arrogance of the perpetrators — their overbearing pride and haughty self-importance, which were deep-seated characteristics that had devastating consequences. What I have in mind is illustrated powerfully in Primo Levi's *Survival in Auschwitz*. Early on in that memorable book, Levi describes his Auschwitz initiation. When he reached out a window to quench his painful thirst with an icicle, an SS guard immediately snatched it away from him. "*Warum?*" Levi asked him, only to be told with a shove, "*Hier ist kein warum.*" Levi's "why?" sought explanation. He got none, because questions of life and death were already settled there. No asking was permitted the likes of Levi. In Auschwitz no "why?" existed — not as a question and certainly not as satisfying explanation, either.

Auschwitz raises every "why?" but it did not tolerate the kind Levi posed. Paradoxically, the Holocaust was beyond "why?" because the minds that produced it were arrogant. They were convinced that they "understood" why. They "recognized" that one religion had superseded another. They "comprehended" that one race was superior to every other. They "saw" what nature's laws decreed, namely, that there was "life unworthy of life." Thus, they "realized" who deserved to live and who deserved to die. Such arrogance doomed Europe's Jews and millions of other "undesirable" men, women and children.

Adolf Hitler and his Nazi followers were beyond "why?" because they "knew" why. Knowing they were "right," their "knowing" made them killers. One can argue, of course, that such "knowing" perverted rationality and mocked morality. It did. And yet to say that much is to say too little, for one must ask about the sources of such perversion. When that asking takes place, part of its trail leads to the tendency of human reason to presume that indeed it can, at least in principle, figure everything out and understand why.

As Leonard Grob helps us to see, people are less likely to savage and annihilate each other, they are less likely to stamp on human faces, when they ask "why?" instead of "knowing" why, when their minds are less made up than opened up through questioning. Philosophy helps or hinders such awareness to the degree that it puts ethics first, emphasizes the claims and responsibilities that your humanity places upon mine, and relinquishes an obsession with knowing that too often leads to judgments that kill. Philosophy can be part of the problem or part of the solution. In that regard, everything depends on whether philosophy breeds arrogance or encourages gentleness. The gentleness we need makes us vividly aware of the fallibility and incompleteness of our own perspectives. It responds with care to the particularity of human faces, which express the preciousness of human life as nothing else does or can.

What obstacles have to be overcome if philosophy is to make human existence less arrogant and more gentle? What may happen if it cannot do so? If gentleness becomes more widespread, and arrogance less so, how would philosophy and our world change? Leonard Grob's responses shed important light on those issues, but significant questions remain, and he needs to address them further. To draw out these points, consider three of Grob's most important views.

With the help of the contemporary French Jewish thinker, Emmanuel Levinas, Grob believes that arrogance stands at the heart of "the *ideal* of Western thought." This ideal holds that, in principle, everything is knowable. It does not follow, of course, that particular persons and specific communities ever possess such knowledge with finality and completeness. From Socrates onward, philosophy has often criticized human pretension when excessive knowledge claims are made. It does so imperfectly, however, because philosophy's thirst for knowledge and thus its inclination to theorize typically entail "totalizing" tendencies. Those tendencies appear in dispositions to see things—"human nature," for example, or "Jews," "Germans," and "Americans"—as being essentially this way or that. Dedicated so much to knowing, philosophy has a hard time becoming fully self-critical because it assumes — arrogantly — that everything, at least in principle, is knowable.

If philosophy could overcome the arrogance of its fundamental ideal, which is to say if philosophy changed fundamentally, it could become more gentle and thereby spread a gentler spirit among us. Again following Levinas, Grob thinks that the desired change can take place if philosophy places its emphasis, first and foremost, on ethics. The ethics that Levinas and Grob envision, however, is not the ethics of philosophical theory. Instead, the ethics they have in mind arises from human encounters. It emerges from "face-to-face" meetings in which "my *very right* to exercise power" is challenged. As persons meet in this way, arrogance fades and gentleness beckons. The philosophy worth having, the kind that the world desperately needs, helps us to see each other. It does so not in ways that deface but in ones that unmistakably recognize the gift and preciousness of life, a recognition that comes to us especially through the particular embodiment of spirit that only a face can express. Then knowing becomes less important than caring, self-sufficiency looms less large than sharing, and gentleness replaces that arrogance that breeds divisions of race and ethnicity that have wasted so much human life.

If philosophy cannot succeed in making itself — and us — more gentle, then the wasting of life will continue its dreary and deadly accumulation, and the twenty-first century may prove to be more genocidal than the twentieth. Here it is instructive to note that, while Nazi Germany and other genocidal regimes rarely epitomize what are regarded as the highest expressions of philosophy, they are usually steeped in theory nonetheless. The theory is usually totalizing in the extreme as well. Nazi Germany was theory-drenched. Theories about racial purity, the inferiority of Jews, the superiority of Germans, and countless other totalizing topics were part and parcel of the context that was necessary for the "final solution." Post-Holocaust philosophy, Grob rightly argues, has to take stands against theory and in favor of the gentleness that never loses sight of the human face. To the extent that this change takes place, people will thwart each other less and help each other more. They will take better care of one another. There will be less cruelty and more kindness.

A gentler world is one that all of us need. While nothing makes that point more clear than the Holocaust, it is also true that the destruction of the European Jews and the cruelty and genocide that continue to infect the post-Holocaust world create doubt—even despair—about whether such high and idealistic hopes have much of a chance for realization. Ethics, says Grob, is about optics. It involves learning how and what to see; it entails vision and revision. He counts on education and particularly on dialogue to keep alive the hope that ethics will come first in all that we say and do. Seeing the face of the Other as "the absolute, the end of all ends" is the goal of Grob's gentleness, but the big questions that cry out for response include the following: How can we approach this goal more fully? How can we do so, in particular, when the views of Levinas and Grob unavoidably contain as much theory as they do? Education and dialogue may be the way, but these ideas have been around for a long time. How can they best help us to keep "the face of the Other" from becoming yet another theoretical concept? How can they actually make us see each other better and more deeply as human beings who must receive the gentleness that we need?

As far as Hitler and his followers were concerned, Primo Levi's face—to the extent that they saw it at all—was indeed the face of the Other. It had absolute status, too—absolute worthlessness because it was a Jewish face. Like Levi, Emmanuel Levinas, the philosopher who has done so much to remind us of the preciousness of the human face, survived the Holocaust, but many in his family did not. To the Holocaust's perpetrators, "the face of the Other" was scarcely a compelling ethical reality, except insofar as they took it to be "good" to destroy the Jews and other inferior creatures.

What can Grob's gentle philosophy do in the midst or aftermath of such powerful and wasteful disrespect for human life? So much needing gentle touches, how can we sustain them against the onslaught that seems always to lay in wait to crush them? We need to hear whatever Leonard Grob's gentle voice can say about such important concerns.

Grob's Response to Critiques

I begin my reply to my co-authors with a reaffirmation of the importance of the work of Emmanuel Levinas in helping to inaugurate a post-Holocaust ethics. Levinas dedicates a late major work, entitled *Otherwise Than Being or Beyond Essence*, to the victims of the National Socialist persecution. Although this may be the only work *explicitly* dedicated to these victims, the *whole* of Levinas's philosophical and religious corpus, I have argued earlier in this book, *implicitly* honors the memory of six million murdered Jews and others who suffered their own forms of persecution at the hands of the Nazis. The event that is the Holocaust—if only seldom discussed at any length within the body of Levinas's work—remains ever-present to that corpus as a whole: If Levinas's proclamation of the primacy of ethics challenges the Western "totalizing" tradition; and if totalizing thought can be the harbinger of totalitarian action; and, finally, if Nazi genocide lies at the end of a totalizing/totalitarianism continuum, then how could it be otherwise than that the Holocaust remain horizonal to all of Levinas's thought?

Several questions arise at this point, questions which are raised, most appropriately, by my co-authors addressing my earlier chapter in this text. Can, indeed, the Western philosophical tradition be dismissed as coinciding with an ontological thinking which refuses to acknowledge the primacy of an ineffable Other? If we are to seek a post-Holocaust ethic, must we reject, as Levinas appears to do, the body of Western thought?

Although so often marginalized within mainstream philosophy, some philosophico-religious strains in Western thinking do, without doubt, contain allusions to that which is both Unknown and Unknowable, before whom the human subject remains humble and awestruck. Levinas speaks of signs, hints, foreshadowings of speech about that which is beyond-Being in the thought of traditional philosophers and religious thinkers, from Plato onward. Yet, in the eyes of Levinas, both philosophic and religious thinking remains fundamentally suspect: "Philosophy," he tells us in his *Nine Talmudic*

Readings, "derives from religion. It is called into being by a religion adrift, and probably religion is always adrift." The name of God, for Levinas, is "subject to abuse." Although faith must be "purged of myths," Levinas turns to faith traditions for much of his inspiration. The frequent use of the images of "call" and "command" of the Other, for example, celebrates biblical "hearing" as a mode of relating more fundamental than the Greek notion of (an appropriative) seeing. Indeed, *both* traditional religions and traditional philosophical systems are taken to task by Levinas for their nearly constant failure to acknowledge the primacy of the ethical relation: Ethics-as-first-philosophy must ground both what has been called religion and what has been called philosophy in celebrating that which is truly sacred. In a post-Holocaust world, religion can longer afford the luxury of "the artificial peace of synagogues and churches"; philosophy can longer indulge in serving as a merely "academic" pursuit: Both must resist a totalizing impulse; both must alert us to the sacred task of hearing the command of the Other: "Thou shalt not kill."

Thus Levinas does not claim that there are no harbingers of the Other-who-is-truly-Other in the history of religious ideas; rather, he warns that the developed thought of religious thinkers remains—*most often*—ontological in nature. Whether it be natural theology, or even that mystical traditional which speaks of God's ineluctable nature, God remains, in most instances, an object: God is *part of*, rather than *beyond* being, even in the pronouncement of His absence before my usual modes of comprehension. How to speak of a God who would be truly Other is a task of infinite proportions. Naming God as outside of being, or "Other," is not just another endeavor to posit an Absolute, but rather the end of "positing" altogether. It is the introduction of process, summons, a movement-toward which must place this Other outside the realm of traditional names for God: God is often spoken of by Levinas as *à-Dieu* (to-God), rather than *Dieu*. The Other-beyond-Being is not just a variant on that spoken of in traditional religious thought, but a radical break with all naming which alludes to God as a substantive, present (or even absent!) to the subject-as-referent.

But must a post-Holocaust ethic speak about God at all? My own essay in this volume does indeed fail to speak *explicitly* of God in Levinas's thought. It should be noted that some of Levinas's own philosophical works—as distinguished from essays generally referred to as religious or specifically Jewish—speak little of God outright. Neither Levinas nor I, as interpreter of certain themes in Levinas's work, wish to deny the clear influence on his work of religious and, specifically, Jewish thought. *Implicitly*, the God who is wholly Other *is invoked throughout* Levinas's work—the so-called "philosophical" books and essays included—as it is throughout my essay. The image of God, whether God is called by that name or not, reminds us that the Other who is truly other calls us to account from "on high"; this image keeps us in mind of the radical asymmetry present in the face-to-face relation, disallowing us from identifying the *ethical* relation with something more akin to Martin Buber's dialogical, I-Thou encounter. Indeed, this invocation of God is crucial for establishing a ground of all grounds of alterity, from which can be developed a critique of ontology as helping to establish a potential for genocide.

In alluding to a "potential for genocide," however, I do not wish to imply that the Holocaust has no unique characteristics which would, in some respects, distinguish it from other genocides. At the same time as they set out to exterminate Jews wherever they could be found, the Nazis sought to eliminate from the world the Jewish ethical teaching concerning the sacred nature of the Other-who-is-wholly-Other, that Other who, alone, could call the Nazis to account for their appropriative (and, eventually, genocidal) acts. Further light is shed on the specifically Jewish roots of his ethics in Levinas's essay "Loving the Torah More Than God." Here Levinas takes to task those who would love God in a puerile manner, seeking some easy equivalence of goodness and evil with reward and punishment. Rather than blind obedience, a healthy dose of atheism—freedom from a God who "treats men like children"—is requisite for authentic belief. More concretely, the Torah of the Jewish people demands the "superhuman of man," exacting, through Law, that which is "excessive," thus making the Jewish people nothing short of a "religious category" whose example can teach the avoidance of facile, ultimately idolatrous beliefs.

Whether expressed in terms of the divine or the human—Levinas says, in *Totality and Infinity*, that "there can be no 'knowledge' of God separated from relationship with men"—the Other commands me from a height beyond my own. Yet, as we know so certainly in the post-Holocaust world, *hearing* the Other's fundamental command "Thou shalt not kill" and *obeying* this command are not necessarily the same. Levinas values, though not as an end-in-itself, the "separated" or autonomous status of the "I" who acts with freedom: In response to a question, posed in a 1986 interview, "...is it possible to recognize an absolute commandment as such and to disobey it in spite of this recognition?" Levinas claims that this is indeed the case. Yet, although I am free to kill *others*, as did the Nazis who de-faced their Jewish victims, I cannot succeed in killing the *Other*. The face of this Other is ultimately impervious to all acts of killing: It stands constant, calling me to responsibility even after my attempts to murder it. The Other survives even the genocidal acts of Nazi murderers.

Two questions immediately arise from what has just been said: Is not Levinas's Other just another abstract philosophical concept in the history of ideas? And even if the Other is freed from the charge of serving as "just another concept," is it not small consolation to us, who know of the murder of six million Jews during the Holocaust and who look to Levinas for guidance in developing a post-Holocaust ethics, that *others* can be murdered but that the *Other* cannot? What role in a post-Holocaust ethics can be played, *concretely*, by the depiction of the call of the Other in Levinas?

For Levinas, the presence of the inviolable Other is no abstraction conjured up by academic philosophers; nor is his philosophizing another example of theorizing, subject to the same critique he has leveled at all appropriative thinking. Not that Levinas, as I have indicated in my earlier essay in this volume, is unaware of the tendency of language to congeal into dogmatism. In speaking of the Other, however, Levinas endeavors to do nothing short of "unsaying the said." The depiction of the Other is no mere theory, no positing of one more static absolute in a history of ideas of what constitutes an absolute. It is, rather, a "living" absolute, a summons. Rather than a fixed idea existing on the same plane with other pretenders to the status of an absolute, Levinas's Other is more "call" than theoretical construct: It is to be encountered, rather than posited. More verb than noun, more vocative than indicative in its structure, the Other summons us to be responsible humans.

Finally, if it is not just another abstraction in a history of philosophical abstractions, how does the face-to-face encounter help us to realize our goal of a post-Holocaust ethics? How can it help us to prevent future genocides? Is Levinas's depiction of the ethical relation descriptive or prescriptive in nature?

It must be recalled that Levinas is writing against the backdrop of centuries—no, millennia—within which moral, legal, and religious systems have failed to protect us from the threat and, all-too-often, the reality of genocidal acts. Levinas does not offer us just another set of moral directives akin to those ultimately derived from a base of egoist ontology. Rather, he endeavors to ground all modes of thinking and acting in a ground of all grounds: the call to responsibility sounded by the Other. This call undergirds, and thus stands outside any traditional descriptive/prescriptive distinction. Levinas's thought provides a context of all contexts for what it means to be moral, prompting us to rethink, from the bottom up, where we stand in relation to others.

Where *do* we stand? We stand, in every aspect of our lived experience, as called to account for ourselves. Levinas brings to our attention that which, at bottom, is requisite for action which would refuse our potential for genocide. Whether it be those aspects of my being traditionally analyzed, let us say, by behavioral, social, or any other (alleged) science of humankind, each and every part of my being must now be looked at as founded in a fundamental call to responsibility. The human sciences must indeed be called upon in the endeavor to combat genocide, but they must no longer ground themselves in an *egoist* base. After Levinas, it is not as if I am no longer subject to emotional or social constraints; rather, I must see this "being subject to" as rooted in something more basic than the alleged need to act, in all instances, from mere self-interest. The ethical relation to the Other permeates all that has heretofore been considered rooted in a fundamentally *egoist* ambition.

I speak earlier in this volume of the need to educate our young toward the goal of eliminating genocide. It is certainly true that ideas about education for peace and justice have been advanced, most often unsuccessfully, for centuries on end. What Levinas adds to a discussion of education is the "reminder" that I am, at root, called to account for my conduct by an Other who exceeds my power, infinitely, but whose "power" consists not in coercion but in an "authority" which is an ethical resistance. The perpetrators of the Holocaust exercised their freedom in the attempt to avoid the face of the Other. Levinas argues that without the face of the Other grounding all aspects of my being, I will be constantly subject to the temptation to de-face my world. *Most often*, this de-facing will be a relatively benign "using" of the other with reference to my purposes, my self-interest. *Sometimes* defacing will mean exploiting others, subjecting them to my will on a continuum from verbal to physical coercion. *At its extreme*, as during the Holocaust, defacing will end in genocide. Keeping before me, at every moment, the face of the Other as inviolable is Levinas's contribution to a notion of education which will help renounce our potential for genocide. Levinas gives us no manual suggesting concrete measures to combat genocide; what he *does* give us is a framework of thinking/acting within which what might previously have been thought to be adequate moral or religious guidance can now be re-animated with new ethical force. Nothing short of this radical rethinking of traditional forms of such guidance is needed in our radically-fractured post-Holocaust world.

CHAPTER TWO

Science and the Determination of the Good

Peter J. Haas

In 1615, in the midst of his struggle with the Church, Galileo Galilei wrote a letter to Madame Christina, Grand Duchess of Tuscany, explaining why he thought the Church should allow the publication of his claim that the earth revolves around the sun. The Church, he said, should see no threat whatsoever from what he as a scientist might write. After all, the Church's expertise and legitimate teaching authority concern the salvation of the soul, not scientific doctrine. He told the Grand Duchess that the intention of the Holy Ghost was simply "to teach us how one goes to heaven, not how heaven goes."

In one sense, of course, Galileo was right. Religion deals with matters that are beyond the reach of scientific validation while science must be able to pursue its questions free from doctrinal considerations. Yet on another level, I think Galileo was fundamentally, and dangerously, wrong. We do not hold our view of the cosmos as science reveals it to us, on the one hand, and our notion of religious and moral values, on the other, as utterly distinct epistemological arenas. Quite the opposite. The history of Western thinking shows us that scientific inquiry and religious and philosophical views of what it means to be human and to act justly have always interacted with each other. On the one hand, it is a matter of historical record that as scientific paradigms develop and change, so too do conceptualizations of what constitutes the moral life. At the same time, the social implications of new scientific paradigms have always been open to the critique of religious and moral insights. In short, history has proven Galileo at least partially wrong in his claim to Madame Christina that science and religion are, or ought to be, distinct enterprises. Science and moral philosophy are, and always have been, intimately linked.

It is with this thought in mind that I turn to the Holocaust. The Holocaust can be seen as a prime example of what happens when science and religion are severed, giving scientific paradigms absolute and uncritical authority. I want to argue here that it was precisely by ceding science unassailable moral authority that a modern, Western, twentieth-century, cultured people came to think that the genocide of other Europeans was an appropriate way to solve their problems. In other words, my claim is that the Nazis were able to argue that their policy was based on scientific principles that were beyond question, and on that basis were able sufficiently to convince university students, professors, doctors, lawyers, theologians, fathers (and mothers) to live with the destruction of Jews and others (like Gypsies) because, as distasteful as it might be, that was ultimately what science demanded.

On a simple level, the Nazis were able to establish their radical ethic because it was clear to everyone that none of the received ways was working. After all, Germany as a nation and a society was facing utter collapse in the 1920s and 1930s. In the wake of her defeat in World War I, Germany found herself saddled with an imposed government that was paralyzed by inter-party bickering, with an economy that was in shambles and on the verge of collapse, and with a social climate that tottered on the edge of civil war. It was against this background that we have to understand the attractiveness of the Nazi alternative. So many intelligent people found it appealing, I submit, precisely because it offered a comprehensive, coherent and—in my view most importantly—apparently scientific account of matters. The Nazis were simply able to convince Germans that killing Jews and other racial enemies was the most scientific, and therefore the most advanced, strategy available to them to solve their problems. At a time when other more conventional policies were failing and when people were disposed to place great store in science and technology, these features of the Nazi ethic proved irresistible to many, especially among the intelligentsia. All that was necessary was to suppress any outside source of critique.

In short, what I call the "Nazi ethic" succeeded because normal people chose to ignore their previous moral heritage and to rely instead exclusively on what appeared to be a coherent and cogent social scientific theory. The theory in question, of course, was Social Darwinism. This theory drew together elements of mainline biology and Darwinism, on the one hand, and Romantic theories of nation and *Volksgeist*, on the other, to create a scientific explanation for the social malaise Europe was experiencing. It provided a paradigm within which the new insights of science could be harnessed to manage the deteriorating social situation. By the late nineteenth and early twentieth century, it claimed to offer the most plausible and coherent account both of reality as people were experiencing it and of how that reality might be mastered and reshaped. Nazi racial policy can be seen, in fact, as little more than a large scale and largely successful attempt to institutionalize into social policy this scientific paradigm. The fact that all religious and philosophical grounds for criticizing this paradigm were silenced, along with the fact that the social, economic, and military situation of Germany seemed greatly to improve once the Nazis took over, gave the Nazi claims unassailable authority. To see how closely this scientific paradigm fueled the political and ethical outlook of the Nazis while displacing the received religious tradition, it will be necessary to look at it in more detail.

In effect, as I said, the Nazi ideology wove together elements from two different scientific traditions, one having to do with biology and the other with social science. The biological theories on which Nazism drew had taken shape over the previous century and a half around the question of how to understand the diversity of the natural world. The discovery of the new and strange flora and fauna in the New World, along with the end of Aristotelianism, lent a new urgency to attempts to rethink in a systematic way the character and meaning of the natural world. To be sure, some biologists had come to the disorienting conclusion as early as the late seventeenth century that the natural world made no sense at all, that any classification scheme was simply a human invention, a trick of the mind to give us a sense of purpose in what was really a meaningless cosmos.

But most found this conclusion unacceptable. If the world was really random and senseless, then there would be no point in doing science, in accepting religious teachings, or in talking about ethics at all.

What was becoming increasingly clear through this debate, however, was that finding the supposed order and meaning of the natural world was not going to be easy. The problem, in its simplest terms, was that the variety and diversity of the natural world made it impossible to find any objective scheme of classification. Outer appearance, in particular, turned out to be not only worthless, but downright misleading. A Siberian Husky (for example) looks very much like a wolf, which is a member of a different species, and nothing like a Chihuahua, which is the same species. Biologists concluded that classification could not be based on outer form and appearance, but had to depend on finding some inner essence. The problem then became how to identify scientifically and objectively such an essence. What emerged by the middle of the nineteenth century was a focus on the historical development of extant types. The idea, in brief, was that the species to which any individual belonged could be determined only from its genealogical history. A Husky belongs to the dog family not because of its appearance, but because it carries within itself the genealogical heritage of the canine genotype. The problem biologists now faced was to fashion both a theory and a method for adducing how historical genotypes developed and why they lead to the diversity of individuals we encounter in the real world.

This is where matters stood in the middle of the nineteenth century when Darwin hit upon a scientific way for describing how a common ancestor could generate over time a range of distinct subtypes and individuals. Through the mechanisms of adaptation and survival of the fittest, Darwin showed in detail how change in natural types was both possible and logical. He provided a scientifically sophisticated scheme by which the natural world was finally made subject to human efforts at classification and description.

Darwin was thinking, of course, only of species in the natural world. Yet some social scientist thought that the clash of rival cultures in human history could also be explained "scientifically" through this scheme. The idea was that just as different plants and animals were engaged in a struggle against each other in the natural world, so different human groups were engaged in a struggle on the historical stage for access to resources. It did not in fact take much effort to apply the Darwinian ideas of natural selection and survival of the fittest to the human situation. One simply had to assume that different civilizations were like different species, struggling for dominance against each other. Civilizations, like species, that possessed superior qualities would prevail to reproduce and expand; others would be marginalized or eliminated. Further, each civilization could change and adapt as conditions demanded. Finally, the essence or innate character of a civilization was constant and could be traced over time just as genotypes in the natural world retained their essential characteristics despite outer change. Thus one could study different civilizations, nations or "races" on the human level in the same way one would study different animal species in the natural world. The variety of present-day civilizations could be classified into races, on an analogy with the classification of natural flora and fauna into species, using as markers such traits as skin color, language, cultural creativity and the like. In addition, the historical trajectory of present-day races could be traced through their "fossilized" remains, namely art, literature and architecture and other archeological data. One could, on this view, then not only identify which "species" or "race" a modern person belonged to, but what innate behavioral and mental traits that person was carrying forward.

A major result of reading the human social situation through the lenses of scientific biology was the conclusion that social upheavals and wars were no longer to be seen as merely a matter of economics or politics, but rather a matter of biological necessity. It was the law of the survival of the fittest played out on the arena of human society. On this reading, bearers of a strong genetic endowment, whether the upper classes within a nation or a more advanced nation among less developed ones, had a natural right, even imperative, to prevail so as to carry civilization forward. On the other hand, if the gene pool of any group were to degenerate for whatever reason, then that population would by the very laws of nature undergo decline and would "by right" be eliminated. Such genetic degeneration could come about from within (inferior classes having too many children) or from without (genetic intermingling with members of "inferior" groups). To insure that a nation survive and prosper, this view would demand a scientific social policy of careful eugenic management. These were the ironclad implications of attempting to institutionalize a social ethic adduced from the scientific hypothesis of Darwin.

The conclusions sketched above were precisely what the Nazis proposed to do in order to cure Germany's problems. They were claiming simply to be applying the advanced scientific insights of biology to their social situation. Germany's decline, they claimed, was simply the result of a deterioration of the gene-pool. The inevitable result, by the unalterable law of the survival of the fittest, was that the German people/race would be marginalized or eliminated unless the process of degeneration was reversed. The scientific study of nature suggested a two-pronged attack to engineer a revitalization of the German stock. On the one hand, internal bearers of defective genetic material had to be prevented from reproducing. This led to a range of eugenic policies that included killing or sterilizing undesirable or "degenerate" elements in the population. On the other hand, there was a need to prevent the intermixing, and so dilution, of the German genetic heritage, the so-called Aryan genotype. This could be accomplished only by identifying and segregating out non-Aryans, leading ultimately to the Nazis' vast scheme of ghettos, concentration camps, and death camps. Again, this was perfectly in line with the ironclad laws of nature. It was a "public health" matter different only in focus and scale from exterminating rats or killing germs.

Let me recapitulate where the argument is so far and reflect on what I see as some of its major ramifications. First of all, Social Darwinism (as a social theory) had deep roots in legitimate science, especially biology. Second, because of this, Social Darwinism and the eugenic "sciences" it created constituted an all-encompassing, internally consistent, and apparently objective world view. That is, once one accepted this biological paradigm, there is no way from within to prove it wrong. In a technologically advanced society like Germany's, this gave it a certain compelling quality. Third, Social Darwinism easily yielded what appeared to be a scientifically valid social policy. The result was that the world view offered by Social

Darwinism proved irresistible to a Germany reeling from the defeat of war, social anarchy, and economic collapse. Here was a comprehensive system, allegedly based on a solid scientific theory, that could not only explain what was happening, but also give reliable guidance on how to fix it. And so step by step Auschwitz was built and operated by people just like you and me who in good conscience thought they were doing the ultimately right thing for the greater good as demanded by the laws of nature.

Although this paradigm had a certain compelling internal character, its adoption should not be taken as inevitable. Those who promulgated and accepted this "Darwinian" model of social policy did so despite clear counter-indications. The question thus is not merely why did people act as they did once they had accepted the Nazi ethic; this is fairly easy to explain. The more interesting question is why did they accept it in the first place. This paradigm had, after all, horrific policy implications which were obvious to anyone who cared to look. It established the moral necessity of racial warfare, it justified slavery of inferiors, it called for the sterilization or killing of those declared to be socially useless, and it demanded the murder of any one, or any group, defined to be a racial enemy. It must be remembered that the thinkers who proposed or acquiesced to this paradigm did so in perfect awareness of these ramifications. The real question, then, is why Social Darwinism achieved the acceptance that it did in the first place. It is, I submit, in the very choice of this particular social paradigm that the real foundation of the Holocaust is to be found. Once this choice was made, it seems to me, the move toward racial war and genocide was all but inevitable, but, and this is a major qualification, the choice of Social Darwinism to begin with was not inevitable.

This of course raises the further question of whether some equally compelling, even scientifically-based, grounds existed on which people could have rejected the Nazi paradigm. My answer is that such grounds were in fact available. Why people chose to ignore them is an altogether different question which I do not want to explore here. Suffice it to say for the moment that it seems to me that the choice of this paradigm was not so much rational as emotional. In other words, it was chosen not for any objective, *a priori*, and

disinterested reasons. Rather, the Nazi paradigm was adopted, despite the counter-indications I shall discuss in a minute, because it
offered a seemingly scientific grounding for conclusions to which
many Germans were already committed. These conclusions included
the notion that Germans were ontologically distinct from others in
Europe (in particular the Jews and the Slavs) and that they were
engaged in a brutal war of survival with their neighbors that had to
be won at any cost. The Social Darwinian paradigm averred and
systematized these propositions. This acquiescence, in turn, was encouraged, at least in part, by the deployment of state power and control of the media.

I now want to turn to the elements of the paradigm that I think
offered internal grounds for rejecting it. I want to address in particular two assumptions that undergirded the Nazi program: a) the claim
that the Darwinian hypothesis in biology was applicable to human
society, and b) the more basic assumption that science is objective,
that is, that science could give reliable access to truth (and so by
implication, knowledge of what is right). I want to argue that at the
time of the Nazis' rise to power, both these claims were known to be
questionable if not false. The Nazi ethic was promulgated and accepted despite these basic flaws.

Turning first to the applicability of Darwinism in the biological
sciences to the study of human society, this approach has to presup-
pose a number of homologies which Darwinism specifically denies.
That is, anyone who understood what Darwin was saying already
had the tools at hand for rejecting the claim that this could be applied to the human condition. I will just give three examples. First,
the principle of survival of the fittest never claimed that the best
species in some absolute sense would dominate and vanquish all
inferior species. It was making a much more modest claim, namely,
that in any one ecological niche, the *individuals* best adapted to that
situation would have a greater chance of survival and so to reproduce. Second, Darwin's theory implies that diversity is rewarded in
nature, not strict adherence to a single archetype. Species propagate
and flourish because they are able to adapt and bring forth new characteristics, not because they retain a static genetic purity. In fact,
Darwin's theory was devised in considerable part to explain the very

lack of genetic purity. Finally, the definition of species is not transferable to the human realm. All humans constitute a single species (Homo Sapiens); the distinct races and nations we see may be some sort of sub-category of this species, but they are certainly not distinct species in and of themselves. This can be shown by the simple fact that all humans can interbreed with all others. The Nazi laws against racial-mixing thus stands in open contradiction to one of the basic premises of the scientific system to which they claimed they were committed. On these, and other grounds, it ought to have been clear to anyone that Darwin's theories as regards biology were themselves incompatible to the use to which the Nazis wanted to apply them.

More fundamentally, however, is the fact that natural scientists were already quite aware that scientific inquiry was not yielding an objective reading of the world. Quite the opposite, advances in physics in particular were showing how contingent human perceptions of reality really are. The physical sciences were thus not in any position to claim to offer the basis for adducing moral values.

A good example of the contingent nature of science as recognized by scientists themselves comes from the writings of Ludwig Fleck, a medical researcher, whose major work, *Genesis and Development of a Scientific Fact* appeared in 1935. In the prologue to this study, he wrote that

> we have even lost any critical insight we may once have had into the organic basis of perception, taking for granted the basic fact that a normal person has two eyes. We have nearly ceased to consider this as even knowledge at all and are no longer conscious of our own participation in perception. Instead, we feel a complete passivity in the face of a power that is independent of us; a power we call "existence" or "reality.[1]

What Fleck was getting at, it seems to me, is the unconscious assumption on the part of many that what scientists perceive or experience is objectively connected to what is really out there, that the "facts" of scientific inquiry are given and it is only up to us to articulate their meaning. His book is in many ways a long argument the other way around, namely, that the observer is in fact an active agent in the very formation of the perceived "facts" and the "meaning" they bear. Whitehead paraphrasing John Locke, puts it this way: "nature gets credit which should be reserved for ourselves: the rose for its scent; the nightingale for his song."

The protean and ultimately unknowable (to us) character of whatever reality lies beyond our perceptions was not a new discovery of Fleck's. Western science had long recognized the contingent and even deceptive nature of our perceptions. Plato had already argued in the fourth century BCE that the physical world we sense is but a reflection, and a poor one at that, of a true reality that can only be intuited. The twelfth and thirteenth centuries witnessed the great debate between realists and nominalists as to whether names applied to different things had any objective epistemological status or were only conventions. The great thinkers of the Enlightenment such as René Descartes, Gottfried Leibniz, and Immanuel Kant all struggled with the problem of how to bridge the gap between perceptions and what was really out there. By the beginning of World War I, Einstein had already shown that even such apparently objective components of the cosmos like space and time were really only our mental constructs. By the 1930s, quantum mechanics had even demolished the idea that at the atomic level and below there was any kind of cause-and-effect relationship in operation. In other words, the mechanical and objective reality we think we see is really only the result of probability and chance. This was a well-established principle in science at this point, standing in full contradiction to the claim of the Nazis to have an objective and unassailable lock on what really makes the natural world work.

The argument can in fact be pushed even further. Again, Fleck offers a good example. He went on to argue that in his case the "fact" under investigation was the existence of a disease called "syphilis." For Fleck the nature of this disease, and what it "means" medically and socially, are not defined by the data themselves. Rather, there were, and are, a variety of ways in which the "disease" can be defined. This means that even the one adopted by the scientific community was in fact a subjective choice. To be sure the choice had a certain self-evidence to it because it was part of a larger universe of discourse, but it was a choice nonetheless. The apparently objective conclusions of science are already a social construct.

The danger comes in, Fleck clearly tells us, when the scientist forgets that he or she has had a hand in constructing the facts. The fact becomes dead, a sort of Buberian "it" and ends up dominating the observer rather than the other way around. This is what, I think, happened in the case of the Nazis. Despite all the evidence to the contrary, the biological theories of Darwin, shielded from all outside critique or perspective, simply harden into the "facts" of Social Darwinism and from there into the institutions of the Nazi state. These presumed "facts," despite their innate contingency, were thus ceded the power to structure the moral and social discourse of an entire society. Any counter-indications, internal inconsistencies, and the sheer human horror of the policy this paradigm generated were mentally banished and then made physically invisible.

This brings me back to Galileo and his letter to Madame Christina. The separation between science and religion that he proposed was maybe a necessary claim at his time to free scientific inquiry from religious restraints. But it had an unintended consequence, namely, the separation of science from all external sources of critique. In an age in which science has been given unprecedented power, this separation has had horrendous results. What happened in Nazi Germany stands as a stark historical example of what can happen when the human, and thus inherently flawed, intellectual enterprise of science is allowed to become the unchallenged and unchallengeable source of human values.

Note

[1]Ludwig Fleck, *Genesis and Development of a Scientific Fact*, ed. Thaddeus Trenn and Robert Merton (Chicago: University of Chicago Press, 1979), xxvii.

Critiques

Critique by Leonard Grob

Peter Haas's contention that "what happened in Nazi Germany stands as a stark historical example of what can happen when the human, and thus inherently flawed, intellectual enterprise of science is allowed to become the unchallenged and unchallengeable source of human values," is a compelling one. Haas reminds us that because Nazi pseudo-science was "shielded from all outside critique or perspective," it congealed into an undisputed body of "fact" which then could "structure the moral and social discourse of an entire society." Cut off from interaction with any source of criticism, and most especially from those sources present in ethico-religious traditions, the scientific basis for the Nazi world view assumed the status of an absolute. The demands of adhering to scientific "truth" made the aim of the destruction of a whole people, as well as the murder of large numbers of others, not just acceptable, but a necessary—if rather unpleasant—task. Professionals, such as doctors, attorneys, teachers, and even theologians, could now lend their hands (or, at the very least, their silence) to the "scientific" mission of keeping Germany racially pure.

Haas is certainly correct in speaking of both the historical fact and the moral necessity of interaction between science and religious and moral insights: "Science and moral philosophy," he claims, "are, and have always been, intimately linked." When, during the Holocaust, a total divorce between these seemingly distinct epistemologies was instituted, genocide was given leave to arise. Although I am in basic agreement with Haas's thesis, my response to his work takes a slightly different path. I argue that it was not so much a schism between the disciplines of science and religion that gave rise to the events of the 1930s and 1940s, but rather a failure to apply what I will term the "spirit of critique" *across the disciplines*: Racialist assertions were articulated and received by those who, both within and outside of science, adopted an unreflective, unexamining posture toward these claims. In other words, it is not so much because it was a (social) *scientific* theory that the Nazis found Social Darwinism so compelling as to have it become the basis of an ethic; rather, *any* seemingly coherent theory in *any* disciplinary arena could, on principle, have been generated and could have found acceptance as the ground of an assumed ethic by those willing to abandon the Socratic directive to lead an "examined life." Let me elaborate.

Haas argues that "...what I call the Nazi ethic succeeded because normal people chose to ignore their previous moral heritage and to rely instead exclusively on what appeared to be a coherent and cogent social scientific theory." Reliance on a "previous moral heritage," I contend, is no guarantor of living an ethic which acknowledges the sacredness of each and every human whom I encounter. Reliance on previously articulated religious or moral traditions *may or may not* produce directives which will dispel the threat of genocide from our midst. Indeed, as has been well documented, it has often been an uncritical adherence to ethico-religious systems of the past which has served, and continues to serve, as one cause of much bloodshed in the course of human history. Moral and religious belief systems demand the same self-critical processes as do the sciences in order to prevent them from drying up, from becoming reified. The dividing line, I would argue, exists not, as Haas appears to suggest, between science and moral/religious systems, but rather between critical and uncritical readings of the world.

Incorporating the "spirit of critique" into every facet of one's life is our sole protection against ideas from science, or from any other disciplinary base, turning into ideologies. The fixed ideology of Social Darwinism did not arise, as Haas appears to argue, because Social Darwinism was "shielded from all *outside* critique or perspective (my emphasis)," but rather because this theory was formulated by social scientists who failed, *from within*, to adopt a critical perspective. That is to say, it is from *inside* each discipline that we must adopt the spirit of critique, challenging alleged "truths" at the same moment that we articulate them: *We must be both outside and inside our professions*, for example, what we profess, at one and the same time. Such critical perspective results not necessarily from consulting past ethico-religious systems-as-systems, but rather from a primordial realization of our finitude: In the process of acknowledging our fallibility as humans, we open ourselves to critique. Scientists, historians, theologians—*all* must adhere to the claim, grounded in ontology, that "truths" articulated by limited beings take on an ultimately provisional cast. "Living" truths represent the only sense in which truths are possible for us finite beings. Truths-as-provisional can never become static; they are perpetually forged in the give-and-take of dialogical processes in which ever-new perspectives on the issue in question are progressively disclosed.

Science, Haas implies, perhaps more than any other discipline, must beware of the dangers of reification. The idea of a neutral, objective search for fixed truths about the universe is certainly appealing. However, as Haas also points out, the alleged neutrality of the scientist observing what is real in some "external" world has always been questioned in the history of Western thought; the pace of such questioning has certainly increased during the twentieth century. Yet science still maintains its mystique. To counter this mystique, scientists must adopt a critical posture from *within* their discipline. Chemists, biologists, physicists must ask the questions appropriate to the "perpetual beginner" whom the philosopher Edmund Husserl urges us to become. Scientists must perpetually seek to uncover the values they inevitably bring to their investigations, examining those values in dialogue with others. In so doing, they must seek to expose the tendencies of their own theories to congeal into doctrine or dogma. Through ongoing dialogue with colleagues, scientists must work toward truth-as-a-process.

It is, of course, not merely the creators of reified science who bear responsibility for the efficacy of the "Nazi ethic." The recipients of this ethic—and here I speak especially of those professionals who occupied a leadership position in Nazi society—bear an equal measure of responsibility for receiving Nazi racial theory as an uncontested, indeed uncontestable truth. For Haas, "university students, professors, doctors, lawyers, theologians" adopted the Nazi ethic because "it was ultimately what science demanded." We know that of the 14 members of the Nazi leadership who attended the Wannsee

Conference, during which the "final solution" of the Jewish problem was definitively formulated, eight had doctoral degrees; they had published 35 books among them. Education, understood as the mere transmission of accepted bodies of knowledge, is thus no guarantee that the humanities will humanize or that science will lead to that progress within society as a whole envisioned by Enlightenment philosophers. What was lacking in the education of the Nazi leadership during the Weimar and early Nazi periods was the presence of a critical spirit informing all that was taught. Nazi professors learned and taught racial theories without critical scrutiny; attorneys and jurists practiced law, formulated in accord with these theories, as usual; physicians applied—uncritically—the tenets of an assumed experimental method to the subjects at hand: prisoners at Auschwitz. Without a willingness to examine whatever one is taught, teachings inevitably congeal into fixed doctrine and dogma. Nazi leaders were led to defend such teachings with tools ranging from the verbal harangue to the use of physical force. Only a willingness to examine, with humility, one's own deepest convictions will provide for true dialogical existence which stands in direct opposition to the imposition of force on the other.

But how do we know that adopting a critical, dialogical approach will turn us away from the use of force, and, ultimately, away from the likelihood of other holocausts? How will it support an ethic that honors the other person as a sacred being? Might not the give-and-take of critical processes merely lead to a relativization of knowledge in which nothing is any longer sacred? To engage in the spirit of critique, I argue, is not a morally neutral posture; it is to abandon, from the outset, the quest to dominate the other. To critique one's own and others' beliefs is to acknowledge that such beliefs are human, and thus—in Haas's own words—"inherently flawed." As an incomplete or flawed being, I stand in need of dialogue with an other whose views can contest, complement, or confirm my own. Having grasped the finite nature of my own perspective and the infinite nature of the quest for truth, I, of necessity, reach out to an other in dialogue. In so doing, I must see this other in the fullness of his or her personhood: *The medium of dialogue, in other words, is the message.* Dialogue is not a means adopted to fulfill some end outside itself; rather it assumes the full humanity of the other to whom I speak. In genuine dialogue I refuse to see my interlocutor solely in terms of some conceptual schema within which I would have subsumed him or her in advance. My interlocutor is not my object, but rather my co-subject. To engage in dialogue is to refuse to promote an uncritical allegiance to any set of ideas; it is already to have disarmed myself—both in terms of verbal or physical force—in order to engage in a search for truth with the other. This other cannot become the object of racial, or any other, stereotypes.

Haas is correct when he speaks of the necessity of science and moral/religious views to interact with one another. To prevent science from becoming "the unchallenged and unchallengeable source of human values," we must work not only to nourish science from sources whose locus is "outside" itself. We must strive, as well, to realize the ontological claim which would locate the ground of science, and all human pursuits, in the spirit of critique. For science to be authentic science—indeed, for any discipline to be authentically itself—it must discover its wellspring in a call to dialogue.

Critique by David Hirsch

As Peter Haas is well aware, his original thesis, that the Nazis acted ethically, even as they were constructing and utilizing the death camps, represents a troubling paradox; indeed, in the present essay his purpose is precisely to address some of the troubling elements in the original thesis, first propounded in his book, *Morality after Auschwitz*. He proposed, originally, that there was a "Nazi ethic," and that this ethic constituted a serious and viable code of behavior. The code of behavior was internally coherent, and those who acted according to the code believed that it was supported by scientific theory, specifically by the Darwinian theory of natural selection and survival of the fittest. As a consequence, Haas feels that it can be argued that those who murdered, and those who were complicit in the murder of Jews and other undesirables, acted in a "normal" way, that is, in a way consistent with their beliefs.

Because of the alleged (for the sake of clarity, I should stress "alleged" by Nazi theorists, not by Haas) scientific underpinnings of Nazi racist views, "normal people chose to ignore their previous moral heritage and to rely instead exclusively on what appeared to be a coherent and cogent social scientific theory.…Nazi racial policy can be seen…as little more than a large-scale and largely successful attempt to institutionalize into social policy this scientific paradigm."

In his present essay, Haas goes further than he did in the book, by showing that the German people had strong grounds for rejecting the Nazi "paradigm." It should have been obvious to any thinking person, and certainly to a true scientist, that the "science" was flawed, and, in fact, was not even science. Haas points out that the laws of "'biological necessity' did not, and were not intended to, apply to human beings and human societies." Second, German thinkers had provided ample reason, even as early as the twenties and thirties, for Germans to question the very notion that scientific "truth" is "objective."

The "truly interesting question," Haas proposes, is not, "Why did people act as they did once they had accepted the Nazi ethic," but "Why did they accept it in the first place?" They accepted the paradigm, according to Haas, for irrational "emotional reasons" that

Haas prefers not to "explore here." The paradigm, in fact, "offered a seemingly scientific grounding for conclusions to which many Germans were already committed." I take this to mean that at least certain German people (and other people as well) already harbored a desire to get rid of the Jews (not necessarily with murder and extermination), and therefore found the pseudo-scientific paradigm a convenient fiction which would enable them to conceal their unseemly desire under the cloak of "neutral science."

In citing the anecdote about Galileo, Haas attempts to resolve a dilemma. His point is that when Galileo wrote that "the intention of the Holy Ghost was simply 'to teach us how one goes to heaven, not how heaven goes,'" he established a fatal separation between science and religion, and created what Haas sees as an unwarranted division between the human individual as a being who clings to scientific truth, on the one hand, and a being who embraces "religious and moral values," on the other.

Returning to Galileo in his conclusion, Haas feels he has now reached the point where he can solve the mystery—let us call it, for the sake of brevity—the "mystery of Auschwitz." Galileo's claim "had as an unintended consequence,…the separation of science from all external sources of critique.…This separation has had horrendous results. What happened in Nazi Germany stands as a stark historical example of what can happen when the human, and thus inherently flawed, intellectual enterprise of science is allowed to become the unchallenged and unchallengeable source of human values."

I agree, basically, with Haas's portrait of the human being. I take Haas to be saying that, in order to act as a human, the individual must negotiate the world of science, as well as the world of values. Therefore, while I do not agree that the "mystery of Auschwitz" lies solely in the runaway locomotive of scientific inquiry, yet I am in agreement with Haas's assumption that the truly human individual must be more than a scientific inquirer. Instead of disagreeing, then, I should like to examine the notion that the mystery of Auschwitz is to be explained as the consequence of a rupture in man's dual nature.

I am not sure what alternative Haas offers to the "intellectual enterprise of science." We may infer from the first two paragraphs of his essay that the alternative is religious faith. But the moment we say so, all the questions Haas has submerged rise up to haunt us. He writes that "The Nazis were simply able to convince Germans that killing Jews and other racial enemies was the most scientific, and therefore the most advanced, strategy available to them to solve their problems."

Who were these "Germans" who could be so easily convinced to implement so cruel and horrendous a solution to their economic, political, and social problems? To repeat a cliché, but one that expresses an undeniable truth, these were, after all, the Germans of Bach, Mozart, Kant, Hegel, Gunkel, Bultmann, and Heidegger, among many others. In other words, we are not talking about a people of illiterate peasants, but of the greatest and most profound minds in Europe, not only in the sciences, but in philosophy, theology, and in the historical study of the Bible and Christianity. Moreover, even among peasants, were there not among them Christians who put more faith in Jesus than in science? If we descend from the level of "Germans" to just one specific German, the last of the august thinkers named above, we can see clearly the difficulties in Haas's thesis. We now know that Martin Heidegger, considered by some to have been the most powerful thinker of the twentieth century, was a committed and loyal Nazi from 1933 to 1945. Who convinced him that "killing Jews and other racial enemies was the most scientific" way of solving Germany's problems? How is it possible that this great mind should have been persuaded to share an ideology with the likes of Adolf Hitler, Joseph Goebbels, and Alfred Rosenberg?

But even those Germans who were not great thinkers were usually practicing Christians. In fact, it is common knowledge that Heinrich Himmler constructed the ideology and discipline of the SS on the model of the Jesuit order. Given these undeniable facts, what is the evidence that would support the contention that "normal people chose to ignore their previous moral heritage..."? In fact, quite the contrary seems to have been the case. That is, many of the "normal people" who supported Nazism, and even some who were Nazis, still thought of themselves as Christians. And not only ordinary people. In his book, *Theologians under Hitler*, Robert P. Ericksen points out that the three theologians he studied (Gerhard Kittel, Paul Althaus, and Emanuel Hirsch) "saw themselves, and were seen by others, as genuine Christians acting upon genuine Christian impulses." He adds that all three of these Protestant theologians practiced "a Christianity…in which the love of Christ cannot be readily perceived." How is that possible, we may ask? Can we blame runaway science for a Christianity lacking the "love of Christ"? On the Catholic side, we may recall Cardinal Faulhaber's well-known sermon on "Judaism, Christianity, and Germany," preached in 1933, in which he threw Germany's Jews to the raging mob, declaring that "Christianity does not become a Jewish religion" merely by retaining its belief in the message of the books of the Old Testament. In this same sermon, Cardinal Faulhaber declared that "the Christian…is not forbidden to stand up for his race and his rights."

The Nazis, to be sure, clouded the issue by adding their crackpot racial theories to traditional Christian antisemitism. But the point is that we are not in a position to say that the Germans believed they were giving up their "moral heritage." In fact, Haas himself argues, in his book on Nazi ethics, that Germans did not think they were giving up their moral heritage. The point Haas makes in his book is that Germans were able to believe that in killing Jews they were acting in conformity to a higher ideal that was consistent with a moral imperative, which called for the purification of the human race. The truth of the matter is not easy to get at, since perpetrators, accomplices, and bystanders have never been very forthcoming about what happened, or in describing sincerely why they acted as they did in the terrible years, 1939-1945.

Haas's thesis, as I understand it, is that the Nazi atrocities were made possible, at least in part, by the split that occurred in Germany between a value-laden religious faith and value-free science. A most penetrating analyses of this split in human beings (not just in Germans), derived from a reading of the creation narrative in Genesis, is Rabbi Joseph Soloveitchik's essay, "The Lonely Man of Faith." Soloveitchik locates this dichotomy in the two creation stories of Genesis, which present "two Adams." Rabbi Soloveitchik attributes the two Adams, not to various biblical documentary sources (J, E, Priestly, for example) but to the biblical understanding of the human as a "dual" personality. The first Adam ("God created man in His own image"), Soloveitchik says, represents "majestic man," who seeks to subdue the natural world (man the scientist). In gaining mastery over his natural surroundings, this first Adam affirms his human dignity.

The second Adam ("And God shaped man from the dust of the ground") is what Rabbi Soloveitchik refers to as redemptive man, man in need of "cathartic redemption." "Cathartic redemptiveness," writes Rabbi Soloveitchik, is attained "through man's exercise of control over himself. A redeemed life is...a disciplined life.... Redemption is achieved when humble man makes a movement of recoil, and lets himself be confronted and defeated by a Higher and Truer Being." Certain Germans (it would be foolish and untrue to say all Germans) lost sight of *both* Adam One *and* Adam Two. That is, these Germans made it their goal to destroy the dignity of certain of their fellow human beings, and in so doing they inevitably destroyed their own. These same Germans also were blinded to the Judeo-Christian essence of redemptive man, and whether they were Christians or not, they no longer permitted themselves to be confronted and defeated by a Higher and Truer Being. These Germans violated the spirit of Christianity as much as they violated the principles of science.

Since almost all of these Germans (including the highest leadership) had been born Christians and brought up as Christians, they must be held responsible for what happened. It was not science or modernity that created the Holocaust, it was Christians, who made choices and decisions.

Critique by David Patterson

In his essay "Science and the Determination of the Good," Peter Haas offers an accurate explanation of Darwin's theory in the contexts of biological science. He also presents an insightful discussion of issues surrounding that theory in the nineteenth century, particularly with respect to the problem of determining the essence of a species apart from the physical appearance of the members of that species. To be sure, such a determination would become a major point in the Nazis' understanding of what made a Jew Jewish. It was not merely looking like a Jew that was critical; rather, according to the decree of 14 November 1935, identification as a "full" Jew included anyone "descended from two fully Jewish grandparents" (defined according to religious affiliation) and who "belonged to the Jewish religious community when the law was issued or has subsequently been admitted to it,"[1] which, of course, would include converts. Haas is keenly aware of the biological portion of this definition of the Jew; indeed, his interest is in how biological science shaped Nazi racial theory, which in turn led to the adoption of a certain "Nazi ethic." But he ignores the religious definition of the Jew, one which indicates that the Nazis viewed the Jew not only as a racial enemy but also as a metaphysical enemy.

This metaphysical dimension of Nazi ideology reverses the direction of influence: science did not determine the "Nazi ethic," but rather Nazi ideology determined the agenda for Nazi science. The Jew's status as a metaphysical enemy rests upon a transcendent Good—*Ha-El Ha-Tov*, we say in our prayers—that the Jewish religious community both signifies and attests to. Because it is transcendent, this Good is not determined by science but rather determines the value of science and every other human endeavor. In their assault on the Jew, the Nazis undertook an assault on this transcendent Good. Therefore, contrary to what Haas maintains, they did not adopt a science that would justify a certain morality or ethic; rather, they embraced an anti-morality that determined how they would manipulate science until it was no longer science at all but just another expression of an anti-moral ideology.

While Haas is mindful of a Nazi perversion of science, he does not acknowledge that it was perverted to the point of no longer being science. When Darwinian thought is applied to human societies "engaged in a struggle on the historical stage," it becomes Darwinism; and when it becomes Darwin*ism*, it is no longer science. As the word implies, it is an *ism*, an ideological construct calculated to serve the interests of a predetermined political agenda. While the Nazis may have viewed the advance of civilization as the advance of the fittest, they understood the fittest to be those who belonged to a particular race and who had surpassed morality through a will to power. This ideological agenda shaped their scientific world view—not the other way around.

It was their hatred of the Jews, and not science, that led Germans to believe that their gene pool was being threatened by the Jews, since there was no scientific evidence of such a threat: the Jews constituted less than one percent of the population of Nazi Germany, and most of them did not intermarry. Haas suggests further that from the Nazi standpoint the racial issue "was a 'public health' matter different only in focus and scale from exterminating rats or killing germs." But even where science tells us that rats and germs cause disease, we are usually content to purge our home or our community of such vermin; we do not go from Norway to the Black Sea to seek out, torture, and destroy every rat we can find. The Nazis may have viewed the extermination of the Jews as a genetic necessity, as Haas points out, but a moral imperative cannot be generated out of a genetic necessity. If science determines that it is a good thing to get rid of rats or Jews, it cannot determine it to be a *morally* good thing. Nor does Nazism regard the extermination of the Jews as a moral good; rather, it is a racial, biological, cultural—that is, an *ontological*—good.

Hence Haas's references to a "Nazi ethic" are not only misleading; they are wrongheaded. If "ethic" means rooted in moral good, moral sensibility, or moral understanding, then there is no Nazi ethic. For the Nazis took themselves to be beyond morality and viewed moral conscience, "monotheistic religion," and "the rule of law" as a Jewish invention.[2] What Haas refers to as "the moral necessity of racial warfare" was not a moral necessity even in the minds of the Nazis. Although they may indeed have regarded it as a measure necessary to their own survival, survival alone is never the basis of moral necessity; the interest in one's own survival is a form of self-interest, whereas moral necessity rests upon an interest in the other. Nor can racial warfare be construed as a scientific necessity. It is an ideological necessity.

Haas himself makes an important statement supporting the position that ideology had more to do with the Nazis' understanding of the necessity to exterminate the Jews than did science. He argues that opting for Social Darwinism resulted in an inevitable compatibility between science and genocide; but, he rightly points out, "the choice of Social Darwinism to begin with was not inevitable." If, however, it was not inevitable — if it was *chosen* rather than concluded — it is not science. A scientific theory is not something we choose or approve; it is something we prove or disprove. To settle on one scientific position over another is not a matter of moral decision; it is a matter of calculation, observation, and experimentation leading to conclusions drawn from those activities. And if scientific investigation is to proceed in an honest and objective manner, then it cannot guide but must be *guided by* a moral order.

Mistakenly maintaining that scientific outlook shapes moral outlook, Haas adopts the equally mistaken position that, like moral values, scientific systems are subjective social constructs; just as life has no intrinsic meaning, the world harbors no intrinsic facts. While it is true that modern scientists have called into question the paradigms of objective observation and cause and effect, they have not concluded that there is nothing out there to observe or that scientific theory has no connection to physical reality.[3] Yes, Einstein once said, "As far as mathematics refer to reality, they are not certain; and as far as they are certain, they do not refer to reality."[4] But he did not say that there is no objective, factual reality to refer to. While it may well be the case that "the apparently objective conclusions of science" are a conceptual construct, it cannot be concluded, as Haas concludes, that such scientific explanations of the world "are already a social construct." That is why a theory on quarks or on the causes of cancer can be proven wrong.

Rightly, if not intentionally, Haas implies that one may invoke an objective moral good when he says that separating science from religion, or from "all external sources of critique," can have "horrendous results." But he does not refer to any sacred text or teaching that would lend an external source of critique the authority of truth. Indeed, his argument for the subjective nature of scientific inquiry tends to undermine any appeal to an external authority by which the moral integrity of science may be judged. For if, like science, morality is merely a social or external construct, then it is not an *external* source of critique. Such a critique is viable only where *external* means *metaphysical*. Omitting the metaphysical dimension from his examination of the Nazis' assault on the Jews, Haas loses the grounds for any absolute moral objection to that assault. What, then, is left to make the results of the divorce of science from religion horrendous, and not just a matter of academic curiosity?

But perhaps that is just the point that Haas wishes to make: we must not allow an ideology thinly veiled as science to be the source of moral value. If that is the case, it is because Nazi "science" neither shaped German morals nor justified German atrocities. Rather, the Nazis' anti-moral stance and the atrocities they committed and planned shaped their ideologically-driven pseudo-science.

Notes

[1]See Yehuda Bauer, *A History of the Holocaust* (New York: Franklin Watts, 1982), 104.

[2]Ibid., p. 330.

[3]See, for example, Niels Bohr, *Atomic Theory and the Description of Nature* (Cambridge: Cambridge University Press, 1934), 56-57, 119.

[4]Quoted in P. A. Schlipp, *Albert Einstein: Philosopher-Scientist* (New York: Harper, 1959), 250.

Critique by Didier Pollefeyt

Peter Haas's *Morality after Auschwitz: The Radical Challenge of the Nazi Ethic* is one of the most provocative and pioneering works in contemporary post-Holocaust ethics.[1] In Haas's interpretation, the Nazis were neither "diabolical" nor "banal" but remained "ethical" throughout the war. For the Nazis, the development of genocidal policy followed an ethically logical progression with which they could identify consciously, voluntarily, and even enthusiastically. In the light of this ethical framework, the efforts to persecute and exterminate the Jewish people were for the Nazis an ethically acceptable part of a greater good. Given this outlook, the Holocaust demonstrates the exceptional human capacity for redefining good and evil and for reconstructing reality in the light of these new ethical categories. It also shows the danger of subsequently calling this new ethical construction "objective" or "natural."

Haas's theory includes the role Social Darwinism played in the construction of the "Nazi ethic." He argues that the Holocaust developed progressively and got support from ordinary people who sincerely judged they were doing what was ethically and socially necessary in the light of a number of coherent principles of biology and nature. Once all other possible sources of criticism were silenced and the Social Darwinian interpretation of society was generally accepted, Haas contends, genocide became inescapable.

The innovation in Haas's present contribution is that he responds to the criticism that has been formulated against his interpretation, especially that his theory leads to an apology for Nazi evil.[2] He argues that the acceptance of the "Nazi ethic" should not be seen as inevitable. Those Germans who promulgated and accepted the Darwinian model of social policy did so despite clear counter-indications about its validity. But I want to ask whether Haas's new position adequately answers the old criticism.[3]

I think that the characteristics Haas uses to describe an "ethic," namely a "comprehensive, coherent and apparently scientific account of matters," does not sufficiently identify the essence of authentic moral discourse. Thus, Haas's use of the word Nazi "ethic" is erroneous. In a critical essay, Emil Fackenheim has similarly argued against Haas's position, arguing that Haas's use of "ethic" is inaccurate.[4] Fackenheim takes the concrete content of Haas' s use of "ethic" to be closer to the German notion of *Weltanschauung* (world view).[5] A *Weltanschauung* includes some formal attributes that are close to Haas's description of an "ethic": cosmic dimensions, internal coherence (*Geschlossenheit*), and an unconditional devotion. A *Weltanschauung* provides an all-embracing system of meaning according to which all natural and social facts can be interpreted. Furthermore, it is characterized by a self-grounding, closed, and internal coherence where external criteria to evaluate its truth do not exist. A *Weltanschauung* requires total dedication and obedience from its followers. It establishes a system of values by which one can live and for which one is prepared to die. The devotion of its followers is necessary because a *Weltanschauung* (in contrast to religion and metaphysics) is never true as such but always needs to be made true. Hence difficult struggles ensue when elements of the *Welt* (world) do not fit into the *Weltanschauung* but must be made to do so. This understanding fits Haas's remark that all counter-indications and horrific consequences of the Nazi paradigm were expelled from sight.

According to Fackenheim, Nazism was built upon such a *Weltanschauung*, which was formulated by Hitler. In Fackenheim's interpretation, the Holocaust is certainly not seen as working toward a greater good, but it was a component of a system that sought to establish itself with a vengeance. As Haas's analysis rightly shows, all other religious and philosophical grounds for criticizing the "Nazi ethic" were silenced. Such silencing is a typical characteristic of a *Weltanschauung* but not of an ethic. In my view, an ethic does not acquire its validity primarily from the coherent pattern of thinking and speaking it incorporates but, on the contrary, from the openness it bears for its coherence to be questioned. In this view, counter-indications and inconsistencies are crucial to real ethical experiences. They are the place where coherent systems are broken up for "Something Else": a beyond being (*autrement qu'être*), the Other, or the Good.[6] By contrast, a *Weltanschauung* provides its followers with a closed framework that enables them to legitimate their actions.

As a consequence of this distinction between ethics and *Weltanschauung*, one cannot conclude from the fact that the Nazis legitimated their crimes, that they also acted out of *ethical* concerns. Perhaps Haas too readily accepts the way the Nazis presented themselves. Their so-called "ethical" language could also be the expression of the need they felt to legitimate themselves in the face of what they recognized as unambiguous evil—and this for themselves as well as for others. The real question, Haas says, is why Social Darwinism achieved the acceptance that it did in the first place? I would answer that question as follows: to do evil in the name of a pseudo-good. The Nazi *Weltanschauung* can then be interpreted as the supplier of an arsenal of skillful pretexts and ethical sophisms for doing evil (and not good) with a more peaceful (but not good!) mind. Here we encounter the universal phenomenon of self-justification that becomes extreme self-deception.[7]

For Haas, good and evil are determined by the ruling and entirely contingent ethical paradigm. Once one accepts this paradigm, there is no way from within to prove it wrong. If the Nazis did what was good in their eyes, they could not be held responsible for *the evil* of Auschwitz. It even becomes difficult to call the Holocaust evil. Haas is well aware that speaking of a "Nazi ethic" can be interpreted as an excuse for evil, and thus he has added a major qualification to his theory: "the choice of Social Darwinism to begin with was not inevitable." He argues that other and equally strong scientific foundations existed by which people could have questioned and rejected the Nazi paradigm. The implicit idea is that because the Nazis did not do so, they can still be held morally responsible for the evil of the Holocaust.

Examine Haas's thesis more closely. He argues that the Nazi ethic was promulgated and accepted despite the fact that two of its presuppositions were known to be questionable and even false: first, that the Darwinian biological hypothesis is applicable to human society; second, that science is the objective access to (physical and ethical) truth. Haas adds that he does not wish to explore (here) why people chose to ignore such grounds for rejecting the Nazi paradigm. In my view, however, this is precisely the crucial question, and the reason for this deliberate blindness is neither rational nor emotional, as he suggests, but fundamentally an ethical issue. In my opinion, the applicability of Social Darwinism in Nazi social views was not a question of an honest and neutral scientific discussion, which was subsequently open to different ethico-political outcomes, but rather a search for a "good" excuse for genocidal evil, *a priori, in medias res,* and *post factum.*

Moreover, *when* and *how* must scientific knowledge criticize the wrong political use of Darwin's theory? *Who* had the tools and the power at hand for rejecting this application of Darwin's theory to social reality? Haas speaks of "people" or "anyone," but I am not persuaded that the masses had the interest or capacity to enter into such complex scientific discussions. Nor do I think people *need* such intellectual falsifications of applied biological theories for developing a moral opposition to the Holocaust. Its horrific implications were sufficient and clear enough for that.

How does Haas understand the terrible consequences of the Holocaust and the reactions of (some) bystanders and perpetrators to them? More generally, what is the meaning of disturbing moral emotions if human (ethical) experience is ultimately built on the collective, scientific framework of a particular society that can be so dominant? In his view, emotions can disrupt ethical performance, but they do not play a positive, constitutive role in the genesis of moral choices.[8] Still, one can ask whether the periodic, spontaneous emotional disgust of the Nazis for their own crimes should not have been a warning or counter-indication in their own moral life. For that reason, it is not certain that once the choice for the Nazi paradigm was made, the move toward genocide was inevitable. There are considerable differences between violent theories and physical violence. The face of the other always stands between these two dimensions. "Once this choice was made," Haas writes, "the move toward racial war and genocide was all but inevitable." Against this strong determinism, I believe that people—even if they lack scientific arguments—always retain a potential ethical capacity to break through certain preordained ideological frameworks that give so-called ethical reasons for evil.

Haas's determinism brings me to another key element in his argument: the Nazis wrongly presented the scientific theory of Social Darwinism as objective truth. Haas argues that human perception of reality is always "innately contingent" and a human construction.

In Nazism, the (scientific and moral) facts become dead (objects) which end up "dominating the observer rather than the other way around." Even if it is true that objectivities can determine the thinking and acting of individuals, often with very destructive consequences, one should never forget that, first, people always *give* the power of objectivity to certain facts. Otherwise, we end up again in a one-directional determinism of the subject by the "frozen objectivity" of (Nazi) reality. What happened first was a manipulation of reality *by* the subject before a manipulation *of* the subject by reality took place. Social Darwinism was not "simply" hardened into facts that then became independent and deterministic powers. Social Darwinism was first of all constructed and continuously given power by subjects.

One can illustrate this relationship by referring to one of the most important Nazi philosophers, Alfred Rosenberg. In *Der Mythus des 20. Jahrhunderts (The Myth of the 20th Century)*, which appeared in 1930 and sold more than a million copies, Rosenberg strongly attacked the objective truth of modern philosophy and argued for a more organic conception of truth: the truth of blood and race. For Rosenberg, values were not to be discovered in logical analysis but were to be created by a race. Moreover, no communication between the races could be possible. When detached from its racial origins, Rosenberg claimed, humanity became a senseless notion. Rosenberg took truth to be always culturally relative and subordinated to the practical purposes of the *Volk*. Nazism, then, is not so much a domination of the observer by a frozen reality (extreme objectivism), but the tyranny of active subjects—with very ambiguous and evil intentions (extreme subjectivism)—over reality.

There is another problem with the argument that scientists only make constructions of reality. If one takes this claim seriously, it becomes unclear what basis there would be for saying that the Nazi construction of reality is less acceptable than another construction. When the construction of reality (and thus of ethics, too) is only at the disposal of groups that are capable of controlling reality, then there is no longer any ground for protesting against such constructions of reality (including ethics), except from another construction that is, in turn, vulnerable to the same relativism. In short, we need a more complex theory about the relation between construction and reality, freedom and determinism, subjectivity and objectivity.

Haas challenges every student of the Holocaust to discover the nature of true morality and to ask whether, after Auschwitz, there is a perspective that transcends moral relativism. I think that Haas's reflections point toward such a perspective by forcing us to argue carefully why Nazism is not ethical. After studying Haas's insightful essay, the answers of diabolization, which say that Nazis did evil because they were evil, become simplistic and tautological. Historical analysis indicates that the Nazis showed a kind of "ethical" interest. In this sense, they are not fundamentally different from us. But ethicists should also demonstrate how ethics was perverted in Nazism.

As Lacan has indicated, language is only possible in confrontation with otherness. Similarly, the precondition for the production of ethical meaning is not a closed and absolute self-satisfied system but the irreducible difference between any system and the possibility of meanings that deviate from it (for example, the stranger who, without asking, interrupts my safe and righteous life). Ultimately, no system can be closed and definitive, because there are always productions of meaning that may escape the rules and power of the system. Haas's analysis teaches that an authentic ethical discourse differs precisely from a *Weltanschauung* thanks to the former's fundamental openness for new meaning, for otherness, for that which calls the totality of the system into question, time and again. True, human morality always takes form within a particular and contingent context, with its own history, language, social structure and political interests, but nevertheless an ethic cannot derive its validity from this community itself. On the contrary, the concrete ethic of a community receives its legitimacy precisely from a point that lies outside, and can never be captured by, its homogeneous structure. An ethic becomes immoral when it eliminates or strangles this point of transcendent otherness, especially when it does so in the name of some immanent good alone. The evil of the "Nazi ethic" precisely fitted this description.

Notes

¹Peter J. Haas, *Morality after Auschwitz: the Radical Challenge of the Nazi Ethic* (Philadelphia: Fortress Press, 1988). Hereafter abbreviated as *Morality*. Some important reviews can be found in: *The Scottish Journal of Theology* 46 (1993): 550-553 [M. Brearley]; *Journal of Religion* 71 (1991): 119 [L. Rasmussen]; *Journal of the American Academy of Religion* 60 (1992): 158-61 [Richard L. Rubenstein]; *Expository Times* 101 (1990): 220 [A.M. Suggate]; *Nouvelle Revue Théologique* 115 (1993): 420 [A. Toudobeau]; *Journal of Spiritual Formation* 15 (1994): 121 [M. Baird]; *The Jewish Quarterly Review* 83 (1992): 167-172. See also my review in *Driemaandelijks tijdschrift van de Stichting Auschwitz* 32 (1992): 78-80.

²Didier Pollefeyt, "The Morality of Auschwitz? A Critical Confrontation with Peter J. Haas's Ethical Interpretation of the Holocaust," in *Good and Evil after Auschwitz: Ethical Implications for Today*, ed. A. R. Crollius (Rome: Gregorian University Press, 1998).

³Emil Fackenheim, "Nazi 'Ethic': Nazi Weltanschauung and the Holocaust," *The Jewish Quarterly Review* 83 (1992):167-72.

⁴See "*Weltanschauung*," in *Die Religion in Geschichte und Gegenwart: Handworterbuch für Theologie und Religionswissenschaft*, 2d ed., ed. H. Gunkel and L. Zscharnack (Tübingen: Mohr, 1927-1932), 5:1911-18.

⁵See my response to Leonard Grob in this volume.

⁶S. Hauerwas and D.B. Burrell, "Self-Deception and Autobiography: Reflections on Speer's *Inside the Third Reich*," in S. Hauerwas, R. Bondi, and D. B. Burrell, *Truthfulness and Tragedy: Further Investigations in Christian Ethics* (Notre Dame, IN: University of Notre Dame Press, 1977), 82-98.

⁷Haas, *Morality*, 86: "To hear the perpetrators themselves explain their reactions and experiences is to hear how fully the Nazi ethic was allowed to override contradicting feelings and moral concerns."

Critique by John Roth

"What happened in Nazi Germany," writes Peter Haas, "stands as a stark historical example of what can happen when the human, and thus inherently flawed, intellectual enterprise of science is allowed to become the unchallenged and unchallengeable source of human values." Haas is correct, and his judgment is all the more devastating because what happened in Nazi Germany depended to a considerable degree on widespread acceptance of a scientific paradigm that had, as he says, "horrific policy implications which were obvious to anyone who cared to look."

Haas identifies the paradigm as Social Darwinism. The implications of the Nazi interpretation of that paradigm, he rightly understands, included racial warfare and the enslavement of "inferiors" as well as the sterilization or killing of any person or group defined as a racial enemy. Extending his analysis, Haas remains on solid ground when he claims that "the thinkers who proposed or acquiesced to this paradigm did so in perfect awareness of these ramifications." Indeed, the paradigm gave those ramifications moral legitimacy and hence political urgency, too.

Haas tracks the connections among scientific theory, public policy, and genocide in Nazi Germany for reasons of historical clarity but primarily because he is profoundly concerned about ethics—then, now, and in the future. Thus, the most fundamental and important issue that governs his essay is the following: Especially given the fact that the lethal implications of their fundamental choice were not obscure, why did so many Germans allow the Nazi ethic—grounded by Social Darwinism at its roots—to become normative for them?

As Haas handles that issue, clearly he is no determinist. Nor does he think that only Germans could have succumbed to such temptations. He does find that the socioeconomic situation in Germany during the 1920s and 1930s, including what he takes to be a divorce between science and religion, created circumstances in which Social Darwinism made a strong appeal in that country. Nevertheless, Haas denies that the Nazi ethic's dominance was inevitable, and he also makes clear his belief that "Auschwitz was built and operated by people just like you and me who in good conscience thought they were doing the ultimately right thing for the greater good as demanded by the laws of nature."

What remains less clear, however, is Haas's answer to the crucial issue he has raised. We need him to address that issue further, because versions of it exist wherever choices, especially public policy decisions, are made. Those choices and decisions are driven by what individuals believe is good and by what groups think ought to be the case. But here is the rub: To what extent does an ethical code or a moral theory influence such decisions and to what extent do human desires, wants, ambitions, even prejudices and hatreds sway ethical codes or moral theories so that they legitimate the choices people want to make, the goals they desire to pursue, and the policies and deeds they enact?

Haas tends to see the paradigm of Social Darwinism as the driving force behind a Nazi ethic that eventually authorized, indeed necessitated, the destruction of the European Jews and millions of others who were regarded as threats to Nazi Germany's interests. He makes us wonder, however, why that paradigm and the Nazi version of its ethic became normative. As a result, Haas implicitly invites consideration of issues that his essay has not entirely resolved, sometimes because of historical particularities that he underplays. One example involves antisemitism, a reality to which Haas pays surprisingly little attention. That oversight seems to affect his treatment of the relationships between science, religion, and politics. By asking Haas to focus on these issues further, it may also be possible to see more clearly what is needed for the vitality of post-Holocaust ethics.

To advance this inquiry, consider that in 1879 and 1880, Heinrich von Treitschke (1834-1896), an influential German historian, published a series of articles that drew attention to a fateful phrase: *"Die Juden sind unser Ungluck"* (The Jews are our misfortune). Eventually that slogan would be festooned at Nazi Party rallies. Just before Treitschke's essay appeared, another German writer, anti-Jewish journalist Wilhelm Marr, coined the term *antisemitism*. But what that term denotes—discrimination and hatred against Jews—is arguably the world's longest hatred.

Anti-Jewish hostility was inflamed by a "teaching of contempt" that early Christianity promoted. Christians often called Jews "Christ-killers." Violence against Jews was common. They were expelled from England in 1290, from France in 1306, and from Spain in 1492. As human equality, religious toleration, and civil rights developed in eighteenth-century Europe, Jews became almost equal citizens under the law. These liberal trends, however, did not eliminate antisemitism. In the late 1800s, anti-Jewish pogroms broke out in Russia and Poland.

Antisemitism has taken different but related forms: religious, political, economic, social, and racial. Jews have been discriminated against, hated, and killed because prejudiced non-Jews believed they belonged to the wrong religion, lacked citizenship qualifications, practiced business improperly, behaved inappropriately, or possessed inferior racial characteristics. These forms of antisemitism, but especially the racial one, all played key parts in the Holocaust. Without antisemitism the Holocaust could not have happened.

These historical points, well-known to Peter Haas but not always specified in his essay, are important because they contextualize the racial theories that infested Nazi ideology. Its bedrock included virulent hatred of Jews. Hitler and his followers were not antisemites because they were racists driven by Social Darwinism. The relation worked more the other way around: Hitler and his followers were racists who embraced Social Darwinism because they were antisemites looking for an anti-Jewish stigma deeper than any religious or economic prejudice alone could provide.

Antisemitism, nearly all of it steeped in Christianity's anti-Jewish traditions, preceded the racial views that some theorists linked to Darwin's evolutionary biology. Especially as events unfolded with the rise of Hitler and the Nazi Party, German antisemites who wanted a more "rational" antisemitism of the kind that Hitler himself called for as early as 1919 saw that the scientific paradigm identified by Haas could be embraced with open arms. That step would deface Jews and other despised groups so indelibly that they could do nothing to escape classification as deadly threats to the health of the German people. Meanwhile, in the 1930s, if not thereafter, advocates of eugenics, "race hygiene," and other forms of Social Darwinism could admire Hitler's rise to power, for it meant that scientific theory and political practice—both still blessed by influential forms of religion—could support each other. After the Second World War began in 1939 and the mass killing of Jews got under way in the early summer of 1941, many in Nazi Germany and in its collaborating regimes were prepared to take this wedding—its arrogant glorification of the Aryan master race even amplified by the antisemitic strains of Wagnerian opera—all the way to Auschwitz.

It is nearly impossible to understand why the European Jews were targeted through racial thinking unless one emphasizes the hatred of Jews that preceded the grafting of racial theory onto antisemitism. But given the previous existence of antisemitism, the temptations of racial thinking were nearly irresistible. Once linked, the two energized each other, and the "final solution of the Jewish question" ultimately took its genocidal form. What this line of thought suggests, and it will be helpful if Peter Haas responds to the suggestion, is that the Nazi ethic—perhaps the same is true of any ethic—has roots deep down in human desires and feelings, which can include persistent prejudice and hatred.

Our desires and feelings yearn for justification, rationalization, and legitimation. Ethical codes and moral theories emerge to do that work. They can do so powerfully, because they invariably urge that some things must be done and others must be avoided. Those teachings, moreover, can be underwritten by a society's most influential institutions: schools, laws, popular opinion, the arts, even medicine and science. As Haas shows, the Nazi ethic performed that function in uniquely lethal ways.

Ethics depends on the shifting sands of human desire. As the Holocaust shows, human beings can develop ethical theories to justify destruction that remains nearly unimaginable despite the undeniable fact that it has taken place already. So the most crucial question that always faces human beings is this: What do we want?

Utterly simple, that question is also as complex and ambiguous as it is unavoidable and decisive. Critical thinking can help us to answer it, and if such thinking is absent, no one is likely to answer that question well. The Holocaust can inform critical thinking in ways that nothing else can, which is why post-Holocaust ethics is so important. That event surely tells us what we do not want—or it seems unlikely that any event can. Who can study Birkenau and still defend racism? Who can learn about Treblinka and want anything that might promote genocide? Who can confront Mauthausen, Dachau, Ravensbrück, Sachsenhausen and the hundreds of other Nazi sites that destroyed defenseless human life—Jewish life foremost—and not be put on alert to evaluate scientific paradigms and the implications for public policy that flow from them so that what we want and identify as good will be for the sake of respecting and saving human life?

How can we best govern, evaluate, and implement what we want? Given the excellent beginning that his essay makes, that question, I believe, is the most important one that Peter Haas's insightful essay invites him—and all of us—to contemplate further.

Haas's Response to Critiques

One continuing criticism of my writings on the subject has been that they seem to leave no grounds for declaring the Nazi ethic to be wrong. On this point Didier Pollefeyt and I have been wrestling back and forth for years. His proposal here moves the discussion forward in what I think is a promising direction, and so I want to concentrate on his remarks.

First, let me say that I am ready for the most part to accept his argument that what I have called in my book the "Nazi ethic" might be more accurately captured by Fackenheim's sense of *Weltanschauung*. I say for the most part because there is a residue of meaning in the phrase "Nazi ethic" that is not in the phrase "Nazi Weltanschauung" and that both Pollefeyt and I take very seriously, namely, its implications for how we understand ethics and moral philosophy in the post-Shoah world. To me, the term "Nazi Weltanschauung" seems to refer more to the Nazi construction of reality in an intellectual or philosophical sense. To be sure such a world view carries with it implications for behavior, but these are implications, not directly the *Anschauung* in itself. My investigation, in contrast, was designed specifically to address the behavioral aspects of the Nazi system, its ability systematically to override and redefine the received Western moral tradition. In other words, my interest is in someone like Rudolf Hoess at Auschwitz, who not only acted in a manner consistent with the Nazi "Weltanschauung," but also did so with good "ethical" conscience. And Hoess was not a dolt or a moral cripple; he was a thoughtful, introspective, educated, sensitive, aware human being. So the real problem posed by the Nazis, in my mind, goes deeper than Weltanschauung. My point in using "ethics" rather than "Weltanschauung" is to stress that aspect of the Holocaust.

The central thrust of Pollefeyt's response, however, has to do with the question of how we are to judge objectively any one "ethic" or "Weltanschauung." In other words, if, as I have claimed, the Nazi "ethic" is coherent, internally consistent and self-sufficient, then on what basis do I decide that in the end it was wrong? There would seem to be no internal source of critique, and external ones are irrelevant. To get at this, Pollefeyt turns to the concept of the "other." As articulated in Pollefeyt's essay, it is a brilliant and powerful move. The "other" is always within the system (that is, any ethic) and so always a source of internal critique and at least potential correction. From this perspective it follows that what the Nazis promulgated was not an "ethic" because it systematically excluded that necessary component: the other. So the question on the table for me becomes whether consideration of "the other" is in fact what makes an ethic an ethic and not merely a Weltanschauung.

It seems to me that it is at precisely this point that Leonard Grob's response has real purchase. The point of always considering the other is precisely never to allow scientific or moral claims to become uncritically and unqualifiedly accepted and reified. For Grob (as for Pollefeyt) it is just this lack of space for critical reflection within the Nazi system which allowed the Holocaust to proceed to its awful conclusion. So for both Grob and Pollefeyt, the absolute need for inclusion of consideration of the other is the overriding ethical lesson of the Nazi system.

In many ways this seems to be a powerful answer to the question of how we can show objectively that the Nazi ethic was bad, or at least, not an ethic in the true sense. There still seem, however, to be at least two points that I would like to see addressed. One has to do with the claim that concern for the "other" must *by definition* be part of an ethic. There is certainly a growing body of modern and postmodern thought that claims that consideration of the "other" is, or should be, part of our post-Shoah moral thinking. Both Grob and Pollefeyt base their arguments on this significant and growing philosophical position. My question is how do we know that something without this concern for the "other" is *ipso facto* not an ethic?

The second piece of unfinished business, inextricably bound up with the first, is a clearer definition of what it takes for an other to really be "other." On the one hand, the argument that we must always make room for the "other" assumes that the other has a moral claim on us. But if the "other" can be tolerated in an ethic, then is it actually "other" in any really significant way? The alternative, it would seem, is to hold that the "other" is other in such an absolute sense that according to our ethic it is utterly evil and so must be fought against: the devil or Nazism, for example. In this sense, it could be argued that the Nazis did take "the other" seriously into consideration and then decided that that other was dangerous and evil and so had to be eliminated. In short, adding in consideration of the other *simpliciter* does not seem to me to yet get us out of the conundrum.

A second issue that often emerges in response to my book has to do with the power an ethic, or a Weltanschauung, has to determine human action. My explanatory use of Social Darwinism has often been taken to mean that I am claiming that people were "predisposed" or even "predetermined" by Social Darwinism to choose the Nazi ethic and that once they made that "choice" they were willy-nilly condemned to act as Nazis. One answer is to assert that it is in my scheme just as possible to reverse the poles and argue that people accepted Social Darwinism precisely because they had already adopted prior racist and antisemitic postures which Social Darwinism could now justify scientifically. But that leaves open the deeper question as to whether it is sufficient in any event to explain one's Nazi behavior as the inevitable result of some prior choice. It is precisely this foundational question that I hear John Roth raising in his response to me, and one with echoes in David Patterson's response. Does one choose a science on the basis of ethic, an ethic on the basis of science, or both on the basis of some third something altogether? And in either case, does that explain and/or justify a person's moral behavior? The point of my argument is simply that all of this works together and that Social Darwinism was but one component, albeit a powerful one, in the Nazi justification of their program of genocide. I mean to make no claim as to which came first, and certainly I do not mean to absolve anybody for bearing responsibility for the choices they made while acting in support of the Nazi program. In this I agree with the arguments advanced by both Roth and Patterson.

But Patterson goes on to offer a sort of hierarchy between science and ethics, namely, that scientific investigation must be guided by a moral order. If by that he means we should treat experimental subjects morally, there is no argument. But on the higher level of how humans go about making sense of the world, I am not sure his proposal works. After all, as I have been arguing all along, I can easily concede that science must serve moral ends, and then still justify the Holocaust on the grounds that killing inferior humans is a moral good. The question of what defines a "real" morality still stands. This seems to me to be in fact precisely the point that David Hirsch is trying to make, and I agree with him wholeheartedly. There are simply no scientific (or, for that matter, moral) "facts" out there independent of the human interpreter (as relativity and quantum mechanics have now made abundantly clear). Science is as much a human intellectual construct as I am saying that ethics is. This means that we can give neither priority. So we are back where we started, with the question of how we can objectively define a standard that allows us to declare an "ethic" to be wrong. This question has to be answered before we can do science morally.

This is why the caution that Roth leaves with us is powerful and central. In all these deliberations, we are dealing with the logic of a network of ideas, interests, inclinations and historical understandings rather than with a linear and objectively logical progression from axioms to premises to conclusions. The Nazi road to Auschwitz was infinitely complex, and so infinitely fascinating. It has of yet yielded no easy answers.

Chapter Three

The Gray Zone or The Banality of Evil

David H. Hirsch

Primo Levi was a reluctant moralist, an objective observer whose description of the persecutions and injustices he witnessed and endured as a *Häftling* in Auschwitz owes much of its effectiveness to the detached analytical tone of his writing. Trained as a chemist, Levi tried to come to terms with the camp experience from the perspective of a scientist.

Nevertheless, Levi's observations are not value free, and his memoir of Auschwitz has a powerful moral center. Gian Paolo Biasin has observed that "*Survival in Auschwitz* is...ultimately a moral treatise on certain aspects of the human soul studied in the most extreme conditions. The moral backbone of the book is undoubted: every page, every character, every event is presented on the basis of an assumption which is firm and unshakable at the core of the writing: the value of man, the value of the human personality, the value of the moral responsibility each of us has toward others—the common bond of humanity."[1]

While I agree wholeheartedly with Biasin's characterization of Levi as a moralist, I sometimes find myself wondering if Biasin and I mean the same thing by that term. For example, Biasin cites a passage, which I shall reproduce only in part, as an example of the moral dimension in Levi's writing:

> Sooner or later in life everyone discovers that perfect happiness is unrealizable, but there are few who pause to consider the antithesis: that perfect unhappiness is equally unattainable.... As [inevitable material cares] poison every lasting

happiness, they equally assiduously distract us from our misfortunes, and make our consciousness of them intermittent
and hence supportable.[2]

Levi's view is striking, especially so because one would not expect
that the condition he describes would apply to the Jewish inmates of
Auschwitz, of whom Levi was one, but rather to human beings living in normal circumstances.[3] Yet, incisive as Levi's observation may
be, it is not clear in what sense it expresses a moral vision. Biasin
considers this passage an example of Levi's moral beliefs because he
finds in it Levi's determination to approach Auschwitz from the standpoint of "our human condition: not the Jewish condition, or the
anti-fascist situation, or Italian nationality" (128). That is, Levi's observation endorses what Biasin sees as Levi's universalism, his refusal to limit his own situation in the camp, and the concentration
camp experience in general, to a narrow Jewish perspective. What
Biasin most admires in Levi is his "distance from any transcendence
and yet his uncompromising fidelity to a human—and humane—
morality which is all the more remarkable precisely because it is
thoroughly immanent" (129).

Biasin values Levi's universalizing tendencies, his conversion of
the Auschwitz experience into a laboratory experiment that may be
applied to all of humankind. I do not wish to contest the validity of
Biasin's contention, but I would like to examine Levi's treatment of
the moral issues of the Holocaust from a slightly different perspective.[4] I should like to start with what might be called Levi's moral
awakening in the camp, which crystallizes in a single moment, a
moment of the kind readers of James Joyce might describe as an
"epiphany." This scene, which is well-known and has been discussed
by previous commentators, occurs in a chapter entitled, "The Last One."

The main subject matter of the chapter is a hanging, a commonplace occurrence in Auschwitz narratives. This particular hanging
takes place toward the end of Levi's Auschwitz ordeal. Moreover, it
occurs at a most incongruous moment for Levi, and is registered by
Levi as an anticlimax to the "high point" of his life in Auschwitz. He
has been in the camp almost a year, and has succeeded in surviving
the most dangerous phases of the camp regimen, arrival and the first
selection, and has managed to get himself assigned to a good job in

the "Chemical Kommando."[5]

The episode in Levi's narrative starts on a high note, with the announcement that "Christmas is approaching." Levi and his friend Alberto have solved some of the most vexing problems of survival in Auschwitz. In addition to getting into good work details, they have found a source of extra food to supplement the Auschwitz starvation diet, and even a means of transporting the food; they have "procured…what is called a 'menaschka,'…a zinc pot." They have come to resemble a happily married couple, gossiping about their jobs and other matters after work. "As for the moral aspect of the new state of affairs," Levi then observes, "Alberto and I are forced to agree that there is nothing to be very proud of; but it is so easy to find justifications! Besides, the very fact that we have new things to talk about is no negligible gain" (132).

Levi even allows himself a bit of irony, indulging in a somewhat inflated description of his and Alberto's newly found confidence in their camp situation. Alberto, he tells us, "has just crowned his achievements with his masterpiece" ("*E infine, ha coronato in questi giorni il suo capolavoro*"). Alberto's crowning masterpiece is a scam to outwit the camp guards by selling them worthless trinkets he has learned to manufacture, in exchange for bread rations, thus securing a camp treasure, a practically unlimited supply of food.

But at this moment of triumph, Alberto and Levi are brought crashing to earth. They are about to witness a hanging, accompanied by all the "pomp and ruthless ceremony" customary on such occasions. "I have already watched thirteen hangings since I entered the camp," Levi notes, "but they were for ordinary crimes.…Today it is different"(134). The difference this time is that "The man who is to die in front of us today in some way took part in the revolt" (135). Levi's choice of words is quite deliberate, "The man who is to die" ("*L'uomo che morrá*"). That is, the person about to be hanged is going to die like a *man*, like a human being, unlike the other *Häftlinge* in attendance, whose spirits have been broken, and whose humanity has therefore been extinguished, or at least diminished.[6]

Actually, this man who was hanged for resisting the Nazis seems to stand outside the categories of drowned and saved delineated by Levi himself, and elaborated by Biasin. "Perhaps," Levi observes, "the Germans do not understand that this solitary death, this man's death which has been reserved for him, will bring him glory, not infamy"(135). Though Levi's writings in general tend to downplay the notion of individual acts of heroism, in this instance he does seem to attribute heroic status to the resister. The one about to be hanged stands apart from Levi and Alberto and the other compliant *Häftlinge*. He is a man, not a prisoner, and his ceremonial death, as opposed to the anonymous industrial killing awaiting the prisoners who look on passively, "will bring him glory," because he has "earned" it by resisting the essence of evil embodied in the dehumanizing killers who have staged the hanging. And the hanged man dies without having yielded, his last words being shouted out: "'*Kameraden, ich bin der Letzte!*' ('Comrades, I am the last one!')."

Ever the realist, however, Levi turns from his description of the heroic resister (an anomaly in the camp) to the rest of the *Häftlinge*, including himself: "I wish I could say that from the midst of us, an abject flock, a voice rose, a murmur, a sign of assent. But nothing happened. We remained standing, bent and gray, our heads dropped, and we did not uncover our heads until the German ordered us to do so" (135). Having described the hanging of the hero and the passivity of the ruined ones, Levi continues with one of the more striking paragraphs in all of Holocaust literature:

> To destroy a man is difficult, almost as difficult as to create one: it has not been easy, nor quick, but you Germans have succeeded. Here we are, docile under your gaze; from our side you have nothing more to fear; no acts of violence, nor words of defiance, not even a look of judgment. (135-36)[7]

One of the problems in dealing with Holocaust memoirs, even the most truthful and thoughtful of them, is that it is difficult to determine at what exact moment an author's moral insight has taken place: at the time the act being described takes place, or during that later period when the act is being recorded (or at some moment between these two). But at least at the time of the writing of his Auschwitz memoir, Levi was evaluating both the perpetrators and the victims who participated in this particular hanging ceremony; the latter were

no longer men because they had become docile; they were no longer
capable of resisting evil, but even worse, they were no longer even
capable of *judging* those who *were* evil. In other words, the prisoners
had ceased being human because they had been stripped of their
moral sense. The Germans, in this scene, are the perpetrators of
evil, the enemies and destroyers of all that is human. They have
extirpated the victims' inherent moral sense, but they, too, have lost
their moral bearings, and are lacking in the moral dimension that
would have made them human.

Years later, Levi would return to this motif in a collection of
essays entitled *The Drowned and the Saved*, a title he had used as a
chapter heading in the Auschwitz memoir. Biasin writes that, "The
second major concern of *Survival in Auschwitz* is the moral problem of salvation." This is so, but in *Survival in Auschwitz*, the "moral
problem of salvation" is dormant, while in the later work, Levi addresses the "moral problem" in greater detail, and with greater
subtlety. In the earlier text, "The Drowned and the Saved" referred
primarily to physical survival. Each of the four types of survivor analyzed in the Auschwitz book was concerned only with physical survival, and each used his particular natural gifts (physical, mental or
social) to that end: the "saved" survived on the basis of sheer physical endurance, cunning, or psychological strength. And, of course,
as Levi keeps reminding us, on luck, or inexplicable favors of fortune.

It is only in the later essay that Levi turns his attention to "moral"
survival, or what amounts to the same thing for Levi, to the possibility of retaining, against all odds in the camp, one's humanity, the
very element the Nazis wanted to destroy (and that Levi testifies, in
the aforementioned hanging scene, the Germans had indeed destroyed in all of the remaining *Häftlinge*, except for that one last
hanged man). That basic component of humanity, as it emerges from
the hanging scene, is the will to resist evil.

Levi addresses this problem of moral survival most acutely in
"The Gray Zone," a profound meditation on human moral fragility,
to which is appended, almost as an afterthought, a version of an
earlier essay on the so-called "King of the Jews," Chaim Rumkowski,
the eldest of the Jews of the Lodz ghetto. The essay collection in
which the Rumkowski material first appeared was *Moments of Re-*

prieve, where it bore the title, "The Story of a Coin." Now, Levi reprints the essay, with some changes, immediately after having cautioned the reader not to be too hasty in passing moral judgment on the members of the Special Squads, who assisted the SS in the killing process. "Each individual is so complex," Levi warns, "that there is no point in trying to foresee his behavior, all the more so in extreme situations; nor is it possible to foresee one's own behavior. Therefore I ask that we meditate on the story of 'the crematorium ravens' with pity and rigor, but that judgment of them be suspended" (60).

Why did Levi believe that it was appropriate, at this point, right after his disquisition on the *Sonderkommando*, to reprint an essay about Rumkowski that he had already published once before? To answer this question, we must examine more carefully the subject of "the crematorium ravens," that is to say, those Jews who worked in the gas chambers and crematoria, sometimes ushering their own dearest relatives into the maw of the death machine.

Though Levi positions the members of those special squads in one of the murkiest enclaves of the gray zone, he entertains no such equivocations about those who created the Special Squads. "Conceiving and organizing the squads," he writes, "was National Socialism's most demonic crime" (53). Despite the fact that his scientist's training has provided him with the ability to distance himself from certain phenomena and examine them objectively, suspending value judgments; and despite his delicate nuancing of the various kinds of behavior engaged in by different levels of the prisoner hierarchy in Auschwitz (from *Oberkapos* down to prisoners without rank), Levi leaves no doubt about his moral condemnation of those who conceived and directed the concentration camp enterprise. And he leaves no doubt that the authors of the system are not to be confused with those who were destroyed by it. As a writer Levi was a consummate craftsman who chose his words carefully, and here he clearly accuses "National Socialism" of having committed a "most demonic crime."

Levi also leaves no doubt about what it is that constitutes this "demonic crime." The "institution" of the *Sonderkommando*, he continues, "represented an attempt to shift onto others—specifically the victims—the burden of guilt, so that they were deprived of even the solace of innocence. It is neither easy nor agreeable to dredge this abyss of viciousness." (53). To drive his point home, Levi introduces a description of a soccer game first narrated by Miklos Nyiszli, a Jewish physician from Hungary, who survived Auschwitz by working for Dr. Mengele in the crematorium laboratory.

The game was a contest that took place between the SS and "the veterans of the squad" (54). In these veterans of the *Sonderkommando*, Levi observes, the SS men

> recognized to some extent colleagues, by now as inhuman as themselves, hitched to the same cart, bound together by the foul link of imposed complicity.
>
> Nothing of this kind ever took place, nor would it have been conceivable, with other categories of prisoners; but with them, with the "crematorium ravens," the SS could enter the field on an equal footing, or almost. Behind this armistice one hears satanic laughter: it is consummated, we have succeeded, you no longer are the other race, the anti-race, the prime enemy of the millennial Reich; you are no longer the people who reject idols. We have embraced you, corrupted you, dragged you to the bottom with us. You are like us, you proud people: dirtied with your own blood, as we are. You too, like us and like Cain, have killed the brother. Come, we can play together. (54-55)[8]

Having invoked the horrors of the situation in which "the crematorium ravens" found themselves, and having urged that the reader "suspend judgment" in their case, Levi moves on to Rumkowski. In the case of Rumkowski, as in the case of "the crematorium ravens," Levi advises that we should not be too hasty to judge. Although Levi never alludes directly to Hannah Arendt's *Eichmann in Jerusalem*, it is as if it suddenly occurred to Levi that Rumkowski, like the members of the Special Squads, belonged in "the gray zone," and that the Jewish leaders, whose role in the genocide had been condemned by Arendt as "undoubtedly the darkest chapter of the whole dark story," also belonged there.[9]

Scientist that he was, Levi reasoned inductively from the data to the theory. Unlike Hannah Arendt, who saw in the Eichmann trial an opportunity to verify and disseminate her theories of totalitarianism, Levi arrived at his theory of evil on the basis of what he had experienced in Auschwitz, that is, on the basis of seeing the Nazis in action, and not on the basis of seeing one now-pathetic former Nazi official being tried in a court of law.

Richard J. Bernstein has argued that Arendt was not "passing moral judgment on the reasons or motives of the members of the Jewish Councils," and both his reading of her text and his argument are plausible.[10] Nevertheless, it is not unfair to point out that Bernstein reads the passages from *Eichmann in Jerusalem* out of context; the many intelligent and perceptive readers who felt strongly that Arendt was indeed passing moral judgment were not unjustified in thinking so. Bernstein concedes that "there is a great deal in her book that can legitimately be criticized—both what she says and how she says it. Throughout, she employed sarcastic irony" (159). It is, of course, precisely the pervasive "tone" of Arendt's style, her slashing "sarcastic irony," which leaves the reader, inevitably, with the impression that she looks down on the members of the Jewish Councils with an air of haughty contempt and moral disdain. As a philosopher, Bernstein must know that "tone" is part of the meaning of a text. Perhaps Arendt did not intend to pass moral judgment, but one can hardly argue, on the basis of the full text, that she did not do so.

Levi's interpretation of the soccer game between the SS and the *Sonderkommando* constitutes a radical critique of Arendt, and of the "functionalist" position, to which *Eichmann in Jerusalem* became a crucial contributor.[11] Adopting the functionalist perspective, Arendt interpreted the Nazi manipulation of the Jewish Councils and of Jewish leaders as a policy, partly of necessity, and partly of opportunism. It would have been impossible, so her argument goes, for the Nazis to have murdered six million Jews using only the German manpower that was available. The drain on personnel would have been too great, and therefore, the Nazis were compelled to enlist Jewish collaborators in order to facilitate the extermination process. This, of course, was to overlook the contributions to the mass killing made by collaborating Ukrainians, Latvians, Estonians, Lithuanians, Poles, Hungarians, the French, and others. There was, in fact, no lack of volunteer executioners eager to participate in implementing the "final solution." But, as so many of her critics have already pointed out, Arendt was never one to let historical data interfere with her cherished theories.

As a scientist and a humanist, Levi weighed in on the side of the "intentionalists," not that he ever used that term (or perhaps even thought about it).[12] He recognized that the forced involvement of victims in their own destruction was not a matter of mere functional expediency on the part of the killers, but a deliberate subversion of the moral order, and therefore, an act of unambiguous evil: in Levi's own words, "National Socialism's most demonic crime."

Readers of *Eichmann in Jerusalem* were immediately troubled by what they perceived to be Arendt's exculpation of the criminals and indictment of the victims. Critics pointed out that Arendt analyzed Eichmann's psyche ad nauseam to demonstrate only that he was pretty much what he claimed, in his own defense, to be: a mediocre (banal) functionary who simply carried out orders. Yet, while she accepted Eichmann's functionalist portrait of himself as a mindless bureaucrat, Arendt embellished this image with the seemingly contradictory notion that Eichmann was also an "idealist" who felt compelled to have Jews rounded up and transported to death camps, not simply in obedience to orders, but in fulfillment of the Nazi ideal of racial purity, which he had come to believe.

What disturbed the readers of *Eichmann in Jerusalem* still more was their impression that while Arendt accepted Eichmann's portrayal of himself as a mere functionary and, at the same time, an idealist, she denounced Jewish leaders and the Jewish Councils as collaborators. Of course, Arendt was not the first to denounce Jewish leaders and the Councils. Jews living in the ghettos had done so in no uncertain terms, in their diaries, journals, essays, and memoirs. But there was also an issue of authenticity. The Jews living under the yoke of Nazi oppression, "governed" by Jewish Councils appointed by the Germans, which were to serve as intermediaries between the Jewish populace and their German masters, had a right to denounce the Jewish leaders which, in their view, had betrayed them. But Arendt was not one of the Jews living under the Nazi yoke. She was, on the other hand, someone who had chosen to run away from the struggle, rather than enlist in the fight against evil. Is it, then, not possible that Arendt was projecting her own concealed guilt, a guilt she never explicitly acknowledged, even to herself, onto the Jewish leaders?[13] And may not her theory that totalitarian systems cannot be overthrown from within (now, of course, proved wrong by history) reflect a measure of self-justification on her part?

Arendt seems to have lacked Levi's exquisite sensitivity, his ability to factor his own consciousness and existential situations into his analyses of objective data. Everywhere in his writings, Levi is agonized by a sense of "guilt" for having survived, while others who may have been no less worthy, and perhaps even less tarnished spiritually, perished; thus, Levi makes sure to calculate a consciousness of inevitable human complicity in evil into his account of "the gray zone." Even Rumkowski, egomaniacal, lusting for power, doing the dirty work of selecting Jews for the transports, even he, still falls into the "gray zone." But this does not mean that Levi does not allow for the possibility that there are some evil-doers who are outside of it.

Levi himself brings up the case of an SS man named Muhsfeld, who showed a "single, immediately erased moment of pity." That one fleeting moment of pity is enough, according to Levi, to "place him, too, although at its extreme boundary, within the gray band, that zone of ambiguity which radiates out from regimes based on terror and obsequiousness" (58).[14]

In a sense, "The Gray Zone" constitutes a reversal of Arendt's argument. By psychoanalyzing Eichmann's testimony and behavior, Arendt, probably without realizing what she was doing, allotted Eichmann a comfortable niche in "the gray zone." On the other hand, she tarred all Jewish leaders with one brush, and banished them pitilessly from "the gray zone" by peremptorily dismissing them all as having, "almost without exception, cooperated in one way or another, for one reason or another, with the Nazis."[15]

Levi, on the other hand, reinstates the Jewish leaders in "the gray zone," while making it clear that it was only the Nazis themselves, those who had conceived and implemented a political and social system grounded in evil, who were outside the "zone." Now that the laboriously created mythology of ubiquitous French resistance, and of Swiss benign neutrality, are crumbling, we are beginning to see how well the Nazis succeeded in implementing their policy of leaving no human within their power uncontaminated. This was evil on a grand scale, and there was nothing banal about it.[16]

Since Arendt's book on Eichmann was first published, her tantalizing phrase, "the banality of evil," has continued to puzzle readers; Richard J. Bernstein's attempt to clarify the vexatious phrase is both sympathetic and detailed.[17] But while he is sympathetic to Arendt's cause, Bernstein does not try to dodge embarrassing realities. Thus, he reminds the reader of Martin Heidegger's infamous assertion, "Agriculture is now motorized food industry—in essence the same as manufacturing of corpses in gas chambers and extermination camps...," and concludes, "This is the mentality that Arendt believed she was facing in Eichmann, and which she claims we must confront if we are to understand the new type of criminal that he represents"(169, 170). Bernstein seems to suggest that Arendt perceived a parallel between Eichmann and the mentor she once worshipped, and perhaps still loved, Martin Heidegger.[18]

Bernstein's intimation that Arendt was able to perceive a parallel between the mentalities of Heidegger and Eichmann is intriguing, but he does not pursue it. Rather, he goes on to "distinguish two issues...concerning the banality of evil...which have frequently been confused"(170). The first of these issues is "conceptual...showing that individuals can commit evil deeds on a gigantic scale without these deeds being traceable to evil or monstrous motives." The second issue "is whether Eichmann fits this description." Bernstein seems to feel that the first proposition is valid: "individuals can commit evil deeds on a gigantic scale without these deeds being traceable to evil or monstrous motives"; but, at the same time, he does not consider Eichmann a good example of this proposition. That is, Bernstein believes Eichmann may have been more motivated than Arendt concedes. This anomaly leads Bernstein to conclude that

> perhaps the most troublesome perplexity in Arendt's attempt to account for the banality of evil, the phenomenon she claimed to have witnessed in Eichmann, concerns what she has left *unsaid*. On the one hand, she tells us that thinking and judging are faculties that can be ascribed to everyone, in that everyone *potentially* has the capacity to think and to judge. This is a crucial presupposition in her attempt to show that

> there is an "inner connection between the ability or inability
> to think and the problem of evil." On the other hand, she
> claims that Eichmann's specific characteristic was "a curious,
> quite authentic inability to think." Presumably this is also true
> of all the members of "respectable society" who could switch
> so effortlessly from one set of mores to another—from the con-
> viction that one ought not to kill to the conviction that killing
> was permissible or even required for racial reasons. (176)

Finally, however, Bernstein is forced to concede that "Arendt never
satisfactorily answers the questions she raises concerning the 'inner
connection of thinking and the problem of evil'" (177). In other
words, she never succeeds at all in clarifying what she meant by "the
banality of evil." Yet, that phrase, in association with Arendt's claim
that Eichmann was not a monster, has fueled the functionalist view
that the Holocaust was simply an unfortunate side-effect of "modernity," in which "no human agent can...be held responsible for decisions or for their consequences," thereby eliminating the possibility
of individual "exercise of free will in human society and depriv[ing]
men and women of their capacity to choose between good and evil."

Arendt's misguided thesis is the motivating force behind *Facing
the Extreme*, by Tzvetan Todorov, who maintains that, "we cannot
understand the evils of the concentration camps by interpreting them
in terms of abnormality unless we define abnormality tautologically—
as the behavior in question: nothing about the personalities or actions of the authors of evil, apart from this behavior, allows us to
classify them as pathological beings—in other words as monsters,
whatever our definition of the terms *pathological* and *normal*."[19]
Either Todorov does not understand the uses of metaphorical language, or he has not checked conventional *pre-Holocaust* definitions
of the term "monster," as, for example, substantive, #4 in the *Oxford
English Dictionary*, which defines the term as "A person of inhuman and horrible cruelty or wickedness" and cites a usage in this
sense as early as the sixteenth century. I do not want to get hung up
on who is or is not a monster; I simply want to make the point that at
least one conventional usage of the term fits Eichmann quite well.
The term does not necessarily designate a "pathological being," and
using it to describe Eichmann is not necessarily "tautological." Nor

is it true, as Todorov claims, that "we cannot understand the evils of the concentration camps by interpreting them in terms of abnormality." In what other terms *can* we interpret them? Would Todorov wish to argue that the "social regimen" (if it can be called that) created by the Germans throughout the *Konzentrationslager* system is what he would consider a "normal" social order?

I cannot think of a single camp narrative that would support that view, not even those written by the Nazi overlords themselves. On the other hand, it is not unreasonable to argue that the camps constituted a grotesque parody of normal social orders. That is the point that is conveyed so beautifully in "The Gray Zone." Those who find themselves among both the "drowned" and the "saved" in the camps behave in ways that are analogous to the way people behave in normal societies. Soccer is played in normal societies. And often soccer games are played involving opposing teams who may not like each other. But when, in normal society, has a soccer game ever been made possible only by the fact that the members of one team recognized in their opponents, "colleagues, by now as inhuman as themselves, hitched to the same cart, bound together by the foul link of imposed complicity,...dirtied with your own blood, as we are"?

According to the definition of "normality" favored by Todorov, "nothing about the personalities or actions of the authors of evil, apart from this behavior, allows us to classify them as pathological beings." But is this not saying, simply, that if we overlook the fact that the overlords of the camps often engaged in what is generally considered pathological behavior, then we would not think of them as pathological beings, that is, as monsters? Todorov's point seems to be that the camp overlords did not behave pathologically all the time, only when they were in the camps or in their dealings with Jews. In all their other dealings, these people were "normal."

It was exactly this split between civilized and uncivilized behaviors engaged in almost simultaneously by the same person that Erich Kahler considered to be the key to the rupture in normal behavior that characterized the Nazis. Kahler identifies this split as a "phenomenon which has much broader significance. It concerns a peculiar mode of behavior on the part of the executors of the Nazi crimes, a novel kind of schizophrenia which, in a rudimentary or potential form, is present everywhere in our modern civilization, but has grown to extremes only in the Nazi situation." Kahler sees this alternation between subhuman cruelty and brutality, on the one hand, and a sophisticated civilized sensibility on the other, as a new kind of behavior, an "uncanny suspension of all human sensibility."[20]

I would like to bring these ruminations to a close by raising what seems to be an obvious question about Arendt's methodology in *Eichmann in Jerusalem*, though it is one I have not yet seen raised. Supposing we grant Arendt's contention that Eichmann was what she says he was: not a monster, just a bureaucrat obeying orders; or, alternatively, an idealist who believed he could purify humanity by doing his bit in the nasty job of exterminating Jews. Is it possible to generalize on the basis of one instance, in this case Adolf Eichmann, that among the perpetrators of these most heinous Nazi crimes there was not a single person who could be designated a "monster," in the sense given by the *OED*, that is, "A person of inhuman and horrible cruelty or wickedness"? Suppose the Israelis had put Dr. Josef Mengele on trial, instead of Eichmann, would it then have been possible for Arendt to discover the same "banality of evil" in Mengele that she did in Eichmann?

Notes

[1] Gian Paolo Biasin, "Till My Ghastly Tale Is Told: Levi's Moral Discourse from *Se questo e un uomo* to *I sommersi e I salvati*," in *Reason and Light: Essays on Primo Levi*, ed. Susan Tarrow (Ithaca, NY: Cornell University Press, 1990), 127.

[2] Ibid., 128. Quoted from Primo Levi, *Survival in Auschwitz: The Nazi Assault on Humanity*, trans. Stuart Woolf (New York: Collier, 1976), 13.

[3] It is not self-evident, however, that this remarkable insight applies to the situation of the Jews living in the ghettos the Germans set up almost everywhere in Poland. When one reads the final entries in the diaries Chaim Kaplan and Abraham Lewin kept in the Warsaw ghetto, or Dawid Seriakowiak's Lodz ghetto diary, or the agonies of Calel Perechodnik, who, as a Jewish policeman, sealed his wife and two-year-old daughter into the freight train that transported them to their doom, or the short stories Isaiah Spiegel wrote in the Lodz ghetto, then it is by no means clear that for

these individuals, at least, it is accurate to say that "inevitable material cares" rendered the "consciousness...of...[their] misfortunes...supportable." On the contrary, it was these very "inevitable material cares" that compounded the misery, and indeed, did bring them to what may be described as a state of "perfect unhappiness."

[4]It is, however, worth noting that while Levi was interested in discovering universals, he explicitly rejected the kind of universalization that maintains, "Anyone is capable of doing anything." In what is, perhaps, the greatest of his essays, "The Gray Zone," Levi asserts that "This mimesis, this identification or imitation, or exchange of roles between oppressor and victim, has provoked much discussion. True and invented, disturbing and banal, acute and stupid things have been said.... The film director Liliana Cavani...declared: 'We are all victims or murderers, and we accept these roles voluntarily....' She also said she believed 'that in every environment, in every relationship, there is a victim-executioner dynamism more or less clearly expressed and generally lived on an unconscious level.'"

"...I do not know," Levi continues, "and it does not much interest me to know, whether in my depths there lurks a murderer, but I do know that I was a guiltless victim and I was not a murderer. I know that the murderers existed, not only in Germany, and still exist, retired or on active duty, and that to confuse them with their victims is a moral disease or an aesthetic affectation or a sinister sign of complicity; above all, it is a precious service rendered (intentionally or not) to the negators of truth." *(The Drowned and the Saved* [New York: Vintage Books, 1989], 48-49.)

[5]Auschwitz memoirs invariably stress the dangers of the arrival and absorption process. Levi himself refers to the "entire sinister ritual," made up of "kicks and punches right away, often in the face; an orgy of orders screamed with true or simulated rage; complete nakedness after being stripped; the shaving off of all one's hair; the outfitting in rags." ("The Gray Zone," *The Drowned and the Saved*, 38-39.) There are graphic descriptions of this process in Wieslaw Kielar, *Anus Mundi*, Tadeusz Borowski, *This Way for the Gas, Ladies and Gentlemen*, and Sara Nomberg Przytyk, *Auschwitz: True Tales From a Grotesque Land*, among others.

[6]Levi's description of this scene would seem to cast some doubt on Biasin's assertion that Levi, though he never actually says so explicitly, considered himself one of those who are "saved both physically and spiritually" (Biasin, "Till My Ghastly Tale Is Told," 133).

[7]Here one is reminded of Herman Melville's description, in *Moby-*

Dick, of the valor-ruined first mate of the *Pequod*, Starbuck. Ishmael asserts that a whaling ship was his Yale and Harvard, but in a sense Melville's whaling ship was also a precursor of the concentrationary universe. When Starbuck permits himself to be intimidated by the crazed Ahab, Ishmael laments that "it is a thing most sorrowful, nay shocking to expose the fall of valor in the soul....Man, in the ideal, is so noble and so sparkling, such a grand and glowing creature, that over any ignominious blemish in him all his fellows should run to throw their costliest robes." But in the fictions he wrote after *Moby-Dick*, Melville seems to have lost his faith in "man, in the ideal," and in that "just Spirit of Equality, which hast spread one royal mantle of humanity over all my kind!...thou great democratic God!" Ahab himself was the antithesis of that "great democratic God," as were, of course, the Germans who ran the ghettos and the death camps. In a way, Levi, like Ishmael, begs indulgence for the exposure of the valor-ruined man. In Auschwitz, and specifically at the moment he heard the words, "I am the last one," Levi, too, lost his faith in "man, in the ideal." The absence of any reaction from the rest of the prisoners to this particular hanging, coming when it did, and being a direct consequence of the resistance to evil, signified, for Levi, the demise of "man, in the ideal." In what may be the best known of all accounts of a hanging in Auschwitz, Elie Wiesel watches a young boy die a slow agonizing death on the gallows. As the boy dangles alive on the noose, a man standing behind the narrator asks, "Where is God, now?" Whereupon, the narrator continues, "And I heard a voice within me answer him: 'Where is He? Here He is—He is hanging here on this gallows...'" (*Night* [New York: Bantam Books, 1986], 61-62). Just as one particular hanging signified for Levi, the humanist, the death of "man, in the ideal," so for Wiesel, the believer and student of Jewish mysticism, another particular hanging signaled the absence of God. It may be argued that the highly productive creative lives both Levi and Wiesel lived after their Holocaust experiences indicate a remarkable recovery from these epiphanic moments. Both men continued to live their lives, one as if "man, in the ideal" still lived, and the other as if God, though absent, must still be reckoned with.

[8]The game is described in Miklos Nyiszli, *Auschwitz: An Eyewitness Account of Mengele's Infamous Death Camp* [also, *A Doctor's Eyewitness Account*, 1993], trans. Tibere Kramer and Richard Seaver (New York: Seaver Books, 1986), 57-58.

[9]Hannah Arendt, *Eichmann in Jerusalem* (New York: Penguin Books, 1983), 117.

[10]Richard J. Bernstein, *Hannah Arendt and the Jewish Question* (Cambridge: The MIT Press, 1996), 161.

[11]The "intentionalist" and "functionalist" interpretations of the Holocaust have been summarized by Lucy S. Dawidowicz, in her "Introduction" to the "Tenth Anniversary Edition" of *The War Against the Jews: 1933-1945*. Dawidowicz herself, along with Leon Poliakov (*Harvest of Hate*), was one of the early and effective contributors to the intentionalist position. She summarizes the functionalist position, in part, by pointing out that in this view, "no human agent can...be held responsible for decisions or for their consequences. The Structuralists [aka, functionalists] have thus eliminated the exercise of free will in human society and deprived men and women of their capacity to choose between good and evil." The functionalist position eventually modulated into what may be called the gradualist position, as represented by Karl A. Schleunes, *The Twisted Road to Auschwitz*. Schleunes carefully traces the many major and minor decisions that finally led to Auschwitz. According to this account, Auschwitz came into being as the result of many blunders, missteps, miscalculations, and thwarted aims. What is most troubling about Schleunes's thesis is that in essence it boils down to the horrendous conclusion that after all other Nazi "solutions to the Jewish problem" failed, genocide and industrial killing turned out to be the last and most logical option, albeit an unpleasant one.

[12]Biasin asserts that Levi's "major moral themes [were]...derived...from the humanistic education of the Italian *liceo*.... (*Reason and Light*, 128).

[13]One is struck by Arendt's stunning lack of introspection or self-knowledge when she condemns Pinchas Freudiger for having "fled to Rumania, because he was rich and Wisliceny helped him" (*Eichmann in Jerusalem*, 124). Was this not approximately what she herself had done, having fled first to France, then to the United States?

[14]See Nyiszli, chapter 19.

[15]Arendt, *Eichmann in Jerusalem*, 125.

[16]Collusion with the Nazis was very widespread, as the Swiss are now finding out, to their sorrow. But one might also say that "the gray zone" applies to the phenomenon of collusion, which sometimes was voluntary, sometimes coerced, sometimes fallen into on the basis of trickery or deception. Two works that portray the phenomenon of the ubiquity of collusion brilliantly are the film, *The Sorrow and the Pity*, and Harry Mulisch's novel, *The Assault*. These two works of art also make it clear why it was so difficult to deal with collaborators after the war. Any attempt to root out

everyone who collaborated in any way would have led to endless recrimination and bloodshed. The most sensible solution was to bury the past, and pretend that everyone had in one way or another resisted the Nazis.

[17]Bernstein, *Hannah Arendt and the Jewish Question*, chapter 8.

[18]See Elzbieta Ettinger, *Hannah Arendt/Martin Heidegger* (New Haven: Yale University Press, 1995.

[19]Tzvetan Todorov, *Facing the Extreme* (New York: Henry Holt, 1995), 121.

[20]Erich Kahler, *The Tower and the Abyss* (New York: George Braziller, 1957), 68, 72.

Critiques

Critique by Leonard Grob

David Hirsch argues, with some passion, that we must make distinctions between the thought of Primo Levi who "leaves no doubt about his moral condemnation of those who conceived and directed the concentration camp enterprise" and that of Hannah Arendt, the author of *Eichmann in Jerusalem*, whose readers "were immediately troubled by what they perceived to be Arendt's exculpation of the criminals and indictment of the victims." This is not to say that Arendt does indeed free Nazi perpetrators of the Holocaust from blame, but rather that her use of the phrase "banality of evil," combined with her contention that Eichmann was no "monster," has given added weight to "the functionalist view that the Holocaust was simply an unfortunate side-effect of 'Modernity,' in which 'no human agent can...be held responsible for decisions or for their consequences.'" While I agree with the general thrust of the distinctions drawn by Hirsch, I will pursue the thesis that a depiction of those elements of modernity which were *necessary* (but not *sufficient*) for the Holocaust to occur—including those elements which manifested themselves in the career of Adolph Eichmann—in no way contradicts a blatant condemnation of the perpetrators' "grand" evil. On the contrary, I believe that a portrayal of the bureaucratic work of "desk killers" can be understood as moral censure of deeds ultimately no less "monstrous" than those committed by the wielders of clubs, guns, or pellets of Zyklon B.

Whether or not Adolph Eichmann precisely fits the characterization given him by Arendt, it remains true that functionaries, with no particular hatred of Jews, played an important role in the mass murder of Jews during the Holocaust. Modernity had indeed given birth to a brand of killer who could kill without passion and, what is even more startling, without acknowledgment of responsibility.

Arendt is certainly correct in characterizing Eichmann as someone uniquely instructive for us in our time. Eichmann was not ruled by raging hatred, but rather proceeded in a largely matter-of-fact manner to carry out his daily duties, meticulously attending to detail, adhering to all the rules. Eichmann, in other words, is typical of modern bureaucrats who use their thought processes as functional tools, as mere instruments to devise means for achieving unexamined ends. Only such instrumental—as opposed to authentically reflective—thinking could support a killing machine on a scale unthinkable in the times of Attila the Hun or Genghis Khan, grand killers of those periods of barbarism allegedly eclipsed by Enlightenment rationalism.

The entire bureaucratic culture surrounding Eichmann contributed to his ability to separate moral from technical concerns. Typical of such a culture is a division of labor: Those Nazis working on the railway lines or in the manufacture of Zyklon B or in a variety of administrative offices—all were removed, both physically and psychically, from the outcome of their actions. This distancing, for Zygmunt Bauman, "achieves more than the suspension of moral inhibition; it quashes the moral significance of the act and thereby preempts all conflict between personal standard of moral decency and immorality of the social consequences of the act."[1] Such functionaries saw themselves as proverbial "cogs" in a machine. Amoral thinking allowed for, indeed demanded, the continuation of "business as usual." Contrary to those who see the Holocaust as the triumph of the irrational in humankind, Bauman, in the tradition of Arendt, claims that "the Final Solution did not clash at any stage with the rational pursuit of efficient, optimal goal-implementation."[2] "Morality" boiled down to the desire to obey one's superiors in the service of carrying out tasks with optimal efficiency.

The notion of serving one's superiors without question is another theme sounded long and loud by Arendt in her *Eichmann in Jerusalem*. Arendt documents Eichmann's depiction of himself at his trial as nothing other than a citizen who abided strictly by the law: "What he had done was a crime only in retrospect, and he had always been a law-abiding citizen, because Hitler's orders, which he had certainly executed to the best of his ability, had possessed 'the force of law' in the Third Reich."[3] A movement from the rule of *efficiency* in the technological order to the adoption of *compliance* in the social order was inevitable. In the words of Herbert Marcuse: "Autonomy of reason loses its meaning in the same measure as the thoughts, feelings and actions of men are shaped by the technical requirements of the apparatus they have themselves created."[4] The abandonment of individual autonomy in the face of a faceless bureaucracy, coupled with the realization of the power of the modern nation state, should sound a warning to us who inhabit the post-Holocaust world: Modernity has bequeathed to us a legacy—one which helped make the Holocaust possible, and one which presages future genocides.

Although I am in agreement with Hirsch that Arendt's phrase "the banality of evil" is "puzzling," I believe that there is much to learn from her about a particular guise that evil can take. I would not, as does Hirsch, term the results of her analysis of Eichmann "misguided." To argue that Eichmann was not pathological, or to claim that his motives were not rooted in hatred, is not to free him, or any other perpetrator, of the charge of gross immorality. The evil of the desk killer may fail to register with immediacy upon our consciousness, ever-ready to find in raging passions the sole motives for monstrous acts. For that reason Eichmann's brand of evil is more insidious than those forms which preceded it. What we must remember is that the bureaucrat *chose* his or her bureaucratic culture. The complicity of the railway worker, whose sole concern was to make certain that the trains ran on time, was a *chosen* complicity. Modernity did not "come upon" the murderers; they were not unwitting accomplices to acts forced upon them by their (inevitable) embeddedness in the givens of time and place. The fact that we are encultured beings does not mean that we are *determined* by culture. It is we ourselves who construct—and sustain or fail to sustain—cultural constructs. The characteristics of modernity detailed by Arendt and Bauman, are, like all human characteristics, given whatever meaning they have by human agents. To deny one's agency—to remain passive in the face of the bureaucratic structures of modernity—is itself to choose a course of action: In acts of denial we reaffirm the very agency we deny.

If, as Hirsch argues, proponents of a functionalist analysis have seized upon such concepts as the banality of evil and the desk killer in order to attempt to deny the personal responsibility of the killers for their deeds, we must not lay the blame for this at the feet of Hannah Arendt. Arendt uses the word "banality" in juxtaposition with "evil" in order to alert us to a possible new attire in which evil can cloak itself. We are shocked at this juxtaposition of words; I believe this is Arendt's intent. Far from distancing the desk killers from our moral outrage, Arendt, I would argue, has helped alert us to the need to fight evil in several of its manifestations. While Arendt, as quoted by Hirsch, may say that Eichmann's deeds are not "traceable to evil or monstrous motives," I contend that she is alluding here only to evil as-it-has-traditionally-been-understood. It was ultimately nothing short of "monstrous" for the desk killers to have followed orders unthinkingly, to have done their duty, to have made mere efficiency their goal. They *chose* the modernity within which they acted—and they must be judged accordingly.

Finally, Hirsch points to a difference in method between the two writers who serve as the key figures in his essay. Primo Levi, Hirsch tells us, "reasoned inductively from the data to the theory"; Arendt, on the other hand, used the Eichmann trial merely to confirm what she had already embraced as theory. Whether or not there is a central difference in *method* between Levi and Arendt is less important than the endeavor to understand differences in the way each takes his or her total stand as an author. I agree with Hirsch when he claims that "Arendt seems to have lacked Levi's exquisite sensitivity, his ability to factor his own consciousness and existential situations into his analyses of objective data." Here, I believe is a key to differences between the two authors, differences which extend beyond the arena of mere method. Levi's "engagement" as a survivor haunts his writings; he lacks the "leisure" to engage in theorizing—with the ever-present temptation it offers to leave the *Lebenswelt* behind. Although her theorizing is allegedly triggered by a phenomenology of Eichmann's behavior at his trial, Arendt flirts with the dangers inherent in all attempts to address the Holocaust from some "position." Having said this, I would argue that we must remain open *both* to the witness of the survivor (itself mediated in a number of ways) and to the frameworks of thought offered by the more detached theorist. In the case of Arendt, as in the case of Levi, we must not close any doors to the variety of endeavors to say what ultimately cannot be said.

Notes

[1]Zygmunt Bauman, *Modernity and the Holocaust* (Ithaca, N.Y.: Cornell University Press), 25.

[2]Ibid., 17.

[3]Hannah Arendt, *Eichmann in Jerusalem: A Report on the Banality of Evil* (Harmondsworth, Middlesex, England: Penguin Books, 1977), 24.

[4]Herbert Marcuse, "Some Social Implications of Modern Technology," in *The Essential Frankfurt School Reader*, ed. Andrew Arato and Eike Bebhardt (New York: Urizen Books, 1978.) For a more detailed discussion of the notion of technological rationality in Marcuse, see Alan Milchman and Alan Rosenberg, "Hannah Arendt and the Etiology of the Desk Killer: The Holocaust as Portent," in *History of European Ideas*, 14 (1992), 222.

Critique by Peter Haas

David Hirsch raises one of the central philosophical issues of the Holocaust, namely, the nature of the evil it represents. The two extremes can easily be spelled out. On the one side is the view that the Holocaust represents absolute evil in its most pure and direct form. On this view the perpetrators were fully aware that what they were doing was evil and yet proceeded with full intention and even relish. They were doing evil for its own sake and enjoyed doing it. On the other side stands the view, in this essay identified with Hannah Arendt (whether rightly or wrongly), that the perpetrators were not moral monsters but normal people like you and me who, because of historical circumstances and a misguided system, ended up committing acts of shocking cruelty as simply part of their daily routine. The cruelty and evil of the Holocaust dissolve in the banal activity of everyday existence.

This simple dichotomy is here associated with another binary debate among scholars of the Holocaust, namely, that between the "intentionalists" and the "functionalists." In simple terms, the intentionalist side argues that the utter destruction of European Jewry and the mass murder of its members were clearly intended by the perpetrators from the very beginning. The period between 1933 and 1942 was taken up simply with developing the technology and setting up the mechanisms for so doing, but the goal remained constant throughout. Here we have fully evil intent being carried out consciously, systematically, and unswervingly over an extended period of time. In contrast is the functionalist argument which holds that the massiveness of Nazi atrocities was not foreseen at first, but developed over a ten-year or so period of having to devise more and more radical solutions to the increasingly pressing question of what to do with Europe's Jewish population. According to this view, the Holocaust began with the more modest aim of simply getting Jews out of Germany, but as the world moved towards war, and as Germany found herself in control of millions of Jews living in conquered territory, the solutions grew more massive and radical until a policy of full-scale genocide emerged. This view Hirsch sees as promoting the notion of the banality of the Holocaust's evil. It simply grew out of the everyday evolution of Nazi policy and bureaucracy.

Although each side of each dichotomy has its defenders, there has been little debate as to whether these binary oppositions in and of themselves make academic sense. It seems to be that even presupposing that one explanation or the other would give an adequate accounting of the Holocaust is to engage in massive oversimplification. On the one hand, claiming that any population can easily and fairly accurately be broken down into two groups: the evil and the non-evil, glosses over the multilayered complexity of the human condition. Now it is possible to say that we can apply this taxonomy only to one population: that of Central Europe in the 1930s, as if this population—the population of Holocaust perpetrators—is somehow unique and distinct in history. That, however, seems to me an enormous historical leap. On the other hand, it also seems oversimplistic to say that the Holocaust in all its detail was simply routine business committed by well-meaning state employees who were dutifully carrying out policy. There clearly was evil being done by many for the sheer joy of being able to exercise life and death power in an environment that sanctioned it. There was something more than normally accepted behavior going on among the perpetrators, something that is missed when we dismiss the Holocaust as banal but not evil in any real sense of that word.

In short, my problem with the essay is not so much that it portrays the Holocaust as "pure" evil rather than as "banal"; rather my problem is that it casts the moral problem of the Holocaust in such simple either-or terms. A closer look at the myriad of individual events that make up the Holocaust reveals a whole universe made up of good, evil, banality, and indifference altogether, and a whole cast of characters who are sometimes good, sometimes evil, sometimes banal, and sometimes indifferent, and sometimes all of these with greater or lesser intensity and consistency over time. To be sure, there is the occasional Nazi leader or middle-level bureaucrat or camp guard who does seem to be consistently, purposefully, and even eagerly evil, just as there are those purely good souls who stood up to the Nazis at considerable personal risk. But against these extreme types there are the millions of others at all levels and in every role who do not fit such neat categories: the rescuers who later demand payment, the SS guards who protected prisoners and so on. In fact, one of the most challenging aspects of the study of the Holocaust in its detail is how often good and evil, right and wrong, blend together seamlessly in the course of everyday life in the conditions of Nazi Europe.

It is also this complexity that makes the Holocaust such a potent teaching tool. It seems to me to be already too easy for students to distance themselves from the perpetrators and bystanders: they are people of a different time and a different place and of a different character; what they did seems to have precious little to do with us. By refusing to allow students to erect this barrier and instead showing them that otherwise normal people could be, and so can be, drawn into an evil system despite their own best intentions, is a powerful tool for teaching the need for moral vigilance. It is not only the absolutely evil we have to watch out for (and I must say I find it a moral problem to define another human being, created in the image of God, as purely and ontologically evil), but the seemingly ordinary and routine as well.

Hannah Arendt did release a fire-storm of protest with her reflections on the trial of Eichmann. It can still remain a question as to whether the man Eichmann was really banal (in whatever sense) or whether he was (at least for a time?) the devil incarnate. That may be an issue that we can never resolve. But Arendt also forces us to confront a broader and more important question, even if we disagree with her about the banality of this one individual. She sensed through him that matters were not as simple as the apocalyptic battle between the sons of light and the sons of darkness, between absolute demons and absolute angels. The victims may have been pure victims, as Elie Wiesel once said, but the fact remains that each perpetrator was a perpetrator in his or her own way. In the end the Holocaust was a human event played out in human history by human actors. The evil was neither diabolic nor banal, but both together at the same time. Maybe the real lesson of the Holocaust is that the demonic and the angelic, as well as the banal, are inextricably interwoven and integrally a part of what it means to be human, and so are within each of us as well.

Critique by David Patterson

David Hirsch's essay "The Gray Zone or The Banality of Evil" is a valuable, thought-provoking critique of what frequently passes for common "wisdom" among students of the Holocaust, particularly those who have been infected by the ontological outlook that pervades most of twentieth-century thought. If Hirsch falls short in his investigation, it is because he does not drive home his most crucial point forcefully enough, namely, that the essence of human being is moral being. If the human being is created in the image of God, then he is created in the image of the Good; if the Nazis undertake an assault not only on man but on the "idea of man," as Elie Wiesel argues,[1] they do so through an assault on the Good. They did not simply have a different concept of the Good; rather, they opposed a concept of power to every notion of the Good. What constitutes Nazism as a monstrosity, then, is not so much their pronounced embrace of evil but their implicit rejection of good *and* evil: from the standpoint of the Nazis, there is no good or evil but only power and weakness, only master race and slave race. That is what constitutes their evil.

Pursuing the link between the assault on the moral and the assault on the human, Hirsch correctly understands the key to Primo Levi's insight as an insight into the Nazis' attack on the human image. He does not, however, take his critique of Gian Paolo Biasin's claim regarding Levi's universalism far enough. Indeed, he appears to accept the misleading either/or of *either* universal or particular, failing to note, for example, that a particular paradigm—such as the revelation of the Good at Sinai or the assault on the Good at Auschwitz—may have universal implications.

Hirsch does point out, however, that Biasin's view of Levi rests upon two key matters: (a) Levi was concerned not with the Jewish condition but with the human condition and (b) Levi kept himself at a distance from any transcendence. Yet Levi *does* distinguish the Jewish condition in the camps from the condition of non-Jewish inmates, noting, for example, that for the Jews "the Lager is not a punishment" but is "a manner of living assigned to" them.[2] Levi's sense of urgency about something transcendent, moreover, can be seen in the chapter titled "The Canto of Ulysses" in *Survival in*

Auschwitz. There Levi recalls the passage from Dante's *Divine Comedy* in which Ulysses invokes the will of God with the phrase "as pleased Another" in order to come to some deeper understanding of his plight. "I keep Pikolo back," says Levi, "it is vitally necessary and urgent that he listen, that he understand this 'as pleased Another' before it is too late....I must explain to him about the Middle Ages, about the so human and so necessary and yet unexpected anachronism, but still more, something gigantic that I myself have only just seen, in a flash of intuition, perhaps the reason for our fate, for our being here today."[3] In the Middle Ages the reason for our being here always entailed an element of the transcendent.

Both the peculiarity of the Jew and the higher will of Another are significant to Levi's—and Hirsch's—contention that our humanity is rooted in our moral sensibility. As the people chosen to bear the Torah—that is, God's teaching and law—into the world, the Jews, in their peculiarity, signify the transcendent, higher will of Another, from whom all human beings receive the commandment to live in accordance with the Good. Living in accordance with that commandment, every human takes on a human image. Stripping the Jew of moral sense, Hirsch rightly notes, the Nazis stripped them of their humanity precisely by transforming them into the monstrous likeness of the Nazi himself.[4] Contrary to what may seem to be the case, the human image is not destroyed by transforming a person into a walking corpse; rather, it is undone by undoing his morality. This the Nazis accomplished by various means: through the appointment of Jewish Councils, Kapos, *Sonderkommandos* (SK), and through soccer games between the SS and the SK.

As Hirsch rightly notes, Levi sees these activities as part of a calculated undoing of the Jew's humanity through an undoing of the Jew's morality. He is also right when he sees Levi's example of the soccer game as "a radical critique of Arendt, and of the 'functionalist' position," that is, the position that the Holocaust unfolded as the by-product of a social, political, and cultural bureaucratic system, and not as the explicit intention of a person or persons. Levi, says Hirsch, "recognized that the forced involvement of the victims in their own destruction was not a matter of mere functional expediency on the part of the killers, but a deliberate subversion of the moral order, and therefore, an act of unambiguous evil." Here Hirsch enables us to see how feeble is the defensive position that the Nazis thought they were doing a "good" thing or that they thought they were serving a higher duty. While one may find examples of Nazis claiming to seek a higher "good" through the annihilation of the Jews, there is no evidence to show that they believed they were serving a higher "good" by forcing the Jews to participate in their own destruction—or that forcing members of the SK into soccer games was a necessary outcome of a bureaucratic system.

Just as the Nazis undermine the Jew's humanity by undermining his morality, so does the functionalist eliminate the Nazi's humanity by eliminating his moral responsibility. Assaulting morality by reducing it to yet another by-product of a social and cultural system, the functionalist becomes something of an accomplice to the Nazi. Thus, in the case of Arendt, the functionalist not only defends Nazis by making them into the products, if not the victims, of a system, she attacks Jews who fled Europe or who served on Jewish Councils. Contrary to what may seem to be the case, there is a logical consistency in this position. For, adopting a position opposed to moral responsibility, the functionalist adopts a position opposed to Jewish teaching, so that there are important similarities between functionalist thinking and Nazi thinking; hence the functionalist's defense of the Nazis and attack on the Jews.

Similar to the functionalist Arendt, as Hirsch points out, is the post-modernist Tzvetan Todorov, who maintains that there is nothing in the personality or behavior of the Nazis that would allow us to classify them as monsters, since any definition of monstrosity is tautological and therefore arbitrary.[5] One culture's monster is another culture's hero. Like Nazi thinking and functionalist thinking, this post-modernist thinking constitutes an assault on moral being and therefore on human being. This is not to say that functionalists or post-modernists are Nazis. It is to point out, however, that all three replace morality with that which is *determined*—culturally, socially, politically, racially, bureaucratically, or whatever. In this respect, all three positions are antithetical to Jewish teaching and tradition, according to which morality is commanded from above and either embraced or rejected from below—according to which, in short, human being is moral being, and anything that perverts the moral is monstrous. Todorov, however, frees himself from the monstrous, so that he does not have to face evil; he has only to face "the extreme." Indeed, he has left the ethical far behind, arguing in terms of "normal" and "pathological," rather than in terms of good and evil.

Like the normal and the pathological, good and evil—in the eyes of Arendt and Todorov, as well as the Nazis—are matters either of cultural convention for the weak or of a will to power for the strong. What Hirsch does not make sufficiently clear, then, is that, with regard to the premises of their thinking, Arendt and Todorov are much closer to the Nazis than they are to the Jews. Not only do ontology and its post-modern corollaries leave us with an inadequate means of responding to the ethical implications of the Holocaust—such means of responding play into the hands of those who would annihilate Jewish souls along with Jewish bodies. For in its *human* being, the being of the Jewish soul is moral being as commanded from on high, and not as determined by the accidents of nature or culture.

Notes

[1]Elie Wiesel, *Legends of Our Time* (New York: Avon, 1968), 230.

[2]Primo Levi, *Survival in Auschwitz*, trans. Stuart Woolf (New York: Touchstone, 1996), 82-83.

[3]Ibid., p. 115. In a later work Levi elaborates on the importance of Dante for his effort to "reestablish a link with the past, saving it from oblivion." See Levi, *The Drowned and the Saved*, trans. Raymond Rosenthal (New York: Vintage Books, 1989), 139-40.

[4]One recalls here the story from the Warsaw ghetto about the Nazi officer who went to a woman's apartment to take her two children away. After listening to her pleas for the lives of her children, the Nazi told the mother, "If you can guess which of my eyes is a glass eye, then you may have one of your children back." "Your right eye is made of glass," the woman immediately answered. "Why, yes," the Nazi replied, "how could you tell?" "It looks more human than the other one," she explained. See Emmanuel Ringelblum, *Notes from the Warsaw Ghetto*, ed. and trans. Jacob Sloan (New York: Schocken, 1974), 84; also Alexander Donat, *The Holocaust Kingdom* (New York: Holocaust Library, 1978), 103ff.

[5]See Tzvetan Todorov, *Facing the Extreme* (New York: Henry Holt, 1995), 12.

Critique by Didier Pollefeyt

David Hirsch's challenging essay reveals how the confrontation with Hannah Arendt's controversial study, *Eichmann in Jerusalem: A Report on the Banality of Evil,* has been and remains a decisive moment for all post-Holocaust ethicists. In an extraordinary way, he criticizes Arendt's presentation of Adolf Eichmann as a banal functionary. He strongly argues for understanding the Nazi as a "monster" who "deliberately subverts the moral order," choosing "unambiguous evil," and who even attempts to make the victims responsible for their own fate by forcing them to "collaborate" with the perpetrators.

Hirsch knows that Primo Levi's influential essay, "The Gray Zone," can easily be read as an argument in favor of Arendt's notion of the banality of evil and as a critique of the idea of the monstrosity of the Nazis. He asserts that this parallel between Levi and Arendt is erroneous and that Levi does not exclude the possibility that some evil-doers, such as Eichmann, fall outside of the gray zone and can be called "monsters." I will argue that the theories of Arendt and Levi are not as incompatible as Hirsch claims.

Hirsch correctly holds that we should always take notice of the *style* an author employs. Similarly, it is also important to take into account the *context* in which one writes. In 1961, Arendt covered the Eichmann trial in Jerusalem as a reporter for *The New Yorker.* Listening in the House of Justice to the public prosecutor, Gideon Hausner, she was struck by the contrast between the person of Eichmann in Jerusalem and the public prosecutor's portrayal of him. Hausner stripped Eichmann of every human characteristic and presented him as nonhuman and with almost satanic features. Disregarding the sociohistorical and everyday context of Eichmann's actions, Hausner concentrated the evil of the Judeocide into one spectacular image: Eichmann became "the Nazi who murdered six million Jews."[1] The conclusion of this selective and condensed presentation was that Eichmann did his job "not as a blind tool, but with passion."[2] All objections to Hausner's cherished theory about Eichmann were seen by Hausner as "nothing but lies."[3] In his later book, Hausner went on to call Eichmann the "arch monster" and "the strongest personification of satanic principles."[4]

In this way, at the cost of setting aside more complex ethical and historical considerations about the Holocaust and the important role of Eichmann in it, the Eichmann trial was reduced to a Manichean confrontation between "Beauty and the Beast," the "world of humanity" and the "world of cruelty." It is relevant to quote here from Levi's essay, "The Gray Zone": "We…try to simplify history,…we have such a strong need to divide the territory into 'we' and 'they'…that this…duality friend-enemy has priority over all others."[5]

Arendt's position can only be understood in the light of its being a critique against this extreme Manichean discourse, against the desire to divide the world in "we" and "they." It is a response to the ruling theory of diabolization that thrived in the Jerusalem trial. Arendt argued the opposite of Hausner: Eichmann was also a victim (in part) of a greater Nazi system, and, similarly, some of the victims were also involved (in part) as perpetrators in the Nazi genocide. Her theory about the historical complexity of good and evil was so controversial because it fundamentally challenged the ruling paradigm. True, Arendt's analysis was one-sided. In her work, there is a disproportion between her negligible sensitivity for the moral dilemmas of the victims and her great empathy for the person of Eichmann. Hirsch rightly criticizes this moral imbalance in her theory and can be summarized with the similar objections raised by Norman Podhoretz immediately after the publication of Arendt's book: "In place of the monstrous Nazi, she [Arendt] gives us the 'banal' Nazi; in place of the Jew as virtuous martyr, she gives us the Jew as accomplice in evil; and in place of the confrontation of guilt and innocence, she gives us the 'collaboration' of criminal and victim."[6]

It is important, however, to see that Arendt's one-sidedness is the inverse of Hausner's one-sidedness. While Hausner tried to adapt the person of Eichmann to the cruelty of his acts, Arendt tried to adapt the acts of Eichmann to the banality of his person. I do not think, however, that we should return to Hausner's demonic representation of Eichmann, as Hirsch seems to argue, to respond adequately to Arendt's theory. We do not need to explain how evil people do evil things. This is self-explanatory: demons can only do demonic things. What we should try to understand is how (potentially) *good* human beings can do (factually) *evil* things. Ethics after Auschwitz should try to understand the complex relation between act and person, between evil and evil-doer. Act and actor cannot be separated or destroyed (for Arendt, in a totalitarian context, there is no act, because there is no independent actor), but neither can they be identified with each other, as Hirsch claims.

I see no contradiction in the statement that banal ("normal") people can do demonic ("abnormal") things. It is important not to confuse the "banality of evil" and the "banality of the evil-doer." The (sub)title of Arendt's book was deceptive (moreover, the notion is not developed further in her book). For Arendt, it is not evil that is banal, but the people who do evil. As Arendt put the point elsewhere, "the acts were monstrous, but the perpetrators...were rather ordinary."[7] Thus, speaking about the "banality of evil," Arendt intended to say that the criminal was banal, not evil itself. She never called the evil of Auschwitz itself banal. On the contrary, she meant to say that just because evil is such an ordinary human reality, we can never banalize it, but should always take it seriously as a universal human possibility.

Criticizing Arendt's hypothesis, Hirsch argues that there are some people, such as Eichmann, who fall outside of the gray zone that separates and connects victims and perpetrators at the same time, and who can in a way be considered *absolute perpetrators*. He sees this possibility also in Levi's position. On the other hand, Hirsch argues with Levi in favor of the Jewish victims, who cannot be considered morally responsible for collaboration in their own destruction, for they were, in a sense, *absolute victims*. Accordingly, Hirsch tries to re-establish the clear distinction between (absolute) perpetrator (choosing "unambiguous evil") and (absolute) victim. Even if this is a very valuable position, I would criticize the dualistic understanding of good and evil implied by it.

My critique against a dualistic moral understanding of the Holocaust does not mean that there is no longer a difference between wrong-doers and innocent victims. Rather, my basic contention is that one should better distinguish between *the capacity to act* and *the act itself*—otherwise, as Todorov properly argues, we risk mistaking anthropology (human nature) for jurisprudence (human acts) and *vice versa*.[8]

Regarding the perpetrators, Hirsch argues that Arendt "allotted Eichmann a comfortable niche in 'the gray zone'." Even if I am not so convinced that Arendt really gave Eichmann a "comfortable" place in the gray zone—at the end of her book, she demanded the death penalty for Eichmann—the more fundamental question is whether there are people who are moral monsters (Eichmann or others) and who do not belong in the gray zone. Hirsch bases his argument on Levi's consideration that the creation of the (forced) Jewish "collaboration" was "National Socialism's most *demonic* crime." It is remarkable that Levi speaks here of a *demonic* crime (adjective), not of crimes of *demons* (substantive). This is not a mere game of language: the former expression ("demonic") is about ethics (a qualification of human acts), the latter ("demons") about anthropology (an assertion concerning human nature).

At this point, it can be helpful to reflect upon the story Levi tells five pages later in his essay on "The Gray Zone." The "fable of the onion" is not mentioned in Hirsch's essay. This is already an illustration that not only Arendt's but every theory on the Holocaust is—inevitably—based on a selection of the data. In Levi's selective version of this fable from Dostoevsky's *The Brothers Karamazov*, a malicious woman dies and goes to the lake of fire, but her guardian angel remembers that she once, one time, gave an onion to a beggar.[9] As Levi tells the story, the guardian angel holds out this onion, the old woman latches onto it, and she is lifted out of hell's flames. "Which human being is such a monster [substantive]," asks Levi, "that he didn't give one time in his life an onion to someone else, even if it were only his children, his wife or his dog?" He applies his (rhetorical) question to Muhsfeld, an SS-man who worked at a crematorium, and who had just killed a young girl, after a moment of hesitation: "That one moment of immediate repressed compassion [of Muhsfeld] is surely not enough to discharge him, but to count him, at the very extreme limit, of the gray zone."[10] Implicitly, Levi is making a distinction between ethics and anthropology. Muhsfeld, working at a crematorium, the center of Nazi evil, is conclusively morally responsible for the evil he did (human acts), yet (even!) he is not a monster, but belongs instead to the gray zone (human nature). If the criterion for including someone in the gray zone is the fact of having once given an onion to a dog, then we can conclude that for Levi, every Nazi, including Hitler himself, belongs to the gray zone.

One could counter-argue that this fable is only meant metaphorically. However, the possibility of giving an onion, even to a dog, seems a profound statement. Humans distinguish themselves from nonhumans by their capacity to distance themselves fundamentally from their own self-development by the possibility "to give." Only humans are capable of experiencing "transcendence," which means perceiving reality in terms other than instincts, survival, and social determinations. The giving of an onion to another is thus a decisive act that makes someone a human being forever. It testifies to a distance, an openness between a person and him- or herself. A person is always greater or other than his or her gender, place of birth, history, and even his or her own acts. Thanks to this openness between what is determined biologically and socially and what is not, one irreversibly becomes a human being, capable of doing and experiencing good—even stronger, *called* to do good (Levinas), and precisely therefore also capable of doing (even demonic) evil. Accordingly, only a human being can *do* evil. A monster cannot do evil, he or she *is* evil.

Human evil, then, is always secondary to goodness; evil deviates from what was (and remains) originally good. Even during the greatest evil, or better, precisely then, the Nazis did not abandon their human efforts to "ethicize" their criminal behavior, but tried to do evil under the pretext of good, as is vividly illustrated in Peter Haas's contributions to this volume. Therefore, the Nazis did not do evil for evil's sake, as only monsters can do, but evil in the name of a good, or better, a so-called good (see my critique of Haas's position).

On the other side of the continuum, Hirsch argues against Arendt's critique of the "collaboration" of the Jewish victims in their own destruction. Even if in the original edition of *Eichmann in Jerusalem*, only eight of the 260 pages were devoted to this subject, the discussion, or better, the "civil war" about her book was concentrated primarily around this topic. She contended that the Jews, and especially the Jewish Councils (*Judenräte*), "collaborated" in the process of extermination by their lack of moral and military resistance, by delivering administrative support to the Nazi destruction machine, by deceiving themselves about the reality of the situation, and by all kinds of self-enrichment, corruption, and class privileges. If the Nazis had been obliged to use their own forces to select, to gather, and to register the victims, Arendt argues, there would have been fewer victims.

Arendt's argument is important ethically as well as historically. It suggests that good and evil cannot be separated absolutely, and that those who move in a world of evil, even if they are victims, and even if they attempt to do good, inevitably risk infection by evil. In this way, Arendt has also criticized the other side of the moral dualism of Hausner's discourse: the Jew as absolute victim.

Hirsch does not deny the (forced) cooperation of the Jews in the Holocaust, but he does criticize the severe moral condemnation in Arendt's interpretation. On this point, he can find appropriate support not only in the work of Primo Levi but also in the work of Zygmunt Bauman, whose position is close to Arendt's. Bauman argues that the attitude of the Jews and the Jewish leaders ultimately did not influence the outcome of the war.[11] For Bauman, the Jews' cooperation in their own destruction was not a question of immorality but of rationality. The victims tried to anticipate the reactions of the Nazis, so as to increase their chances for survival. An important principle in their reaction to anti-Jewish measures was the calculation of how many lives could be saved. The survival of a greater number of people would be better than the survival of a smaller amount. So some decisions seemed more rational than others. By such calculation, the victims came to accept the bureaucratic rules of their oppressors. Because the Nazis had all the power, they could manipulate this Jewish rationality as a useful bureaucratic tool for realizing their own goals. They could organize the bureaucratic system so that every logical step taken by the Jews brought them nearer to their own destruction.

For Bauman, it would be unfair and misleading to use the ethical criteria of normal daily life to evaluate human choices that were made under such extreme circumstances. Rationality and even the ethical concern of the victims became instruments in the hands of the perpetrators. For the victims, it became impossible to take an option that did not at the same time serve the goals of the perpetrators. Bauman's analysis is interesting because it shows that we should not interpret the manipulation of the victims purely in terms of intentions, as Hirsch does. The reality of Jewish cooperation also leaves room for some functionalistic elements. The distinction between Hirsch's and Bauman's analysis is that Hirsch understands this manipulation immediately as a "deliberate subversion of the moral order," as an "act of unambiguous evil," which it is, of course, and Bauman sees here, more in agreement with Arendt, the efficiency of modern (totalitarian) bureaucracy. For Bauman, to reduce their victims to manipulatable and controllable objects, the Nazi bureaucracy had to let them act rationally. At every moment, the victims had to be confronted—at least subjectively—with different possibilities of choice. Even if their alternatives were not between good and bad choices, the Nazi bureaucrat let the Jews think they could choose between a better or worse situation. Meanwhile, the rational bureaucratic system could realize its goal with a minimum of cost and resistance. In this way, the Holocaust is for Bauman a unique product of modernity. While the collaboration of the victims for a classic pogrom was impossible, the Holocaust provides a manual for the modern manager because that event illustrates how a maximum of benefit can be realized with a minimum of cost. Of course, the question remains: With what intention did the manager, the Nazi, act? Intentionalism and functionalism need not exclude each other: indeed, only together can they explain how the Holocaust became possible.

Lawrence Langer has likewise indicated that the victims simply were not given a *real* opportunity to choose and did not have an autonomous ethical life because of the extreme context Nazism created.[12] One of the major aims of Nazi camp life was to deprive the victims of their personality before killing them. When prisoners succeeded in surviving, then this was not so much a victory but a violation of the basic aim of the camp. Langer's central idea is the "choiceless choice." In the camps, the victim was offered a choice that was, in fact, no choice at all. According to Langer, camp life for the victim was beyond good and evil. He gives the example of a Jewish woman in Auschwitz whose "choiceless choice" was to drown a newborn boy to save his mother from the gas chambers when the infant's life endangered the mother's and saving both was impossible. Making such a decision cannot happen without a loss of human dignity.

Nevertheless, I would still argue that even in the camps some ethical choices—and thus also evil acts—sometimes remained possible, although in situations less extreme than Langer's agonizing examples. Many camp prisoners could not choose the purely good any longer, and many times their choices were manipulated by the system. But often it still remained possible to choose between more or less evil. In fact, some victims did choose for good (or lesser evil), while others chose for evil. In the end, the freedom of real ethical choice could never be *totally* controlled by any power. This fact implies that we should also avoid too quickly and too simply silencing morally the less admirable sides of Jewish cooperation with the Nazi regime. Ultimately, even the victims remain in the gray zone.

Viktor Frankl, the Viennese psychiatrist who survived Auschwitz and Dachau, goes even further. He argued that people could be deprived of everything in the camps, except for one thing: the ultimate freedom of adopting a personal attitude towards the imposed circumstances. Like Frankl and unlike Langer, I believe that even in the camps "places of freedom" remained where "daily virtues" (Todorov) could be developed. Frankl believes that humans can always maintain a certain form of spiritual independence, interhuman involvement, and creativity even under extremely heavy mental and physical pressures. Frankl's insights make clear that the victims must also be seen within the gray zone. For the most part, however, the victim only remained at the *very border* of this gray zone. Because Frankl does not develop this idea, his theory leaves an undeserved moral stain on all victims who have not survived with ethical purity. He underestimated how drastically the extremely miserable situation affected most victims of Nazism. Hirsch is right that Arendt's and Frankl's interpretation of the victims protects the violence used by Nazism against the moral premises that we use to organize our life, shifting the guilt and responsibility of the cruelties from the criminals to the victims. The value of an act does not depend exhaustively on the motive of the person who did it, but also on the (in)humanity of the world in which this action takes place.

I summarize. On the anthropological level: perpetrators and victims are human beings; they both have the capacity to do good *and* evil, and both are always conditioned *and* free. On the ethical level: there is a *clear difference* between perpetrators and victims. These two levels are both real, but they must not be equated or confused. Primo Levi can rightly see himself as within the gray zone and also call himself a "guiltless victim" of the Holocaust. This distinction means that he recognizes in himself (anthropologically) the potentiality for good and evil, but also that in the Nazi camp he was (ethically) an innocent victim who was in no way a perpetrator. It is also no contradiction to see a Nazi in the gray zone and also to call him (to a greater or lesser degree) a guilty perpetrator of the Holocaust. These views exclude neither the option that the victim had the possibility to do (and sometimes did) some evil before, during, or after the Holocaust nor the option that the perpetrator had the possibility to do (and sometimes did) some good before, during, or after the Holocaust. But it is wrong to use these anthropological considerations to relativize the clear ethical distinction between victim and perpetrator, just as it is wrong to use the ethical considerations about the camps to absolutize *anthropologically* the difference between victim and perpetrator. This analysis means that, even if from an ethical point of view there is an irreducible difference between victims and perpetrators, from an anthropological point of view this gap is never total and complete.

My final objection against a dualistic presentation of victims and perpetrators is that it bears a remarkable resemblance to the Nazis' own demonology. With the diabolization of the perpetrators, we risk reproducing the Nazi *Weltanschauung* itself. The Nazis used precisely such Manichean categories of good and evil, *Übermenschen* and *Untermenschen*. Of course, there is a vast moral difference between Nazis demonizing innocent Jewish victims and us demonizing guilty Nazis. Yet at the same time, we risk becoming vulnerable to the same dangers as the Nazis—not seeing the same possibility of evil in ourselves, which is the very basis of every evil. We can thereby make the perpetrator's inhumanity so aesthetic that we create a safe Manichean distance between ourselves and them. In this way we can strategically absolve ourselves of every possible evil, and, when confronted with Auschwitz, simply reorganize our own identity without blemish. But by combating evil only in monsters, we risk rendering evil permanent in ourselves.

Nevertheless, Hirsch's analysis challenges me with the question of whether there are no exceptional beings who have completely lost the possibility of openness and in whom there is no longer a difference between act and actor, in short, whether there are people who are monsters. First, even if such people would exist, their existence would never be able to explain the Holocaust, because there were surely not enough such people to account for such a radical genocide. And even if such monsters do exist, the real question is how such people became monstrous, since no one is born a monster. Hirsch tries to understand the context in which the Jewish "collaboration" took place, but he is not prepared to undertake the same effort to understand the psychological background and socio-historical genesis of the evil-doers, as if understanding would automatically mean excusing. For the Nazis, he uses the notion of choosing "unambiguous evil." I would contend, however, that people never choose evil "as such." We always need to ask the question *why* people do evil, and then we consistently discover a mixture of will and determination, of inability and power, of ill-will and self-deception. Of course, this outlook, as well as Hirsch's notion of "unambiguous evil," involves anthropological and, in my case, even theological presuppositions, which can be neither proved nor falsified by the Holocaust's facts. In this sense, then, I cannot agree with Hirsch's criticism that the deductive character of Arendt's theory is inferior to the inductive character of Levi's reflections (based on his own Holocaust experiences). *Every* observation of the Holocaust is already an interaction of induction and deduction, of subject and object. Different survivors have developed different accounts of the same happening as a consequence of the different eyes with which they looked upon the experienced suffering.

Hirsch's essay risks implying a form of "insiderism"; a way of giving to the survivor a special right to speak and of imposing a respectful silence on the nonsurvivor.[13] Insiderism postulates an unbridgeable gap between insiders and outsiders. This gap results from the outsider's inevitable failure to empathize and understand. Central to insiderism is an absolute monopoly of knowledge, the result of making experience supreme. The danger of this insiderism is that one finally ends up in complete solipsism. Because every individual is unique, every individual becomes a noncommunicable monad and is thereby doomed to an absolute solitude. The result is "conceptual apartheid" in which the contribution of "unexperienced" outsiders (Arendt, for example) is seen as a dangerous form of infiltration. *Insiders* are given an unmeditated and transperspectival access to the reality of experience. If we radicalize this principle, we end up with a "Balkanization" of human sciences in which different individuals or social groups (for instance, women, blacks, Catholics) close themselves off in a schizophrenic way and condemn themselves to an autistic, self-enclosed speech. Arendt's perspective is crucial to nuance and correct the potentially exclusivistic perspective of the victim (survivor) and his or her ethical story. Arendt's approach has helped new aspects of the Holocaust to be understood, but it has inevitably obscured others as well. Hirsch's essay correctly uncovers the black holes in her theory, but his important insights cannot dismiss hers. I think it is neither necessary nor possible to negate Arendt's theory. Ethical reflection about the Holocaust needs many supplementary or even conflicting paradigmatic approaches. This process can bring to light different, sometimes paradoxical, elements of the Nazi genocide, and thereby after Auschwitz it can reveal the importance of an ethical openness for *constructive* plurality itself.

Notes

[1] Gideon Hausner, "Eichmann and His Trial," *The Saturday Evening Post*, 3 November 1962, 19-25 and especially 19.

[2] Gideon Hausner, *Justice in Jerusalem: The Trial of Adolf Eichmann* (London: William Clowes & Sons, 1966), 279.

[3] Gideon Hausner, "Eichmann and His Trial," *The Saturday Evening Post*, 17 November 1962, 85-90 and especially 88.

[4] Hausner, *Justice in Jerusalem*, 13.

[5] Primo Levi, *De verdronkenen en de geredden. Essays.* Translated from the Italian by F. De Matteis-Vogels (Amsterdam: Meulenhoff, 1991), 31.

[6] Quoted from D. MacDonald, "More on Eichmann," *Partisan Re-*

view 31 (1964): 262-269 and especially 263.

[7]See Hannah Arendt, "Thinking and Moral Considerations: A Lecture," *Social Research* 38 (1971): 417-446.

[8]Tzvetan Todorov, *Face à l'extrême*, 2d ed. (Paris: Seuil, 1994), 167.

[9]Primo Levi, *De verdronkenen en de geredden*, 53-54. See F.M. Dostoevsky, *The Brothers Karamazov*, Book VII, Chapter 3 ("An Onion"). Translated by Constance Garrett (London: Oxford University Press, 1985), 389-407 and especially 400.

[10]Levi, *De verdronkenen en de geredden*, 53. It is important to note that Levi's version of the "fable of the onion" does not end in the same way as it does in Dostoevsky's novel. In *The Brothers Karamazov*, Grushenka tells the story, and she says that when the woman began to be pulled out of the lake of fire, other sinners, hoping they might also be saved, caught hold of her. But the woman kicked them back, the life-saving onion broke, and the woman fell back into the flames. The redeeming angel left the scene in tears, but, Grushenka observes, the woman in hell is burning there to this day. It is remarkable that neither Levi nor Hirsch mentions this more pessimistic or realistic ending of Dostoevsky's fable, because this conclusion can be very illuminating for ethical reflection on the Holocaust. I learn from it that everyone receives the possibility of salvation, but people can refuse that possibility finally.

[11]Zygmunt Bauman, "On Immoral Reason and Illogical Morality," *Polin* 3 (1988): 294-301.

[12]Lawrence L. Langer, *Holocaust Testimonies: The Ruins of Memory* (New Haven: Yale University Press, 1991).

[13]Robert. K. Merton, "Insiders and Outsiders: A Chapter in the Sociology of Knowledge," *American Journal of Sociology* 78 (1972): 9-47.

Critique by John Roth

Emphasizing how Primo Levi "reasoned inductively from the data" and "arrived at his theory of evil on the basis of what he had experienced in Auschwitz," David Hirsch's essay, "The Gray Zone or the Banality of Evil," shows why no survivor has written about the Holocaust in more perceptive ways. Accurately describing Levi as "a reluctant moralist," Hirsch correctly adds that Levi's writings have "a powerful moral center." Hirsch helpfully identifies that center, a task that his essay's title sets for him by posing an either/or dilemma. More light can be shed on that dilemma by calling attention to a fascinating and, I believe, pivotal question in Hirsch's account. In addition, by asking about that question, I want to encourage Hirsch to expand his observations on two significant issues: (1) How do confrontations with the Holocaust produce moral vision? (2) What do the most important insights of that vision turn out to be? Such issues are crucial for post-Holocaust ethics. My comments will make some suggestions about them, but, given the thinking that David Hirsch has already done in "The Gray Zone or The Banality of Evil," he is well-positioned to say more about those fundamental questions, too.

Hirsch's provocative question is embedded in his discussion of an execution that Levi witnessed in Auschwitz. In that context, Hirsch remarks that "one of the problems in dealing with Holocaust memoirs, even the most truthful and thoughtful of them, is that it is difficult to determine at what exact moment an author's moral insight has taken place." Does the insight arise at the moment a particular event took place, or does it emerge in later reflection on one's experience, or at some point in between?

Such inquiry leads to other significant topics. For example, whenever moral insight comes, what is its most important content? Furthermore, in what ways, if at all, could Primo Levi's moral insight—grounded in his particular experience—be transferrable to others, generalized, or universalized? To what extent could such insight inform post-Holocaust ethics? I hope that David Hirsch will expand his essay along these lines.

To focus this inquiry further, note that Primo Levi was not a reluctant moralist because he doubted that Auschwitz denoted unprecedented evil. As Hirsch points out, moreover, Levi distinguished between perpetrators and victims, between the guilty and the innocent, in ways that clearly distanced him from Hannah Arendt's tendency to blame the Jewish victims for their Holocaust fate and to find that a perpetrator such as Adolf Eichmann was a bureaucratic functionary who so routinized murder that evil itself became ordinary, unremarkable, and banal. The Holocaust's evil may have been routinized, but ordinary, unremarkable, and banal it was not. Levi also took little interest in abstract theorizing about the possibility that all human beings are potential perpetrators of genocide. His skepticism about such speculation, however, never made him an optimist who regarded Auschwitz as an anomaly. Since the Holocaust had happened, Levi understood, genocidal violence can repeat, and no person or place automatically possesses immunity from it.

This outlook kept Levi's attention focused primarily on choices, actions, and events that actually took place. Their reality was a warning for the future. He recalled crimes committed by particular individuals and groups who knew what they wanted, took decisions accordingly, and were well aware of the consequences. Their culpability should alert future generations to the fact that it is essential for people to hold one another morally responsible for their actions. Levi also remembered real people who had suffered and rarely survived — Jews, in particular, who were intentionally put in devastating circumstances by Germans and their collaborators during the Nazi years. Their experiences — Levi used his writing to forestall our forgetting them — provided the testimony that might encourage resistance against the wasting of precious life.

Still, Levi was a reluctant moralist. In fact, his reluctance is essential for understanding the distinctive moral quality of his insights about the Holocaust. Hirsch stresses this point by underscoring the importance of what Levi called "the gray zone." When Levi asks his readers to consider the *Sonderkommandos* (the Jewish squads who were forced to work in the gas chambers and crematoria) — the formation of these squads, Levi says, was Nazism's "most demonic crime" — or the leaders of the Jewish Councils in the Holocaust's ghettos, he also asks his readers to suspend judgment and instead to meditate with "pity and rigor." He seems to suggest that the most important insights will be lost if judgment, especially a condemning moral judgment, takes place too fast. First and foremost, he urges that an unusual combination—pity and rigor—should focus one's analysis.

Put into practice well, that combination shows itself to be the right one. It deserves a governing role in post-Holocaust ethics. When one considers why it is appropriate to pity the *Sonderkommandos* or members of the Jewish Councils, the answer is found in an ever-more rigorous analysis of the conditions in which they were put. Likewise, when one explores what those Jews faced, what they were required to do, how can they not be pitied? Only in such a context of pity and rigor, if at all, can moral judgment about the Holocaust and its aftermath be properly honed to do the work that needs to be done.

In the right time and place, that work must be done. Two examples cited in Hirsch's essay make clear that Levi minces no words about it. First, Hirsch points out that Levi's "gray zone" could include even an SS sergeant identified as Muhsfeld. Amazingly, a sixteen-year-old Jewish girl was still alive when *Sonderkommandos* cleared out one of Auschwitz's gas chambers.[1] As a Jewish doctor assigned to Dr. Josef Mengele was bringing her back to life, Muhsfeld discovered what was happening.

The SS sergeant was not a compassionate man. Noting that Muhsfeld was justly executed in 1947, Levi shows little pity for him. Nevertheless, Levi's rigor makes him dwell on the fact that Muhsfeld hesitated, if only briefly, before deciding what to do with the Jewish girl who had momentarily eluded her Holocaust fate. Muhsfeld ordered her shot, but in the SS man's hesitation, Levi detected something that made him write, "Had he [Muhsfeld] lived in a different environment and epoch, he probably would have behaved like any other common man."[2]

Unfortunately, Muhsfeld's epoch was Hitler's. A death camp was his environment. For Levi, however, it does not follow that Muhsfeld was utterly determined to become a killer whose acts were marked by what Levi calls "refined cruelty." In Muhsfeld's hesitation, I think that Levi saw an element of choice, even a chance for resistance to assert itself. Unfortunately, that opportunity disappeared almost as quickly as it came. The decisions that Muhsfeld actually took, and which were his responsibility, rightly condemned him to death.

The other example of moral judgment that David Hirsch highlights is even more important, because within it Hirsch locates Primo Levi's moral center. This example takes us back to the previously mentioned execution that Levi witnessed in Auschwitz. The man to be hanged by the SS had been part of a revolt that had destroyed a crematorium in Birkenau in October, 1944. Uttered just before the gallows' trap door opened beneath him, his final words were: "*Kamaraden, ich bin der Letzte!*" (Comrades, I am the last one!)

Primo Levi did not forget those words. They resounded for him in a doubly painful way: first, out of deep respect for the condemned resister; second, out of deep regret that, as he puts it, "nothing happened" as his fellow prisoners watched the hanging.[3]

Levi's regret was not a judgmental condemnation of his fellow prisoners or of himself, but it does contain profound sadness and quiet rage about the fact that the Germans so much succeeded in destroying the will to resist the Holocaust's evil. Of course, Levi understood that the very effort to endure Auschwitz for one more day was a form of resistance to that evil. Nevertheless, in the example cited by Hirsch, he advances an especially demanding line of thought by lamenting the fact that the Germans had "nothing more to fear" from the Jews at Auschwitz because the will to resist evil more forcefully was nearly destroyed.[4]

Remaining in "the gray zone," Levi ponders the significance of that Auschwitz hanging with pity and rigor far more than quick moral judgment. Hence he suggests that the Germans' "success" took its dehumanizing toll not only—perhaps, in fact, not even primarily—on their Jewish victims. In devastating ways it erased within the German perpetrators themselves—the ones who most easily could have stopped or prevented the Holocaust—a will to resist the Holocaust's evil. Primo Levi's moral center, then, exists where David Hirsch finds it, namely, in his belief that no component of humanity is more important than "the will to resist evil."

The night before beginning this commentary on Hirsch's astute essay, I finished reading a book by a caring doctor—and my good friend—named Joseph Rebhun. He survived the Holocaust by jumping from a train bound for Auschwitz in September 1943, recovering miraculously from a bullet wound to his head, and passing as a gentile in his native Poland until liberation came. Dr. Rebhun sometimes visits my Holocaust courses at Claremont McKenna College. He always shares his hope that the students will receive his testimony like an immunization that can prevent disease from harming them and those around them. In his book, *Crisis of Morality and Reaction to the Holocaust*, Dr. Rebhun states his belief that when people are "directly confronted with the reality of human suffering, their compassion and concern become evident."[5]

Primo Levi would agree that Dr. Rebhun's judgment deserves to be true. At the same time, Levi would point out, and Dr. Rebhun would agree, that the Holocaust calls that judgment into question. How, then, can we make his proposition more true than it is? How might the moral center that David Hirsch identifies in Primo Levi's writing help us to do so? How can pity and rigor in analyzing the gray zone of Auschwitz assist in clarifying how to articulate and practice a post-Holocaust ethic rooted in the conviction that no component of humanity is more basic that the will to resist evil?

In her Afterword to *Nightfather*, a remarkable novel about a young daughter's poignant attempts to understand her Holocaust-survivor father, the Dutch writer Carl Friedman—her father was a Holocaust survivor—quotes poet Remco Campert, another author from the Netherlands. "Resistance does not start with big words," Campert says, "it starts with small deeds. Asking yourself a question / that is how resistance starts / then putting that question to somebody else."[6] David Hirsch's essay makes me ask myself questions. They are questions about resistance. I hand some of them to him, because I believe that his deeds of writing, which are not small, can help to expand our understanding of the will to resist evil, a basic component of humanity on which the best post-Holocaust ethics profoundly depends.

Notes

[1]As Hirsch points out, Levi reports this singular incident in *The Drowned and the Saved*. The source for Levi's account is *Auschwitz: A Doctor's Eyewitness Account*, which Miklos Nyiszli published in 1960. Nyiszli identifies the SS man as Mussfeld. See Miklos Nyiszli, *Auschwitz: A Doctor's Eyewitness Account*, trans. Tibere Kremer and Richard Seaver (New York: Arcade Publishing, 1993), 114-20.

[2]Primo Levi, *The Drowned and the Saved*, trans. Raymond Rosenthal (New York: Summit Books, 1988), 57.

[3]See Primo Levi, *Survival in Auschwitz: The Nazi Assault on Humanity*, trans. Stuart Woolf (New York: Collier, 1961), 135.

[4]Ibid., 136.

[5]Joseph Rebhun, *Crisis of Morality and Reaction to the Holocaust* (Claremont, CA: OR Publishing, 1998), 120.

[6]Carl Friedman, *Nightfather*, trans. Arnold and Erica Pomerans (New York: Persea Books, 1994), 134.

Hirsch's Response to Critiques

After reading my colleagues' essays and critiques, I hope I have achieved a deeper understanding of some Holocaust issues. At least, I seem to see certain problems more clearly. Roughly speaking, the essays and responses represent two basic attitudes, one attitude views the events that took place in Europe from 1939 to 1945 in the perspective of sacred history, and the other views those same events in the perspective of secular history.

From the standpoint of sacred history, the events may be represented by the term Holocaust (or Shoah) and are considered to be unique in Western, if not human, history. These events add up to a fully conscious attempt to exterminate an entire people in order to erase from the face of the earth, not only a gene pool, but a moral vision, the moral vision of biblical religion, including, explicitly, Judaism, and more vaguely, Christianity. In this context, the extermination of the Jews is perceived as "intentionalist," that is to say, as an extermination that was planned from the very start and carried out, at each stage, to the extent that conditions allowed. Because this plan was so monstrous in itself (from the standpoint of biblical morality, but not from the standpoint of the planners themselves), and because it was conceived, plotted, and carried out by one of the most intellectually and technologically advanced peoples in the world, it remains, from the standpoint of sacred history, inexplicable. Because those who conceived the plot and implemented it were so thorough in its planning and so merciless in its execution, the event remains, from the standpoint of sacred history, a unique instance of radical evil, and those who participated in it willingly, because they were raised in an enlightened Christian culture, are conceived as creatures beyond the bounds of "the human," insofar as "the human" includes the quality of mercy in each "human being." It should be made clear, however, that this accusation of being beyond the bounds of the human is directed only against perpetrators, and is no way to be taken as a blanket condemnation of a people or a nation.

From the standpoint of secular history, the events of 1939 to 1945 were not unique but universal. What happened in Europe during those years was a genocide, not a Holocaust. That is to say, the European events of 1939 to 1945 represent only one more instance, albeit an extreme one, of violence in a long history of human conflict. Nor was the extermination of the Jews planned from the very start, as claimed by the sacralists; the genocide emerged, rather, as a series of steps and missteps, a "twisted road," as it has been called by one historian, in which events were determined by historical circumstance rather than human choice. If these events have not yet been fully explained, the secularist historians claim, they certainly can be. All it would take to explain them would be patience and careful, objective research. Moreover, far from being an example of "radical evil," this genocide demonstrates, rather, the "banality of evil." No one has been able to define this phrase precisely, including the person who coined it, but the secularists cling to it as they would to the flimsiest of shelters in a storm. One way of defining the phrase is to say that "banality" really modifies not evil, but the evildoers themselves, though if that was what the author of the phrase really meant, she could just as easily as have subtitled her book, "the banality of the evildoers."

Finally, the secularists refuse to condemn the perpetrators "as evil," but would rather speak of them as "ordinary men" who happened to do evil deeds. From this perspective, once again, the secularists are able to preserve the notion that the genocide of the Jews committed by the Germans was one more instance of normal human violence. They maintain that since these unprecedented acts of cruelty and destruction were committed by people just like you and me, and since even we ourselves and, in fact, all human beings, are quite capable of committing these very deeds in the very same way and with the very same serenity and absence of conscience, therefore the Holocaust is universal.

To put the matter somewhat differently, and admittedly more provocatively, to preserve the notion of the universality of the Holocaust, the secularists seem to go so far as to insist that Dr. Josef Mengele is Everyman, qualifying this claim, however, by explaining that it was not some inherent personal quality, but rather the system, that made Dr. Mengele what he was. That is, anyone living within the political and social system the Nazis brought to Germany could not help but become a Dr. Mengele, though, at the same time, these very same secularists deny that all Germans were Dr. Mengeles.

But if it was the system that created Dr. Mengele, and if Dr. Mengele was an "ordinary man," then how is it that a Dietrich Bonhoeffer could have come into being within that same system, and what was he? Was Bonhoeffer, too, an ordinary man? And if there had been a million Bonhoeffers rather than a million Mengeles, could the Holocaust have happened? If there had been ten thousand Bonhoeffers, could the Holocaust have happened? And why weren't there more Bonhoeffers than Mengeles, since we are all "ordinary men"? And may we not ask who created the system? Was it killers who created the system, or the system that created killers?

For sacralists, the events of the Holocaust are extraordinary, a rupture in Western, if not human, history. But for the secularists, the events that took place in Europe from 1939 to 1945 are part of the flow of normal history, and the claims of the secularists are a distortion caused by excessive focus on the extremes of the Holocaust. The secularist position, which has been advanced most notably by Ernst Nolte, amounts to the claim that from the vantage point of micro history, there really was no Holocaust at all. If we would only agree to immerse ourselves in the infinite number of details that made up the life of hundreds of millions of Europeans during the years 1939 to 1945, if we could focus our attention on the infinite number of errands and chores conducted by hundreds of millions of people over a period of six years, which is 365 days multiplied by 24 hours multiplied by sixty minutes multiplied by sixty seconds, then we would see that concentrating on the mere thousands of witness accounts testifying to ghettos and concentration camps and *Einsatzgruppen* distorts history. And let us face it, even the war criminals themselves were not committing criminal acts twenty-four hours a day over a period of about two thousand days. Out of a total of about 48,000 hours, even the most industrious killers could have spent no more than a hundred or so of those hours in the act of committing murder. The rest of the time they were ordinary men, which means, I take it, that they ate and slept, defecated and urinated, even made love, just as we ourselves might do. Thus, the Holocaust is normalized. It is restored to the flow of normal human history, which, as we all know, has always been generously spotted with outbreaks of violence.

And the voices of the victims are muted. I do not know of a single witness account by either a survivor or a victim that describes the situation in which the victims found themselves as normal. But, the secularists tell us, we are not to pay too much attention to these accounts. They are not reliable. Yet the philosopher Emmanuel Levinas, who is invoked by both the secularists and the sacralists, has said, in commenting on a short work of fiction, "Yossel Rakover's Appeal to God," that, "I have just read a text that is beautiful and true [*beau et vrai*], true as only fiction can be." I would like to cite, in this context, another work of fiction that is "beautiful and true, true as only a work of fiction [as opposed, I assume Levinas means, to history] can be."

In her brilliant short fiction, "A Scrap of Time," Ida Fink creates a narrator who distinguishes between a "second" kind of time "which is measured in months and years," as opposed to a "first" kind of time. "This [first] time was measured not in months but in a word—we no longer said 'in the beautiful month of May,' but 'after the first *aktzia*, or the second, or right before the third.'" Fink conveys very beautifully, nowhere more beautifully than in the image of the title itself, "a scrap of time" [*skrawek cziasu*] the sense that the moment the Holocaust started, normal time was suddenly suspended. For the victims at least, time was now measured not as points along a continuum of seasons and years, but in scraps of time defined by the German word *Aktion*, Yiddishized into *aktzia*: "We, who because of our difference were condemned once again, as we had been before in our history, we were condemned once again during this time measured not in months nor by the rising and setting of the sun, but by a word—*aktzia*, a word signifying movement, a word you would use about a novel or a play."

Fink's narrator describes the moment the rupture in time took place, that is to say the first *aktzia*: "I had left my house after eating a perfectly normal breakfast, at a table that was set in a normal way...." The Jews of the town, we learn, have been ordered to assemble in the town square to be "conscripted" for "labor." "This beautiful, clear morning that I am digging out of the ruins of my memory," she writes, "is still fresh." On this beautiful clear morning, the Jewish men of the town are rounded up in an *aktzia*, presumably for forced labor, and are trucked out to a field and murdered, no doubt by ordinary men. But for Ida Fink and her "impatient" cousin, who believed the lie and turned himself in and was subsequently among those murdered, normal time has stopped and has been replaced: for Fink, with discontinuous scraps, and for her cousin with oblivion. What normalizing historians have to say to this is that we should put this event into the context of the hundreds of millions of people who were not in the least affected by the *aktzia*, who did not even know it was happening. If we include them in our narrative, then we will gain the proper perspective, which is, no doubt, that a few men were murdered by a handful of killers on a clear beautiful morning while millions of other people were going about their normal activities. Therefore, it is a distortion to dwell on Fink's scraps of time.

I believe there is one sentence in Didier Pollefeyt's response that I should comment on specifically. "Hirsch tries to understand the context in which the Jewish 'collaboration' took place, but he is not prepared to undertake the same effort to understand the psychological background and sociohistorical genesis of the evil-doers, as if understanding would automatically mean excusing."

In all honesty, I do not really know whether I believe that "understanding" is tantamount to "excusing." But I do know that I have seen many "explanations" for Nazi behavior and have found none convincing or enlightening. To rerun some of the old tapes: a lost war, an unfair treaty, depression, inflation, social upheaval, the threat of communism, nationalism. But as has been said many times, many of these ills were felt worldwide, but only one nation believed these problems could be solved only by implementing the "final solution," that is, by exterminating the Jews.

Is it strange that I should try "to understand the context in which the Jewish 'collaboration' took place," but am "not prepared to undertake the same effort to understand the psychological background and sociohistorical genesis of the evil-doers"? Robert Jay Lifton, an eminent psychiatrist, conducted extensive research into the question of "medical killing," interviewing both Nazi and prisoner doctors who had worked in the camps. Yet the best explanation Lifton could come up with was a vague concept called "doubling," which amounts to little more than saying in psychobabble that the killers were quite capable of creating psychological mechanisms that enabled them to kill without feeling either guilt or remorse. Erich Kahler had defined this phenomenon with greater clarity and effectiveness thirty years earlier, as what he termed a "split from without" and a "split from within." But these explanations describe rather than clarify.

Scholars, by nature of their occupation, cannot be satisfied by simple explanations, and certainly not by obvious ones. There is a point in Edgar Allan Poe's famous story, "The Purloined Letter," when Auguste Dupin explains the thinking that led him to discover the stolen missive. "There is a game of puzzles," he tells the narrator,

> which is played upon a map. One party playing requires another to find a given word—the name of a town, river, state or empire—any word, in short, upon the motley and perplexed surface of the chart. A novice in the game generally seeks to embarrass his opponents by giving them the most minutely lettered names, but the adept selects such words as stretch, in large characters, from one end of the chart to the other. These, like the over-largely lettered signs and placards of the street, escape observation by dint of being excessively obvious; and here the physical oversight is precisely analogous with the moral inapprehension by which the intellect suffers to pass unnoticed those considerations which are too obtrusively and too palpably self-evident.

The subtlety of scholars who have been studying and trying to explain the Holocaust by employing the methodology of microhistory falls precisely into the purloined-letter trap, that "moral inapprehension by which the intellect suffers to pass unnoticed those considerations which are too obtrusively and too palpably self-evident." The obvious and therefore true explanation is ignored. I believe we need go no further than David Patterson's observation that "the Nazi project to exterminate the Jews came about not in spite of but, in part, because of the sophisticated German civilization as it had been shaped by German philosophy."

In another of those fictional texts that is, as Levinas would say, beautiful and true, as only a fiction can be, this same point is made with the inspired passion of a great writer. Chaim Grade's short story, "My Quarrel With Hersh Rasseyner," is a debate between the narrator, a secular writer who is a former student in a Musarist yeshiva, and Hersh Rasseyner, a pious Jew who has remained within the fold of Musarist beliefs. These beliefs call for strict observance of the 613 commandments and intense self-examination to assure the maintenance of the individual's spiritual purity. At one point, responding to the narrator's praise of Western culture in general, and German philosophy in particular, Hersh asks,

> ...Do you know why [Western thinkers] haven't been able to rise to a higher level of moral perfection? Because they are driven by an irresistible desire to experience only pleasure in their lives. And since they had to strive so hard to experience all the pleasures that life offered, they gradually discovered inside themselves, a new source of pleasure—the joy of murdering human beings. And they despise us with an implacable hatred, because we came into the world and declared that there are certain things one is not permitted to do. As soon as we uttered the first "Thou shalt not!", the commandment, "Thou shalt not murder!" they targeted us as the eternal enemy. Some of them eventually accepted the commandment, "Thou shalt not kill!", and that did have a beneficial effect on them. But the rest became even more resolved in their intractable enmity toward us. (The Yiddish version of the story was first published in *Yidisher Kemfer* [*Jewish Fighter*], September, 1951; the English version, translated by Milton Himmelfarb appeared in *A Treasury of Yiddish Stories* [1954], edited by Irving Howe and Eliezer Greenberg. This passage was omitted, either by the translator or the editors. The abridged translation has been reprinted in two anthologies of Holocaust Literature.)

Philippa Foot, a Nietzsche scholar, provides a convenient and lucid summary of the extent and significance of Nietzsche's hostility to Christianity and to the Christian ethical values that had their source in Judaic thinking. "Nietzsche," she writes, "wanted to show Christian morality as a 'slave morality' rooted not in anything fine or admirable but rather in weakness, fear and malice...." Here we have the long and short of Nazi behavior toward the Jews. The Nazis wanted to uproot two thousand years of Judeo-Christian ethics, and to achieve this goal they believed that they first had to exterminate the people who introduced the "Thou shalt nots" into Western culture. It does not matter that the Jews of the 1930s and 1940s were not necessarily identical with the Israelites who first gave the world the "Thou shalt nots." The point is that the Nazis believed it, and therefore launched a campaign to exterminate the carriers of the virus of Judeo-Christianity. What is truly remarkable is that masses of European Christians joined in the campaign.

Because it is so obvious, this explanation has yet to be discovered by Holocaust microhistorians. Instead of reading the answer written large on "the motley and perplexed" Holocaust map, they are still looking for the answer in the smallest print. In *The Cunning of History* (1975), Richard Rubenstein accepted the view of Lord Moyne, that "Hitler's 'final solution' was the most convenient way of solving the problem of disposing of one group of surplus people." But since then, Rubenstein has come around to the view that "the Holocaust was a holy war in which post-Enlightenment European Christendom's goal of eliminating Jews and Judaism from its midst was fulfilled by Hitler, albeit by means other than most European religious authorities would have preferred"("Religion and the Uniqueness of the Holocaust," in *Is the Holocaust Unique?*, ed. Alan S. Rosenbaum, [p. 16]).

In pointing out the inconsistency between my defense of the Jewish Councils, on the one hand, and my condemnation of the Nazis, on the other, Pollefeyt suggests that I show compassion for the Jewish victims but not for the Nazi perpetrators. In this matter, Levi seems clear enough to me in "The Gray Zone." Those who created the system (and can it be denied that it was indeed human beings who created it?) are outside the gray zone. Only the victims, in varying degrees, belong in the gray zone, and the creation of the *Judenräte*, like the creation of the "crematorium ravens," was one of National Socialism's most demonic crimes. That is the connection between the Special Squads and Chaim Rumkowski. Pollefeyt feels that the phrase, "one of National Socialism's most demonic crimes," suggests that the demonic crimes were committed by National Socialism itself, and not by National Socialists. I cannot believe that this is what Levi intended, for it makes no sense. Reading this objection to my point of view, I am reminded of a couple of sentences Gershon Scholem wrote to Hannah Arendt after reading her report on Eichmann. "In the Jewish tradition," he pointed out, "there is a concept, hard to define and yet concrete enough, which we know as *Ahabath Israel*: 'Love of the Jewish people…' In you, dear Hannah, as in so many intellectuals who came from the German Left, I find little trace of this."

Perhaps, then, I am guilty of *Ahabath Israel*. On the other hand, it seems to me that regardless of *Ahabath Israel*, there is no way, from any point of view, that the vile and murderous behavior of the Nazi war criminals can be compared to the pathetic and contemptible behavior of some of the Jewish leaders and the Jewish police. At the very worst (and granted, it is bad enough), the Jewish Councils cooperated in delivering the lambs to the slaughter, but they did not commit the slaughter and they did not initiate the events that led to the slaughter, and in the overwhelming majority of cases, it may truly be said of the Jewish leaders that, literally, "They knew not what they did." When Adam Czerniakow finally realized the truth, that he would be handing children over for destruction, he committed suicide. Even Rumkowski, arrogant petty dictator that he was, deluded himself into believing that by cooperating with the Germans, he was working to save the Jews, not exterminate them. Is it possible, let us say, to compare the behavior of Adam Czerniakow with that of Reinhard Heydrich and say both are worthy of our understanding sympathy? For is it not true that I cannot understand another human being without feeling sympathy for that person's humanness?

At one point in Grade's "My Quarrel With Hersh Rasseyner," Hersh, the Musarnik, who is himself a survivor of a camp, contemplates the question of forgiveness for the perpetrators:

> And if a hundred years from now, [Hersh says,] one of the
> murderers were to awaken one of the murdered victims in his

grave, and were to say to the martyred one: "Your innocent blood is choking me, and I can't find rest until you grant me forgiveness. After all, more than a hundred years have gone by since I murdered you, so you would have been dead by this time, anyway." Even if that were to happen, the martyred victim would still have no right to forgive the murderer; he would be bound to withhold forgiveness for his own sake, and for the sake of his unborn children, who had been cut off from life because the one who was to have been their father had been murdered. And if the victim did indeed pardon the murderer, then his fellow victims would be obliged to bar him from re-entering paradise; indeed, they would not even let him enter gehenna. Because if he forgave the murderers he would be murdering the victims again, and this time the murder would be even more painful because it would have been committed by brother against brother.

This is a hard sentence. But is it less than just?

CHAPTER FOUR

Nazis, Philosophers, and the Response to the Scandal of Heidegger

David Patterson

Martin Heidegger's involvement with National Socialism is well known, and many thinkers have responded to the scandal of that involvement. Interestingly, the most famous of these thinkers—those who have had a significant impact on current thinking in a variety of fields—have generally responded most scandalously by fervently defending the Nazi philosopher.

Hans-Georg Gadamer, for example, notes that Heidegger felt no responsibility for the "ignominy of the extermination camps," since "that was the corrupted revolution, not the great renewal from the spiritual and moral strength of the people that he dreamed of and that he longed for as the preparation for a new religion of human-kind."[1] Although Gadamer attempts to dissociate Heidegger from the Nazis, he also tries to interpret his teacher's unbroken silence on the whole affair as an admission and therefore a repentance of his error and delusion.[2] Similarly, in *De l'esprit* Jacques Derrida suggests that Heidegger's turning to Nazism in the early 1930s was a sign of his involvement not with that incarnation of evil but with metaphysics; once Heidegger renounced metaphysics, argues Derrida, he renounced Nazism and moved beyond philosophy.[3] Like Gadamer, Derrida views Heidegger's silence as a form of renunciation and repentance; thus the philosopher's saying nothing gets deconstructed into confession and expiation. Derrida adds his own silence to the silence of Heidegger, however, for he never mentions

Heidegger's comment on "the inner truth and greatness" of Nazism, which appears at the end of the 1953 edition of the *Introduction to Metaphysics*.[4] Nor does he mention Heidegger's response to Rudolf Bultman's advice that, unlike Saint Augustine, the great philosopher should write his *Retractions* before the advent of his last years: in reaction to the suggestion, "Heidegger's face froze over, and he left Bultman without saying a word."[5] Shall this silence too be construed as a confession? And how should Derrida's silence on this silence be construed?

Thinkers such as Gadamer and Derrida insist that, no matter how we may regard Heidegger's affiliation with the Nazis, he cannot be ignored merely because of that affiliation. Of course, they are right: Heidegger must be dealt with. He is the most prominent philosopher of the twentieth century. And these prominent figures who follow him and defend him are infected by his ontological, amoral thinking. But they are not the only ones. With very few exceptions (most notably Emmanuel Levinas, whose entire philosophy opposes ethics and infinity to Heidegger's ontology and totality), even those who either critique or attack Heidegger remain under his spell. For they understand the scandal of Heidegger primarily in terms of a relation between philosophy and politics, and not between philosophy and ethics. Recall, for example, some of the titles of their works: *The Heidegger Case: On Philosophy and Politics* (Tom Rockmore and Joseph Margolis), *The Politics of Being* (Richard Wolin), *The Political Ontology of Martin Heidegger* (Pierre Bourdieu), *Heidegger's Confrontation with Modernity: Technology, Politics, Art* (Michael Zimmerman), *Heidegger's Crisis: Philosophy and Politics in Nazi Germany* (Hans Sluga).

This focus on politics is symptomatic of an outlook ruled by power and the will to power, by an ontological outlook that continues to be enthralled by "the call of Being." It is a way of thinking inherited from a line of German philosophers traceable to Kant's notion of the autonomous will, culminating in Nietzsche's insistence on the will to power, and exemplified in Heidegger's emphasis on resolve as the mark of human authenticity. "Dasein *is its own self*," he maintains, "in the original isolation of silent resolve."[6] Here, as Hans Jonas points out, "decision in itself is the greatest virtue.…[Heidegger] identified the decisiveness (of the *Führer* and the Party) with the principle of decisiveness and resoluteness as such. When I realized, appalled, this was not only Heidegger's personal error but also somehow set up in his thinking, the questionability of existentialism as such became apparent to me."[7] Now a key category in existentialism is freedom. And, infected by the existentialism that Heidegger so profoundly influenced, some of his critics, such as Rockmore, see the Nazism that Heidegger embraced primarily as a threat to human freedom,[8] so that in our reply to Heidegger and the Nazis, "we must hold fast to humanism."[9] Others, such as Sluga, skirt the ethical issue altogether by declaring that "truth and the search for truth are not outside the web of power and cannot be fully conceived apart from it."[10] The web of the Good having been left behind, truth too gets swallowed up by the only "genuine" reality that remains: power.

Attempting to stir our moral outrage, John Caputo rightly points out that "nowhere in the call of Being is the cry of the *victim* to be heard, nowhere the plea for mercy, the summons for help. The silent peal of Being is deaf to the appeal of suffering."[11] But here too something is missing, and it is missing from nearly every reply to the scandal of Heidegger: the Jew. Despite his concern for the victim, Caputo speaks as if the victim's status as Jew were incidental. Others, such as Alan Milchman and Alan Rosenberg, not only de-Judaize their thinking on the ethical and philosophical implications of the Shoah but "Heideggerize" it, so that a form of thinking entirely consistent with Nazi thought infects their thinking about the Jewish victim. These authors maintain, for example, that "Heidegger's insights make it possible to understand that the *Muselmann* is denied the possibility of facing his finitude, of facing up to his freedom toward death."[12] As a Jewish victim, however, the *Muselmann* is denied a *Kiddush Hashem* and a cry of the *Shema* in his last hour—the possibility of facing not his own finitude but the infinity of his Creator, of facing up not to his freedom toward death but to his responsibility in a dying for the other. Thus some of the well-meaning respondents to the scandal of Heidegger talk as if it were mere coincidence that not only Jews but Judaism and all it stands for were targeted for destruction. The Jews have no place in their discourse because philosophy—and very often Heidegger himself—is there instead of Judaism: their discourse is *Judenrein.*

And that is precisely the problem: the history of a major current in Western thought is the history of a struggle to eliminate Abraham and the God of Abraham from human life. Therefore the Holocaust happened not despite but, in part, because of Western civilization, as European philosophy has shaped it. It came not in a breakdown of philosophy but, in part, as its consummation. And at the peak of its consummation stood the Nazi Martin Heidegger.

The Assault on the God of Abraham

"God really died in Auschwitz," argues Philippe Lacoue-Labarthe quite convincingly, "in any case, the God of the Greco-Christian Occident. And it is not by some sort of chance that those that one wanted destroyed were the witnesses within that very Occident, of another origin of God, that had there been worshiped and thought — or, perhaps, it was even a different God who, having remained free of Hellenistic and Roman captation, is, for this very reason, able to thwart the program of accomplishment."[13] The Greco-Christian God "really died in Auschwitz" because the reign of his followers for nearly two thousand years was not enough to prevent such a catastrophe; indeed, nearly all of the millions who participated in the murder were baptized Christians. The God who *really* died at Auschwitz is not the God of Abraham but the God who cannot tolerate the God of Abraham, whose followers declared the children of Abraham to be the murderers of God, and who would exclude from the new Kingdom of Heaven and Earth — from the New Testament — all those who continue to submit themselves to the commandments that come from the Voice at Sinai, rather than from the voice of reason, power, or even faith. As Lacoue-Labarthe suggests, the program to exterminate those who cling to the God of Abraham, Isaac, and Jacob and reject the God of the Christians-turned-philosophers was not accomplished: thousands continue to pray in Hebrew three times a day. But why and in what sense was it undertaken?

"Never," notes Emil Fackenheim, "was a more exalted view of man conceived than that of the divine image, and never one more radically antiracist....It was therefore grimly logical — if to be sure uniquely horrifying — that the most radical racists of all time decreed a unique fate for the Jewish people."[14] The divine image here does not refer to the internalized apotheosis of the ego that characterizes much of the modern thought that derives from Greco-Christian thinking. It pertains rather to the sanctity of the *other* human being; the Holy One is found not in the autonomy of the self but in the need of the widow, the orphan, and the stranger. Authenticity lies not in one's own resolve or will or even faith but in the adherence to the will of God as articulated in the Torah. And freedom lies not in doing what we want to do, as our thought or desire might dictate, but in doing what we must do, as outlined in the commandments of the Torah.

If these concepts are central to a Jewish view of world and humanity, then "the adjective Jewish," as Henri Crétella correctly states it, "does not designate an ethnic group. On the contrary, it signifies that there is no true humanity without being related to divinity—as the Jews have shown us. In other words, it is not blood and soil which properly define us, but rather the possibility of emancipating ourselves from this very blood and soil."[15] Therefore Nazi philosopher Max Wundt is quite right when he asserts that the Jewish view of world and humanity "stands opposed to the folkish world view as its total antithesis."[16] Indeed, the Nazis cannot be Nazis without the notions of the German *Volk*, the master race, the purity of the blood, and so on. Therefore they must eliminate the notion of a higher, divine image within the other human being, and to do that they have to eliminate the people whose presence in the world signifies such a teaching. Thus, Fackenheim observes, "the Nazi rejection of the knowledge of the divine image was translated into law. The law itself came closest to the self-fulfilling prophecy aimed at in the murder camp. The murder camp was not an accidental by-product of the Nazi empire. It was its pure essence. The divine image in man *can* be destroyed. No more threatening proof to this effect can be found than the so-called *Muselmann* in the Nazi death camp....The *Muselmänner* are a new way of human being in history, the living dead."[17] The *Muselmann* is the incarnation of the human being who has no trace of a divine image, of the human being as the one who is simply and indifferently there—of the human being as *Dasein*. This assault on the divine image of the human being was conceived by philosophers and carried out by the SS. First conceptual and then actual, it is an assault on divinity, humanity, and the people chosen to attest to the divine chosenness of every human being.

From the time of Cain, the murder of God has been undertaken through the murder of people. Rashi, the great eleventh-century commentator on Torah and Talmud, writes, "Whoever attacks Israel is as though he attacks the Holy One."[18] This connection between God and Israel and the assault on both is attested to in many Holocaust diaries, including the *Vittel Diary* of Yitzhak Katzenelson,[19] the Warsaw ghetto diary kept by Emmanuel Ringelblum,[20] and the chronicle of the Vilna ghetto recorded by Zelig Kalmanovitch.[21] In these and many other testimonies we discover the uniqueness of the Holocaust: it is an attack not only on human beings but on the Holy One who sanctifies humanity. This singularity manifests itself in the calculated destruction not only of Jewish bodies but of Jewish souls and Jewish prayers, of Jewish texts and traditions, of synagogues and cemeteries. It manifests itself in a murder of God that follows in the wake of Nietzsche's assertion that God is dead.

One recalls, for example, the Nazis' destruction of Torah scrolls wherever they went. Why Torah scrolls? Because, on some level, they knew what the tradition teaches us through the words of the Koretzer Rebbe: "God and Prayer are one. God and Torah are one. God, Israel and Torah are one."[22] The synagogues that house the Torah scrolls were marked for desecration and destruction; those that were not made into latrines or stables were burned down, often with Jews inside them. Judith Dribben recalls one Nazi's remark as he gazed upon a synagogue filled with Jews going up in flames: "The Jewish God is burned to ashes!"[23] Not only are the places of prayer and the people who pray to be destroyed, but prayer itself is to be demolished (Kant's insistence on the worthlessness of prayer comes to mind).[24] On the eve of Tisha B'Av 5700 (1940), for example, Chaim Kaplan writes in his Warsaw ghetto diary, "Public prayer in these dangerous times is a forbidden act. Anyone caught in this crime is doomed to severe punishment. If you will, it is even sabotage, and anyone engaging in sabotage is subject to execution."[25] Hence the Nazis' position: not only shall we torture and slaughter you, but we forbid you to pray beforehand. For prayer is as dangerous to "civilized" Germany as the Jews are.

In addition to assailing the words and the silences of prayer, the Nazis sought to destroy the vessels of the holy, those symbols, rites, and rituals that assist us in our effort to hear the voice of the One who forever speaks. The use of the *mikveh*, the ritual bath, for example, was forbidden. To be sure, as synagogues were desecrated, so were ritual baths, which is a desecration of family and childbearing. For the ritual bath is central to the laws of family purity. As the ritual purity of those who bring life into the world is defiled, so is life defiled; so is the Creator of life defiled. In a diary entry dated 2 February 1941 Ringelblum reports another example of the destruction of a holy vessel: "A group of Jews were locked up in the synagogue until they hacked the holy ark to bits."[26] Forcing the Jews to do this work themselves is a means of forcing them into a destruction of their own image, of their own sanctity, as they destroy the sign of the Holy One in whose image they are created. In all of these cases the divine holiness that shows itself through the symbol opens up to us what is holy in our fellow human being.

The synagogue, the ritual bath, and the holy ark are all components of the sacred center upon which the Jewish community is founded. Tied to that center and sanctified by it is the primary component of the community itself: the home. Therefore, assailing God, the enemy launches an attack on the symbols that consecrate the home. One of the most significant of these is the *mezuzah* attached to the door posts of the home. Containing portions of the Torah, it is embossed with the letter *shin*, which stands for *Shaday* or "Almighty" and is one of the names of God. Yitzchak Ginsburgh offers another reading of the *shin* on the *mezuzah*, explaining that it is "short for *Sh.D.Y.* (the initial letters of the phrase *shomer daltot Yisrael*, 'the guardian of the doors of Israel')."[27] The *mezuzah*, then, is a sign of God's presence at the threshold of the home, a sign of the sanctity and security of home and family. The destruction of the *mezuzah* signifies an attempt to destroy the name of God and with it the Guardian of Israel Himself. Thus, writes Ringelblum, "At the beginning of the Ghetto period, *men of valor* [Nazis] tore down the *mezuzot* from the door posts of Jewish apartments."[28] This destruction of the *mezuzah* is an assault not only on the particular homes violated but on the very notion of home and family as a sanctuary for the sacred.

Indeed, every Jew in Europe was rendered homeless—not only because every Jew was in a camp, in a ghetto, or in hiding but because every space that could be designated as a home was swallowed up by the Nazi leviathan. And every family was broken.

The Nazis took their onslaught against ritual objects to the people who breathed life into them. In his diary from Warsaw and other places in Poland, for example, Rabbi Shimon Huberband records that the Nazis took the Jews' *tefillin* and "ripped them and burned them. They confiscated *talis kotons* in order that they be used by Jews to clean toilets."[29] And: "The Germans collected *taleysim, talis kotons,* and *kitls.* These holy garments were given to Jews to wash floors, automobiles, and windows."[30] When a Jew puts on these holy garments or lays *tefillin* with the appropriate prayers on his lips, his very body is transformed into a symbol of the divine Presence in the world. We are taught that to wrap ourselves in the prayer shawl is to wrap ourselves in the Light of God. Made of eight threads and five knots, the *tsitsit* or fringes on the *taleysim* and *talis kotons* signify the 613 commandments of the Torah, as Rashi explains: 613 equals the numerical value of the word for "fringes" (600) plus five plus eight.[31] The destruction and desecration of such garments, then, are tied to the assault on Torah, on God, and on Israel.

Not only did the symbolic clothing of the Jews become the object of the Nazis' assault, but the symbolic features of the body itself also came under attack. Among Jewish men, for instance, the symbol that distinguishes the face as a face turned toward God is the beard. And so, writes Warsaw diarist Michael Zylberberg, "Saddest of all, perhaps, was the position of the Orthodox. They were ordered to shave their head and face completely, to remove every symbol of Jewishness."[32] Similarly, Rabbi Huberband notes, "If a bearded Jew was caught, his life was put in danger. They tore out his beard with pieces of flesh, or cut it off with a knife and a bayonet."[33] And, describing an *Aktion* staged in the Lvov ghetto, David Kahane writes, "First they seized old men with beards and sidelocks. Not even a work card could save a bearded Jew."[34] The Talmud tells us that the beard is the glory of the face (*Shabbat* 152a). If it is the glory of the face, then it makes the face into a sign of the Holy One, who sanctifies the life of the human being; and if the face is a sign of the Holy

One, then, in the words of Levinas, "the face is what forbids us to kill."[35] Such a prohibition is precisely what the Nazis must eliminate, if they are to get rid of God. And they do indeed eliminate it by eliminating those whose faces signify the glory of the One who, through the face, speaks the prohibition against murder.

These definitive features of National Socialism in action are generally ignored both by Nazi philosophers such as Heidegger and by our own contemporaries who respond to them. In a Heideggerian leveling of Being into the neutrality and sameness of what is merely there, those who mention the Jews usually throw them into the same category as all the other victims of the Nazis, as though the details outlined above were completely insignificant. Hans Sluga is typical. "Given the crimes the Nazis committed against *the Jews and other minority groups*," he maintains, "it may be difficult to accept that racial theory was for them only a means to justify their belief in German privilege. But unless we credit that, we will not understand why philosophers who had no sympathy for biological racism could feel in tune with the aspirations of National Socialism."[36] Sluga's claim rests on a fundamental misunderstanding. In the case of the Jews, the racial theory justified far more than a belief in German privilege; it justified the assault on the God of Abraham and everything He signifies. Unlike the terrible atrocities inflicted on other groups, the Nazis' assault on Jews and their Judaism is not simply about biology or race but is primarily about metaphysics. That is why the philosophers could be in tune with them; that is why, despite his opposition to biologism, Heidegger could complain about the "Jewification" of the German mind.[37] Let us consider, then, the philosophers' complicity in the assault on Jews and Judaism.

The Philosophers' Complicity in the Assault

It is a matter of record that no major protest was raised against the Nazis on the part of the philosophers of Germany. Indeed, by 1940 nearly half of them were members of the Nazi Party, and several of them, including Heidegger, from a variety of schools of thought competed with one another to emerge as the philosophical spokesman of the National Socialist movement. The philosopher who, for example, in 1923 became the first to publicly support the Nazis was

Hermann Schwarz, a thinker influenced by Meister Eckhart and Jacob Boehme. There were the Kantian Idealists such as Bruno Bauch, Max Wundt, Hans Heyse, and Nicolai Hartmann; the noted Hegelian Theodor Haerung; and those, such as Alfred Bäumler and Ernst Krieck, who turned to Nietzsche for their inspiration.

These Nazi philosophers are the avowed heirs to the thinking handed down to them from a number of German philosophical giants. What these thinkers have in common is their embrace of a philosophical tradition that is fundamentally atheistic and that takes individual autonomy to be the measure of human freedom and authenticity. As Theodore Kisiel has pointed out, the basic atheism of philosophy that Heidegger proclaimed in 1922 is what attracted him to "the full-blown antireligious attitude of the German *Geist* ripened from German Idealism."[38] We have already mentioned Kant's aversion to prayer; in a letter to Johann Caspar Lavater dated 28 April 1775, for instance, he refers to prayer as "the so-called worshipful supplications which have perennially constituted the religious delusion."[39] Insisting that religion derives from morality, and not the other way around, Kant embraces a rationalist theology that is opposed to anything resembling a revealed religion such as Judaism. Indeed, in *The Conflict of the Faculties* Kant declares, "The euthanasia of Judaism is the pure moral religion."[40] According to his view, where you have reason, you have no need of religion, since reason is the basis of human autonomy and therefore of human freedom. To be free is to be moral—not, however, subject to moral law but authoring moral law through the will to universalize maxims from one's actions. The law that binds us, says Kant, comes from nowhere but within ourselves; the human being is "determinable," as he states it in *The Critique of Practical Reason*, "only by laws which he gives to himself through reason."[41] Kant insists, therefore, that Judaism lacks the inner moral imperative characteristic of freedom because it relies on externally given laws.[42] Judaism is the opposite of Kantian Idealism.

Like Kant, G. W. F. Hegel was a rationalist who associated freedom with human autonomy. His writings, as Paul Lawrence Rose has noted, "conform to the basic Kantian idealist and moralist critique of Judaism. Judaism is seen as the epitome of an unfree psyche."[43] In Hegel's *Life of Jesus*, for example, the title character addresses the Jews, saying, "This inner law is a law of freedom to which a person submits voluntarily, as though he had imposed it on himself....You, however, are slaves. You stand yoked by a law imposed on you from without."[44] Going beyond Kant, however, Hegel draws on the Christian notion of the Christ as the Incarnation to develop a view of God that denies the otherness of the divinity. Hegel's "denial of divine otherness," Fackenheim explains, "issues not in an atheistic rejection of the Divine, but rather in its internalization. Divinity comes to dwell, as it were, in the same inner space as the human self."[45] Resisting this internalization, Jews insist on a fundamental distinction between God and the "inner space of the human self." In Hegel's eyes, then, Jews live an "animal existence," are in a "state of total passivity, of total ugliness," and should be faulted for refusing to "die as Jews."[46] The philosophical result of this internalization of God and deprecation of the Jews unfolds in the thinking of atheistic neo-Hegelians such as Ludwig Feuerbach and Karl Marx, where, says Fackenheim, "divinity vanishes in the process of internalization, to be replaced by a humanity potentially infinite in its modern 'freedom.'"[47] From there it is a short step to Nietzsche's proclamation that God is dead and his notion of the will to power as the basis and substance of human—or superhuman—being.

In a logical sequence proceeding from Kant and Hegel, there unfolds in Nietzsche's thought a drive to be a god unto oneself as the legislator of good and evil "He has discovered himself who says, 'This is *my* good and evil'"—thus spoke Zarathustra.[48] And *my* good and evil means as I have willed it, not as I have received it from the teaching and the tradition of my mothers and fathers. The will to power is a will to freedom, where freedom is understood as an autonomy beyond any law, resolute and decisive. Indeed, "the expression 'will to power,'" says Heidegger in his study of Nietzsche, "designates the basic character of beings; any being which is, insofar as it is, is will to power. The expression stipulates the character that beings have as beings."[49] And so after Nietzsche's will to power as the *character* of beings we have Heidegger's resolve as the *authenticity* of beings.

"For Kant," Rockmore points out, "to determine oneself to act according to a principle applicable to every possible rational being is already in a sense to be moral; so for Heidegger, merely to be resolute is already to be authentic."[50] For to be resolute is to be autonomous and free. "Resolve," says Heidegger, "is the loyalty of existence to its own self."[51] There is, then, a line of progression from the will to make the maxim of one's action into law, to the will to power, to resolve. The thread running through this progression is the accent on the autonomy of the self as the basis for freedom, a notion that was part of the thinking of all the Nazi philosophers—and a notion antithetical to Jewish teaching. For Jewish teaching places its accent not on freedom but on justice, not on ontology but on metaphysics, not on being but on being ethical, which means living in a manner in keeping with God's Torah, and not setting oneself as the author of good and evil. How do we do that? By situating the other human being in a position higher than our own, rather than relegating him to the status of one more being among beings; by seeking the divinity in the need of the other, and not in the deification of the self. The self can no more be a god and a ground unto itself than a man can pull himself up by his own hair.

Once philosophy brings about the eclipse of the divine by the human, the human being is no longer a child of God but a child of the people, of the *Volk*. In Germany his allegiance is not to the Creator of all humanity but to the leader or the *Führer* of the *Volk*. And in German philosophy Heidegger exemplifies that turn of events.

The Scandal of Heidegger

Levinas accurately summarizes the thesis of Heidegger's definitive work *Being and Time* by explaining, "Being is inseparable from the comprehension of Being (which unfolds in time); Being is already an appeal to subjectivity....[But this] is to subordinate the relation with *someone*, who is an existent (the ethical relation), to a relation with the *Being of the existent*, which, impersonal, permits the apprehension, the domination of the existent (a relationship of knowing), subordinates justice to freedom....In subordinating every relation with the existent to the relation with Being the Heideggerian ontology affirms the primacy of freedom over ethics."[52] And Levinas succinctly states the implication of such a philosophy: "A philosophy of power, ontology is, as first philosophy which does not call into question the same, a philosophy of injustice....Heideggerian ontology, which subordinates the relationship with the Other to the relation with Being in general, remains under obedience to the anonymous, and leads inevitably to another power, to imperialist domination, to tyranny."[53] A philosophy that does not call into question the same is a philosophy of injustice because it situates freedom beyond the Law and is therefore lawless. Enclosed within the thought of Being, it is a philosophy entrenched in the Greco-Christian prejudice that "the Other is Being," to borrow from Lyotard; hence "it has nothing to say about a thought in which the Other is the Law."[54] Such is the philosophy of *Volk* and *Führer*, which insists, as Heidegger did, that "the *Führer* himself and he alone *is* the present and future German reality and its law."[55] It shows itself quite starkly in Heidegger's infamous Rectorial Address delivered at the University of Freiburg on 27 May 1933—by which time Hitler had assumed dictatorial powers, Jews were removed from civil services jobs, Dachau was in operation, and Jewish businesses had been boycotted.

In the Rectorial Address Heidegger extolled the "magnificence and greatness of this new departure [Nazism]."[56] It was in the name of that new departure that he summoned his listeners to a "national community" (*Volksgemeinschaft*) rooted in labor service, military service, and knowledge service.[57] "All abilities of will and thought," he declared, "all strengths of the heart, and all capabilities of the body must unfold *through* battle, heightened *in* battle, and presented *as* battle"[58]—where any contemporary German listener would immediately associate the word *battle*, or *Kampf*, with Hitler's manifesto *Mein Kampf*. In the slogan with which Heidegger ends his speech, he falsifies the translation of a famous line from Plato's *Republic*. Instead of the standard "Everything great is at risk" or "Everything great is precarious," he translates it as *"Alles Grosse steht im Sturm,"* misreading the Greek *episphala*. According to Wolin, this mistranslation is "in conformity with the *Sturm* and *Kampf* metaphors he has been promoting throughout the address. When one recalls that the initials 'SA'—used to refer to Hitler's 'Storm Troopers'—actually stand for *Sturm*abteilung, and that one of the most virulently antisemitic publications at the time was called *Der Stürmer*,

Heidegger's manifestly tendentious gesture loses all its innocence."[59] What is also lost is any doubt as to how Heidegger understood his relation to National Socialism.

From the Rectorial Address it is evident that, in Sluga's words, Heidegger considered himself "the born philosopher and spiritual leader of the new movement."[60] This view of himself was not merely a matter of intellectual conceit. More than that, Heidegger believed he was addressing a philosophical vacuum that threatened the new movement and the life of the German *Volk*.

What was to fill that vacuum? Not, according to Heidegger, a "bourgeois" philosophy of values. Values, he claimed, are "the last decadence of the bourgeoisie. Who can commit themselves or show enthusiasm for values? We are enthusiastic about certain tasks. Tasks are tasks of creation, and creation is works. A philosophy of works must arise in opposition to the philosophy of values. Only what is concrete commits us, values never commit us."[61] Opposing himself to Nazi philosophers of values—such as Bauch, who sought to ground values in race—Heidegger understood the Nazi order to be one that "would find secure grounding not in values but in a new unconcealment of Being, a new truth of Being."[62] The "unconcealment of Being" is characterized by a new collision with a profound anxiety over being thrown into a world that is empty of any ground or meaning. The new truth of Being then arises when the individual takes on the re-solve to become his own ground of truth and meaning through an allegiance to his own *Volk* and the *Führer*. Thus Heidegger saw in Nazism a new comprehension of Being that finally frees itself from the appeal to an infinite or divine being, from all revelation of values from on high, from every remnant of "onto-theology." "Existential ontology," he declared, "has as its sole objective the explication of the primordial transcendental structure of the *Dasein* in man," which, in turn, "manifests itself as need of the comprehension of Being,"[63] and not as, say, the need for a moral relation to another (person or God), the responsibility for the life of one's neighbor, or the like.

That is why Heidegger's rare critical remarks about National Socialism concern only its shortcomings as a comprehensive theory of Being, and not its moral depravity. Indeed, if, according to Heidegger, the substance and the good of human being lie in the comprehension of Being and not in the care for the life of our fellow human being—if the interest is in freedom and not in justice, in what *is* and not what is *lawful*—then the only grounds for criticizing any ideology are ontological and not moral grounds. Hence, contrary to what some scholars have argued, neither Heidegger nor his Nazi colleagues thought they were doing a moral good by pursuing the Nazi agenda; on the contrary, they believed they were doing an ontological good beyond good and evil, with its corollary social, political and cultural good. Just as the Nazis spoke of "resolution and mastery" or of "command and obedience," Heidegger invoked "the will to power as the will to will," "self-overcoming," and the "authentic experience of freedom."[64] But nowhere do they claim to be doing what is ethically or morally needful. The Nazis did not believe they were doing a moral good because, like Heidegger, they believed they were transcending all morality.

To be sure, in a comment on a meeting he had with Heidegger in Rome in 1936 Karl Löwith notes that "a partnership for National Socialism lay in the essence of his philosophy. Heidegger agreed with me [about this] without reservation and elucidated that his concept of 'historicity' was the basis of his political 'engagement.' He also left no doubt about his belief in Hitler."[65] Understanding Being in terms of time—and not, say, in terms of Divine Law or the Good—Heidegger views the human being as one who is historically *in situation*. On the ontic level of life, as he states it, the call of conscience that summons us to our own potentiality for being "does not hold before us some empty ideal of existence, but *calls us forth into the situation*."[66] In that situation the human being must be his own ground, generating his own resolve, to uphold his situation, which is his Being-in-the-world. "In resolve," says Heidegger, "*Dasein* takes on its ownmost potentiality-for-Being, which, as thrown, it can project only onto its specific, actual possibilities."[67] And since this "Being-in-the-world exists essentially as Being-with-others," he explains, "its happening is a happening-with and is determinative for it as *destiny*. This is how we designate the happening of a community, a *Volk*."[68] And how does that happening authentically take place? Through the resolve of the individual who wills his way into the body of the *Volk*. The point to be gathered from all this is that Heidegger was not a philosopher who happened to become a Nazi. His Nazism was not a personal shortcoming or a character flaw but a central feature of his ontological thinking, a thinking that was the culmination of German philosophy as it developed from the time of Kant.

The thinking that comes to characterize German philosophy as exemplified by Heidegger is a thinking that eliminates the other human being from its horizons. "*Das Dasein existiert umwillen seiner,*" Heidegger declares: "*Dasein* exists for the sake of itself."[69] Why? Because, according to this thinking, the individual is one whose being is defined by time and by the horizon of his time, which is death. "Since men and women cannot unload their deaths upon someone else," Jacques Taminiaux points out, "it is therefore not vis-à-vis others that individuals declare who they are but only vis-à-vis themselves in the solitude of their inner selves, in a profound absence of relationships."[70] Once the move from being-there to being-with is established, the solitude ascribed to the single individual is ascribed to the *Volk*; one can be only with others who are like oneself, that is, who are German. Left with no room for a relationship to the other human being, we are left with no room for ethics, no room for the Good. While Heideggerian ontology sees time as the inner structure of the self, metaphysical ethics (particularly as articulated by Jewish thought) views time in terms of a responsibility for the other person: as Levinas has said, "Responsibility for the Other signifies an original and concrete temporality."[71] While Heideggerian ontology sees the death that concerns me as *my* death,[72] metaphysical ethics (again, as articulated by Jewish thought) takes the death that concerns me to be the death of the other human being: as Levinas has said, "The fear for the death of the other is certainly at the basis of the responsibility for him."[73]

Hence if there is any room for guilt in Heidegger's thinking, it is not "the result of some moral failing," as Edith Wyschogrod rightly points out, "but rather because the who of *Dasein* is negatively defined as the possibility of its not existing."[74] According to Heidegger, this possibility of not existing is the only thing that can *essentially* interest the individual, and it blinds the individual to all such possibility vis-à-vis the other human being. Yes, in *Being and Time* Heidegger notes that "the world is always the one I share with others."[75] But those others constitute the They that threatens the authenticity of the self. "The *They*," says Heidegger, "by which the everyday *Dasein* answers the question of *who*, is the *no one*."[76] The extent of the Heideggerian blindness to the other human being can be seen in Heidegger's very lame defense of himself on this point. "The fundamental thought of my thinking," he says, "is precisely that Being, or the manifestation of Being, *needs* human beings and that, vice versa, human beings are only human beings if they are standing in the manifestation of Being. With that answer, the question to what extent I have forgotten human beings should be settled."[77] And so, indeed, it is settled: what is needful for me is to stand "in the manifestation of Being" through my own inner resolve in the face of the death that lays claim to me. Everything and everyone are either an annoyance or a matter of indifference.

"In the final analysis," Rockmore points out, "to embrace Being as the ultimate explanatory principle is tantamount to casting off the idea of ethical responsibility."[78] There is much truth in Rockmore's insight, but not for the reasons he thinks. Like many other respondents who, directly or indirectly, invoke Kantian thinking, Rockmore makes the mistake of identifying ethical freedom and responsibility with individual autonomy, as if Heidegger were trying to get rid of autonomy.[79] But the reverse is the case: Heidegger does not get rid of autonomy—he pushes it to its limit. The Enlightenment philosophy of Kant cannot be held up as a response to Heidegger because, as we have seen, it led to Heidegger. What must be opposed to Heidegger is precisely the Jewish metaphysics that the Nazis opposed: not the autonomy of the self but the sanctity of the other, not the universal maxims of reason but the uncompromising commandments of God, not freedom but justice.

One thing that distinguishes Jewish metaphysics is the dimension of height that belongs to the Most High, to the Holy One, to Our Father, Our King, to the Good, who is the Creator of heaven and earth. This dimension "ordains being," in the words of Levinas. "Height introduces a sense into being. It is already lived across the experience of the human body. It leads human societies to raise up altars. It is not because men, through their bodies, have an experience of the vertical that the human is placed under the sign of height;

because being is ordained to height, the human body is placed in a space in which the high and the low are distinguished and the sky is discovered."[80] To be sure, in Jewish thought the capacity to make such distinctions—between high and low, God and man, good and evil, sacred and profane—forms the basis of every notion of the Holy, from which the sanctity of human life is derived. With the advent of Heideggerian ontology, being loses the dimension of height that imparts meaning to it and is leveled into a flatland of neutrality.

Several remarks from Heidegger himself illustrate the implications of this leveling. When Herbert Marcuse wrote to him and asked what he had to say about the gas chambers, Heidegger replied by equating the Nazis' treatment of the Jews with the Allies' treatment of the East Germans. In a letter to Marcuse dated 20 January 1948 he wrote, "To the severe and justified reproaches formulated 'over a regime that has exterminated millions of Jews, that has made terror a norm and that transformed everything connected to the concepts of spirit, freedom, and truth into its opposite,' I can only add that instead of 'the Jews' one should put the 'East Germans.'"[81] And in a lecture given in 1949, Heidegger compared technologically-driven agriculture to the technologically-driven murder of the Jews, saying, "Agriculture is now a motorized food industry—*in essence*, the same as the manufacturing of corpses in gas chambers and the extermination camps, the same as the blockading and starving of nations, the same as the manufacture of atom bombs."[82] And so we can see why Jürgen Habermas complains, "Under the leveling glance of the philosopher of Being, the extermination of the Jews, too, appears as a happening, where everything can be replaced as one likes with anything else."[83] In a world where one is merely a being among beings, anyone can take the place of another, and all are expendable. The German escapes this leveling by assuming the position of philosopher/*Führer*—his is the leveling glance, so that neither "Jewified" thought nor the mongrel Jewish race may corrupt him. Once leveled, the human being is rendered faceless. And since, in the words of Levinas, "the face is what forbids us to kill,"[84] with the loss of the dimension of height in the Heideggerian leveling of Being, we also lose the prohibition against murder. That is why Fackenheim declared the murder camp to be the essence of National Socialism.

That is why the murder camp is a logical outcome of a line of German thought traceable from Kant to Heidegger and into our own time.

The Rabbis explain that the Ten Commandments were inscribed on two tablets to designate two realms of relation: the first five commandments pertain to the human-to-divine relation, and the second five designate the human-to-human relation, which is the realm of ethical relation. The first commandment in the latter category is the prohibition against murder. It is the basis of all other commandments pertaining to our relationship to our fellow human being, the basis of ethics itself. And, according to the Jewish teaching that the Nazis sought to annihilate, it comes not from some tribal chieftain but from God Himself. It is the Most High who commands us not only not to murder our neighbor but to love him as we love ourselves. Through that love, God reveals Himself; revealing Himself, He makes ethics possible. Through that *commandment* to love, our freedom is curtailed to open up the possibility of justice.

As we have seen, however, the German philosophers of autonomy and authenticity place an unlimited freedom over the pursuit of justice. Hence there is no room for ethics in that philosophy, which begins with Kant in an ostensible concern for ethics and ends with Heidegger by leaving ethics behind. "The other for Heidegger," as Wyschogrod has noted, "is the one with whom I share the world: my relation to the other never bypasses the world; rather it passes through the circuit of the world....Such relations as love, sexuality, and friendship, which occur primordially as relations between persons, circumvent the world, and represent a sphere of limited freedom, play no part in Heidegger's analysis."[85] Because such relations play no part in Heidegger's analysis, ethics plays no part—either in his analysis or in Nazi ideology. The Nazis may have believed that they were doing a "good thing" in their extermination of the Jews, but they could not believe they were doing an *ethically* good thing. In keeping with Heideggerian thought, the good they sought was not an ethical good but an ontological good. For they sought a purification of being by overcoming the "Jewification" of the world, and not an ethical relation to their neighbor expressive of a higher relation to God, to the Infinite One, in whose image *every* finite human being is created.

Precisely these distinctions have generally been absent from the attempts both to attack and to defend Heidegger. But these are the very distinctions that have to be made if we are to understand the scandal not only of Heidegger but of German philosophy in the contexts of the Shoah. Indeed, the Shoah is about this very matter: is there or is there not a higher and holy Good?

Perhaps, then, we can now see the truth of Levinas's insight and better understand its implications, when he asserts, "Heideggerian philosophy precisely marks the apogee of a thought in which the finite does not refer to the infinite (prolonging certain tendencies of Kantian philosophy: the separation between the understanding and reason, diverse themes of transcendental dialectics), in which every deficiency is but weakness and every fault committed against one-self—the outcome of a long tradition of pride, heroism, domination, and other to the relation with the neuter, Being, and it thus continues to exalt the will to power, whose legitimacy the other alone can unsettle, troubling good conscience."[86] And perhaps by now we can see that the Nazi project to exterminate the Jews came about not in spite of but, in part, because of the sophisticated German civilization as it had been shaped by German philosophy.

Notes

[1]Hans-Georg Gadamer, "Superficiality and Ignorance," in *Martin Heidegger and National Socialism*, ed. Guenther Neske and Emil Kettering, trans. Lisa Harries (New York: Paragon, 1990), 143.

[2]See Gadamer, "The Political Incompetence of Philosophy," in *The Heidegger Case: On Philosophy and Politics*, ed. Tom Rockmore and Joseph Margolis (Philadelphia: Temple University Press, 1992), 368.

[3]See Jacques Derrida, *De l'esprit* (Paris: Éditions Galilee, 1987), 11, 12, 64, 66, 155, 156.

[4]See Martin Heidegger, *Introduction to Metaphysics*, trans. R. Mannheim (New York: Doubleday, 1961), 199.

[5]See John D. Caputo, "Heidegger's Scandal: Thinking and the Essence of the Victim," in *The Heidegger Case*, 265.

[6]Heidegger, *Sein und Zeit*. (Tübingen: Max Niemeyer, 1963), 322. Translations from this work are my own.

[7]Hans Jonas, "Heidegger's Resoluteness and Resolve," in *Martin Heidegger and National Socialism*, 202-03.

[8]Tom Rockmore, *On Heidegger's Nazism and Philosophy* (Berkeley: University of California Press, 1992), 290.

[9]Ibid., 288.

[10]Hans Sluga, *Heidegger's Crisis* (Cambridge: Harvard Univ. Press, 1993), 254.

[11]Caputo, "Heidegger's Scandal," in *The Heidegger Case*, 277.

[12]Alan Milchman and Alan Rosenberg, "Heidegger, Planetary Technics, and the Holocaust," in *Martin Heidegger and the Holocaust*, ed. Alan. Milchman and Alan Rosenberg (Atlantic Highlands, NJ: Humanities Press, 1996), 224.

[13]Philippe Lacoue-Labarthe, *La Fiction du politique* (Paris: Christian Bourgeois, 1987), 62-63. See also Jean-François Lyotard, *Heidegger and "the jews,"* trans. A. Michel and M. S. Roberts (Minneapolis: University of Minnesota Press, 1990), 80.

[14]Emil L. Fackenheim, *What Is Judaism?* (New York: Macmillan, 1987), 109.

[15]Henri Crétella, "Self-Destruction," in *Martin Heidegger and the Holocaust*, 159.

[16]Max Wundt, *Deutsche Weltanschauung* (Munich: J. F. Lehmans, 1926), 75; see also Sluga, *Heidegger's Crisis*, 113.

[17]Emil Fackenheim, *The Jewish Return into History* (New York: Schocken, 1978), 246.

[18]Rashi, *Commentary on the Torah*, vol. 4, trans. M. Rosenbaum and A. M. Silbermann (Jerusalem: Silbermann Family, 1972), 146.

[19]Yitzhak Katznelson, *Vittel Diary*, trans. Myer Cohen (Tel-Aviv: Hakibbutz Hameuchad, 1972), 122.

[20]Emmanuel Ringelblum, *Notes from the Warsaw Ghetto*, trans. Jacob Sloan (New York: Schocken, 1974), 80.

[21]Zelig Kalmanovitch, "Diary of the Nazi Ghetto in Vilna," *YIVO Annual*, 8 (1953): 52.

[22]Quoted in Louis I. Newman, ed. and trans., *The Hasidic Anthology* (New York: Schocken, 1963), 147.

[23]Judith Dribben, *And Some Shall Live* (Jerusalem: Keter Books, 1969), 24.

[24]See Ernst Cassirer, *Kant's Life and Thought*, trans. James Haden (New Haven: Yale University Press, 1981), 18.

[25]Chaim A. Kaplan, *The Warsaw Diary of Chaim A. Kaplan*, trans. A.

I. Katsh (New York: Collier, 1973), 179.

[26]Ringelblum, *Notes from the Warsaw Ghetto*, 127.

[27]Yitzchak Ginsburgh, *The Alef-Beit* (Northvale, NJ: Aronson, 1991), 319.

[28]Ringelblum, *Notes from the Warsaw Ghetto*, 152.

[29]Shimon Huberband, *Kiddush Hashem*, trans. D. E. Fishman (Hoboken: Ktav, 1987), 44.

[30]Ibid., 35.

[31]Rashi, *Commentary on the Torah*, 76-77.

[32]Michael Zylberberg, *A Warsaw Diary*, trans. M. Zylberberg (London: Valentine, Mitchell, 1969), 21.

[33]Huberband, *Kiddush Hashem*, 35.

[34]David Kahane, *Lvov Ghetto Diary*, trans. J. Michalowicz (Amherst: University of Massachusetts Press, 1990), 45.

[35]Emmanuel Levinas, *Ethics and Infinity*, trans. R. A. Cohen (Pittsburgh: Duquesne University Press, 1985), 86.

[36]Sluga, *Heidegger's Crisis*, 103, italics added.

[37]Reported in *Die Zeit*, 29 December 1989; see Theodore Kisiel, "Heidegger's Apology: Biography and Philosophy and Ideology," in *The Heidegger Case*, p. 12.

[38]Kisiel, "Heidegger's Apology," 34.

[39]Quoted by Cassirer, *Kant's Life and Thought*, 377.

[40]Immanuel Kant, *The Conflict of the Faculties*, trans. Mary J. Gregor (New York: Abaris, 1979), 95.

[41]Kant, *The Critique of Practical Reason*, trans. Lewis White Beck (New York: Macmillan, 1985), 101.

[42]For a good discussion see Paul Lawrence Rose, *German Question/Jewish Question* (Princeton, NJ: Princeton University. Press, 1990), 93-94.

[43]Ibid., 109.

[44]G. W. F. Hegel, *The Life of Jesus* in *Three Essays, 1793-1795*, trans. Peer Fuss and John Dobbins (Notre Dame, IN: University of Notre Dame Press, 1984), 127.

[45]Emil Fackenheim, *Encounters between Judaism and Modern Philosophy* (New York: Basic Books, 1993), 190-91.

[46]See Hegel, "The Spirit of Christianity and Its Fate," in *Early Theological Writings*, trans. T. M. Knox (Chicago: University of Chicago Press, 1948), 201-05.

[47]Ibid., 191.

[48]Friedrich Nietzsche, *Thus Spoke Zarathustra*, trans. Walter Kaufmann (New York: Penguin, 1978), 194.

[49]Heidegger, "Will to Power as Art," in *Nietzsche*, vol. 1, trans. D. Krell (San Francisco: Harper, 1979), 18.

[50]Rockmore, *On Heidegger's Nazism and Philosophy*, 46.

[51]Heidegger, *Sein und Zeit*, 391.

[52]Emmanuel Levinas, *Totality and Infinity*, trans. Alphonso Lingis (Pittsburgh: Duquesne University Press, 1969), 45.

[53]Ibid., 46-47.

[54]Lyotard, *Heidegger and 'the jews,'* 89. By "Greco-Christian prejudice" I have in mind the attempt to appropriate the Being of God through such concepts as the God-man and human autonomy rather than to submit to the Law of God.

[55]From the *Freiburger Studentenzeitung*, 3 November 1933 (see *Martin Heidegger and National Socialism*, 45).

[56]Ibid., 13.

[57]Ibid., 10.

[58]Ibid., 12.

[59]Richard Wolin, *The Politics of Being* (New York: Columbia University Press, 1990), 90-91.

[60]Sluga, *Heidegger's Crisis*, 4.

[61]See "Martin Heidegger: A Philosopher and Politics: A Conversation," in *Martin Heidegger and National Socialism*, 178-79.

[62]Ibid., 217.

[63]Martin Heidegger, *Kant and the Problem of Metaphysics*, trans. J. S. Churchill (Bloomington: Indiana University Press, 1962), 244.

[64]See Pierre Bourdieu, *The Political Ontology of Martin Heidegger*, trans. Peter Collier (Stanford, CA: Stanford Univ. Press, 1991), 33-34.

[65]Karl Löwith, "Last Meeting with Heidegger," in *Martin Heidegger and National Socialism*, 158.

[66]Heidegger, *Zein und Zeit*, 300.

[67]Ibid., 299.

[68]Ibid., 384.

[69]Heidegger, *Vom Wesen des Grundes*. 5th ed. (Frankfurt am Main: Klostermann, 1965), 38.

[70]Jacques Taminiaux, "Heidegger and Praxis," in *The Heidegger Case*, 190.

[71]Emmanuel Levinas, *Time and the Other*, trans. Richard A. Cohen (Pittsburgh: Duquesne University Press, 1987), 104.

[72]See, for example, Heidegger, *Sein und Zeit*, 240.

[73]Levinas, *Ethics and Infinity*, 119.

[74]Edith Wyschogrod, *Spirit in Ashes* (New Haven: Yale University Press, 1985), 167.

[75]Heidegger, *Sein und Zeit*, 118.

[76]Ibid., 128.

[77]Heidegger, "Martin Heidegger in Conversation with Richard Wisser," in *Martin Heidegger and National Socialism*, 82.

[78]Rockmore, *On Heidegger's Nazism and Philosophy*, 237-38.

[79]Ibid.

[80]Emmanuel Levinas, *Collected Philosophical Papers*, trans. Alphonso Lingis (Dordrecht: Martinus Nijhoff, 1987), 100.

[81]Quoted by Rockmore, *On Heidegger's Nazism and Philosophy*, 242.

[82]Quoted by Caputo, "Heidegger's Scandal," in *The Heidegger Case*, 266; emphasis added.

[83]Quoted by Neske and Kettering, *Martin Heidegger and National Socialism*, xxxi.

[84]Levinas, *Ethics and Infinity*, 86.

[85]Wyschogrod, *Spirit in Ashes*, 166.

[86]Levinas, *Collected Philosophical Papers*, 52.

Critiques

Critique by Leonard Grob

David Patterson makes an important contribution to our exploration of post-Holocaust ethics with his argument that "unlike the terrible atrocities inflicted on other groups, the Nazis' assault on Jews and their Judaism is not simply about biology or race but is primarily about metaphysics." "The Holocaust," Patterson continues, "happened not despite but, in part, because of Western civilization, as European philosophy has shaped it. It came not in a breakdown of philosophy but, in part, as its consummation." As I have endeavored to show in my own chapter in this volume dealing with the thought of Emmanuel Levinas, Western philosophy, understood as ontology, has been nothing other than an "egology." As such, it is unable to respond to the ethical challenges posed by the Holocaust. Yet more is claimed by Patterson: Amoral European thought has, in some measure, laid the groundwork for appropriative thinking and action which found its ultimate expression in the destruction of six million Jews. Grounded in a vision of an *autonomous* subject exercising its "totalizing" powers vis-à-vis the other-as-object, Western philosophy has helped to prepare the way for the *autocratic* subject of the Nazi era. In Patterson's words, "This assault on the divine image of the human being was conceived by philosophers and carried out by the SS. First conceptual and then actual, it is an assault on divinity, humanity, and the people chosen to attest to the divine chosenness of every human being."

Patterson has succeeded well in showing the influence of German philosophy, from Kant to Heidegger, on philosophers who supported the Nazi cause; the silence of so many other thinkers may be attributed to this same chain of thought. Although the modern German philosophers discussed by Patterson give clearly new emphases to ontology as an uncritical, ultimately *unjustified* celebration of human autonomy, the roots of these teachings—so antithetical to

Jewish thought—are most certainly to be found in the more than two thousand year-old tradition across Europe. The Western consciousness *as a whole* has been fundamentally "allergic," fundamentally given over to the endeavor of removing from the world its alien character. Nazi philosophers are indebted to Kant, Hegel, Nietzsche, and Heidegger—each of whom is in debt himself to a history of philosophy as an imperialist enterprise.

Having made the above observation, I wish, in the Levinasian tradition of continually "unsaying the said," to pose a question with regard to it. Although the history of Western thought-as-ontology can indeed be characterized as a totalizing enterprise, we must beware of possible dogmatic tendencies of our own in the uncovering of alleged dogmatics. May there not be some "leaky margins" in the totalizing activity of philosophers depicted by Patterson, in accord with Levinas? Levinas himself speaks of prefigurings of the "rupture of being" present in both the concept of the Platonic good beyond being and in the Cartesian discussion of thinking the infinite. While I am firmly in accord with Patterson's analysis of Heidegger's work as a culmination of German (and, in general, Western) ontological thought antithetical to Judaism, I believe that Patterson's depiction of a seemingly inexorable movement from Kant to Hegel to Nietzsche to Heidegger fails to do justice to certain elements of the thought of Immanuel Kant, first-in-line in this progression toward "the murder camp." In his representation of Kant as a key player in the anti-Jewish bias of the history of modern German philosophy which precedes Nazi thinkers, Patterson is silent regarding the possibility of a Kantian prefiguring of Levinasian thought. Just as Levinas, as quoted by Patterson, notes that "Heideggerian philosophy marks the apogee of a thought in which the finite does not refer to the infinite (*prolonging certain tendencies of Kantian philosophy...*" (my emphasis), so Patterson himself claims that "there is no room for ethics in that philosophy which begins with Kant *in an ostensible concern with ethics...*" (my emphasis). I wish to point to elements of Kant's thought which, in my view, call into question the observation that Kant's concern with ethics is merely "ostensible."

Although it is true that Kant's autonomous subject derives its ethical being from *within itself,* from reason—Kant would abhor a founding of ethics in a heteronomy embraced by Patterson, Levinas and the Jewish tradition—it is nonetheless the case that Kant's realization that the noumenal cannot be *known* but rather *enacted* deserves further consideration within the context Patterson has set for himself. For Kant, as for Levinas, it is a *doing* which opens me to the *Sache selbst*, the thing-in-itself which philosophers have traditionally sought. (Having said this, it must be remembered, as Patterson emphasizes, that for Kant ethical *praxis* is initiated by the self; for Levinas, self lacks ethical import until invested with such by the call of the Other. This summons, while not an act of knowing, situates itself, ultimately, beyond any theory/*praxis* dichotomy.) Kant's distinction between phenomenon and noumenon, between that which is accessible to *pure* and that which is enacted by *practical* reason, is ultimately inimical to the Levinasian embrace of the noumenal *within* the phenomenal. Yet it remains the case that Kant's aim to "deny knowledge in order to make room for faith,"[1] has in common with Levinas the desire to place ethical concern (albeit one which, for Kant, is rooted in an autonomous subject) at the center of philosophy.

That this is so is brought home by the second formulation of Kant's categorical imperative: "So act as to treat humanity, whether in your own person or in that of any other, always at the same time as an end, and never 'merely' as a means."[2] Although Kant arrives at his notion of human dignity from the purely formal claim of a necessarily shared rationality among all autonomous agents—Kant remains captive of an Enlightenment philosophy itself captive to a tradition of philosophy-as-ontology—he nonetheless gives expression to a dictum which echoes through the ages as a summons to regard the other as an absolute. For Kant, others are never present merely to-be-used, to be incorporated into meaning systems within which they are subject to ends beyond their own personhood. There is most certainly a familiar ring for Levinas scholars in Kant's notion of subjects living in a "kingdom of ends" in which they are not merely *makers* of laws, but also beings *subjected to the laws of others*. That ethical obligation is not rooted in considerations of the *consequences* of actions and that an ethical relation between two persons is direct, unmediated by societal norms—these Kantian thoughts possessed, and still possess, the potential to resound mightily through the modern and contemporary Western consciousness. That mainstream German philosophers who succeeded Kant failed to develop *these* aspects of his thought does not negate their significance as a celebration of human dignity. Though for Patterson, as for Levinas, humans can ultimately be invested with true dignity only through the rupture of the totality occasioned by the appeal of the Other, Kant's hallowing of human individuals as ends-in-themselves marks an important juncture in Western thought: To be human, Kant tells us, is to treat the other as an *end*. That Kant's thought led to Heidegger, as Patterson claims, is less a comment on the inevitability of a concept of autonomy being pushed to its limit, and more a statement of Heidegger's selection, in the name of a totalizing-cum-totalitarian ontological enterprise, of certain elements of Kant's thought—and his disregard of others.

The German philosophical "assault on the divine image" is inaugurated, for Patterson, in part, by Kant's embrace of a "rationalist theology that is opposed to anything resembling a revealed religion...." Patterson goes on to cite Kantian references to prayers as "worthless," and as "worshipful supplications which have perennially constituted the religious delusion"; more particularly, Patterson depicts Kantian idealism as the opposite of Judaism, since the latter rests on "externally given laws." I would contend that, in the spirit of Levinas, we must be cautious in any censure of those of who would proclaim the "death" of prayer or of revealed religion. Levinas himself speaks of the need to distinguish between authentic religion (which he appears at times to unequivocally identify with ethics, in his use of the term) and degenerate religion, *both rationalist and revealed*. The dividing line, I would contend, following Levinas, lies not between natural and revealed religion, but between both the "ontotheology" of philosophers and the "theosophy" of mystics, and an authentic theology rooted in the call to responsibility of the Other. Levinas seeks a religion "purged of myths,"[3] a religion "no longer adrift,"[4] a religion in which God's name is not "subject to abuse."[5]

In this sense, then, the antireligious Kantian quotations cited by Patterson lose some of their significance as evidence of a train of thought leading inexorably to Heidegger and the Nazi thinkers. Rather, it can be understood that Kant, like Levinas, is endeavoring to clear a path toward the possibility of a religion no longer "adrift." Kant shares with Levinas the desire to expose *false* heteronomy. Kant joins Levinas in the endeavor to rid religion of a notion of eminence modeled on the static image of the physical height of the heavens. Only after the "death" of idols which pose as gods—only after we have dethroned those pretenders to divinity who come from a height defined by power—only then can the potential arise for welcoming a Transcendence which hails from beyond all being.

Patterson is certainly correct that Kant's religious vision remains within the realm of ontology: Kant did not succeed in piercing the totality of being in order to ground my ethical existence in the call of the Other; the autonomy of the rational self remains, for Kant, the source of all that constitutes the ethico-religious realm. Prefigurings of the sacred, however, can and do occur in many forms—perhaps even in disguise—both in Kant's thought and elsewhere in the tradition. Both in his endeavor to open a clearing in which false gods are exposed for who they are and in his imperative depicting the other as one to be treated as an "end" and never merely as a means, Kant opens the door to a body of thought capable of spurring a movement of thought beyond itself. Kant's philosophy did not *have* to lead to Heidegger's celebration of resolve as humankind's chief virtue. Perhaps we may learn to seek traces of (in Patterson's words) "the Infinite One, in whose image every finite human being is created" even within a philosophical tradition given over to the *logos* of being.

Notes

[1]Immanuel Kant, *Critique of Pure Reason*, trans. Norman Kemp Smith, 2d ed. (New York: The Modern Library, 1965), 22.

[2]Kant, *Groundwork of Metaphysic of Morals*, trans. H.J. Paton (New York: Harper Torchbooks, 1964), 96.

[3]Emmanuel Levinas, *Totality and Infinity: An Essay on Exteriority*, trans. Alphonso Lingis (Pittsburgh: Duquesne University Press: 1969), 77.

[4]Emmanuel Levinas, *Nine Talmudic Readings*, trans. Annette Aronowicz (Bloomington: Indiana University Press, 1990), 182.

[5]Ibid., 14.

Critique by Peter Haas

One underlying thesis of David Patterson's essay is that Nazism, at least as read through Heidegger, stands in complete metaphysical opposition to Judaism. His contention is that Nazism, for its part, is built on an ontology, on the assertion that the center of human concern is Being. On this view, human life is taken to revolve around the struggle to comprehend and consequently control Being. This plays itself out on the political level by the attempt of people to conquer, control, and even eliminate other representatives of being, in this case other people. It follows that the death camps are but a logical extension of Nazism. Judaism, on the other hand, is about the submission of the self to the commandments of an outside deity. Dealing with others thus takes place not in the realm of politics (as is the case with Nazism) but in the realm of ethics. Justice, in this reading of Judaism, takes precedence over Kantian autonomy or Heideggerian freedom. It is precisely because of this duality, this fundamental opposition between Nazism and Judaism, Patterson tells us, that Nazis were obsessed not only with Jews but with Judaism. It was a struggle between two mutually exclusive metaphysics and in this struggle, Heidegger takes his place firmly on the side of Nazism, and in fact represents what may be one its clearest articulations.

While this is a compelling argument, I am not sure it captures the historical complexity of the relationship between Nazis and Jews/Judaism. My objection circles around two foci, one having to do with the nature of Nazism in its historical manifestations and the other with the character of the Judaic communities which Nazi thought and bureaucracy encountered. On the operational level, it seems to me, the events of the Holocaust do not resolve into the simple dichotomy of Heideggerian *versus* Jewish metaphysics.

Turning first to the question of the character of Nazism, it should be said right off the bat that there is some question in my mind as to whether there was really an "ism," in any rigorous philosophical sense, behind Nazi initiatives (a few philosophical apologists excepted). To be sure there was a general feeling that all non-Aryans were inferior and that Jews in particular posed an immediate threat to Germany and German culture. There was also clearly a process of increasingly systematic and extreme attempts to separate Jews from German life, culminating in Auschwitz. But as the "functionalist" vs. "intentionalist" debate tells us, this does not mean that there was a clearly perceptible philosophical imperative from the very beginning to kill all Jews. The records and rhetoric of the Nazis from 1933 to at least 1942 reveal a much messier and more historically contingent struggle to deal with the ever-changing parameters of the "Jewish Question." And these records also show, it seems to me, that Patterson overstates matters when he says "the Nazis' assault on Jews and their Judaism is not simply about biology or race but is primarily about metaphysics." This may be, in fact, the way that Heidegger saw matters, but it is not how the upper echelons of Nazi policymakers talked about what they were doing. For them it clearly *was* primarily about biology and race (and at times economics). At the rare times when they contemplated the metaphysics or ethics of what they were doing (rather than the pragmatics), their speculation stopped at general references to "might makes right" or some vague claim to the "laws of nature" and the "imperatives of biology." At no point did the Nazis themselves seem to be struggling with working out an ontology of Being.

There is a similar complexity on the side of the "Judaism" the Nazis were opposing. For Patterson, Judaism represents the exalted view of the human as created in the image of, and responsive to, the divine. The rage of the Nazis against this view is illustrated, for Patterson, in (among other things) the Nazis' physical attacks on Torah scrolls, Taleysim, talis kotons, and kitls. But these are accouterments of only one type of Judaism, and one the Nazis only encountered en masse after 1939, namely, East European traditional Judaism (whether Orthodox or Hasidic). The German Jews, over against which Nazi policy was shaped for the first six or seven years of its development, were fundamentally different. They were by and large liberal Jews, Jews who in their personal and communal philosophies drew heavily and explicitly on Kant and Hegel and not on, say, the Kotsker Rebbe. Outwardly, they were fully German. If matters are to be put on a metaphysical level, it might be more accurate to say that the early Nazi muggings of German Jews were "in house"; it was one group of Kantians and Hegelians against another group of

Hegelians and Kantians. It is simply not accurate to say, at least in reference to German Reform Judaism, that "Judaism is the opposite of Kantian Idealism." German Reform Judaism was in fact a *form* of Kantian Idealism.

Along these same lines I have to take strong exception to Patterson's approval of Max Wundt's quote that the Jewish view of the world and humanity "stands opposed to the folkish world view as its total antithesis." The reason I take exception is that Zionism is an authentic expression of Judaism in the modern period, and it in fact *is* a folkish world view and *not* its antithesis. In short, there were many forms of Judaism that the Nazis encountered that shared foundational metaphysical assumptions with a lot of other Germans. This is hardly surprising since in all events we are speaking of a population made up of twentieth-century Central Europeans. In short, the issue here was not, and could not have been metaphysical; it was much more explicitly racial and biological.

Now where I do agree with Patterson is that Nazism was an assault on the God of Abraham. There was without doubt a bundle of secular, scientific assumptions behind Nazi thinking that was opposed to divinity and the divine. Fackenheim is surely right when he says, as Patterson quotes him, "divinity vanishes in the process of internalization, to be replaced by a humanity potentially infinite in its modern 'freedom.'" There is, in fact, a clear dichotomy that one can draw between Heidegger (autonomy of self, universal maxim of reason, freedom) and the view ascribed by Patterson to Judaism (sanctity of the other, uncompromising commands of God, justice). But it should be noted immediately that these are also *Christian* values. The claim of the One Just God who challenges believers to become participants in the divine by submitting to the divine will is certainly to be found not only in Judaism, but also in Christianity (and Islam, for that matter). If there was a metaphysic that the Nazis were battling, it was one informing Christianity as well and not just Judaism. This is why various Christian denominations, those that refused to "sell out" to Nazism, also were targets of Nazi attacks.

The problem, then, is different from the one Patterson describes. If there was a metaphysical battle going on, it is not so much Nazism against Judaism as one side of nineteenth-century thought (secular, scientific, biological) against another (the religious). But in the end very little of Nazi rhetoric suggests that they really conceived of their mission in these exalted terms. For them, the real struggle came down to race, biology, and economics; it was Aryans *versus* non-Aryans, not Kantians *versus* theists.

The scandal of Heidegger lies elsewhere. I don't think that in the end Heidegger shaped Nazism. Rather, the problem he represents is that as a thinker he found a way within modern Western philosophical tradition to make sense of Nazism. That is, he represents a whole generation of early twentieth-century philosophers— and *theologians*, it must be noted—who found Nazism compatible (or at least not incompatible) with the most advanced metaphysical thinking of the day. The real scandal, in my view, is that philosophers and theologians allowed themselves to be hijacked by a modern, secular, scientific paradigm that simply denied the received religious and ethical tradition of the West (the "God of Abraham"). These thinkers, represented powerfully by Heidegger, gave up their positions as critics and became apologists for a sustained policy of rape, pillage, plunder, torture, and murder in the name of a higher Good. The scandal is that in light of this, Heidegger can still be regarded as a philosopher worthy of being listened to.

Critique by David Hirsch

Since I agree in all essentials with the main thrust of David Patterson's argument, and have already written to that effect, it would be foolish and counterproductive for me to try to concoct a critical argument solely for the purpose of fulfilling an assignment.[1] What I would like to do, instead, is apply some of Patterson's fine insights into the Heidegger scandal to two American writers, thus continuing the line of thought I have pursued in responding to John Roth's positioning of the Holocaust within the context of the doctrine of human rights enunciated in the Declaration of Independence.

First, however, I would like to make clear what I take to be points of agreement. I accept without reservation Patterson's observation that "Nazism was a central feature of [Heidegger's] ontological thinking, a thinking that was the culmination of German philosophy as it developed from the time of Kant." Second, I accept Patterson's assertion that Heidegger "pushes...[the] autonomy [of the individual self]...to its limit." Third, I accept Patterson's characterization of Judaism as a religion and a way of life centered in ethical behavior and self discipline, a religion requiring the individual to accept a "curtail[ment of] freedom." Finally, I accept Patterson's contention "that the Nazi project to exterminate the Jews came about not in spite of but, in part, because of the sophisticated German civilization as it had been shaped by German philosophy."

Returning to the Enlightenment doctrine of unalienable rights that is the bedrock of the American ideology, I would like to focus on two major nineteenth-century American writers who both stand in a paradoxical relation to the Enlightenment doctrine of unalienable rights and also in antipodal relation to each other. The first of these writers, Ralph Waldo Emerson, was the central figure in the constellation of authors constituting the literary era that later came to be designated as the "American Renaissance." The other is Edgar Allan Poe, Emerson's slightly younger contemporary, who was excluded from the American Renaissance because he "was bitterly hostile to democracy."[2]

Writing in the first half of the nineteenth century, they represent the antipodes of the Romantic sensibility in a newly established demo-

cratic nation. Emerson's idealistic expansion of Enlightenment political principles inspired the individualist moral perfectionism of
Thoreau ("I should not talk so much about myself if there were any
body else whom I knew as well."[3]) and the all-inclusive democratiz-
ing of Walt Whitman ("I speak the pass-word primeval, I give the
sign of democracy.…Through me many long dumb voices, / Voices
of the interminable generations of prisoners and slaves.…"[4]). Poe,
on the other hand, inspired mainly dismay and hostility among his
American peers.[5] Emotional and ideological opposites, each of them
powerfully affected an influential nineteenth-century European
thinker.

In one of his unpublished writings, Nietzsche wrote, "Emerson.
I have never felt so much at home in a book, so much in my own
house.…" Hermann Hummel remarked that as one "long familiar
with Nietzsche," he found "many of Emerson's passages…to be so
familiar at first sight that the question of [Emerson's] influence on
Nietzsche became a crying one."[6] Nietzsche valued Emerson's thinking sufficiently so that "he always carried a volume of Emerson when
he traveled.…"[7] Hummel contends "that Emerson was more than 'a
brother soul' to Nietzsche;…he exercised a continuous influence
stronger than that of any other writer on Nietzsche."[8] Among the
most important ideas that Nietzsche could have found in Emerson's
essays were the notion of man as a god, who was "beyond good and
evil." An Emerson essay that Nietzsche "undoubtedly knew and
used," according to Hummel, was "Self Reliance"(1840-41), which
anticipated both Nietzsche and Heidegger, in "push[ing…the] autonomy [of the individual self]…to its limit" ("No law," Emerson
wrote, "can be sacred to me but that of my nature"). Emerson's essay
also anticipated the two Germans in pushing individual humans
beyond good and evil ("He who would gather immortal palms must
not be hindered by the name of goodness, but must explore if it be
goodness"; "good and bad are but names very readily transferable to
that or this; the only right is what is after my constitution; the only
wrong what is against it.").[9]

The impression Poe made on Baudelaire seems to have been as
forceful as Emerson's impact on Nietzsche. Baudelaire thought of
Poe as "his *alter ego*, his brother." "The first time I opened one of

[Poe's] books," he wrote to a friend, "I saw, to my amazement and delight, not simply certain subjects which I had dreamed of, but sentences which I had thought out, written by him twenty years before."[10] Baudelaire translated Poe's stories into French and wrote prefaces to the translations, so we know exactly what qualities he admired in Poe. "More important than anything else," he wrote, "we shall see that this author...has clearly seen, has imperturbably affirmed the natural wickedness of man." As Baudelaire understood him, Poe had issued a powerful reminder to "misguided equalitarians, that we are all born marked for evil!"[11] Through his alter-ego, Baudelaire, Poe may be said to have originated symbolist poetry and the decadent movement in literature. Discussing the "Futurist" movement of the early twentieth century, Erich Kahler writes that, "we easily recognize in these manifestoes the traces of Nietzsche's barbarism, of Baudelarian satanism...."[12]

Though two great American writers may be said to have anticipated the intellectual and emotional roots of European barbarism and satanism, and though American culture has not been immune to either of those forces, nevertheless neither have those forces ever become a dominant factor in American ideology. It has been pointed out that, in at least one respect, Nietzsche was the opposite of Emerson. Nietzsche, "in his transvaluation of values, sought to do away with [the] Christian ethic and return to pagan standards." Emerson, however, "instead of revolting against his Christian heritage,...attempted to raise its ethic into the realm of the universal."[13] Likewise, Poe, unlike Baudelaire and later symbolist poets, did not celebrate the "Flowers of Evil," but rather portrayed, in many of his tales, the catastrophic consequences of man's designating himself as a god.[14] Even at its fringes, American ideology never embraced the most amoral and dehumanizing elements of European thinking.

What kept American ideology from falling into the more dehumanizing aspects of modernity was its enshrinement of Enlightenment ideals of human rights and individualism in the Declaration of Independence, the Constitution, and the Bill of Rights. It was Emerson, not Poe, who became not only a literary master, but the inspiration for what George Kateb has called "democratic individualism," which is, as I understand it, a fusing of the principles of political egalitarianism with biblical moral consciousness: "The rights anyone has, others must have. That is democracy."[15] "Democratic individuality," Kateb insists, "is not egotism.... The consummation of democratic individuality is therefore a passage beyond self-concern."[16] Compare Deuteronomy 10: 18-19: "The Lord doth execute justice for the fatherless and widow, and loveth the stranger....Love ye therefore the stranger...." Kateb's only reservation about "democratic individuality" is that "the rapture of [Emerson, Thoreau, and Whitman] is sometimes marred by a still-too-religious proclivity," but he believes that "we can sever the words from their theological or metaphysical preconceptions without violating them."[17]

It is doubtful whether the writers Kateb is referring to would have agreed with him on this point. Even the most rationalist of the framers of the Constitution accepted the basic moral precepts of the Torah, and the law that they created is not incompatible with the Commandments, which, as Patterson says, can be divided between those that pertain to the human-to-divine relation (the first five), and those that pertain to the human-to-human relation (the second five), the first commandment in the latter category being the prohibition against murder.

Patterson adds that, "According to Jewish teaching, [the commandment] comes not from some tribal chieftain but from God Himself." While the drafters of the Declaration and Constitution expressed the view that "all men...are endowed by their creator with certain unalienable rights," they believed that these rights were guaranteed, not by the Creator but by a social contract. They took the view that while God may have commanded, not all human beings behaved consistently with their claims to have accepted those commands or even the existence of God.

The Nazis were determined to destroy biblical morality, but they also planned to do away with democratic individuality and human rights. It was the liberal democracies that defeated Nazism. The religious systems based on biblical religion and the ethical code based on the Ten Commandments did little to stop the spread of Nazism.

Notes

[1]David H. Hirsch, *The Deconstruction of Literature: Criticism After Auschwitz* (Hanover & London: University Press of New England, 1991. See especially, chapters 3, 6, 7.

[2]F. O. Matthiessen, *American Renaissance* (New York: Oxford University Press, 1941) xii.

[3]Henry David Thoreau, *Walden*, "Economy," second paragraph.

[4]Walt Whitman, "Song of Myself," Section 24.

[5]This is not to say that Poe did not have admirers and imitators among contemporary American writers, but Poe managed to dismay even his admirers.

[6]Hermann Hummel, "Emerson and Nietzsche," *The New England Quarterly*, 19 (1946), 63.

[7]Ibid., 73.

[8]Ibid.

[9]*Selections from Ralph Waldo Emerson,* ed. Stephen E. Whicher (Boston: Houghton-Mifflin, 1957), 150, 149, 150. Hummel, "Emerson and Nietzsche," 74.

[10]Quoted in Patrick F. Quinn, *The French Face of Edgar Poe* (Carbondale: Southern Illinois University Press, 1957), 15. Previous quotation from the same source.

[11]Charles Baudelaire, "New Notes on Edgar Poe" [1857], reprinted in *The Recognition of Edgar Allan Poe*, ed. Eric W. Carlson (Ann Arbor: University of Michigan Press, 1966), 46, 47.

[12]Erich Kahler, *The Tower and the Abyss* (New York: George Braziller, Inc., 1957), 147.

[13]Grace Foster, "The Natural History of the Will," *The American Scholar*, 15 (1946), 285.

[14]See David H. Hirsch, "Poe as Moralist: The Cask of Amontillado and the Transvaluation of Values," in *The American Short Story: New Perspectives*, ed. Constante Gonzalez Groba, Cristina Blanco Outon, Pratricia Fra Lopez (Universidade de Santiago de Compostela, 1997), 13-34.

[15]George Kateb, "Democratic Individuality and the Meaning of Rights," in *Liberalism and the Moral Life*, ed. Nancy L. Rosenblum (Cambridge: Harvard University Press, 1989), 183-206 and especially 193.

[16]Ibid., 192, 196.

[17]Ibid., 195.

Critique by Didier Pollefeyt

In one of his table speeches (*Tischgespräche*), Hitler called "conscience" a "Jewish invention."[1] A Jewish survivor of Bergen-Belsen, Abel Herzberg, who later became a famous Dutch writer on the Holocaust, quotes Hitler's full statement: "We abandon the wrong tracks of mankind. The tables of Mount Sinai have lost their legitimacy. Conscience is a Jewish invention."[2] Herzberg comments that Hitler's persecution of the Jews "can only be understood as the revolt of a pagan against the abstract monotheistic idea and its far-reaching consequences....Whatever may be the origin of Hitler's hatred, his theory of races, his propaganda, his political system obtained an almost metaphysical character and thereby a raging power. Hitler's origin was anti-Semitic....In his doctrine, he became anti-Judaic. Religious people speak about a revolt against God and we understand this."[3] Reading David Patterson's powerful contribution to this volume, one begins to understand the depth of the Nazis' "metaphysical assault" on Jews, Judaism, and the idea of the Good itself.

Ethical interpretations of Nazi genocide, however, are never without presuppositions. They always imply certain anthropological, historical, ethical, and theological *a priori*'s. In this response, I want to identify some of the presuppositions that govern Patterson's reflections on post-Holocaust ethics (such as stereotyping, intentionalism, Judeo-centrism, uniqueness). I will argue that if we start from other presuppositions, we do not need "metaphysics" to understand the evil of the Nazi genocide. More generally, I hope to show that every view of the Holocaust always entails a re-construction of the facts, which is done with this or that (ethical) goal. Finally, I will finish my response with some remarks on the non-metaphysical character of Nazi evil.

First, Patterson's interpretation begins from a "stereotyped" presentation of the Nazi crimes. His ethical reflections are built on a selection of the most extreme and individualized forms of Nazi aggression, specifically those committed on particular (orthodox) Jews and (orthodox) Judaism (Torah scrolls, for example), which are condensed and presented as *the* picture of Nazism for ethical reflection.

Of course, these particular Nazi cruelties against Jews and the Jewish religion *did* happen, but one can question the selection and the presentation of only these historical facts of the Nazi genocide and the motives that drive this organization of facts. Are these facts really the most representative for the Nazi genocide? Are humiliations and persecutions of Jews, even in very extreme forms, not typical for a long and tragic history of Christian and biological antisemitism? Could the Nazis have exterminated millions of Jews if they had humiliated all of them in such an intense, individualized way?

In stereotyping, all that does not fit the presentation of extremity tends to be left out. The relation between the fanatically evil perpetrators and their victims is primordial and maximally polarized. It becomes difficult to see gray zones, or even gradations in evil, in different Nazis or during different periods of the Hitler years. The more routine, technical aspects of Nazism and its genocidal program, which are less moving and less emotionally volatile, but which are perhaps more representative, become forgotten in favor of the more remarkable facts, which probably do not illustrate the process of destruction in its totality.

By focusing one's attention on the stereotyped extremities, the victims and perpetrators are lifted out of their historical setting. The behavior of the perpetrators is, as it were, mythologized, decontextualized, and explained as separated from concrete circumstances—explained, in short, as pure (metaphysical) evil. By a myopic focus on the ultimate extremes, evil is synthesized, and one no longer needs to analyze the historical escalation of the Nazi regime, which for many had fascinating promises at the beginning. Examination of structures, complex causes, motives, developments, and workings becomes irrelevant.

I do not question the extremity of Nazi evil as described by Patterson. I only want to indicate that his presentation of Nazism is based on a certain *selection* of facts—the extreme cruelties committed against Jews—that fits the point he seeks to prove, namely, Nazism as an attack on the notion of Judaism itself. As Patterson advances his theory, other views and paradigms tend to be disregarded. Varieties, subtleties, and gradations of experience are left behind because these have little relevance to Patterson's picture. The "metaphysical hyperevil" of the Nazi genocide is the consequence of a functional and selective condensation of the historical reality of Nazism. In the end, the motive behind this selection is to argue that Nazism was in essence an attack, not only on the Jewish body, but also on the soul of Judaism itself. The attack, moreover, consisted not only of evil acts but also was a revolt against the notion of the Good itself.

As a consequence of this stereotyping, Patterson approaches the Nazi genocide almost exclusively as a *Judeo*cide, as a war against the Jews. In fact, while it is true that all Jews were victims of the Nazis, not all of the Nazis' victims were Jews. Non-Jewish victims become almost invisible in his ethical reflection on the Holocaust. Moreover, the Judeocide is viewed as the immediate outcome of modern thought that derives from Greco-Christian thinking: "The Greco-Christian God really died in Auschwitz…; indeed, nearly all of the millions who participated in the murder were baptized Christians." Patterson's systematic use of the expression "Greco-Christian" tradition is problematic, however, because the traditions of Greek philosophy and Christianity should not simply be reduced to one expression (anymore than the Jewish and Christian traditions should be). True, there has been a major historical coalition between the Greek (ontological) and the Christian tradition (as there has been a minor coalition between Greek and Jewish thinking as well). But these traditions cannot be simply identified, and the violence that has come from their coalition is likewise a perversion of the message of Jesus, the Jew, as well as an attack on Judaism. As George Steiner correctly points out, Nazism was an upheaval against the *three*fold legacy of Judaism in Western history: the radical monotheism of the Sinai, primitive Christianity, and messianic socialism.

Patterson seems to equate the essence of the Christian message with its anti-Judaic historical development. Thus, his framework makes it difficult to argue that Christianity can survive the Holocaust, as I believe it can (for example, by rediscovering its Jewish roots, without however identifying itself with Judaism). In Patterson's approach, I cannot find any reason why and how Christianity should survive the Holocaust. A hopeful perspective for the Jewish-Christian dialogue becomes lost. Theologically, I see a much deeper Judeo-

Christian, rather than a Greco-Christian coalition, even if, of course, Judaism and Christianity cannot be identified theologically. Still, history and theology are not the same.

Moreover, we should not forget the relative newness of Nazi antisemitism in the light of Christian anti-Judaism. Nazi antisemitism was no longer solely based on religious antisemitism but fundamentally on racial theories and racist arguments instead. Even if the distinction between Christian anti-Judaism and pagan antisemitism has all too easily been used by Christians as an apology (for example, see the 1998 Vatican declaration on the Holocaust, "We Remember"), one cannot deny the historical fact that Nazi antisemitism was situated in the much broader eugenic concerns of the Nazis. The great influence of this larger, biocratic framework is also clear in the Nazi destruction of German citizens with mental deficiencies, the kidnaping of children with desirable race characteristics, and the *Lebensborn* project. Neither exclusively nor essentially can the Nazi genocide be easily considered as Judeocide alone, as the quantitative extension or end-point of traditional anti-Judaism. This theory cannot explain how not only Jews but also Roma and Sinti, Jehovah's Witnesses, Poles, Russians, the mentally disturbed, and homosexuals were victims of the Nazis, even if we cannot speak here of the same quantity and intensity of persecution. Where are the non-Jewish victims in Patterson's analysis? Does his plea for the "cry of the victim" end in a plea only for the *Jewish* victim?

Historians debate to what degree antisemitism can be the final explanation of the Holocaust. In Western history, antisemitism is omnipresent and not geographically restricted to Germany. In Russia, Poland, and France, strong antisemitic traditions developed, but in those places genocidal extermination of Jews did not became state policy. Thus what part did antisemitism play in the fact that German Jews in the twentieth century became the victims of Nazi genocide? This question suggests that hatred of Jews was perhaps not the only and ultimate force behind the Nazi extermination campaign. These considerations can make clear that at least one important precondition of the Holocaust cannot be found in antisemitism, or that antisemitism is perhaps only the most clear form of Nazi violence, a form that speaks most strongly to our historical sensibilities.

In addition, Patterson does not make a clear distinction between the fanatically antisemitic ideas of the elite and those of the German people more generally. Even if traditional antisemitism was a global phenomenon (although in its mild, latent, and non-murderous form) before the war, historical research shows how a great part of the German electorate in the early 1930s preferred political parties that struggled against antisemitism.[4] During the elections of 1932, the Nazi propaganda was unambiguously anti-Jewish, but antisemitism was not its ultimate argument. As historian Yehuda Bauer points out, the Nazis never thought that their anti-Jewish campaign would be their decisive vote-getting argument. People voted Nazi because of the economic crisis, because of the promise of a new Germany devoid of deep social crisis, and because they were promised a strong Germany that would make them proud. This analysis does not mean that the Germans were not antisemitic. As Christopher Browning says, "if the Germans were not fanatical or 'paranoid' anti-Semites, they were 'mild,' 'latent,' or passive anti-Semites, for whom the Jews had become a 'depersonalized,' abstract, and alien entity beyond human empathy and the 'Jewish question' a legitimate subject of state policy deserving solution."[5] It is precisely this ordinary, non-metaphysical antisemitism that was the most dangerous, because it created indifference and gave free hand to extremists. Even if many Germans did not overtly support physical violence against Jews, they showed much tolerance toward administrative measures against the Jewish people. Nazi antisemitism, however, became genocidal only when it came into the hands of technicians and bureaucrats, an aspect of the Holocaust that Patterson does not take into account.

Even if one accepts antisemitism as the central engine of the Nazi ideology, two questions remain: First, to what extent does a theoretical picture of an enemy imply preparedness to carry out violence against the Jews? It remains to be explained how negative attitudes against Jews could become the cause of such mass destruction. Prejudice can exist for a long time against a group without causing violence on such a massive scale.[6] This makes clear that hatred of the Jews was a necessary but not sufficient condition for genocidal violence. A second question concerns the function of antisemitism in Nazi ideology. Against Patterson's hypothesis about its central place in Hitler's ideology (compare Daniel Goldhagen's notion of "eliminationist antisemitism"), antisemitism can be interpreted as a tactical-propagandistic instrument in Nazi doctrine.[7] In this view, the Jew was a necessary but interchangeable enemy.

The Italian historian Enzo Traverso speaks about Nazism as a syncretic movement, in which antisemitic influences are combined with geo-political considerations, Social Darwinism, and anti-Marxism.[8] For the Germans, this combination created the promise of a new and better world. From this point of view, the Jews were not killed because they did something wrong (for example, creating conscience), but because they were simply seen as one obstacle on the route to a utopian world. The death of Jews was then an instrument for bringing perfection to the Nazi world (compare Saul Friedländer's notion of "redemptive antisemitism"). The Jews made the difference between realizing a dreamed utopia and a contemporary world in crisis.

Furthermore, Patterson's analysis presupposes a strong intentionalistic reading of the Nazi genocide: the Judeocide is the outcome of a *calculated* antisemitic vision that had planned from the beginning to exterminate each and every Jew.[9] Intentionalism is born out of an effort to explain genocidal suffering and murder by reference to a never-changing and completely anticipated plan. Complex, multi-factual, ambiguous historical reality—which is always difficult to grasp—is explained with a clear (for ethicists), attractive, and consistent scheme. Nevertheless, such intentionalism is not self-evident. For functionalists, the Holocaust is not the result of a program that was created completely in advance but the result of a progressive radicalization of the Nazi system.[10] In this case, the genocidal process is understood not as the effect of a fully calculated plan but as the product of an accumulation of different measures that developed, at least in part, by trial and error.[11] Far from reducing the Holocaust's tragedy, the fact that not everything was planned in advance makes the catastrophe greater because it shows that mass destruction does not need an integral and uniform preparation or a metaphysically evil intention.

Early on, functionalists argue, the Nazis looked to solve the Jewish question by forced emigration. In the beginning, total extermination was not necessary. It was especially the occupation of Poland and the enormous increase of Jews under Nazi domination that required more radical solutions. Functionalist interpretations contend that the Nazis originally looked for a territorial solution for the Jewish question and that it was the pressure of circumstances of the war that brought the Nazis to experiment with more radically exterminationist ideas.

A last presupposition in Patterson's ethical reflection is found in his view about the uniqueness of the Holocaust. The thesis of the Holocaust's uniqueness is a logical consequence of his Judeo-centric and intentionalistic reading of the Holocaust. The analysis of the Nazi genocide as Judeocide, in combination with the thesis of the uniqueness, runs the risk of giving a different meaning and moral value to the suffering of different people. For instance, Patterson says that "unlike the terrible atrocities inflicted on other groups, the Nazis' assault on Jews and their Judaism is not simply about biology or race, but is primarily about metaphysics." But here we should recall John Donne's words: "every man's death diminishes me." They refuse every kind of hierarchy in human suffering. Is there something worse than suffering "simply" on biological grounds or racial motives? Is "simple" suffering not enough? What is, for instance, the moral difference between trying to kill all Roma and Sinti because they are "Gypsies" and trying to kill all Jews because they are Jews? What, if anything, is more "metaphysical" about the latter?

More and more, the thesis of the uniqueness of the Holocaust is called into question, especially when the Roma and Sinti are considered. They lived in the same inhuman camps as the Jews, and they probably lost proportionally as many of their people, if not more, than the Jews. This analysis is accepted by many Holocaust scholars.[12] Not only the Jews but also the Roma and Sinti were chosen on the basis of their identity. There were many statements of the Nazi regime calling for a total extermination of the Gypsies. In December 1938, for example, Himmler called for the "complete extermination of the Sinti and Roma."[13] Meanwhile, there is no proof to suggest that a very clear plan to exterminate the Jews existed before 1941. Even the great Jewish scholar Fackenheim admits that "*with the possible exception of Gypsies* only Jews had committed the 'crime' of existing at all."[14] An inclusion of the Gypsies in ethical reflection upon the Holocaust makes a very great difference for the question of uniqueness, even if Fackenheim has not fully considered this in his writings.

The danger of the thesis of uniqueness is that it can easily become so dogmatic that it uproots the Holocaust from its historical and human framework, and the event becomes a sacral event in radical discontinuity with general Western history and ordinary human life.[15] In this sense, there is a certain tension between stressing antisemitic history and stressing uniqueness. It also becomes difficult to draw universal conclusions that transcend the framework of that specific event itself. Many Holocaust scholars think that "it is wrongheaded to bend every effort towards making 'the Holocaust' the One Unique Horror of all time—and necessarily a Jewish horror more than a human horror....Thus, we believe that 'the Holocaust' should not be isolated as a *sui generis*, the cataclysmic event, the discontinuity of history."[16]

In my view, Patterson's approach risks confirming the growing gap between historical analysis of the Holocaust and philosophical and theological reflection upon it. I think that ethicists must instead try to bridge the gap between the "science of history" and the "pain of history." It is not my purpose to "settle" the complex (historical) discussion about the uniqueness versus universality of the Holocaust, the debate between functionalism and intentionalism, or the question about the role of antisemitism in the Holocaust. I merely want to show that Patterson's ethical interpretation takes a clear—and respectable—position in these debates but that certain (debatable) *a priori's* determine his ethical conclusion that Nazism is not "only" an attack on particular homes, Jews, and human persons but an assault on the very ideas of home, Judaism, and humanity themselves. In short, Nazi evil *receives* a metaphysical character in Patterson's interpretation.

A post-Holocaust ethics that tries to bridge the gap between the science of history and the pain of history must also try to integrate the more nonstereotypical, universal, and functionalistic elements of the Nazi genocide. Accordingly, we should try to transcend an *exclusively* Judeo-centric approach to the Holocaust.[17] This outcome, however, need not deny that the Jews were a crucial element in the Nazi *Weltanschauung*, or that the Holocaust has unique characteristics, but it would indicate that the Nazi plans were broader than a war against the Jews, and that we need to recognize the universal as well as the unique, the functional as well as the intentional elements in this catastrophic event. Post-Holocaust ethics, then, must seek to assimilate different theories of the Holocaust. An important consequence of such developments will be that the Nazi genocide will appear less as a metaphysical event and more a terribly human one. The Holocaust will be more an extreme example of collective human failure rather than a unique assault on the Good itself. It will be more an analyzable aspect of human history than an incomprehensible mystery about metaphysical evil.

In Patterson's analysis, I see interesting elements to broaden his reflection on the Holocaust, especially where he associates Judaism with "respecting the other," and where he speaks about the attack on Judaism as an attack on ethics. These elements help me to think of the Jew as the representative *par excellence* of humanity and of the Good and to understand, as J. F. Lyotard does in his *Heidegger and "the jews,"* that the attack on "the Jews" is an attack on "the Other." This understanding opens a way between sharp uniqueness and sharp universality and is in the line with contemporary theological interpretations of Jewish election as involving responsibility for the world and solidarity with *all* victims. Such understanding will also help to alert us better that we all can become perpetrators, even if we do not have "metaphysically evil" intentions.

Notes

¹There is one aspect of my critique of Patterson's essay that I will not deal with here. I think that he too strongly stresses the contrast in Jewish tradition between autonomy and ethics. In my response to Leonard Grob, I have joined the Jewish thinker Emmanuel Levinas to argue that autonomy and ethics should not be understood in such strong opposition.

²Quoted in Abel Herzberg, *Kroniek der jodenvervolgingen* (Amsterdam, Meulenhoff, 1978), 31.

³Ibid., 33.

[4]Yehuda Bauer, "Holocaust and Genocide: Some Comparisons," in *Lessons and Legacies*, ed. Peter Hayes (Evanston, IL: Northwestern University Press, 1993), 36-46 and especially 45.

[5]Christopher Browning, *Fateful Months* (New York: Holmes & Meier, 1985), 106.

[6]Ervin Staub, *The Roots of Evil: The Origins of Genocide and Other Group Violence* (Cambridge: Cambridge University Press, 1989).

[7]See H. W. Von der Dunk, *Voorbij de verboden drempel: De Shoah in ons geschiedbeeld* (Amsterdam: Prometheus, 1991), 143.

[8]E. Traverso, "Auschwitz, l'histoire et les historiens," *Les temps modernes* 45 (1990), 19.

[9]See ibid., 13.

[10]H. Mommsen, "Anti-Jewish Politics and the Implementation of the Holocaust, in *The Challenge of the Third Reich*, ed. H. Bull (Oxford: Clarendon Press, 1986) 117-40 and especially 123: "Even the most fanatical anti-Semites within the Nazi elite or the inner circle around the dictator did not conceive the 'Jewish problem' from the aspect of a possible extermination policy before the end of 1939, and even then there was no clear conception of what could be done against the Jews."

[11]Karl A. Schleunes, *The Twisted Road to Auschwitz: Nazi Policy toward German Jews 1933-1939* (Champaign: University of Illinois Press, 1970), 258.

[12]See, for example, David Stannard, "Uniqueness as Denial: The Politics of Genocide Scholarship," in *Is the Holocaust Unique?: Perspectives on Comparative Genocide*, ed. Alan S. Rosenbaum (Boulder, CO: Westview Press, 1996), 169.

[13]In his "Decree for Basic Regulations to Resolve the Gypsy Question as Required by the Nature of Race," quoted in Ian Hancock, "Responses to the Porrajmos: The Romani Holocaust," in *Is the Holocaust Unique?*, ed. Rosenbaum, 41-43. The quote is taken from the State Museum of Auschwitz-Birkenau's *Memorial Book: The Gypsies at Auschwitz-Birkenau* (München: K.G. Saur, 1993), xiv.

[14]Emil Fackenheim, *To Mend the World* (New York: Schocken, 1982), 12 (italics mine).

[15]Hans Küng, *Judaism* (London: SCM, 1992), 225: "The Holocaust must not be made an absolute. For all the shame and sorrow, even this gigantic crime by human beings against human beings must be looked at within the framework of German history and human history."

[16]Zev Garber and Bruce Zuckerman, "Why Do We Call the Holo-

caust 'the Holocaust'?: An Inquiry into the Psychology of Labels," in *Remembering for the Future*, ed. Yehuda Bauer et al. (Oxford: Pergamon Press, 1988), 1889.

[17]Alan Rosenberg, "The Crisis in Knowing and Understanding the Holocaust," in *Echoes from the Holocaust: Philosophical Reflections in a Dark Time*, ed. Alan Rosenberg and Gerald E. Meyers (Philadelphia: Temple University Press, 1988) 379-395 and especially 379.

Critique by John Roth

Near the end of "Nazis, Philosophers, and the Response to the Scandal of Heidegger," David Patterson writes about the sixth of the Ten Commandments: "You shall not murder." His essay explains why the Holocaust remains humanity's most devastating violation of that fundamental ethical teaching. *Violation*, however, barely scratches the surface when the "final solution" and "you shall not murder" confront each other. In that case, violation becomes transgression, defilement, and desecration.

As Patterson shows, the Nazis' genocidal actions—their burning of Torah scrolls and synagogues, their destruction of ritual baths and *mezuzot*, their gassing and burning of Jews, and their dumping of Jewish ashes into ponds and rivers—signified a blasphemous arrogance. That arrogance entailed the death of God (especially the God of Abraham) and the Good. It resolved that specifically Nazi-German humanity ought to be and would become the measure of all things. With the death camp as its essence, Nazism was profane in deadly ways that even now can scarcely be imagined.

The devil is in the details, and details define the Holocaust as nothing else can. Driving these points home, Patterson's account brims full of instructive historical particularity. Contrary to the generalizing tendencies that he deplores in the work of the philosophers he rightly criticizes, Patterson documents specifically what Nazis did to Jews. He also takes his readers into the world of German philosophy from Kant to Heidegger. His interpretation goes on to expose the ambitions and beliefs of Nazi philosophers whose names are barely remembered but who should not be forgotten entirely. Their demoralizing examples show and warn how far and easily philosophers can abandon their responsibility, which is to understand and defend what is just, right, and good.

Thick with content, Patterson's essay is complex. Nevertheless its governing proposition is so basic, so simple, that it deserves elaboration to ensure that no one fails to feel Patterson's penetrating moral point. That point responds to a Holocaust question that keeps coming up in spite of—even because of—increased historical information about the disaster. The question is "Why did the Holocaust happen?" As challenging and disturbing as it is direct and plain, Patterson's response, I believe, is the following: The Holocaust happened because Nazi Germany, a regime that took obedience with the utmost seriousness, disobeyed the principle on which all justice depends, namely, you shall not murder. Put another way—it is morally imperative to acknowledge this point unequivocally because the difference between right and wrong, ambiguous though it may sometimes be, is often no mystery at all—the Holocaust would not have happened, could not have taken place, if more persons (especially but not only in Germany) had obeyed the Sixth Commandment.

Nothing, it seems, could be simpler, but things are not always as simple as they seem, and thus David Patterson's essay reminds me of the work of Raul Hilberg, another important Holocaust scholar. Author of *The Destruction of the European Jews*, a definitive study of the Nazis' systematic destruction process, Hilberg played an important part in *Shoah* (1985), Claude Lanzmann's epic documentary film about the Holocaust. In one of its segments, Hilberg studies a document, one of the many that have been foundational for his work. This particular document, *Fahrplananordnung 587*, is a railroad timetable. It scheduled death traffic: conservative estimates indicate that *Fahrplananordnung 587*, which outlines a few days in late September 1942, engineered the transport of some 10,000 Jews to Treblinka's gas chambers.

Hilberg has spent his life detailing how such things happened. "In all of my work," he explains during his first appearance in Lanzmann's film, "I have never begun by asking the big questions, because I was always afraid that I would come up with small answers; and I have preferred to address these things which are minutiae or details in order that I might then be able to put together in a gestalt a picture which, if not an explanation, is at least a description, a more full description, of what transpired."[1]

Like Hilberg, Patterson is appropriately interested in the Holocaust's minutiae and details. Far from being insignificant, they remind us that the things that matter most are never abstract and general but always concrete, specific, and personal. (The force of the injunction not to murder, for example, does not reside in its generality but in the responsibility that it puts on me and you not to murder persons who are always individual and unique.) It is also true, however, that Patterson's essay deals with big questions—such as "Why did the Holocaust happen?"—and so it is worth probing deeper to make sure that his basic answer is not too small.

Keeping in mind, then, Patterson's conviction that the Holocaust happened because Nazi Germany disobeyed the Sixth Commandment, consider four clusters of detail that can help us to feel more sharply his moral point, particularly if he will elaborate his responses to the questions that they raise. A good beginning for this inquiry involves his interpretation of German philosophy and, in particular, Immanuel Kant's part in that history.

Patterson takes the Ten Commandments to be moral laws that have ultimate authority not because they are decreed by cultural convention, unaided human reason, or even by a general appeal to divinity, but because they are the word and will of the God of Abraham, Isaac, and Jacob. In their perverse ways, Nazis apparently understood this connection, too, at least to the extent that their total disobedience of the Sixth Commandment was inseparable from an intention to destroy the Jewish life that gave humankind the Decalogue in the first place. Be that as it may, Patterson takes Kant— arguably the greatest German philosopher—to be exceedingly problematic because he undermined an ethic based on obedience to externally given laws (specifically to the will of God as it is revealed in Torah) and substituted an ethic based on laws that are legislated internally by human reason alone. However unintentionally, this move paved the way for the human will to be obedient to nothing more than its idolatrous, god-like self. Eventually, Patterson suggests, versions of such thinking led to Auschwitz.

Kant would be puzzled by Patterson's interpretation, and that puzzlement is important. One reason for Kant's deservedly high reputation in the history of philosophy is that he stressed again and again that the moral law legislated by human reason requires each of us to respect every person's life as intrinsically valuable and precious. Whatever his philosophical flaws, Kant understood two more pivotal points. Both are related to his view that every human life must be regarded as an end in itself. First, Kant saw that religion can be one basis for morality, but it is a precarious one because religions are particular. Their appeals will have limited followings, and religious groups can be at odds with one another as well. Second, while everyone is not going to be attracted to a single religious tradition, Kant affirmed that all people can think critically if they work at it. It seemed to him that human reason was an important basis for the development of ethical sensitivity that would make the imperative "You shall not murder" more universal than particular religious traditions might do by themselves.

Lines from Kant to Heidegger and then to the Holocaust can be traced, but they are more complicated than Patterson's narrative admits. Kant's appeals to human reason and to a universalized imperative to respect all human life provided obstacles—inadequate ones as it turned out, but obstacles nonetheless—that the Nazis had to overcome before the Holocaust could be implemented. If twentieth-century human beings had been better Kantians, the Holocaust would have been far less likely. Patterson will probably disagree with this interpretation of Kant, but he needs to respond to it to keep his analysis from being too small.

A second cluster of details raises questions about the place of choice in humankind's moral life. Patterson thinks the Holocaust happened because an over-emphasis on freedom and resolute choice-making created an environment, especially in Nazi Germany, where the will to power was unrestrained by anything but its own desires. When those desires turned genocidal, there were too few moral checks against them. Treblinka followed.

Patterson aptly criticizes Heidegger and other philosophers who were more than ready to embrace and encourage Nazi fortunes, and yet his criticisms may give too small an account because the factor of choice still looms so large. For example, not only does obedience to external moral authority or to the will of God require choice, but it is also true that the very identification of such moral authority or of an imperative as the will of God requires elements of choice as well, for such identifications entail interpretations of experience that are not self-evident. Identifying the proper interpretation—and sticking by it when the supporting evidence is ambiguous—requires choice and resolution.

In this area, Patterson can help us by reflecting further on the following questions: To what extent does post-Holocaust ethics depend, as he suggests, on "the commandments that come from the Voice at Sinai, rather than from the voice of reason, power, or even faith"? What role, moreover, does choice and even resolution play not only in obeying such a Voice but also in identifying and interpreting it? The degree of ambiguity here seems vast, and we need Patterson's help to find ways through it.

A third question-raising cluster of details in Patterson's essay involves the implications about Christianity entailed by his thesis that the Holocaust assaulted the God of Abraham. For instance, he speaks about "the Greco-Christian God," observing that the two thousand year reign of that God's followers did not prevent the Holocaust. To the contrary, the philosophers whom Patterson criticizes for paving the way to Auschwitz, to say nothing of "nearly all of the millions" who made the Holocaust happen, were usually "baptized Christians" or at least significantly influenced by Christian culture even when they rejected it.

Here it is important to contemplate how close Christianity is to Judaism. Like Judaism, Christianity depends on the revealed word of God, it involves obedience to God's will, and it understands God's will to be located in the imperatives of the Ten Commandments, the exhortations of the Hebrew prophets, and in the teachings and life of Jesus, a faithful Jew from Nazareth. When it comes to the Sixth Commandment—"You shall not murder"—Christians, who learned it first from Jews, arguably have spread that word into the world at least as much as any other group, but owing to the tragic disagreement between Jews and Christians about the identity of Jesus within divine revelation, "baptized Christians," especially during the Holocaust, were unfaithful in taking the Sixth Commandment as a mandate to respect and protect Jewish life instead of assaulting it.

Patterson takes heart from the fact that "thousands continue to pray in Hebrew three times a day," which signifies that "the program to exterminate those who cling to the God of Abraham, Isaac, and Jacob...was not accomplished." Every Christian, and here I speak as one, should give contrite thanks for that fact as well. But there is more to say. Jews remain a small percentage of the world's people. That reality is unlikely to change. Because Christian numbers are larger, and Christianity is not going to disappear any time soon, it is important to ask: What does Christianity most need to do to be faithful to its Jewish roots and to stand in solidarity with the ongoing life of the Jewish people? Where post-Holocaust ethics is concerned, few questions are more important than that one. Certainly we Christians must address it again and again. Understandably, David Patterson may be reluctant to join such discussion, but Christians—indeed everyone—could be helped if he would enlarge his perspective to address that question, too.

The fourth and final cluster of details that I hope Patterson will consider further involves his claim that "the Nazis did not believe they were doing a moral good because, like Heidegger, they believed they were transcending all morality." True, Nazism appealed to a triumph of the will that would go beyond traditional morality. SS rhetoric especially emphasized overcoming long-established ethical sentiments so that important Nazi tasks—murdering Jewish women and children, for example—could be accomplished. Here, however, I believe that Patterson's judgment reaches too far. Unless that judgment is better tuned, it risks demonizing and dehumanizing the German perpetrators in dangerous ways.

At least two reasons—one philosophical, the other historical—support this claim. First, human beings are not likely to serve a cause unless that cause makes convincing moral appeals about what is good and worthy of loyalty. Second, Nazi rhetoric overwhelmingly emphasized that the health of the German people and their rightful claims for superiority and hegemony were under deadly threat by Jews. Far from transcending all morality, that outlook urged faithfulness to a new morality, false and genocidal though it turned out to be. Loyalty to its appeal resulted in the death of millions of Jews. Absent Nazi "idealism," or what Peter Haas calls "the Nazi ethic," the Holocaust remained unlikely.

David Patterson probably will disagree with this appraisal, but he needs to respond to the suggestion that the reality of the Holocaust cannot be adequately accounted for in terms of an outlook that simply finds the perpetrators "transcending all morality" or pursuing an "ontological good" but not an "ethical good." Heidegger may have talked about "transcending all morality," but few Holocaust perpetrators were Heideggerians or philosophers of any serious kind. They were, however, men and women who could be motivated to do extraordinarily destructive deeds. Undoubtedly those motives were mixed—greed, ambition, and fear were surely among them—but goals and ideals embedded in the "Nazi ethic" also inspired much of the obedience that implemented Nazi commands. That ethic was murderous, wrong, and immoral in the extreme, but by defining differences between right and wrong, good and evil, it was an ethic nonetheless. The morality needed after Auschwitz must recognize and combat the dismal possibility that, far from honoring the Sixth Commandment, men and women—indeed entire regimes—can accept and act upon an ethic that justifies getting rid of people who are "not like us."

David Patterson's emphasis on the particularity of Jewish fate in the Holocaust profoundly answers the question "Why did the Holocaust happen?" by arguing that the Sixth Commandment was obediently profaned and thereby profanely disobeyed as well. His essay's answer to that big question has never been small, but it can become even larger and more penetrating by further attention to the four areas that these comments respectfully identify.

Note

[1]See Claude Lanzmann, *Shoah: An Oral History of the Holocaust* (New York: Pantheon, 1985), 70.

Patterson's Response to Critiques

Although my insightful colleagues are generally accurate in their paraphrasing of my argument concerning German philosophy's contribution to the Holocaust, it seems that my argument needs some clarification. The cornerstone of the argument lies in the opposition between freedom and justice and how we respond to that opposition. It is an opposition between self and other, between Kantian autonomy and religious heteronomy, between power and truth, between expedience and ethics—in short, between Nazi and Jew. Saying this, I do not mean to suggest anything about "the German character," whatever that might mean; nor do I wish to take to task all of German philosophy or even all of Kant, Hegel, Nietzsche, and Heidegger. I am interested, rather, in this key thread of freedom versus justice that runs through these thinkers—key because how we decide this opposition decides the viability of any ethical relationship among human beings. If the Holocaust poses an ethical problem, it poses a problem for how these thinkers have viewed freedom and justice.

It is clear that Kant's interest in ethics is shaped by his concern for freedom understood as autonomy of the self. Some of my colleagues complain that I am unfair to Kant, especially in characterizing his concern with ethics as "ostensible." Perhaps I do give Kant too little; but my colleagues give him too much. The claim, for example, that in his moral philosophy Kant respects every person's life as precious is not altogether accurate. Kant insists that a rational being must respect the life of all rational beings and must treat any rational being always as an end and never as a means. It is unclear as to what this position implies for our relation to infants, the mentally handicapped, the emotionally disturbed, the insane, and others who do not appear to be rational beings—and who fell prey to the Nazis' T-4 Euthanasia Program. If the value of a human being lies in being rational, then it is a contingent value. It makes perfect sense, for example, to say to someone, "You are not being rational." But what would it be like to say to someone, "You are not being holy"? Only the determination of a human being as an inherently holy being, sanctified by the Creator and not defined by reason or any other contingency, can determine the infinite and absolute dearness of our fellow human being. If such a value cannot be determined, then ethics is eclipsed because its demands are no longer absolute.

There is also a concern among my respondents that I have been too hard on Kant's view of religion. They point out quite rightly that Kant tried to bring clarity and definition to a religion "adrift" by situating it within the parameters of reason, where it is determined by a morality that rests on the autonomy of the rational individual. To be sure, defining religion according to reason appears to be in the interest of a humanity that has often suffered from the collisions that result from religious ambiguities: How do we know which path to God is the right one? How do we know what God really wants of us? On one point, however, there is no ambiguity concerning what God commands: do not murder people—not because such a "maxim" yields no contradiction but because each human being is a child of God. The religion that Kant would deduce from reason has no idea of the God who, out of love, commands us not to murder His children, because reason, according to Kant, has already deduced this prohibition—deduced it before God commanded it. Therefore reason is prior to God—that is the Kantian blasphemy and abuse of the Holy Name. If reason is prior to God, then it can do very well without God; instead of the Supreme Being we have the Superfluous Being. For if the rational self is its own legislator, then it has no need of God's commandments. It is like God. Hence Kant's deprecation of prayer. Surely my colleagues can see the implications of purging the world of prayer.

We know how Judaism would regard such a position; and we realize why Kant called for the euthanasia of Judaism. From the standpoint of the Jewish teaching and tradition slated for annihilation in the Holocaust, there can be no ethics without God and God's commandments; God is prior to ethics, prior to reason, prior to human autonomy. From the standpoint of Jewish teaching, freedom lies not in the authority of self-autonomy but in the commandment that the self receives from its Creator; that is what sanctifies us. Chief among those commandments is the commandment not to murder. From a Jewish perspective, then, Kant's religion, rationally determined and not divinely revealed, is a false religion. Is it the Nazi religion? No. But it shares one important thing with the Nazi religion: the accent on a freedom defined by autonomy. This autonomy of the self may at first include respect for other autonomous selves, but it ends in an eclipse of the ethical relation. For the holiness of the other as one created in the image of the Holy One cannot be derived from the autonomy of the self any more than self-sacrifice or martyrdom can be so derived; only the holy situates the other in a position of height, making the other not equal to but more dear than myself. In this disparity the ethical exigency shows itself. And the ethical exigency is the exigency of the holy: as soon as the ethical becomes an issue, so does self-sacrifice — not for freedom but for justice. There lies the righteousness of the Righteous Gentiles.

If I have given Kant too little credit, some respondents complain, I have given the Nazis too much, particularly in ascribing to them a philosophical position sophisticated enough to wage a metaphysical war against the Jews. After all, it is pointed out, the Nazis were primarily interested in biology, race, and occasionally economics, not philosophy. But to posit these categories as a basis for determining human value; to enjoin the German people to overcome their Jewishly influenced moral conscience and find the resolve to follow their Führer; to insist that *Volk* and *Führer* are one's true mother and father — is to take a philosophical position. And the Nazi philosophers of Germany — Bruno Bauch, Alfred Bäumler, Nicolai Hartmann, Martin Heidegger, Ernst Krieck, Alfred Rosenberg, Max Wundt, and others — were well aware of it. To be sure, by 1940 nearly half the professors of philosophy in Germany were members of the Nazi Party. To say that the Nazis were interested in race and not philosophy is similar to saying they were interested in race and not history, law, medicine, literature, art, and so on; it is to ignore the truth that Nazism is not just a political movement or cultural curiosity but a view of world, reality, and humanity, a view that cannot abide in the same universe with the Jewish view.

What about the Jewish view? Is it not, one respondent asks, sometimes similar to forms of Kantian, Hegelian, and even elements of Nazi thinking? It has been rightly noted, for example, that German Reform Judaism was heavily influenced by the philosophy of Kant and Hegel. But inasmuch as it rejects the revelation at Sinai, the Covenant with Abraham, the prophecies of the Messiah, the resurrection of the dead, the chosenness of the Jews, and other teachings essential to Judaism, German Reform Judaism becomes more German than Jewish. The same can be said of Zionism: to the extent that Zionism departs from Torah, it departs from Judaism, for Torah is the essence of Judaism. With notable exceptions, the Zionists consisted largely of atheists, socialists, communists, and other non-religious Jews; hence Zionism, for the most part, was not an "authentic expression of Judaism," even though its adherents were indeed Jews. As for its folkish or nationalistic features, Zionism is certainly a nationalism; but in no way is it comparable to Nazi nationalism, since it does not adopt the definitively Nazi position that Volk determines value. Zionism, then, may be Jewish, but it is neither a movement within Judaism nor does it resemble Nazism. Of course, German Jews were targeted for murder whether they were Reform, Orthodox, or Zionist. But since people who had converted to Judaism were also subject to extermination, the issue is not reducible to racism. Their crime was being there because the very presence of the Jew in the world—Reform, Zionist, or otherwise—signified a tradition and a truth antithetical to the philosophical foundations underlying Nazi thought. For unlike a Christian, a Jew is a Jew, subject to the testimony of Judaism, as soon as he makes his appearance in the world.

But is not Christian thought, my respondents raise an important question, also antithetical to Nazi thought? Doesn't the presence of Christians signify a teaching similar to the teaching signified by the Jewish presence in the world? Well, yes and no. No one is born a Christian; therefore Christian presence is not implied by the presence of a people chosen from the womb to bring a certain testimony to the world. Nevertheless, the Christian teaching that every human being is a child of God created in the image of the Holy One is certainly antithetical to Nazi ideology. The Christian accent on faith in a single figure who alone can bring salvation, however, is not as antithetical; nor is it as threatening as the Jewish position that righteousness derives not so much from the faith in our hearts as from the work of our hands. When Christians acted they were indeed subject to the dangers of Nazi savagery; but when they kept the fervor of their faith confined to their closets and their cloisters, they were generally left alone. With their accent on faith, the presence of Christians in the world often signifies a retreat from the world, which poses no problems for the Nazis. One respondent asks what Christians most need to do in order to be faithful to their Jewish roots and to stand in solidarity with the ongoing life of the Jewish people. One answer is that they must abandon their insistence on *sola fide*, on the proposition that only faith in Christ can bring salvation. If they would oppose the Nazi threat to ethics, then, like their Jewish brethren, they must understand salvation in terms of ethical action and the pursuit of justice, not in terms of a personal and private faith. Whether Christianity can take such a leap and remain Christianity is a subject for another debate.

Finally, I do not think my colleagues have responded to the most important implication of the opposition I try to set up between freedom and justice: namely, my claim that the Nazis were pursuing not an ethical good but an ontological good. Despite my respondents' insights, it is still not clear to me that all discourse invoking the notion of what is good or bad is ethical discourse. Just as there is a political good, an economic good, a pedagogical good, or a medical good that can be distinguished from an ethical good, so is there an ontological good that may be distinguished from an ethical good. Echoing elements of a view articulated by Nietzsche and Heidegger, the Nazis left behind moral categories in the pursuit of an ontological good. Indeed, a philosophy of will and power eclipsed a philosophy of ethics in Nazi thinking; what was needful, from a Nazi standpoint, was not ethical integrity but fierce resolve. Indeed, people of ethical integrity posed a threat to the Nazis, and the Nazis knew it. Does this view of Nazis as murderers who move beyond good and evil make them into demons, as one respondent fears? I do not think so. One does not have to be a demon to murder or to declare that morality is an illusion and that power is the only reality. On the contrary, it is all too human. For it is the first expression of human frailty: the longing to be as the gods, not only knowing but determining good and evil from a position of power beyond good and evil.

Perhaps that is where the real issue lies for a post-Holocaust ethics. Are we to "modernize" ethics by making the good into an ontological phenomenon of this culture or that, and not an absolute truth or meaning to which all are accountable? Or shall we understand an ethical relation to be part of a higher relation to a metaphysical Good that (or who) sanctifies the life of every human being? If we opt for the former, we are not post-Holocaust; no, we remain in the midst of it, for we remain accomplices to the Nazi project. Only by opposing an ethics grounded in metaphysics—only by using absolute justice to limit autonomous freedom—can we even begin to speak of a post-Holocaust ethics.

CHAPTER FIVE

The Kafkaesque World of the Holocaust: Paradigmatic Shifts in the Ethical Interpretation of the Nazi Genocide

Didier Pollefeyt

The writings of Franz Kafka (1883-1924) have often been understood as a prophetic announcement of the twentieth century's enormous moral catastrophes. For example, *In the Penal Colony*, his short novel from 1914, can be seen as Kafka's anticipatory answer to the question: "How could Auschwitz and Birkenau happen?"[1] In this essay, I argue that this novel can be read from three different perspectives, which can function as points of departure for developing three alternatives for understanding the evil of Auschwitz. I refer to these alternative readings of the Holocaust as *paradigms*.

In *The Structure of Scientific Revolutions*, Thomas Kuhn describes a "paradigm" as a constellation of convictions, values, and techniques, used by a scientific community.[2] A paradigm provides, for a certain time, a successful habit of thought and strong exemplary solutions for scientific problems. Such paradigms contain a specific vocabulary, implicit metaphysical and ethical presuppositions, and pioneering textbook cases. Normal scientific research is understood by Kuhn as the effort to grasp a subject matter within the framework of the ruling paradigm. Difficulties and criticisms are removed by numerous *ad hoc* amendments within the framework of the paradigm itself, so that the paradigm can function under more and more strict conditions. A "scientific revolution" occurs when the majority of scholars leaves a particular paradigm and considers subject matters from another interpretative framework. For the most part, such scientific revolutions are accompanied by serious clashes around the metaphysical and ethical presuppositions entailed by the different paradigms.

In popular and academic approaches concerning the moral aspects of the Holocaust, there have been three successive paradigms. Respectively, they are: the paradigm of diabolization; the paradigm of banalization; and the paradigm of ethicalization.[3] With the 1963 publication of *Eichmann in Jerusalem: A Report on the Banality of Evil*,[4] the Jewish philosopher Hannah Arendt unleashed the first "scientific revolution" in the study of the Holocaust when she provoked a struggle between the defenders of the classic, popular paradigm of diabolization and those who espoused a new and controversial paradigm of banalization. Arendt's ethical interpretation of the Holocaust, especially her concerns for the modern and amoral aspects of genocidal systems, was and continues to be heavily criticized by scholars who place greater stress on the immorality of the concrete, individual perpetrators. In these discussions, it has been largely overlooked that recently a new and at least as provocative interpretation of the evil of Nazism has been developed. It was first articulated systematically in 1988 by the Jewish ethicist Peter Haas in *Morality after Auschwitz: The Radical Challenge of the Nazi Ethic*.[5] In this new interpretation, the Nazis are no longer understood in terms of immorality (first paradigm) or amorality (second paradigm), but described as acting out of "ethical" concerns.

These two historical turning points, the first in modernity, the second at the beginning of postmodernity, make it possible to distinguish three successive ethical interpretations of the Holocaust. Each paradigm can bring to light some aspects of the Holocaust, but at the same time, each paradigm also darkens and even disavows the others. Here I develop these different "portraits" of the Holocaust, indicating their possibilities, presuppositions, and limits, as well as their dangers. One of my goals is to show that any ethical interpretation of the Holocaust is always a vulnerable construction, which—as a *Gestalt*—brings both insight and blindness.

The Cruelty of Torture

Kafka's *In the Penal Colony* is a good point of departure for elaborating the three different paradigms. It helps to show that, just as we can look at the same story with different eyes, we can likewise look at the Holocaust with different eyes. Kafka's story recounts the visit of a foreign traveller to a prison camp, but without mentioning the place or time. Full of pride, an officer of the prison shows the camp's instrument of torture and execution. It is an ingenious construction. Using a rotation mechanism and large needles, it ceaselessly scratches a slogan in the slowly turning body of the condemned, gradually and torturously bringing its victim to death. The visitor is "lucky" since at that moment, a soldier has the "privilege" of being executed by this machine.

Kafka's reader is shocked by the brutal evil inflicted on the victim by the perpetrator and feels morally scandalized by this terrible, random, and incomprehensible violence. How can a human being carry out such a painful execution, such an inhuman crime? One feels powerless in the face of this atrocity, which is so sophisticated, so organized, and so well planned. One experiences deep moral indignation, and even abhorrence, towards the perpetrator of this bloody, sadistic execution in which the executioner seems to find pride and pleasure. One identifies spontaneously with the victim, who not only does not know *why* he will be executed, but does not even know *that* he will be executed. This is precisely the sense of moral recalcitrance we feel when confronted with the Holocaust's horror. The first paradigm offers a suitable language and framework through which we can easily express and interpret our moral revolt and spontaneous revulsion vis à vis the evil of Auschwitz. We immediately recognize ourselves in the language of the paradigm of diabolization, especially when it characterizes the perpetrators of such inhuman acts as "nonhumans," "sadists," "monsters," or "devils." The language of diabolization (from *diabolos*, devil) is morally very powerful and expresses our intuitive moral feelings perfectly. It leaves no room for doubt: "this is evil," "absolutely," even "uniquely."

When people underpin in a more systematic and academic way such a representation in the context of the Holocaust, they usually stress specific characteristics of the Holocaust and use examples that depart from typical historical, anthropological, and ethical presuppositions. In deciphering the basic lines of this *Gestalt* of the Holocaust, certain characteristics emerge: a synthetic approach to evil, ethical Manicheism, intentionalism, a pessimistic anthropology, an optimistic view of civilization, and the incomprehensibility and the uniqueness of the Holocaust. Since this cluster of characteristics constitutes what we call the paradigm of diabolization, concrete interpretations will always have, *to a certain degree*, resemblances with this theoretical construction.

First, the paradigm of diabolization particularly highlights the extreme aspects of Nazism — its excessive crimes, antisemitic teasing, sadistic games, incredible moral excesses, licentious camp guards, and so on. The "order" of the Nazi camps is represented as a very condensed concatenation of terrible horrors, monstrous cruelties, exorbitant pathologies, and satanic inventiveness. From the whole of Nazi politics, one selects the most extreme and traumatic events, bringing them together in one picture that is then presented as the exclusive image of Nazism. In this case, evil is synthesized more than analysed. Stories about senseless slave labor or humiliation of Orthodox Jews, apocalyptic pictures of mountains of corpses, walking skeletons or lamp shades made of human skin are paradigmatic in this stereotypical representation of the evil of Auschwitz.

At the basis of the paradigm of diabolization, there is a prototypical representation of the camps' extremities. Evil is condensed and collected into one, recognizable, and overwhelming picture. This representation enables a description of Nazism as a "revolt against morality" (George Steiner) or as an "orgy of evil for evil's sake" (Berel Lang). The Nazis appear as the perverted figures in the stories of De Sade, as the apocalyptic dragons of Milton's *Satan*, as the ministers of the innermost circle of Dante's *Inferno*, or as fanatic, Teutonic cannibals who carry out their ritual cruelties to the music of Richard Wagner. This paradigm identifies the perpetrator as completely perverted by evil. In his camp testimony, the Polish Jew Klieger, for example, wrote in 1947: "They [the SS in Auschwitz] were no longer human beings who beat us, they were animals, unchained monsters. They shouted and they foamed at the mouth. Their eyes were bloodthirsty. I never saw so close and so precisely the face of men who were so decided upon killing. Only now I saw the face of the murderer, now his mask was taken way, nothing remained but a bloody, deformed, satanic face. See here the *homo sapiens*, when all his instincts are unchained."[6] In a more academic context, Holocaust historian Saul Friedländer wrote that "the perpetrators do not appear...as bureaucratic automata, but rather as beings seized by a compelling lust for killing on an immense scale, driven by some kind of extraordinary elation in repeating the killing of ever-larger masses of people."[7] For this approach to the Holocaust, Eichmann's statement that he "would jump with glee into his grave knowing that over five million Jews had been exterminated"[8] is a revealing case.

It is certainly not my intention to question the fact that extreme cruelties *did* happen in the Nazi camps. The stereotypical picture of the Nazi camps contains few historical errors. The problem, however, is that this extreme picture of the camps is not universally applicable for all places and prisoners. The diabolization is thus based upon a specific *selection* of facts, especially the extreme cruelties, that best fit within the idea of "hyperevil," whereby other, less spectacular aspects may be forgotten in favor of the more striking features. The presentation of the Nazis as "diabolical" or "hyperevil" is the result of a purposeful and selective synthesis of the historical reality of the camps. From other paradigmatic perspectives, one could well question the historical accuracy of this selection and emphasize, for example, the more "daily" aspects of Nazism and its genocidal program, which would show perhaps less "hyperevil" but better exemplify the destruction process.

Ethical Manicheism is a second important feature of the paradigm of diabolization: the distinction between good and evil is extrapolated to a maximum and declared to be an absolute difference. As in historical Manicheism, the paradigm of diabolization posits two completely opposite, irreducible forces at work: our daily world of light and the Nazi counterworld ("planet Auschwitz") of pure wickedness and darkness. For example, Gideon Hausner, the public prosecutor for the trial of Eichmann in Jerusalem, saw the trial as a confrontation between "two worlds": the world of light and humanity and the counter-world of darkness. In his famous study on the rescuers of Le Chambon in France, the ethicist Philip Hallie wrote that there is an unbridgeable difference between those who torture and kill children and those who save children.[9]

People are inclined to agree with extrapolated representations of "good" and "evil," sincerely believing that they would never throw living children into crematoria or be like Eichmann. Nevertheless, descriptions in which the evil-doer is represented as a diabolical, absolutely evil creature obscure the problem since only two extremes remain of what is, in fact, a continuity and since this polarity ignores all the gradations in between, which both separate and link good and evil. When good and evil are dealt with in such a dualistic way, moral indignation risks bringing people to sacrifice all historical, psychological, and ethical nuances to a single and extreme representation. In doing so, ethical dualism meets a fundamental and very old human need to separate humankind into good and evil, "then" and "now," "us" and "them," black and white (Athenians and Spartans, Hutus and Tutsis, Serbs and Croats, "indigenous" and "strangers," "men" and "women").[10] Human complexity in doing good and evil is reduced to the aestheticized and fascinating confrontation between Beauty and the Beast. Such an orderly, dualistic view of good and evil can be very comforting.

The idea that people who do extreme evil are not fundamentally different from ourselves is extremely threatening to our own identity. No doubt this is why it is easy for people to choose a diabolical representation of the Nazis; indeed, in the context of the Holocaust, this representation at least brings some measure of reassurance. We certainly do not want to have anything in common with the "monsters" who do such evil. If I do not look like that stereotypical version of the evildoer, then I am not likely to question myself as to whether I act unethically. The resulting ethical dualism creates a radical difference between good ("us") and evil ("them"). Such a vision situates evil entirely in the other, and every personal identification with evil is strategically evaded. Consequently, diabolization can be a strategy of self-defense; it allows one to envision one's own identity comfortably and to limit oneself to moralization, a very typical attitude for this paradigm. Indeed, defenders of diabolization think that presenting the shocking hyperevil of Auschwitz is the best way to mobilize people against fascism and genocide.

In this vision, a popular myth of civilization emerges. In Hausner's opinion, for example, Eichmann acted from a "desire to obliterate two thousand years of 'Jewish' civilization and 'rationalism' and *to revert to* a mankind guided by instincts."[11] As such, Auschwitz would not be the logical end of the evolution of our modern civilization, but rather a tragic, sometimes called "typically German,"[12] relapse into barbarism, a pitiful deflection of the otherwise progressing trajectory of civilization. Accordingly, Auschwitz would not force us to question our modern way of life. On the contrary, our civilization is presumed to be on the right track, needing only more of that same modern civilization. The paradigm of diabolization thus places civilization and cruelty in opposition to each other, viewing the Holocaust only as an aberration, as a discontinuity with Western history. It was merely a unique "regression" to pure hatred and rage, a kind of pathological deviation of the process of civilization, which is in itself healthy and should not be unduly criticized. The history of humanity is depicted as the progression from a presocial barbarity to a socioethical community. In this progression, the great importance of the Jewish (sometimes the Judeo-Christian) tradition as a factor of civilization is recognized.

This myth of civilization, in turn, goes hand in hand with a certain understanding of human nature. In essence, each human is a "wolf" (Hobbes) in relation to others. The Holocaust is then proof that Hobbes's world is still not (enough) under control, and that the *homo homini lupus* is still a reality. Auschwitz underlines the unethical, egoistic essence of being human, showing how human culture and morality are necessary but unnatural forces that have great difficulties in controlling our egocentric human nature in a structural way. In every human being, then, there is a violent beast that may awaken whenever the flimsy coat of cultural veneer is worn away. From this perspective, our human essence is malicious, and ethics is an unnatural power imposed by civilization. Accordingly, one would think that the extreme evil of the camps reveals our true nature. Such a view can be called "essentialism." In the Holocaust, it concludes, we can see naked, prehistorical, and presocial human beings reduced to their real essence. It entails the conviction that people who were involved in the Nazi project were stripped of all their cultural refinements, and that we are then confronted with "man without morality."

One of the most significant characteristics of the paradigm of diabolization is its preference for an intentionalistic interpretation of the Nazi genocide. Intentionalism is a current in the historiography[13] of the Holocaust[14] that understands the Nazi genocide as the outcome of a carefully planned, methodologically constructed, purposefully prepared, and systematically executed program of extermination, initiated in some way by Hitler himself. It understands Nazi policy as stemming from a central, hierarchical, and monocratic political organization. The extermination is thought to be the result of a coherent, linear, and well-coordinated process in which Hitler had a crucial role. From an ethical point of view, intentionalism is an interesting historical representation, since it reduces the Holocaust to one very clear and localizable political or moral intention. One can then postulate a connection between the unambiguous will of individuals and genocidal evil,[15] and collective evil receives a concrete face. Auschwitz is understood as consciously planned and executed with indisputably evil intentions. Intentionalism shows how the Holocaust was prepared with great precision by a group of immoral beings who did evil—evil for evil's sake—intentionally. Accordingly, genocide was the outcome of a diabolical plan through which evil was systematically realized and with malice aforethought.

As an authoritative historiographical theory, and as characteristic of the paradigm of diabolization, intentionalism tends to explain *everything* the Nazis did in terms of an all-embracing dehumanizing, Machiavellian, and Faustian system. *All* that happened in the camps was planned in advance, methodically programmed with "German *Gründlichkeit*" and "Prussian precision." The elaboration of such a meticulous plan could never have been the work of a normal human being, but requires a diabolical spirit. Even the (exceptional) expressions of humanity of the perpetrators are sometimes interpreted in a contrary way; such moments are attributed to the evil intention that had orchestrated evil in advance, and that did not even shrink from a kind of moral "cunning."

For the most part, intentionalists also deny or relativize the economic dimension of the Nazi genocide. The completeness of evil can be heightened when stressing that the evil was not committed for any material benefits, but for evil's sake alone. In the first paradigm, what is emphasized is that the extermination of European Jewry deprived Nazi Germany's war industry and economy of important labor forces, which was only partially compensated for by the Jewish slave labor and the confiscation of Jewish properties. In *Act and Idea in the Nazi Genocide*, ethicist Berel Lang provides a "textbook case" of the paradigm of diabolization. He shows how the Nazis took trains from the eastern front for transporting Jews to the camps, even though Germany was losing the war at that time and needed the trains more than ever for transporting military machinery and supplies. Similarly, Steiner emphasizes "the deliberate decision of the National Socialist regime, even in the final stages of economic warfare, to liquidate the Jews rather than exploit them towards obvious productive and financial ends. Most enigmatic of all, perhaps, is the persistence of virulent antisemitism where no Jews or only a handful survived....The mystery, in the proper theological sense, is one of hatred without precedent."[16] Here we can see two final characteristics of the paradigm of diabolization: its accent on the incomprehensibility and the uniqueness of the Holocaust and the central place it gives to (German) antisemitism.

The evil and the immorality of Auschwitz are considered unfathomable mysteries that never will yield their secrets.[17] One can find this opinion among historians, philosophers, and theologians. Elie Wiesel is an important representative of this idea.[18] He thinks that one cannot explain Auschwitz, because Auschwitz transcends history. Such a plea for incomprehensibility is an understandable reaction against outsiders who—in a hardly humble way—try to explain and use the Holocaust for their own purposes, and thereby profane it. Elie Wiesel has compared these people to the "friends" of Job. Defenders of diabolization likewise reject comparisons of the Holocaust with other genocides, preferring to reveal the "unique" aspects of the Holocaust. Berel Lang, for instance, points out that it is dangerous for ethical reflection to reduce the Holocaust to one illustration of historical evil. In the Nazi genocide, he finds, "the internal history of evil had at once been asserted and found its end — that this history was now complete, reaching a boundary by which any future instance of evil would be measured. Like the limit set by the speed of light, an outer limit would now have been defined for moral violation."[19] To cite another example, in his article "The 'Unique' Intentionality of the Holocaust" philosopher Steven Katz locates the uniqueness of the Holocaust in the intentionality that drove it, namely, the unique evil intention to kill all Jews — deliberately, continually for a period of twelve years, legally and without geographical limits — *only because they were Jews.*

In the intentionalist model, antisemitism — mostly seen in continuity with Christianity's anti-Judaism — is usually considered to be the primary motive of the Nazi genocide. Antisemitism is not merely one — albeit the most shocking — aspect of a broader Nazi racial policy but the central motive of the Nazi genocide. Often Hitler's "last testament" is thought to be a strong illustration of the central place of antisemitism in his Nazi ideology — just before the end of the war he reiterated the need to fight against international Jewry. The American historian Daniel Goldhagen even stresses the typical German character of this Nazi antisemitism. The evil of Auschwitz is thereby reduced to a very clear cause, embedded in characteristics of German culture or even of the German *Volk*. In this way, Goldhagen's thesis all too easily implies a kind of collective guilt idea. We see here again a mechanism of defense. If we say it's "made in Germany," we need not think that we ourselves could regress to such an immoral level.

The Anonymity of the Torture Machine

To continue our reading of Kafka's novel, one would now recognize from the first paradigm the description of a terrible bloody scene in which the torture is described in detail. Yet, an attentive reading of the description of the execution shows that Kafka is not primarily concerned with the immoral, sadistic character of the event or the perversion of the legal system, but more with the glory of the machine over the human being, for Kafka's story takes an unexpected turn. The officer chooses to demonstrate the machine to the visitor by briefly submitting to it himself. He lays down, starts the machine, and then the machine takes over and tortuously kills him. The visitor watches but does not intervene because it is not up to him to interfere in foreign affairs.

In this part of the story, we discover another perspective on evil: the perfect working of the machine looks endlessly more important than the bloodthirsty hunger of a sadist or any discussion about justice and ethics. Kafka shows a human who is completely given over to instrumental rationality and moral indifference. Herein Kafka's story brings together some crucial themes of the second paradigmatic representation of genocidal evil: the power of technology, the self-destructiveness of modernity, the insensitivity of the executioners, and the moral indifference of the bystanders.

In his ethical analysis of the Holocaust, the Norwegian philosopher Harald Ofstad distinguishes immorality from non-morality. The immoral person of the first paradigm is still within the sphere of morality. He or she knows the difference between good and evil but chooses the later. The non-moral person of the second paradigm, however, lives "beyond good and evil," where moral distinctions are irrelevant.[20] From this perspective, Auschwitz appears as a well-oiled machine, run by people who were not hampered by subjective involvement or specifically evil intentions, but who accomplished in a professional manner what they considered to be their duty. According to the second paradigm, it was not the excessive subjectivity of the Nazis but their purely objective attitude that made their crimes possible. If it is necessary from an economic perspective and it is practical and realizable, for example, why not kill the mentally ill or use Jews and Gypsies as medical experimental guinea pigs, before killing them (anyway)? If the government allows it, why not?

In the context of Nazi genocide, the paradigm of diabolization was critically called into question for the first time by the philosopher Hannah Arendt in her study of Eichmann's trial in Jerusalem.[21] She had been struck by the contrast between Eichmann as a person and the manner in which Hausner portrayed him. Eichmann, she thought, was not a perverted "arch-monster" (Hausner) but an "awfully normal" (Arendt) bureaucrat. Hence, although she was often misunderstood, Arendt spoke of the "banality" of evil. She developed the idea that ethical Manicheism was unable to explain how thousands of people cooperated in the genocide for more than a decade without stopping to consider their humanity in such cooperation. There surely were monsters among the Nazis, but alone they would not have been numerous enough to be really dangerous. It seems that ordinary people are more likely to be the most dangerous in such extreme circumstances, because they enable the system to continue working effectively.

Central to Arendt's interpretation is not the *im*moral, but the *a*moral character of the Nazis. This new *Gestalt* for understanding the Holocaust was severely criticized by the defenders of the first paradigm, and not always in a fair and scientifically correct manner. We can interpret this conflict as a "struggle of paradigms" in which different historical, moral, and metaphysical presuppositions collide. To focus the second paradigm further, consider again its basic points and how the new character of this *Gestalt* of genocidal evil came to the fore.

According to the portrayal of the second paradigm, the perpetrators are not exceptionally evil persons, but "terribly normal." They find no pleasure in transgressing the law, preferring instead to act in perfect accordance with the law. They are even prepared to renounce their spontaneous ethical involvement with their fellow human beings and blindly deliver themselves to an insensitive and amoral system and machinery of murder. In this paradigm, the Nazis were not monsters, but dull, banal, and morally indifferent persons who helped to eliminate suspected enemies of civil order in a rational and thoroughly efficient manner. Arendt's notion of "banality'" was offensive, first, because it criticized an ancient tradition that had invariably understood evil — in agreement with the first paradigm — as envy, hatred, seduction, and pure maliciousness. Arendt argued that evil in the modern (totalitarian) state had lost those characteristics by which people had always recognized it.[22] Her question was no longer how people can do evil, but rather how — in an evil situation — they can rid themselves of the involvement that implicates almost every human when facing human suffering.

In Arendt's opinion, the loss of autonomy belongs to the essence of modern bureaucracy, which reduces each person to a tiny cog in a gigantic machine that is characterized by "the supremacy of no one." The network of bureaucratic rules turns humans into "thoughtless" robots that obey certain laws automatically. Such thoughtlessness is the ideal place for modern evil to take root; it is the "weak spot" (Ricoeur) in our human constitution.[23] According to Arendt, it was difficult for Eichmann to conceive the situation of the other from behind his desk. Nevertheless, one would have thought that he might have followed his human feelings a little more and the regulations a little less. For the first paradigm, sensitivity is the problem and rationality would be the solution; for the second paradigm, rationality is the problem and sensitivity would be the solution.

Behind this second paradigm, moreover, there is not a pessimistic but a more optimistic anthropology at work, namely, the belief that humans are structurally endowed with ethical possibilities and that—for better or worse—the community and culture can manipulate our human capacity of being touched ethically. In the light of the unspeakable suffering in the Nazi camps, the neutralization of our human sensitivity for the good is anything but obvious. To eliminate the inner feelings of moral resistance that one must inevitably have when seeing people being transformed into non-humans, the Nazis used a number of modern techniques of "depersonalization" (Todorov), such as depriving the victims of their clothing and their names. In doing so, the appeal of the face of the victim could be effectively neutralized. This "depersonalization" is not defined as typically German, but is considered to be a fundamental feature of modern warfare and even of modern society as such. The camps merely illustrated the worst possible consequences of this general, modern reality.

In her analysis of "modernity," Arendt does not stand alone. Her "desk killer" bears resemblance to Marcuse's "one dimensional man," Adorno's *subjektlosen Subject*, Heidegger's *das Man-selbst* and Weber's *Ordnungsmensch* and *Fachmann*.[24] In the second paradigm, the "technocratic" qualities of bureaucrats, much more than their personal immorality or evil passions, are what make them "competent" for genocidal evil. As Eichmann's case suggests, those who organized and carried out the murderous system did not feel any particular hatred towards their victims. Technical precision, scientific objectivity, and emotional detachment were much more decisive. Efficiency was the only value of importance, and genocide was part of an intellectual puzzle that had to be solved as adequately as possible. Technology's task was to maximize productivity, not moral value. The second paradigm stresses how individual immorality, hate, and sadism — so central to the first paradigm — were even considered obstacles to the efficient elimination of the enemies of the German people. Albert Speer, for example, defended himself against accusations of cruelties not on moral but simply utilitarian grounds: the use of excessive violence would not have been an intelligent policy in the light of the productive ends of the genocidal system.[25] This attitude shows how the economic dimension of the Holocaust is relevant.

To understand the functioning of this extermination machine, the second paradigm no longer works with a condensed synthesis of some very extreme forms of immediate, concrete, and "intentional" cruelty, which are incomprehensible and even mysterious, but concentrates on the analysis of the large-scale, abstract, functional, and "thoughtless" system that "produced" the evil of Auschwitz. This outlook stresses a functionalistic interpretation of the Holocaust. In contrast to intentionalists, functionalists do not view the Holocaust as a consequence of a planned and monolithic Nazi program but as the (by)product of a progressive radicalization of Nazism as a system.[26] The genesis of extermination is not understood as a conscious and clear plan but as the interaction of successive and heterogeneous measures from different sources that were each submitted to trial and error. In and through the genesis of the genocide, the four most important factors of German society (the party, the army, the economy, and the bureaucracy) interacted with each other in a very complex and sometimes even conflicting way. The results were not clear in advance. For functionalists, the fact that the Holocaust was not planned in advance does not make that event any less horrible. On the contrary, the fact that mass extermination does not require a complete and uniform preparation makes it even more horrendous.

For the second paradigm, the Holocaust is also unique. The uniqueness, however, does not consist in the intentional, even "metaphysical," evil it reveals, but in the unprecedented combination of modern features in a new and massively destructive constellation. By themselves, however, the basic elements of the Holocaust are not unique. The Holocaust is considered the most horrible, but understandable, expression of modern logic in which all "primitive" forms of evil are transcended. Because modern civilization produced Auschwitz, the Holocaust's threats remains an inherent risk to our very way of living. The Holocaust is unique precisely because it is not a kind of "super-pogrom," a new high point in antisemitic madness. The cruelty of the Nazis was entirely different; it was a new kind of evil. Its novelty is not to be located in the unique intentionality of the Nazis but in its uncritical use of modern and potentially genocidal methodologies.

The second paradigm likewise questions the first paradigm's myth of civilization: Auschwitz is not simply a deviation from Western society but its logical consequence. In this context, the true face of the modern world—especially its manipulating rationality—reveals itself.[27] Arendt's analysis, for example, forces us to ask painful questions about *our* (modern) way of life and about *our* Western civilization. It breaks through the comforting dualist distinction between "us" (the good) and "them" (the evil). The second paradigm discloses an understanding that diabolization painstakingly tries to avoid, namely, the inherent potentiality for evil contained in *our* present-day existence. This view makes clear that the distinction between good and evil is not the distinction between Germans ("them") and non-Germans ("us"), or between "then" and "now." Instead, the Holocaust reveals the intrinsic possibility of modern life to rob millions of their human face through technology and modern bureaucracy and, in the process, to restrict human involvement in ethical concerns. Genocide is therefore not a specifically German phenomenon but an actual possibility within modern humanity itself. We do not live in a time "after Auschwitz." We still live in the time "of Auschwitz."

Next to efficiency, obedience to authority is a crucial element for understanding the neutralization of ethics. The perpetrators did not act upon their own initiative; they executed the orders of Nazi policy. In the second paradigm, therefore, it is more difficult to draw a sharp Manichean line between perpetrators and victims, because in the totalitarian system the (obedient) perpetrator can also be considered a victim of the system. Arendt even went further; in fact, she went too far. Insofar as the victims also collaborated in their own destruction, as her analysis argued, their purity and innocence were blemished and the Manicheism of the first paradigm of "absolutely evil perpetrators" versus "absolutely good victims" was further called into question. In the ensuing debate, Arendt's (oversimplified) remarks on "Jewish collaboration" in the extermination process caused considerable controversy.

Kafka's story also illustrates how modernity finally turns against itself. Characteristic of the second paradigm is a philosophical interpretation of the Holocaust that emphasizes modernity's self-destructiveness. What is central here is not so much (Christian) antisemitism but Western thought itself, which is considered responsible—"from Parmenides to Heidegger"—for producing a totalitarian interpretation of reality. Antisemitism is then considered one—very important—manifestation of this Western impossibility to deal ethically with "the other."

In their *Dialectics of the Enlightenment*, Adorno and Horkheimer showed how Western thought tried to submit, exclude, expel, and demythologize the impalpable, foreign, unrecognizable, and unsortable. In that outlook's effort to realize a universal and homogeneous society—which deletes every particularism, renders every infinite finite, eliminates every inexplicable—they understood the whole Western tradition as a striving for total control and thus as a foundation for Auschwitz. In the "dialectics" of the Enlightenment, the "thesis" of a repressive myth and the "antithesis" of a liberating rationality are elevated to a "synthesis" of repressive rationality. All that remains unknowable is considered hostile, and great efforts are undertaken to make the incomprehensible comprehensible. In spite of the great successes of this modern enterprise, there always remain enigmatic entities that withdraw from this effort, thereby creating doubts about the chances of its success. So, for example, the Gypsies' transience escapes the demographics of the state. The absent look of the feebleminded reveals a world that is impenetrable for human reason. The silence of the homosexual evades the statistics of the calculating bureaucrat. The Jew refuses the universal church and continues to cling to "strange habits"—an obscure language and indecipherable books. These "disturbers" of order cause great annoyance, which finally ends in a physical assault on all that eludes "reason." For Adorno and Horkheimer, the Holocaust is an attack on all that is ultimately uncontrollable. Auschwitz is the last step of twenty centuries of Western civilization.

Not only the Jews, but every "disturber of the order" had to be eliminated. The second paradigm breaks open the Judeo-centric approach of the first paradigm, explaining why other people were victims of Nazi genocide as well. In this sense, antisemitism is "only" the most striking and provoking form of the much broader violence of Nazi totalitarianism. The relativizing—not denial—of the role of Christian antisemitism is for the defenders of the second paradigm no reason to absolve Christianity of its role in the Holocaust. One must also look for other elements in Christian tradition that facilitated the Holocaust—for example, an ethic of obedience (especially in Catholicism) or a split between private and public life (especially in Protestantism).

With its critique of modernity, the second paradigm unmasks the mechanisms of mystification and self-defense that are so prominent in the diabolization of evil. In the Holocaust we see the so-called progressive elements of our civilization and our way of life at work: for instance, science and technology, bureaucracy, economics, propaganda, the military industrial complex, anonymity, moral indifference, and instrumental rationality. These are elements with which we try to give our life further form and by which we hope to protect it, elements that for the most part continue to develop today without correction. Every effort to recognize the Holocaust only in the other (in the German, the pre-modern, the subhuman, the sadist, the evil person) reveals itself to be an effort to avoid seeing the Holocaust as a part of ourselves.

Of course, the second paradigm must also be subjected to serious criticism. While the first paradigm (over)emphasized the free choice of evil, despite the psychosocial and historical background of the perpetrators, the second paradigm particularly stresses a number of determining factors that explain evil and to a certain extent even excuse it. This view may imply, for example, that in the long run and because of depersonalization, obedience, and efficiency, the criminal did not know what he or she was doing. He or she was a "thoughtless" creature. Such an approach entails the danger of slipping into determinism. Then the tragic dimension of evil can become a cowardly excuse for crimes committed. Responsibility becomes unthinkable, and human beings become playthings of extrahuman powers.[28] Ethics becomes irrelevant. In our era, evil is "psychologized" and "sociologized." Such views suggest that the criminal who had a difficult youth or who has ended up in a marginal social position is not a perpetrator but a victim. Those who fail are tragic figures needing mercy more than critical moral judgment. This ignoring of ethics shows a fundamental misunderstanding of freedom, a typical human characteristic that is very much celebrated today. The possibility of evil is a condition for the affirmation of human freedom. In short, there is no freedom without the possibility of human failure. If we do not want to reduce humans to pitiful creatures, then we will have to affirm them, in the name of human dignity, not only as victims but also as perpetrators. Moreover, excuses such as "we didn't know" or "we didn't intend *that*" must not be used too readily as justifications. In short, the second paradigm risks too much empathy for the perpetrators and too little for their victims.

Moreover, Arendt's notion of obedience and thoughtlessness is in contradiction to the engaged and even creative way in which the Nazis executed and "re-invented" their duties. Historian Raul Hilberg shows that Nazi orders from Berlin were often not very clear and did not reckon with the difficulties that often arose with their implementation.[29] Without the inventiveness of German bureaucrats, the *Führer*'s orders would have lacked results. The bureaucrats, however, assiduously made the orders concrete, found solutions for unforeseen problems, and generated their own initiatives. If each of them had only waited for orders, probably little would have happened. Obedience was only evil's "outside," not its "inside."

The second paradigm's basic flaw is that technique and rationality are mistakenly presented as the *motivating* forces of genocide, while their actual roles are mainly limited to *simplifying* its execution. Clearly modernity facilitated the Holocaust, but it was not the *reason* for it. Technology was a condition for—but not an *explanation* of—the evil of Auschwitz. It can also be argued that Nazism was more a perversion than the outcome of Enlightenment ideals.[30] In the second paradigm, modernity is divorced historically and analytically from the categories of a universal ethos, human rights, democracy, and tolerance. Only in this way, is it possible to see modernity *only* as a preparation for genocide. In fact, modernity bears a very ambiguous legacy. Hitlerism can be explained as a revolt against modernity, a fight against the ideals of universalism, and as an extreme form of particularism. The same critique can be levelled against "moral indifference" and "obedience" as explanations for the Holocaust. We must ask the question *why* people obeyed. Obedience is mostly motivated by the desire to follow a leader, to be a "good" member of a society or to act in accordance with a ruling system. Such criticisms bring us to the third paradigm, a paradigm that searches for the motivating forces behind obedience and genocidal technology. And to our surprise, with the third paradigm, we will discover *inside* Nazi evil, ethics itself!

The Enthusiasm of the Torturer

In Kafka's novel, we can find a third interpretative perspective. His story need not be read only as a moral warning against "hyperevil" (first paradigm) or as a glorification of the machine over its modern creator (second paradigm) but also as a satire on the moral heroism of human beings. The officer's death on the torture machine is then seen as the tragic story of a man who brings about his own ruin through his passion for certain ideals. The third paradigm provides a similar reading of genocidal evil: The executioners of the Nazi genocide failed to suffer a bad conscience, not because they were perverted completely by evil (immorality), nor because they were thoughtless machines (amorality), but because they devoted themselves consciously, creatively, and with passion to the meaning that the "Nazi ethic" gave their (camp) behavior. According to the third paradigm, the Nazis knew they were violating the ruling norms of the past, but they were nonetheless convinced to do so because of "higher," community-approved values. Their contribution to the "Nazi ethic" was very demanding, and thus deserved moral praise.

Whereas the Holocaust appears as absolute evil to outsiders, for its creators, collaborators, and even bystanders the Holocaust's events were difficult but still a right way to deal with the Nazis' sociohistorical situation.

The third paradigm's *Gestalt* can be summarized as follows. The Nazis knew what they were doing; they found these facts morally acceptable, and they acted consciously and creatively in accord with this new moral sense. The Germans were not suddenly deprived of their capacity to distinguish good from evil. They did not act out of purely immoral desires, or out of moral insensitivity, but *precisely because* they were ethically sensitive. Nazism was sustained by a very strict, almost puritanical, ethical code. The analysis of this code makes clear that the "Nazi ethic" was a new construction, but it was constructed with the building blocks of Western morality. Because good and evil received a new meaning, millions of Germans and non-Germans were no longer able to recognize the evil of Auschwitz as evil. The Holocaust had become an acceptable component of a package of values that, in its totality, was very appealing. Nazism reveals something about the "deceptive beauty of evil."

We can illustrate this paradigm with one "textbook case." On August 15, 1942, when Hitler visited the Lublin camp, Dr. Herbert Linden of the Ministry of Internal Affairs asked him if it would not be better to cremate the bodies instead of burying them, for future generations might think differently about these things. In Hitler's presence, Globocnik, the SS major of the camp of Lublin, answered Linden as follows: "But, gentlemen, if after us such a cowardly and rotten generation should arise that it does not understand our work which is so good and so necessary, then, gentlemen, all National Socialism will have been for nothing. On the contrary, bronze plaques should be put up with the inscription that it was we, we who had the courage to achieve this gigantic task."[31]

In his paradigmatic study, *Morality after Auschwitz*, the Jewish ethicist Peter Haas argues that the fundamental question is not why the Nazis did evil, as in the first and second paradigms, but why they failed to recognize evil as evil, and therefore why they did not distance themselves from it. Haas answers this question by referring to the prevalent patterns of ethical argumentation and acting among the Nazis that predetermined their perception of Jews in a very specific way. In the light of this ethical framework, the efforts to persecute and exterminate the Jewish people appeared to the Nazis as an ethically acceptable part of a greater good. In my view, Haas's pioneering point of departure has introduced an entirely new and original ethical approach to the Holocaust: not regarding it in terms of immorality or amorality but precisely in terms of morality. For him, the development of genocidal policy had an ethically logical progression, and the Nazis identified with it consciously, voluntarily, and even enthusiastically. If so, the Holocaust demonstrates the exceptional human capacity for redefining good and evil and for reconstructing reality in the light of new ethical categories.

Haas's study provides a provocative "picture" of the Holocaust, one that is capable of answering certain questions about the Nazi genocide with great insight. Just as the analysis of Arendt was influenced by thinkers working on modernity (Weber, Adorno, Heidegger), Haas's interpretation has been influenced by postmodern philosophers. It is no accident that this new "paradigmatic" interpretation has received many critical reviews by Holocaust scholars. Still, in this case we cannot as yet speak of a paradigm struggle.

Haas distinguishes an "ethic" from what he calls "morality." Taking "ethic" to mean a systematic way of understanding the bipolarities "good" and "evil," in and by which a society shapes itself, he defines "morality" as those values which we think *should* be incorporated or developed in an ethic. For Haas, when an ethic can produce a coherent and intuitively right discourse about good and evil, and the results of such an ethic meet the wishes and needs of a community, then it becomes possible for people to be ethically motivated to do any action, even the most immoral. In the interpretation of Haas, Nazism developed such a new discourse. This ethical construction, however, was built with key ingredients of traditional Western ethics. Nazism used and reinterpreted—this is a key part of its "uniqueness"—moral ideals that had long been accepted: for example, the idea of just war, patriotism, the ethics of duty, the ethics of labor, and nationalism. Nazism stood for certain values: anti-individualism, obedience, loyalty, anti-pornography, anti-prostitution, and law and order. In its "ethical" construction, it likewise called upon a widespread and deeply rooted religious antisemitism in which the Jews were identified as the ultimate evil. These concepts were complemented by "scientific" arguments from nineteenth-century racial theories. Once the Jew was presented as a lethal threat to German culture, the ethics of lawful self-defense could be put forward to legitimate genocide. Building on these traditions, the Nazi ethic could easily link "good" and "evil" with "Aryan" and "Jew."

The Nazi ethic used a Manichean interpretation of good and evil. "Absolute good" was identified with the Aryan race (*Übermenschen*), and "absolute evil" was identified with the "Semitic race" (*Untermenschen*). In the Nazi ethic, there was no gray area, but only black and white. And for "radical evil" there was only a "radical solution"—a "final solution." This dualism stands as a warning against the first paradigm, which also works with a Manichean representation of the Nazis' "absolute evil." The third paradigm can teach us that a Manichean representation of, and combat against, Nazi genocide may be nothing more than a reproduction of the basic "ethical" logic of Nazism, with all the risks that "ethic" implies.

Like the second paradigm, the third also runs counter to the idea of aberration found in the first paradigm, where the Holocaust is presented as a sudden, formal break with the ideas of the last centuries. Even more so than in the second paradigm, the third emphasizes that the Holocaust was only possible because it was morally acceptable in the light of European history. This continuity made it possible for the Germans to accept the genocide of Jews while still considering themselves to be ethical. Moreover, the "Nazi ethic" mobilized the best ones among its supporters to contribute enthusiastically to the expansion of the "new order."

In this respect, one cannot speak of an intention of doing evil as evil, but rather of achieving the good of the Nazi story. How one dealt with the cruelties in the camps is not explained by a sadistic hunger for evil (first paradigm) or by means of the modern techniques of depersonalization that covered up these atrocities (second paradigm) but as the "necessary price" that had to be paid if one wanted to contribute to a "higher" Nazi goal. There were, of course, complex emotions among the perpetrators, but they were considered human weakness or the necessary price one had to pay in order to be ethical. Every ethic has its painful and emotionally difficult moments. Horror and disgust are therefore not necessarily a vaccine against evil, as the first paradigm would contend. As the Holocaust shows, if there are good reasons to do so, people can continue to do unethical things in spite of their moral revulsion.

Haas can also explain why the Western world protested so little during the war. Despite being told of the atrocities, the Allies were unable to react against the Nazi ethic precisely because, like the Germans, they were caught in the same web of moral presuppositions. Since at that time the entire West reasoned using principles such as race, the sovereignty of the state, the right to self-defense, the importance of battling Bolshevism, and antisemitism, the Allies could not act forcefully and adequately against the Nazi policy of extermination until it was nearly too late.

In a certain sense, the perpetrators were also victims of this all-powerful Nazi ethic. This fact can be illustrated by Eichmann's decision to divert trains from the eastern front at a decisive point in the war in order to use them for transporting Jews. The first paradigm takes this decision as proof of Eichmann's diabolical nature. The second paradigm would argue that this action was a typical example of a machine and a bureaucracy that could no longer be stopped. The third paradigm, however, interprets Eichmann's attitude to be a consequence of his relentless ethical enthusiasm and stubbornness. The third paradigm stresses the strong impact of collective discourse on individuals so that "essentialism" (first paradigm) is not crucial but one's situation is. Even stronger than in the second paradigm, humans are understood as conditioned by the sociocultural framework in which they live. While in the second paradigm one uses modern techniques as though untouched by "good" and "evil," the third paradigm points out how the meanings of "good" and "evil" depend profoundly on social context.

In the end, it was not the power of argumentation of Western ethics that finally eliminated Nazism, but the (contingent) military victory of the Allies. The internal or external critique of morality was entirely powerless. It was only thanks to military intervention that the "Nazi ethic" was finally defeated. With his thesis that an ethic depends upon the political exertion of power, Haas comes very close to Richard Rubenstein's interpretation. In Rubenstein's view, people have no natural rights but only the rights that are guaranteed by an organized community powerful enough to protect those rights. After Auschwitz, Rubenstein contends, it is less than persuasive to think that there is a universal morality by which all peoples and nations will be judged. People only have rights as members of a *polis*. As such, people who have no power to protect themselves must be prepared to become the victims of the obscenities of their opponents.

In the postscript to *Eichmann in Jerusalem*, Arendt developed a notion of moral responsibility in which resistance to social forces would be possible. At this point, an important difference between the second and third paradigms becomes evident. In the second paradigm, human beings must be capable of distinguishing good from evil, even if they can only rely upon their own judgment, a judgment that might well be in conflict with the dominant and univocal opinions of their environment. For Arendt, the normative force of good and evil can never be finally legitimated by referring to the social forces that call them into life, preserve, and sanction them, but for Haas, the Holocaust is a proof of the overpowering influence of the "ethical" framework in which one lives and acts. For the second paradigm, the social foundation of moral authority is not ultimately the most fundamental factor. Of course, this position assumes the optimistic anthropology of the second paradigm, in which people possess intrinsic ethical possibilities, in contrast to the pessimistic anthropology of the first paradigm and the rather deterministic anthropology of the third paradigm.

What Zygmunt Bauman, in the optimistic anthropology (second paradigm) of his *Modernity and the Holocaust*, has called the spontaneous ethical inclination of human beings is for Rubenstein nothing but the expression of a sentimental, yet completely powerless, desire of human beings to be respected. Moral indignation and justice are thus only relevant in situations where people understand themselves as members of the same community. Auschwitz is proof that such considerations become totally senseless in a society where more and more people lose their right to dignity and life. For Rubenstein, under the ethical system of Nazism, it was simply an illusion for victims to think that they lived in the same moral universe as their perpetrators. By exterminating the stateless, the Nazis did not violate any law since these people were not protected by any law. In this way, Rubenstein comes to one of his most paradoxical and controversial, yet logical, conclusions: in Auschwitz, not one crime was committed.

Haas has sought to make his interpretation acceptable by distinguishing "ethic" from "morality." Using this distinction, he can call the Holocaust a component of the "Nazi ethic" without saying that the Nazi genocide was morally permissible. But it is precisely this distinction in his thought that is, in my view, very vulnerable. Since each and every ethical judgment is determined by the ethical system in which one stands, it is not clear *on what grounds* a certain ethical system can be qualified in Haas's interpretation as moral or immoral. A critique of one ethical system can only be formulated from within another ethical system that has the same formal characteristics (coherence, noncontradiction, intuitive rightness). There is no Archimedean point, no universal standard, from which all ethical systems could be evaluated as to their content. Because there is no intra- or trans-ethical touchstone for preferring one ethical system over another, it would be impossible to find in Haas's thinking any real criteria by which to judge Nazism as immoral. The outcome of the third paradigm is the opposite of the first paradigm—not ethical absolutism but ethical relativism. This result brings us to an exceptionally paradoxical conclusion, namely, that such a terrible evil as the Holocaust, which calls out for an immediate and absolute condemnation, brought into life a (sincere) process of thought that seems to undermine the very foundations of morality itself. And if there is no longer a foundation for judging good and evil, why then should not the strongest rule over and even eliminate the weakest?

Against the third paradigm, we would argue that the "Nazi ethic" cannot simply be seen as a reorganization of the values of Western ethics. It is not a rearrangement of the classic values of our moral tradition, but a *perversion* of its ethical principles. In Nazism's abuse and corruption, the basic inspiration and main concerns of Western values were completely lost. Only the veneer of an ethical *form* was left. While in the first paradigm, the discontinuity between Western history and the Holocaust is mistakenly overemphasized, the third paradigm too easily stresses the fact that the Nazi genocide was in continuity with the Christian and humanistic civilization of the West. Nazism, however, is more a manipulation than a continuation of Western ethics.

As a result, even if the Nazis legitimate their crimes, one should not conclude that they acted out of ethical concerns. Perhaps Haas too quickly believes the way the Nazis presented themselves. Their so-called ethical language could also be the expression of the need they felt to legitimate their actions in the face of what they still recognized as unambiguous evil. The Nazi ideology should be interpreted as the supplier of an arsenal of skillful pretexts and "ethical" sophisms to facilitate the implementation of evil (and not good) with a more peaceful (but not good) mind. With this last remark, we come to the heart of our critique of the third paradigm. Haas's distinction between "ethic" and "morality" is best replaced by the distinction between "ideology" and "morality" (the latter in Haas's sense). Ideology is a way of legitimizing the evil in one's own story. If the Nazis had submitted their ideology to a genuinely moral questioning, one can doubt if the ideology would have come through this test successfully. In other words, it is not certain that the Nazis really believed in their own story. For the most part, their "ethical" (ideological) discourse was nothing more or less than a legitimation of evil.

Another criticism against the third paradigm is that it has very deterministic implications. For Haas, ethical choices are always given *within* the story in which individuals situate themselves. If so, the Nazis, given their framework, could not have possibly made other choices. Within the third paradigm, it becomes difficult to explain how different individuals, coming from the same story, can arrive at entirely different ethical attitudes, as some did even in Nazi Germany. One must remember that people always live in complex, even contradictory and mutually questioning, ethical stories.

Conclusion: Ethics after Auschwitz

In this essay, I have taken Kafka's *In the Penal Colony* as a point of departure to identify three paradigms for ethical approaches to the Holocaust. However conflicting or even incompatible these para-

digms may be, we should not forget that each reveals a part of the
Holocaust's ethical complexity. The first paradigm stresses the objective side of the Nazi genocide: *evil* in its most unambiguous and
extreme form. The second and third paradigms explore the subjective side of the Nazi genocide: *evildoers* who are human beings with
moral capacities. The first paradigm describes evil from the *outside*;
the second and third paradigms attempt to understand evil more
from the *inside*. The first paradigm places greater emphasis on the
most extreme *outcomes* of the genocide; the second and third paradigms are more sensitive to its *genesis* and *daily aspects*. The first
paradigm better portrays the experience of the *victims*; the second
and third paradigms bring in the perspective of the *perpetrators* and
the *bystanders*. Each of the three paradigms can also shed light on
the *different* perpetrators: the sadism of the camp hangmen (first
paradigm); the ordinary Germans, working in the Nazi (war) industry (second paradigm); and the convinced Nazi or the bystander
outside of Germany (third paradigm).

To nuance and correct its own deficiencies, each approach requires the other two. My analysis entails a plea to recognize the many
faces of genocidal evil, to see the explosive mixture of hatred (first
paradigm), moral indifference (second paradigm), and ideological
conformity (third paradigm) that made the Holocaust possible. Post-
Holocaust ethics needs to do justice to the different tensions in the
understanding of (genocidal) evil and to recognize the historical and
philosophical presuppositions (such as intentionalism versus functionalism, essentialism versus situationism, synthesis versus analysis
of evil, pessimism versus optimism about humanity and culture) that
are at work in every elucidation of good and evil.

Ethics after Auschwitz must particularly attempt to develop a
theory for understanding the complex relationship between the objective and subjective sides of evil. The Holocaust is not simply about
evil people doing evil things (first paradigm), nor about people doing what they took to be good things (third paradigm). Post-Holocaust ethics must make clear how (potentially) good human beings
(in terms of anthropology) can (factually) do inhuman and evil things
(in terms of morality).[32] It is thus not enough that we call the perpetrators "monsters" to recreate ethics after Auschwitz.

The problem is that our moral discourse *itself* has been involved in and perverted through the Holocaust. As a result, the Holocaust is not simply a lesson about immorality, but as much about the vulnerability of ethics. In this way, the Holocaust can become more significant for *our* lives and *our* time. Indeed, Auschwitz is not *completely* ("qualitatively") different from our "daily" misuse of ethics. It would have been much easier if the Holocaust was the work of moral monsters. The problem and the challenge are that this inhuman evil was the work of human beings. If we overemphasize the discontinuity, uniqueness, and incomprehensibility of the Holocaust's hyperevil, the contemporary moral significance of the Holocaust will disappear. In the end, such an approach risks that the moral meaning of the Holocaust will die together with the last survivor. We must *try* to understand, *try* to see the relevant universal elements in the Nazi genocide, even when this process is difficult, painful, and ultimately impossible. As is the case in every human enterprise of understanding, this effort to understand should never destroy the uniqueness and ultimately impenetrable character of the particular event, surely not of such a complex and extreme event as the Holocaust. In this sense, uniqueness and universality need not exclude but can fruitfully challenge each other. Uniqueness without universality leads to moral irrelevance; universality without uniqueness leads to banality and superficiality.

Every ethical reflection on the Holocaust must not only meet the duty of continuously seeking a good balance between the polarities of uniqueness and universality but also between detached observation and sensitive human involvement, between reflection and experience, between comparability and incomparability, between analysis and synthesis, between scientific neutrality and prephilo-sophical sensitivity, between moral universalism and particularism. Hermeneutical problems begin when we (inevitably?) disturb this balance.

One of the most important challenges that post-Holocaust ethics must address is the moral relativism so typical of the third paradigm. Why do I refer to the Holocaust not as involving an ethic, but as depending upon an ideological misuse of ethics? I think that the beginning of an answer to this question can be found in the distinction between *openness* and *closedness*. The difference between a

community based on biblical-humanitarian values and a community based on totalitarian and racist values is not that the former has
ethical concerns, and the latter does not. On this point, the third
paradigm is correct—Nazism did have a concept of goodness. What
makes the difference is that the basic structure of the Judeo-Christian ethic, for example, is characterised by openness—specifically
by an openness toward the vulnerability of the face of the other,
which, as Levinas points out, continually and unpredictably calls
my closed system into question. By contrast, totalitarian and extremely
nationalistic discourses are typified by closedness. In biblical and
humanitarian ethics, centrality is given to the unpredictable encounters of fellow humans and God, always in new, different, and challenging ethical perspectives, so that people and communities might
perpetually grow in their own humanity. Here God is not the *Gott
mit uns*, who can be used for one's own ethical-ideological purposes,
but the totally Other who always refers to what is irreducible, what
escapes my power and the power of my story, what can never be
defined in terms of economic value, gender, national identity, religious belief, or race. This God is One who can never be used to legitimate evil in any form.

In a totalitarian ethic, priority is given to sameness. Closed totalitarian stories always seek to reduce otherness to sameness. In this logic,
"difference" is the greatest danger; it is even a crime. Everything that
cannot be assimilated into the beautiful, safe, and closed system of
absolute good and absolute evil must be excommunicated and even
exterminated. All that is unprepared or unable to integrate into the
"wonderful harmony," thereby questioning the closed system, must
be destroyed. A closed ethic knows neither gray areas nor mercy.
Instead, it becomes ideological, bringing with it a legitimation of
the evil that is anxiously directed against the disturbers of the closed
black-white order. In such a system, God is not the Other who constantly challenges self-righteousness in the name of more and more
humanity, but a *Gott mit uns*, a pseudo-God who legitimizes the
closed and murderous order. Such a God does not, indeed cannot,
know mercy.

Because it had no respect for alterity, and it required the eradication of everything that could not be reduced to the closed system

with its extreme good-evil polarities, Nazism was a politics without an ethic. Misappropriating ethics and God for the ideological ends of its own ("good") group, Nazism was an idolatrous effort that radicalized itself and eliminated everything that did not conform.

Therefore, the basic structure of ethics after Auschwitz should be openness to the vulnerability of the other. This criterion can be an efficacious touchstone for testing every ethical system after Auschwitz: Is it open for (positive) alterity, growth, discussion, questioning, hesitation, falsification, new challenges, for the vulnerability of the weakest? What the third paradigm reveals is *how* human beings and systems can convert ethical openness to closedness by anxiously creating a Manichean system of (good) super- and (evil) subhumans that eliminates every hesitation and every gray area. The first paradigm shows the ultimate consequences of this development from ethics to idolatry: inhumanity on an unlimited scale. Nevertheless, the first paradigm is problematic because it creates a new kind of ethical Manicheism. In fact, the first and the third paradigms are very close to each other in their definition of ethics. They both approach ethics as a system of binary oppositions of good and evil. Ethics then risks becoming an overly simple means for situating oneself on the side of the good and forgetting one's own evil potentialities. The Nazis are not the only ones susceptible to this temptation. We need to ask whether this binary *system* of good and evil is the central characteristic of ethics. My approach proposes another way for ethics, a way of *living* in openness for (positive) alterities. In the final analysis, my position is closest to the second paradigm, since this paradigm can best explain how good people can do evil things, namely, by neutralizing and destroying—both passively and actively—our ethical openness by eliminating the "face of the Other" (Levinas) that inherently and continually challenges our human closedness.

Notes

[1]Franz Kafka, *In der Strafkolonie: eine Geschichte aus dem Jahre 1914. Mit Quellen, Abbildungen, Materialien aus der Arbeiter-Unfall-Versicherungsanstalt, Chronik und Anmerkungen von Klaus Wagenbach*

(Berlin: Wachenbach, 1975). I quote the English translation as found in Franz Kafka, *The Judgment and In the Penal Colony* (London: Penguin Books, 1995).

[2]Thomas Kuhn, *The Structure of Scientific Revolutions* (Chicago: University of Chicago Press, 1970).

[3]A point of departure for using the ideas of Kuhn in Holocaust studies can be found in G. M. Kren and M. Rappoport, *The Holocaust and the Crisis of Human* Behavior (New York: Holmes and Meier, 1980), 128: "In *The Structure of Scientific Revolutions*, T. Kuhn suggests that this occurs in science when a dominant paradigm for theory and research is overturned by new ways of thinking about scientific phenomena. It is being suggested here that an analogous process occurs in history when real events outstrip the conceptual structures of historians, philosophers, and laymen alike." See also D. Marmur, "Judaism after the Holocaust," *Toronto Journal of Theology* 9 (1993): 211-220.

[4]Hannah Arendt, *Eichmann in Jerusalem: A Report on the Banality of Evil* (New York: Viking Press, 1963), 5.

[5]Peter J. Haas, *Morality after Auschwitz: The Radical Challenge of the Nazi Ethic* (Philadelphia: Fortress Press, 1988).

[6]B. Klieger, *Le chemin que nous avons fait (Reportages surhumaines)*, 2d ed. French translation by Noah. (Brussels: Editions Beka, 1947), 82: 'Ce n'étaient plus des hommes [de SS in Auschwitz] qui frappaient là, c'étaient des bêtes, des monstres déchaînés, ils criaient et l'écume leur sortait de la bouche. Les yeux étaient injectés de sang. Jamais encore je n'avais encore vu de si près et si précises les figures d'hommes décidés à tuer. Maintenant seulement je vis la figure de l'assassin; maintenant qu'ils avaient enlevé leur masque il ne restait qu'une face sanglante, déformée, satanique. Voilà donc, 'l'homo sapiens' quand ses instincts primitifs étaient déchaînés!'.

[7]Saul Friedländer, "The 'Final Solution': On the Unease of Historical Interpretation," in *Lessons and Legacies: The Meaning of the Holocaust in a Changing World*, ed. Peter Hayes (Evanston, IL: Northwestern University Press, 1991), 23-35 and especially 30.

[8]In L. Abel, "The Aesthetics of Evil: Hannah Arendt on Eichmann and the Jews," *Partisan Review* 30 (1963): 211-230 and especially 224. Cited in Berel Lang, "The History of Evil and the Future of the Holocaust," in *Lessons and Legacies*, 90-105.

[9]Philip Hallie, *Opdat geen onschuldig bloed vergoten wordt…: goedheid en gerechtigheid in Le Chambon sur Lignon in de jaren 1939-1944*. Dutch

translation by H. M. Matter. (Kampen: Kok, 1981), 36.

[10]To express the notion of human "averageness" in criminality, the Italian essayist and survivor Primo Levi developed the category of "the gray zone." See, Primo Levi, *De verdronkenen en de geredden: Essays* (Amsterdam: Meulenhoff, 1991), 33-38.

[11]Gideon Hausner, "Eichmann and His Trial," *The Saturday Evening Post*, 3 November 1962, 19-25.

[12]See also Daniel Goldhagen, *Hitler's Willing Executioners: Ordinary Germans and the Holocaust* (New York: Knopf, 1996).

[13]Representatives of this position include: L. Dawidowicz, E. Jäckel, G. Fleming , and K. Bracher.

[14]Tim Mason, "Intention and Explanation: A Current Controversy about the Interpretation of National Socialism," in *Der 'Führerstaat': Mythos und Realität. Studien zur Struktur und Politik des Dritten Reiches*, ed. G. Hirschfeld and L. Kettemacker (Stuttgart: Klett-Cotta, 1981), 23-42.

[15]Saul Friedländer, "From Anti-Semitism to Extermination," *Yad Vashem Studies* 16 (1984): 1-50 and especially 28: "...The intentionalist position implies a key element: premeditation. Planning and premeditation at the top lead, of necessity, to planning and premeditation at various levels of the hierarchy and to...awareness of the events within the various agencies involved....".

[16]George Steiner, *In Bluebeard's Castle: Some Notes Towards the Redefinition of Culture* (London: Faber & Faber, 1971), 35.

[17]See D. Magurshak, "The 'Incomprehensibility' of the Holocaust: Tightening Up Some Loose Usage," in *Echoes from the Holocaust. Philosophical Reflections on a Dark Time*, ed. Alan Rosenberg and Gerald E. Myers (Philadelphia: Temple University Press, 1988) 421-431; Alan Rosenberg, "The Crisis in Knowing and Understanding the Holocaust," in *Echoes from the Holocaust*, 379-395.

[18]Elie Wiesel, *One Generation After*, trans. L. Edelman (New York: Random House, 1970), 167: "We shall never understand how Auschwitz was possible"; and Elie Wiesel, "Trivializing the Holocaust: Semi-fact and Semi-fiction," *New York Times*, 16 April 1978, 29: "The dead are in possession of a secret that we, the living, are neither worthy of nor capable of recovering."

[19]Berel Lang, "The History of Evil and the Future of the Holocaust," in *Lessons and Legacies*, 103.

[20]Harald Ofstad, *Our Contempt for Weakness: Nazi Norms and Values —and Our Own* (Gothenburg: Almquist and Wiksell, 1989), especially

92-104 ("Idealism and Indifference") and 105-125 ("Non-moral versus Immoral"), 105.

[21]Hannah Arendt, *Eichmann in Jerusalem: A Report on the Banality of Evil* (Harmondsworth: Penguin Books, 1984).

[22]Ibid., 156-157.

[23]Hannah Arendt, *The Life of the Mind* (London: Secker & Warburg, 1978) and Paul Ricoeur, *Philosophie de la volonté. Finitude et culpabilité I: L'homme faillible,* (Paris: Aubier-Montaigne, 1960), 157.

[24]Alan Rosenberg and Paul Marcus, "The Holocaust as a Test of Philosophy," in *Echoes from the Holocaust*, 201-222.

[25]*Trial of the Major War Criminals*, London, HSMO, 1946-1948, 16 volumes.

[26]Hans Mommsen, "Anti-Jewish Politics and the Implementation of the Holocaust," in *The Challenge of the Third Reich*, ed. H. Bull (Oxford: Clarendon Press, 1986), 117-140 and especially 123: "Even the most fanatical anti-Semites within the Nazi elite or the inner circle around the dictator did not conceive the 'Jewish problem' from the aspect of a possible extermination policy before the end of 1939, and even then there was no clear conception of what could be done against the Jews."

[27]Zymunt Bauman, *Modernity and the Holocaust* (Cambridge: Polity Press, 1989).

[28]This criticism, however, should not be applied to Hannah Arendt, who thought of Eichmann as personally responsible for the loss of his ability to think. See Arendt, *The Life of the Mind*, 187-216.

[29]Raul Hilberg, "La bureaucratie de la solution finale," in *L'allemagne Nazie et le génocide juif,* ed. F. Furet (Paris: Gallimard, 1985), 219-235 and especially 220.

[30]R. Bucher, "Hitler, die Moderne und die Theologie. Überlegungen in Anschluß an ein umstrittenes Hitler-Buch," *Zeitschrift für Religions- und Geistesgeschichte* 44 (1992): 157-176 and especially 167.

[31]In E.A. Cohen. *Human Behavior in the Concentration Camp*, trans. H. M. Braaksma (London: Free Association Books, 1988), 229.

[32]Didier Pollefeyt, "Auschwitz or How Good People Can Do Evil: An Ethical Interpretation of the Perpetrators and the Victims of the Holocaust in Light of the French Thinker Tzvetan Todorov," in *Confronting the Holocaust: A Mandate for the 21st Century?*, ed. G. J. Colijn and Marcia L. Littell (Lanham, MD: University Press of America, 1997), 91-118.

Critiques

Critique by Leonard Grob

Didier Pollefeyt has undertaken to examine three paradigms within which ethical analyses of the Holocaust can be situated. His spirited, critical study of these paradigms points to strengths and weaknesses of each, and demands of us that we neither accept nor dismiss any one framework of thought out of hand. Pollefeyt warns us against feeling unduly comfortable taking our stand within any of the given paradigms. All need to be examined, at least in part, in light of the contributions of every other: "Each approach," he tells us, "requires the two others in order to nuance and correct its own deficiencies."

Having argued this point with great clarity, Pollefeyt concludes a chapter in a volume devoted to post-Holocaust ethics by asking himself, in light of what has just been discussed, how a true ethic might be derived. The concept of an alleged "Nazi ethic" has just undergone severe criticism. An assumed Nazi ethic is identified by Pollefeyt as no ethic at all, but rather an "ideological misuse of ethics." Having made this claim, Pollefeyt proceeds, appropriately, to pose a question regarding the basis for establishing an authentic ethic. His reply to his own query: "We think the beginning of an answer...can be found in the distinction between openness and closedness." I wish to reflect on this openness/closedness distinction as a supposed ground for building a post-Holocaust ethic.

Pollefeyt is certainly correct to point to openness as a critical dimension of any ethical system worthy of the name. We must be careful, however, in our use of the term "openness," a term which, in common parlance, is overused and often misused. As a catchword of some contemporary psychological movements, "openness" is often employed casually and, sometimes, mindlessly. If it is to be not merely a needed, but also, as Levinas would have it, a central characteristic of any system which calls itself ethical, the word "openness" must be uttered with great care. How can we be certain that being open to another will result in a manifestation of the "biblical-humanitarian values" of which Pollefetyt speaks? How can we be assured that an "open" ethic will lead us, inevitably, to honor the personhood of the other person in the post-Holocaust world?

In the concluding pages of his essay, Pollefeyt occasionally speaks of openness as if it is akin to *any* questioning of fixities of thought. Openness to "new, different, and challenging ethical perspectives" may not, however, *in and of itself*, lead humans to "perpetually grow in their own humanity." Sensitivity to what is "unpredictable" and a willingness to be "open...for growth, for discussion, for questioning, for hesitation..." need not *in itself* thrust me upon a truly ethical plane of existence. To be open in a Levinasian sense, as Pollefeyt proceeds to emphasize in the main thrust of his argument, is to do more than lead an "examined life." This latter sense of openness does not necessarily bring us to embrace the other in his/her sanctity of being. In fact, openness of this sort can lead to a facile give-and-take of discourse in which knowledge is relativized: We can become "open," as an end in itself, to any and all views. If, in the name of openness, all moral stances are ultimately to be held but tentatively, what, for example, becomes of the Kantian absolute—so critical for all post-Holocaust ethical thinking—that we must treat others not only as means but also *as ends*?

Pollefeyt implicitly acknowledges the difficulties in our use of the word "openness" in the course of pointing to openness, not in any generic sense, but rather "openness for the vulnerability of the face of the other...." He grants this radical or root sense of openness, as well, when he speaks of the touchstone for post-Holocaust ethics as openness to a *"positive"* alterity. (My emphasis) Openness, in other words, is not openness to "challenge" as such. Within traditional philosophical schemas, I am "challenged" by an other who confronts me only as part of a play for power. Hobbes and Freud are but two of the many Western thinkers who take the self-interest of the ego as the ground of all human endeavor. As Jean-Paul Sartre, for example, never tires of telling us, the other wishes to encompass me within his/her meaning system at the same time as I wish to encompass him/her within my own meaning systems. Although there *is* also a "challenge" hurled by the Levinasian Other, such a challenge—if it is to bring us to an ethical plane of being—must exist outside a fixed or closed system within which the nature of the relation derives whatever meaning it has. To break through this system, an asymmetry must arise between myself and an other who is truly Other.

As Pollefeyt emphasizes in his conclusion, this Other at one and the same time commands me *and* appeals to me from his/her vulnerability. If I am called to responsibility, it is not because I am overwhelmed by the might of the other person. In Levinas's terms, he or she disarms me nonviolently, soliciting ethical responses by an appeal from the vulnerable states of the "poor one," the "widow," the "orphan." Rather than the individual person being compelled to alternate, within a closed system, between the status of challenged and challenger, it is now the play for power itself which is called to account. The Other jolts me out of an unjustified existence and propels me onto the plane of ethical being. Were I to remain within the totalized system, within a system of ideas-become-ideology, I would be unable to assume that ethical status which alone is worthy of its name in the post-Holocaust world.

With Levinas and Pollefeyt, I would argue that openness is not just one among many touchstones of an authentic ethical system. Openness differs fundamentally from all other potential touchstones in that it is not something *posited,* and thus relativized as something *for me*—but rather *an enactment* which exhausts itself in its everrenewed will to submit itself to the command of the Other. The command to be open has no fixed content which would locate it as one idea among many in a history of philosophy. The medium of openness is also its message: It is more verb than noun. Openness, further, is not a characteristic of ethics which would lead to some ethical end outside itself. Indeed, Levinas would make openness not just a *necessary* but also a *sufficient* condition for ethics: To be "open," in his sense of the word, is already to have acknowledged the sacredness of the Other before whom I speak my word; it is already to have exchanged the arbitrary existence of a free, egoist being for the justified existence of a person who now knows, existentially, that he/she must not harm the Other.

Pollefeyt's presentation of a post-Holocaust ethic of openness to the Other ends with a brief discussion of the differences between this ethic and the alleged ethics forged within the three paradigms examined throughout the course of his chapter. Pollefeyt concludes by arguing that "in the final analysis, my position is closest to the second paradigm, since this paradigm can best explain how good people can do evil things, namely, by neutralizing and destroying—both passively and actively—our ethical openness by eliminating the 'face of the Other' (Levinas) that inherently and continually challenges our human closedness." It is certainly true that concepts such as the banality of evil and the desk killer do much to illuminate how we hide from the face of the Other. I would argue, however, in the spirit of all that Pollefeyt has said, that while the second paradigm may involve sophisticated analyses of the depersonalizing process, all three paradigms bear ultimately equal responsibility for giving rise to an ethics without the face of the Other at its core. At the foundation of all three is a failure to see the other-as-Other, making distinctions between them merely second-order or derivative.

The first paradigm fails us by giving rise to ethics as a "system of binary oppositions of good and evil." Its *root* shortcoming, however, is its failure to ground the good-evil distinction in the primordial difference between an egoist ambition, which totalizes all that is, and a justified existence, ever open to the Other as a sacred being. The first paradigm spawns an ethic of demonization, within which "a sadistic hunger for evil" must be combated by those who have retained a sense of their heritage as "civilized" beings. The second paradigm, by contrast, allows only for that evil which is disguised, transformed into amoral actions by those technocratic means so characteristic of modernity. Yet, here again, I (with Pollefeyt) would argue that the essential failure of an ethic which speaks of the banality of evil and of an unthinking obedience to authority lies not in the distinction between the amorality of modern thought processes and traditional (binary) moral concerns; rather, it lies in the contrast between keeping the naked face of the Other before us and covering it over with the masks supplied by bureaucratic and instrumentalist thinking. Finally, the third paradigm is responsible for our understanding how the traditional binary opposition of good and evil can be reorganized in accord with the situation at hand—in this case, according to the dictates of Nazism which gave new twists to such traditional concepts as the sovereignty of the state and the right to self-defense. To say that the Nazis had an "ethic," however, is to neglect to locate the foundation of anything that can call itself "ethical" in openness to the call of the Other. The failure of the third paradigm lies not in its continued use of the opposition of good and evil, nor even in a resultant ethical relativism. Like the two other paradigms discussed by Pollefeyt, the third paradigm suffers, at bottom, from the failure to acknowledge the Other's call to responsibility as what we, in conclusion, may call nothing less than "the ground of all grounds" of ethical concern.

Critique by Peter Haas

In his essay, Didier Pollefeyt suggests that there are three broad paradigms for understanding the moral question raised by the Holocaust: diabolization, banalization, and ethicalization. He places my thought into the third category, as a matter of fact as the paradigmatic example of this paradigm. Yet upon reading his descriptions of the three, I am no longer sure I belong there. What I tried to say is so close to what Pollefeyt describes as the second paradigm, that I see myself as more of a variation on that than a wholly new approach.

A couple of examples from Pollefeyt's description of the second paradigm will suffice to make my point. He notes, for example, that "behind the second paradigm, moreover, there is not a pessimistic but a more optimistic anthropology at work, namely, the belief that humans are structurally endowed with ethical possibilities and that the community and culture can manipulate our human capacity of being touched ethically, for the better or for the worse." This is, of course, precisely the presupposition of my own work. The beginning point of my paradigm was that the Nazis could not have been entirely amoral and diabolical because that would have made them nonhuman. We all work within ethical systems, and we all respond positively or negatively to what we regard as good and evil, respectively. So, my claim is, the Nazis too must have been endowed with a moral structure. Further, their ethical possibilities were manipulated by their culture, albeit for the worse. As regards this characterization of the second paradigm, then, I think I belong to it rather than to another altogether.

Later, Pollefeyt associates the second paradigm (I think quite correctly) with functionalism. He believes that holders of the second paradigm "do not view the Holocaust as a consequence of a planned and monocratic Nazi program, but as the (by)product of a progressive radicalization of Nazism as a system." He goes on to note that "in and through the genesis of the genocide, the four most important factors of German society (the party, the army, the economy and the bureaucracy) interacted with each other in a very complex, sometimes even conflicting way." Again, this was precisely the point I was trying to lay out in my book. These institutions, I tried to show, struggled with each other for power and resources within a broad consensus of basic values. In years of debate and infighting, none questioned the basic premises of Nazi policy, including its racism and eventually its genocide. In fact each of these bureaucracies, and others as well—the universities and the churches to name two most egregious examples—assumed the "higher good" represented by the Holocaust to advance their own interests. My underlying contention is that members of these segments of German society (except maybe the Nazi Party) would have been shocked in 1933 by the mere notion of genocide, but by 1942 had come to accept it as "business as usual."

One last example along these lines appears when Pollefeyt concludes that under the second paradigm "it is more difficult to draw a sharp Manichean line between perpetrators and victims, because in the totalitarian system the (obedient) perpetrator can also be considered a victim of the system." Without belaboring the point, let me say that I made the same claim in my book. One of my conclusions was that the "ethic" of the Nazi became the discourse within which all discussion took place, and it entrapped its perpetrators as well as the victims. This is why otherwise normal and good people became implicated in the Holocaust, maybe much to their own subsequent bewilderment. The almost standard response of "I didn't know" does not in this reading mean simply that they did not know what was going on, a virtual impossibility in any event given the enormity of what was transpiring. It may mean also that they did not "know" at the time that what was happening was wrong and that now they don't even know why they didn't know that.

I do, of course, have differences with the second paradigm as described by Pollefeyt. He holds that according to the second paradigm "because of depersonalization, obedience, and efficiency, the criminal did not know what he or she was doing. He or she was a 'thoughtless' creature." This seems to me to be slipping into a form of the first paradigm: regarding the perpetrators as different now not on the grounds of being diabolic, but rather on the grounds of being simply thoughtless and mindless. One of the major thrusts of my argument was that in many, even in most, cases this view is not supported by the evidence. To the contrary, the perpetrators seemed to be quite thoughtful and had fully in mind what they were doing. My conclusion, in rejecting the first paradigm, was to reason that if they were not diabolic, then they must have somehow thought that what they were doing, and were mindful of doing, was really not so bad. So if the second paradigm must entail banality on the part of the perpetrators (which is what I take "thoughtless" and "mindless" to mean), then I do part company with it.

I also feel at this point that I need to make a few comments about how Pollefeyt characterizes my "third" paradigm. He argues that against the third paradigm what the Nazis did was not a rearrangement of classical Western values, but a *perversion*. I think this is a quibble rather than a substantive disagreement. My argument was that the Nazi ethic maintained the form of the received morality, but inserted a new content. Whether you call this a rearrangement or a perversion, or more of what I described as an *in*version, is a matter of semantics; the underlying mechanics of ethical transformation is the same in any case.

I am also not sure that I am ready to agree that my "third" paradigm means that Nazis could not have made other choices. I will agree that once one is in a paradigm it is hard to think "outside the boundaries," but I think we all always have choices and other options; even new paradigms are devised by people thinking within the old paradigm. But in all events, we know that there were other ethics around and available to Germans of the Nazi period. The Nazi paradigm, after all, was imposed from the top, on a society which had to be "Nazified." As a simple example, churches, universities and the professions did have other ethical perspectives, perspectives which they consciously had to give up in order to conform to Nazi norms. As far as I am concerned, they made a choice. In short, I fully agree with Pollefeyt that "people always live in different, even contradictory and mutually questioning ethical stories." My model does not require us to say that the perpetrators had no choice.

In short, I am not sure in the end that Pollefeyt's taxonomy really does my argument justice in placing it in its own, "third" paradigm. According to his description, at least, I see it much more as a variation of the second paradigm.

There is of course an advantage for Pollefeyt to having my view distinguished from the second paradigm and put into its own "third" paradigm. The advantage is that it allows Pollefeyt to isolate the problem of relativism solely in this new "third" paradigm, thus making it possible for him to accept the second paradigm under the assumption that it has been freed of the problem of relativism. In point of fact, the basic tension between Manicheism (the first paradigm) and relativism is still there.

By assuming to have dismissed the problem of relativism, Pollefeyt in the end backs into a sort of Manicheism of his own. At the end of the essay, Pollefeyt makes a sort of meta-normative claim, namely, that all ethics, *to be ethics* "must" adopt a stance of openness. Now as a matter of fact I find this an attractive argument, and I must admit that I find his approach to be an interesting and potentially useful way of getting around the problem of relativity vs. Manicheism. Yet I still think it avoids the big issue. After all, one is already within a paradigm of ethics of some sort to find openness rather than closedness a metavalue that does nothing less than define ethics. I suspect that we have here postponed the problem, but not really solved it yet. I would want to know what arguments we could put to the truly thoughtful and intelligent Nazi sympathizer (say Heidegger) that would convince him or her that our system is objectively right and his or hers objectively wrong. My hunch is that the appeal to openness is still *within* our paradigm of moral understanding, not beyond it.

In the end, then, we are still stuck with the binary opposition between holding onto an absolute good at the expense of being Manichean and being open to the contingency of human ethical discourse at the expense of becoming relativists. We have yet to find a really third paradigm that can encompass and transcend this opposition.

Critique by David Hirsch

With dazzling clarity, Didier Pollefeyt outlines three approaches to Holocaust ethics. He calls these approaches "paradigms," and designates the three paradigms as "diabolization," "banalization," and "ethicalization." Pollefeyt does not accept any of the paradigms uncritically, but argues, rather, for a new synthesis that would combine all three paradigms to arrive at an authentic post-Holocaust ethic. Since I agree with Pollefeyt that none of the three paradigms is adequate as a totality, there is no point in disputing his acceptance or rejection of each one, as such. Nevertheless, I would like to state my own reservations about the paradigms and examine, from my own point of view, the ways in which they relate to each other. I would like to contest Pollefeyt's apparent belief that the three paradigms can be equally weighted, and also to challenge his privileging of the second paradigm.

The diabolization paradigm represents the point of view of the victims. According to Pollefeyt, it consists of "a synthetic approach to evil, ethical Manicheism, intentionalism, a pessimistic anthropology, an optimistic view of civilization, the incomprehensibility and the uniqueness of the Holocaust." In this paradigm, the perpetrators are conceived as criminals, even monsters, who deliberately undertook to exterminate a particular group of human beings; the perpetrators are perceived, here, as having acted with savage fury and as having taken pleasure in humiliating, torturing, and murdering their victims.

Pollefeyt points out, correctly I believe, that "the paradigm of diabolization particularly highlights the extreme aspects of Nazism: its excessive crimes,…sadistic games, incredible moral excesses." He does not question the accuracy of these reports of "incredible moral excesses," but he does believe that it is precisely this highlighting of the extreme aspects of Nazism that leads to diabolization. That is, "diabolization is thus based on a specific *selection* of facts, especially the extreme cruelties." This concentration on the evil deeds of the perpetrators has led certain people to view them as monsters.

It seems to me, there are several problems in Pollefeyt's formulation. To begin with, he does not make a sufficiently sharp distinction between witness accounts and later historical, sociological, and philosophical narratives that use witness accounts as the evidence out of which they weave their own narratives. It is one thing to say that certain historians or other Holocaust commentators consider only one kind of evidence (the witness accounts of survivors and victims), and another to say that the victims themselves describe only the extremes of evil.

The problem here is that once we enter the world of the *Kazetlager*, via first-hand narratives or memoirs, or even fiction, we are left only with extremes of evil. That is precisely what makes the *Katzetlager* a *novum* in human experience. The extremes of evil became routine; they were pervasive. The implication of Pollefeyt's assertion is that there must have been a normative life in the camp that the witnesses do not mention in their descriptions. But where are we to find this normative life? I cannot think of a single witness account that is not a journey through a realm of pure evil, where there is only a constant fluctuation between greater and lesser evils. If we take any day at random in the life of any *Häftling*, as described in any witness account, there is never a moment that we can call "normal." Evil is pervasive in the *Kazetlager*. It is the essence of the *Kazetlager*. I do not know of a single witness account that does not make this clear, whether written by a Jew, a Christian, a Communist, an empirical scientist. In order to have made the point decisively that there is an unwarranted concentration on evil, Pollefeyt would have been obliged to present a significant body of evidence that would contradict all known accounts of life in the camps. But he does not present such evidence, nor do I believe it is possible to do so. Pollefeyt, therefore, assumes that there must have been moments in the *Kazetlager* when evil was not the norm.

When Pollefeyt writes, "The presentation of the Nazis as 'diabolical' or 'hyperevil' is the result of a purposeful and selective synthesis of the historical reality of the camps," I believe he is referring to historians rather than first-hand witnesses. But the same need for evidence applies here as in the case of witness accounts. Even if it is true that "diabolization is…based on a specific *selection* of facts, especially the extreme cruelties," it is also true that *all* historical representations are based on a "a specific *selection* of facts." It cannot be otherwise. No account is ever complete in the sense of presenting every single act that takes place within a specific time frame (the "stream of consciousness" novel, as we know, pretends to do this). Consequently, a narrative that de-diabolizes the Nazis would also have to be based on a "selection of facts." The question, then, is, which selection of facts would be closer to reality. Even the Nazis themselves spoke of the *Kazetlager* as *anus mundi*. What they did not acknowledge, and it is precisely this lack of acknowledgment that pushes them across the line dividing mere heinous criminals from monsters, is that they themselves were responsible for creating this *anus mundi*.

For the most part, the perpetrators were reticent about their deeds, but when they speak we cannot help but be shocked by their absolute moral obtuseness. For example, Kremer, a physician, records in his diary some of his activities one day in Auschwitz. "This night," he recalls, "was present at the 6th and 7th special actions. *Obergruppenführer* Pohl with suite arrived at the Waffen SS club-house in the morning. The sentinel at the door presented arms in front of me for the first time. At 8 o'clock in the evening supper in the Home with *Obergruppenführer* Pohl, a truly festive meal. We had baked pike, as much of it as we wanted, real coffee, excellent beer and sandwiches."[1]

Pollefeyt believes that the tendency to "diabolize" the Nazis is not dictated by evidence, but is, rather, a defense mechanism: "The idea that people who do extreme evil are not fundamentally different from ourselves is extremely threatening to our own identity. No doubt, this is why it is easy for people to choose a diabolical representation of the Nazis." This explanation of "diabolization" is purely speculative. Even if we believed that the evil-doers were "not fundamentally different from ourselves," it would still be possible to condemn them. In fact, one could argue that it is precisely because we recognize common ground with the perpetrators that we can condemn them. We may have recognized within ourselves the same inclination to do evil, and yet have realized that we have struggled to resist this inclination.

Certainly, narratives of both the *Kazetlager* and the gulag confirm that human beings are vulnerable, and are quite likely to commit acts under severe pressure that they would not commit otherwise. These ordinary human beings with an inclination to do good, but who are capable of doing evil for a piece of bread when starving, or who will "drown" another human being just to keep themselves afloat, even for just another moment, these are the denizens of Primo Levi's "gray zone." But for the true perpetrators, those who acted of their own free will, who ran the camps and took pleasure in human suffering, for them there is no room in the gray zone. May we not say of Dr. Kremer, who describes his attendance at a gassing of men, women, and children, and in the same breath records the fact that he later ate "a truly festive meal," that he is not quite an ordinary man? Which anthropology is more pessimistic, one that maintains Dr. Kremer is ordinary, or one that hopes he is not?

Pollefeyt's contention, with no real evidence in support of it, that those who "diabolize" the SS do so only because they are threatened by the thought that they could have done what the SS men did, launches a line of argument that all too easily dissolves into moral relativism. Primo Levi has made this point very strongly in commenting on the assertion by the film maker, Liliana Cavani, that "We are all victims or murderers, and we accept these roles voluntarily." Levi's response was to assert, "…I know I was a guiltless victim and I was not a murderer. I know that the murderers existed, not only in Germany, and still exist, retired or on active duty, and that to confuse them with their victims is a moral disease or an aesthetic affectation or sinister sign of complicity…."[2]

With space running out, I shall skip, at this point, to two closely related arguments against "diabolism," Pollefeyt's rejection of the intentionalist argument and of the representation of the Holocaust (of Auschwitz) as an unfathomable mystery. As for intentionalism, it is my impression that "intentionalists" and "functionalists" have more or less arrived at a compromise position. The Nazis did indeed intend to exterminate the Jews, but not necessarily in 1933, or even in 1939. The question, then, is, when did the Nazis arrive at this momentous decision? When did they shift from the intention to "cleanse" to the intention to exterminate?

The "two final characteristics of the paradigm of diabolization," according to Pollefeyt, are "its accent on the incomprehensibility and the uniqueness of the Holocaust and the central place it gives to

(German) antisemitism. The evil and the immorality of Auschwitz are considered unfathomable mysteries that never will yield their secrets." Neither of these issues can be resolved here, so I wish only to reiterate that they have not been resolved. The debate over "uniqueness" can get ugly, since it inevitably touches on issues of comparative victimization, that is, who was a more abject victim. Those who argue for the "uniqueness" of the Holocaust are not unjustified in deploring the trivialization that is all too often attendant on attempts to compare genocides, and to work out a hierarchy of victims. As far as I can tell, Auschwitz still has not yielded its secrets. But why should a Christian balk at mystery? For two millennia, Christian religions have based their existence on mystery: the three-personed God, the resurrection, and transubstantiation. Is it any less a mystery that those who professed themselves Christians would crucify an entire people to avenge a God who permitted Himself to be crucified in order to remove the lust for revenge from human consciousness?

Jorge Semprun, who was neither a Jew nor a Christian, but a rationalist and a Marxist, maintained (after he had become disillusioned with Marxism) that

> One could have spent hours testifying to the daily horror of the camp without touching upon the essence of this experience [of radical Evil].... One could recount the story of any day at all, from reveille...to curfew,...yet never manage to deal with the essential thing, or reveal the icy mystery of this experience, its dark shining truth: *la tènèbre qui nous ètait èchue en partage.* The darkness that had fallen to our lot, throughout all eternity. Or rather, throughout all history.
>
> "What is essential," I tell Lieutenant Rosenfeld, "is the experience of Evil. Of course, you can experience that anywhere....You don't need concentration camps to know Evil. But here, this experience will turn out to have been crucial, and massive, invading everywhere, devouring everything....It's the experience of radical Evil."[3]

Unlike the first paradigm, which has the force of the cumulative testimonies of a wide range of first-hand witnesses, the second paradigm, "banalization," is nothing more than a construct after the fact. I do not have space to re-hash the Arendt controversy, which ex-

ploded after the publication of *Eichmann in Jerusalem,* and continues to this day. But I would like to make two points. First, while it is
true, as Pollefeyt says, that some of Arendt's detractors were not "fair
or scientifically correct," it is also true that some of them were. Jacob
Robinson's *And the Crooked Shall be Made Straight* gives a closely
documented account of Arendt's contradictions and inconsistencies,
and of her many blunders in discussing the legal issues that arose
during the trial. Second, I should say that it is the moral (not amoral)
character of the Nazis that is central to Arendt's interpretation. That
is, if we accept her portrait of Eichmann (which I hasten to say I do
not), he was a man not only doing his job, but a man who believed
in the moral rectitude of the job he was doing.

It is not entirely true, as Pollefeyt states, that, "As was seen in
Eichmann, those who organized and carried out the murderous system did not feel any particular hatred towards their victims." In order to believe this, we must ignore the testimonies of innumerable
victims who testify that the killers acted out of hate. It is true, however, that the killers often murdered in cold blood, without any dis-
play of emotion. Erich Kahler describes this kind of emotionless
systematic mass killing as a "new psychic phenomenon." He cites
an incident described by Ernst von Schenck, of a punitive action
against the French town of Oradour-sur-Glane. "'The peak of horror,' said the Swiss informant,…'is not reached by the fact that as an
act of revenge, a whole town has been reduced to ashes.…If such a
thing had been done in a delirium of hatred, aroused by a savage
fight, it would have been gruesome enough, but somehow understandable.… But the Elite Guards who had received this order…carried it
out with utter calmness and placidity (*seelenruhig*).'"[4]

Finally, it should be said that, even if Arendt's perception of
Eichmann were correct, it would apply to only one high Nazi official. It is hardly possible to say of the highest of Nazis, Hitler, Göring,
Goebbels, Himmler, Heydrich, among others, that they acted without hate. And it is plausible to argue that they were able to communicate their hatred to millions of Germans. Unfortunately, Arendt
never undertook to understand the solid commitment to the ideals
of Nazism of her mentor and lover, Martin Heidegger. Was Heidegger
also an ordinary man, or an ordinary Nazi?

I agree with Pollefeyt that the chief weakness of the "banalization" position is that it is deterministic, which makes it impossible to apply any ethical standards to the behavior of the perpetrators. I disagree, however, with Pollefeyt's later contradictory assertion that "the second and third paradigms explore the subjective side of the Nazi genocide: *evildoers* who are human beings with moral capacities." As the progenitor of the second paradigm, Arendt left it in sublime ambiguity. In fact, the most glaring flaw in Arendt's book is her inability to choose between a universally exculpating determinism and a severely narrow moralism. While Eichmann is presented as a pathetic victim of forces beyond his control, the leaders of the Jewish Councils are condemned for having intentionally contributed to the "darkest chapter in Jewish history."

The third paradigm seems to me the most tantalizing and most problematic. In this paradigm, the Nazis are seen as having acted with intention, but they also acted as idealists who truly believed they were eradicating an evil from the world. Pollefeyt solves this vexing problem by arguing that the Nazis acted not out of idealism but out of ideology. I can accept that. He also points out that "the outcome of the third paradigm is the opposite of the first paradigm, it is not ethical absolutism, but ethical relativism." Again, I agree. Let me add that I also agree that the three paradigms may yield interesting insights when used in conjunction ("Each approach requires the two others in order to nuance and correct its own deficiencies").

I have one objection here, and that is to Pollefeyt's assumption that the three paradigms are of equal value, and are equally true (or not true). I should like to argue that the third paradigm stands on the shakiest legs, for the reason that the evidence used to establish the paradigm comes from the least reliable of sources, the Nazis themselves, who built into their ideology a total disregard for truth. As we know, the Nazis believed in propaganda, not truth. Can we believe them, then, when they say that they acted to fulfill a high ideal? Pollefeyt's "textbook case" to illustrate the third paradigm, for example, is a statement Odilo Globocnik is purported to have made in front of Hitler: "But gentlemen, if after us such a cowardly and rotten generation should arise that it does not understand our work which is so good and so necessary, then, gentlemen, all National

Socialism will have been for nothing. On the contrary, bronze plaques should be put with the inscription that it was we, we who had the courage to achieve this gigantic task."

In every rational court of law, the character of the witness is taken into account. But what kind of a witness is Globocnik? Who was he? Philip Friedman writes that "this Austrian SS leader gained a reputation among the Nazis as 'the man with the iron hand.' He was an organizer of the Nazi terror in Austria and of the assassination of Chancellor Dollfuss." Globocnik later became "head of all the extermination camps in the G[eneral] G[ouvernment] (Treblinka, and the three camps which he had founded in the Lublin district: Belzec, Majdanek, and Sobibor) and was entrusted with the task of annihilating the Jews of the whole GG (Operation Reinhard). Late in the summer of 1943, after the fall of Mussolini, Globocnik was dispatched to carry out the important mission of 'pacifying' the provinces of northern Italy."[5] Is it possible to believe that such a man, an unprincipled mass killer, acted out of some sublime ideal, like the officer in Kafka's story? When he made the statement cited above in front of Hitler, was he giving truthful testimony, or currying favor with Hitler, while at the same time indulging his sadistic appetite?

Of the three paradigms, Pollefeyt prefers the second ("banalization"), because "it can best explain how good people can do evil things, namely, by neutralizing and destroying—both passively and actively—our ethical openness by eliminating the 'face of the other' (Levinas) which inherently and continually challenges our human closedness." I cannot agree with Pollefeyt on either the validity of, or the moral instruction provided by, the second paradigm. The paradigm does not explain the behavior of the perpetrators, but rather the behavior of people who were relatively powerless, low grade bureaucrats who did their jobs even when the job was to carry out some minor function in the killing apparatus. But Eichmann was certainly not a low grade bureaucrat.

It was, after all, not only good people who did evil things, but evil people who did very evil things, and egged on the others. What the second paradigm illustrates is not so much that good people are capable of doing evil things (we have always known that), but that most of us are weak and indecisive, and we cower under threats from the strong and the ruthless. It is in this, not in the doing of evil deeds, that I (and I believe most people if they would admit it) identify with the gray robots of the second paradigm. The Nazis knew human weakness, and how to play on human fears. They were brilliant psychologists, and they ruled by terrorizing: first other Germans, then the rest of Europe. That, of course, was one of the purposes of the *Kazetlager*, not only to exterminate, but to intimidate. I can accept the view that the Nazis "eliminated 'the face of the other.'" But they also did more than that. They terrorized the many good Germans, and others, who might have been prepared to be open to the face of the other, but not at the cost of their comfort, the curtailment of their freedom, or their lives. Can we blame those who committed evil under the threat of terror? No! But we should not confuse those all-too-human weak souls with the criminals who brought about their moral humiliation.

Notes

[1]"Diary of Dr. Kremer," in *KL Auschwitz Seen by the SS*, ed. Jadwiga Bezwinska and Danuta Czech (New York: H. Fertig, 1972), 220.

[2]Primo Levi, *The Drowned and the Saved*, trans. Raymond Rosenthal (New York: Vintage, 1989), 48.

[3]Jorge Semprun, *Literature or Life*, trans. Linda Coverdale (Penguin Books, 1998), 138, 139.

[4]Erich Kahler, *The Tower and the Abyss* (New York: George Braziller, 1957), 71.

[5]Philip Friedman, *Roads to Extinction*, ed. Ada June Friedman (New York: Jewish Publication Society, 1980), 135.

Critique by David Patterson

In his essay "The Kafkaesque World of the Holocaust," Didier Pollefeyt has made a very important and insightful contribution to our thinking about the ethical dimensions of the Shoah. Taking his usual care, Pollefeyt has put together a well organized, highly articulate argument on the strengths and weaknesses of the three main paradigms of ethical response to the Holocaust: the paradigms of diabolization, banalization, and ethicalization. In the course of his investigation, moreover, he makes some very astute points about the ramifications of these paradigms.

With regard to the second paradigm, for example—especially as it is expressed by Hannah Arendt—Pollefeyt notes quite rightly that it leads to a confusion of victims and perpetrators. Working from the paradigm of banalization, one might suppose that the Nazis were merely the victims of a bureaucracy run amok, that they did not mean for things to go so far, or that their hands were tied by red tape. "Arendt's notion of obedience and thoughtlessness," Pollefeyt points out, however, "is in contradiction with the engaged and even creative way in which the Nazis executed and 're-invented' their duties." Members of the SS were not banal; they were highly qualified, highly educated, innovative, versatile, and, as Pollefeyt says, creative people. Pollefeyt observes further that, like Arendt, the second paradigm can lead one to view the Jews themselves as perpetrators, inasmuch as the Jewish Councils or Jewish police cooperated with the Nazis. The perverseness of Arendt's thinking is that, on the one hand, it presents the Nazis as mundane officials caught in the grips of a totalizing system and thus free of responsibility, while, on the other hand, it suggests that Jews such as those who served on Jewish Councils are as culpable as the Nazis.

Pollefeyt also offers a sound critique of the paradigm of ethicalization, a paradigm that would make any value system into a system of ethical values, as Peter Haas appears to do with his notion of a "Nazi ethic" in *Morality after Auschwitz*. "Haas's distinction," says Pollefeyt, "between 'ethic' and 'morality' can be best substituted by the distinction between 'ideology' and 'morality' (in the sense of Haas). Ideology, not ethics, is a way of legitimizing the evil in one's

own story." That is why "within the third paradigm, it becomes difficult to explain how different individuals coming from the same story
can arrive at entirely different ethical attitudes." The distinction between ideology and morality must be made in this instance, because
the Nazis took themselves to be operating beyond good and evil,
beyond the ethical, and not within it. Their interest lay in an ontological good, not a moral good: the crimes of the Jews—the pathological condition that the Nazis would correct—did not lie in having committed an ethical transgression that the Nazis set out to correct. No, the Jewish "crime" that the Nazis tried to correct was the
crime of *being there*.

Pollefeyt, however, does not take his critique of the paradigms
far enough; indeed, portions of his critique are flawed. With respect
to the paradigm of diabolization, for example, he argues that it is
wrongly "based upon a specific *selection* of facts, especially the extreme cruelties, that best fit within the idea of 'hyperevil.'" But
Pollefeyt ignores, for example, the *standard* procedure of the *Einsatzgruppen* that followed the German army eastward in the summer of
1941. After examining the materials that went into *The Black Book*,
for instance, Vasily Grossman came to the conclusion that "executions were carried out [by the *Einsatzgruppen*] in identical fashion
in places separated by each other by hundreds and even thousands
of kilometers. Such total uniformity is evidence of secret instructions worked out in advance."[1] Pollefeyt also ignores what is at work
everywhere in Nazi actions, namely, the general assault on the Good,
an assault that reveals itself in such things as the Nazis' use of the
holy calendar to plan their actions, the prohibition against prayer,
and the destruction and desecration of holy sites, religious texts, and
sacred artifacts.

Nor does the first paradigm necessarily imply a historical
Manicheism, as Pollefeyt claims, since one does not have to be a
Manichean to view the Nazis and their actions as evil. The
concentrationary universe was not created by an independent force
of evil—it was created by the Nazis, who *decided* to act as they did
and who therefore might have acted otherwise. That is why they are
responsible for their evil. Pollefeyt's chief suspicion of the first paradigm, however, lies in the propensity to make the Nazis into mon-

sters and thus not human, that is, not like us. But one does not have to be a monster to act in a monstrous manner. Expressing this concern, moreover, Pollefeyt overlooks the example set by the Righteous Gentiles, those angelic saviors with seemingly superhuman courage who after all were neither angels nor superhuman. If, as human beings capable of evil, we are implicated by the actions of the Nazis, we are no less implicated by the deeds of the Righteous, who were radically *unlike* the Nazis. In addition, to suggest that all of us resemble the Nazis in our potential for evil might lead us to more readily excuse their actions, which are inexcusable. Nor is it self-evident that if the Nazis are human, then *any* human being could be a Nazi; indeed, would we want to maintain that *any* of us could be an Adolf Hitler or a Mother Theresa? While any human is subject to doing evil, I am not sure that any human being could throw infants into flaming pits. To be sure, as already noted, the SS and *Einsatzgruppen* were often carefully selected for the task of extermination, since not everyone was suited to serve the *Führer* in such a manner. They were neither banal bureaucrats nor heinous monsters; they were people who decided to act in a monstrously evil manner.

Looking further at Pollefeyt's critique of the paradigm of diabolization, we see the danger, as Pollefeyt points out, of opposing Auschwitz to civilization, as if it were an aberration and not an outcome of modern civilization. Inasmuch as modern civilization is totalizing and reduces the human being from one created in the image of God to an accident of nature, Auschwitz is modern civilization. Pollefeyt, however, does not make a distinction between Jewish civilization and modern civilization. Yet, as Emil Fackenheim has shown, the modern philosophy that has shaped Western civilization stands in sharp opposition to Jewish thought and tradition,[2] which understands the ethical to be commanded by God and not conditioned by culture. Viewing the human being as the autonomous product of reason and resolve, the thinking that characterizes modern civilization, from Kant to Heidegger, opposes itself to Jewish teaching and testimony. And the advent of the machinery that would annihilate that teaching and testimony by murdering those who signify it is perfectly consistent with modern and post-modern civilization.

Another feature of the first paradigm that Pollefeyt critiques is its intentionalist position. While it is true, as Pollefeyt maintains, that not every atrocity in the camps was specifically planned, it is also true that the murder of every Jew in Europe *was* intended, planned, and nearly carried out. Witness the Wannsee Conference held on 20 January 1942. And what was the stated mission of the *Einsatzgruppen*? To kill every Jew they could find. It is also true that, if not every atrocity was planned, every atrocity was in keeping with the intended annihilation of the Jews, body and soul; under the laws of the Reich, everything that was done to the Jews—even the spontaneous atrocities—was *legal*. Opposite the intentionalist view is the functionalist position, which Pollefeyt rightly critiques but does not fully challenge. According to this position, as Pollefeyt explains, the Nazi evil "is not to be located in the unique intentionality of the Nazis but in its uncritical use of modern, genocidal methodologies." What Pollefeyt fails to consider is the question of what makes the functionalist evil an evil, and not just the unpleasant by-product of bureaucracy. Is it evil to be uncritical? And even if we are critical, does that mean we can recognize something to be evil, rather than inefficient, heretical, absurd, or subversive? The evidence is that the Nazis assessed their programs and methods in a very critical manner. But their assessment, of course, was not guided by an ethical good.

The position that Pollefeyt ultimately adopts comes closest to the second paradigm, "since this paradigm can best explain how good people can do evil things, namely, by neutralizing and destroying—both passively and actively—our ethical openness by eliminating the 'face of the other' (Levinas) which inherently and continually challenges our human closedness." If good people do evil things, one might wonder what makes them good. Further, the invocation of Levinas here is perhaps appropriate, but it is weak. For in his critique of the paradigm of banalization, Pollefeyt demonstrates its propensity to occlude the very responsibility that, according to Levinas, announces itself through the face of the other person.[3] Therefore, it would seem that, rather than settle on one of the three paradigms, we should consider moving beyond all of them. Indeed, Levinas, does just that in his opposition of totality and infinity, of ontology and metaphysics. What is conspicuous by its absence from Pollefeyt's essay is, moreover, essential to Levinas's thinking. It is the holy, the very essence of the ethical and the very thing slated for destruction in the Shoah. Says Levinas, "The face signifies the Infinite. It never appears as a theme, but in this ethical signifyingness itself; that is, in the fact that the more I am just the more I am responsible....It is the exigency of holiness."[4] None of the paradigms critiqued in Pollefeyt's essay approaches an exigency of holiness, and being chosen by the Good before we make any choices, or being commanded from on High through the face we encounter. And thus Pollefeyt himself could take his investigation a step further.

Notes

[1] Vasily Grossman, Introduction to *The Black Book*, ed. Ilya Ehrenburg and Vasily Grossman, trans. John Glad and James S. Levine (New York: Holocaust Library, 1981), xxxvi.

[2] See Emil L. Fackenheim, *Encounters between Judaism and Modern Philosophy* (Northvale, NJ: Aronson, 1994).

[3] See, for example, Emmanuel Levinas, *Ethics and Infinity*, trans. Richard A. Cohen (Pittsburgh: Duquesne University Press, 1985), 95.

[4] Ibid., 105.

Critique by John Roth

The tides of war had turned against Nazi Germany by the time Heinrich Himmler, head of the SS, addressed his officers in the Polish city of Poznan on October 4, 1943. Still confident that Germany would win the war, Himmler recorded the speech—it lasted for more than three hours—that his handwritten notes had carefully outlined. "One basic principle must be the absolute rule for the SS men," he emphasized. "We must be honest, decent, loyal, and comradely to members of our own blood and to nobody else."

Two hours into his speech, Himmler turned to what he called "a very grave matter." Referring to "the extermination of the Jewish race," he stressed that "we had the moral right, we had the duty to our people, to destroy this people which wanted to destroy us." That work, Himmler acknowledged, had been as difficult as it was imperative. "Most of you must know what it means," he said, "when one hundred corpses are lying side by side, or five hundred, or one thousand. To have stuck it out and at the same time—apart from exceptions caused by human weakness—to have remained decent fellows, that is what has made us hard." Although this page of history would never be written, Himmler claimed, it would be nonetheless "a page of glory in our history."[1]

Reflecting on Didier Pollefeyt's "The Kafkaesque World of the Holocaust: Paradigmatic Shifts in the Ethical Interpretation of the Nazi Genocide," I remembered Heinrich Himmler and his Poznan speech. Although the SS leader's oration shows that the Holocaust's realities exceed what fiction can credibly imagine, Kafka's *Penal Colony* might have anticipated rhetoric similar to Himmler's. More importantly, Himmler's speech makes us wonder about the interpretive paradigm that would best fit or be embodied by the life and career of the Nazi who has appropriately been called "the architect of genocide."[2]

Examining paradigmatic possibilities, Pollefeyt implicitly asks questions such as the following: Was Himmler a monster? Was he demonic? Richard Breitman, one of Himmler's biographers, says that Himmler spoke "clearly, deliberately, and emphatically, but for the most part dispassionately" at Poznan.[3] So, did Himmler epitomize instrumental rationality? Did he personify moral indifference when he urged that, apart from duty to "our people and our blood," SS men "can be indifferent to everything else"?[4] Or was Himmler—according to Breitman, he could sound "much like a schoolmaster"[5]—a key teacher of the Nazi ethic that idealized, motivated, and legitimated European Jewry's destruction? Or to move in the direction that Pollefeyt sketches in his essay's final pages, could Himmler see "the face of the other"? If he could see that face, why did he celebrate the annihilation of the Jews? If he could not or did not see that face, why was he so blind? How, in short, can Heinrich Himmler best be understood?

Pollefeyt's wisdom flows from the fact that he identifies interpretive paradigms but avoids entrapment by them. At the end of his essay, the temptation of a paradigmatic turn nearly snares him, but he gets back into the openness that his writing shows to be a vital element in post-Holocaust ethics. As for understanding Himmler, Pollefeyt suggests that a totally definitive analysis will elude us—no final biography can be written about him—but we can comprehend enough about the SS leader and his followers to discern what some of the major ingredients and tasks of post-Holocaust ethics ought to be.

Pollefeyt highlights one of those ingredients when he echoes a theme emphasized by Holocaust survivor Elie Wiesel, who says that the expression "and yet…and yet" is the most important in his work.[6] Pollefeyt and Wiesel share the view that inquiry must not stop too soon. However persuasive explanations seem, they must be questioned lest they settle too much too fast. However complete theories appear to be, they must be criticized lest they rest on too little too long. Such wisdom is especially important in Holocaust studies, because that catastrophe's vastness defies paradigms that seek to explain what took place.

These insights, it must be emphasized, do not imply that sound understanding about the Holocaust cannot be obtained. Nor do they mean that interpretations of the Holocaust are relativized so that one is no better or worse than another. Even less do they dictate paralysis when decisive action is needed most. To the contrary, sound understanding and trustworthy action come about most reliably when inquiry is dialectical. Such inquiry keeps looking for what is overlooked. Hunting for the puzzle's missing pieces, it is governed by awareness that human thinking is finite, fallible, perspectival, and thus in need of testing and correction. When—but only when—such sifting and sorting guide reflection, we can be confident, but not too confident, that our vision is straight and true.

The Nazis sought a "final solution," the very thing that self-corrective inquiry rejects and must actively oppose because solutions of that kind are antithetical to the spirit of inquiry. Practiced in its most profoundly rational way, inquiry is a deeply moral act, one of the most important for post-Holocaust ethics to defend, teach, and respect. Such inquiry calls us to account and saves us from destructive arrogance. It does so by asking: Is our judgment true? Are our policies good? How do we know? Can we find better ways to act? At least in part, Heinrich Himmler became the architect of genocide because he ignored, or never learned, the rhythm of Wiesel's expression "and yet…and yet."

Pollefeyt sees correctly that no single paradigm can provide an interpretation of the Holocaust that will be sufficient by itself. At the same time, his dialectical inquiry permits him to identify other key points from the three paradigms he discusses. Although skeptical about what he calls "the paradigm of diabolization," whose specific selection of facts leads to a misleadingly dualistic view of good and evil, Pollefeyt senses that the abhorrent deeds of torture and murder enacted by the Nazis and their collaborators remain at the core of ethical judgment. Contrary to the moral sensibilities reflected in this first paradigm, presenting "the shocking hyper-evil of Auschwitz" may not be "the best way to mobilize people against fascism and genocide." Nevertheless, confronting that evil and letting its shock be felt are surely necessary ingredients for post-Holocaust ethics.

Himmler knew that the SS had committed shocking deeds. Thus, as his Poznan speech testifies, he had to cloak those deeds in "decency"; he had to make them less shocking than they were by putting them in the category of dirty-work-that-someone-has-to-do because a supposedly greater good hinged on that action. Post-Holocaust ethics depends on recognizing that the deeds Himmler acknowledge at Poznan were as wrong as they were shocking. Not only that point must be made, however. It must also be underscored that the universal is found in the particular. If Himmler's mass murder is wrong—and if it is not, what could be?—then that awareness should help us to see that wrong is done whenever life is wasted.

Pollefeyt's second paradigm tries to explain the Holocaust by showing how a constellation of modern ingredients—science and technology, bureaucracy and instrumental rationality, propaganda and emphases on efficiency, to name only a few—led to a totalitarian politics in which difference was despised to the point of genocidal annihilation. Here, too, he finds that these ingredients offer less explanatory power than the proponents of the second paradigm believe. Pollefeyt thinks, for example, that technology simplified the execution of genocide, but he questions whether technology, and the instrumental rationality that accompanied it, provided motivation for the Holocaust. Still, the second paradigm does offer moral warnings that we ignore at our peril.

The Holocaust shows that people can become cogs in political machines. Even worse, they can become operatives within political regimes who are willing to use their expertise to invent ways to make mass killing more thorough and efficient. Such work, moreover, need not entail striking a physical blow or pulling an actual trigger. The Holocaust's "desk murderers"—professionals who established policies, gave orders, and implemented decisions with strokes of a pen—were a necessary condition for the "final solution." No task for post-Holocaust ethics is more important than alerting ourselves to, and holding ourselves responsible for, abuses of professional expertise. In that regard, if we want to know whether we are on the right or wrong track, individually or collectively, we can help to hold ourselves responsible by asking: Would action like mine, would policies like ours, have tended to help or harm the Holocaust's victims? For post-Holocaust ethics, helping or harming those in need measures the difference between right and wrong.

Peter Haas, one of the contributors to this book, is the source of the third paradigm that Pollefeyt assesses. Pollefeyt ultimately dissents from Haas's belief that the Nazis had what really deserves to be called an ethic. He notes that even Haas himself seems uneasy about the implications of his own position, for Haas distinguishes between an *ethic* and *morality*, a differentiation intended to keep the Holo-

caust from being morally permissible even if that genocide was en-
joined by the Nazi ethic. Pollefeyt worries that Haas's outlook lacks
the resources necessary to defend this crucial distinction. If Haas's
interpretation of the Holocaust discloses that we have a plurality of
conflicting ethical systems, and that there is, as Pollefeyt says, "no
Archimedean point from which all ethical systems could be evaluated," then Pollefeyt thinks that Haas cannot provide "any real criteria by which to judge Nazism as immoral." One outcome is a relativism in which might determines right.

Pollefeyt clearly appreciates the force of Haas's perspective. Nazism did have ideals. It differentiated between good and evil, right
and wrong, duty and irresponsibility. Its beliefs, plus the power that
backed them up, prepared Germans by the millions to kill and die
for causes that many of them deemed worthy of loyalty. Thus, the
appeal of the Nazi ethic offers an important perspective because it
helps to show why so many Germans were prepared to follow Hitler
into genocidal warfare. Nevertheless, Pollefeyt is rightly skeptical
about the ethics of the Nazi ethic, and he prefers to emphasize the
Nazis' perversion of ethics, which they used to put a legitimating,
but fundamentally false, moral gloss on what was, in fact, a murder-
ously immoral political ideology.

In addition to showing that the vocabulary of ethics can be used
to undermine ethics and to legitimate immorality, the most morally
corrosive effect of the Holocaust is arguably that the devastation it
unleashed calls into question the status—especially the functional
status—of moral claims about right and wrong. The Nazis were losing World War II when Himmler spoke at Poznan, but it may be too
easy to say simply that they lost because they were morally wrong.
Absent military force from outside, the Third Reich probably would
not have been toppled from within and would have triumphed instead. Even before that regime was crushed militarily, its destructive
might all but destroyed European Jewish life. True, there was German resistance to Hitler and along with the military force that stopped
Nazism this opposition was buttressed by moral sensibilities at odds
with the Nazi ethic. Nevertheless, no post-Holocaust ethic can easily dismiss the question, "What if the Nazis had won?" For reasons
related to that question, Pollefeyt seeks a moral standpoint—not nec-

essarily an Archimedean point, but a kind of foundation nonetheless—from which to say with confidence that the Nazis really were fundamentally wrong and that their "ethic" was thoroughly immoral.

At first, Pollefeyt's standpoint looks like a fourth paradigm, but it is not, because his outlook is less an attempt to explain why or how the Holocaust happened and more an effort to pay attention to moral content that is as fragile as it is basic. Pollefeyt seems not to embrace a moral philosophy that guarantees the triumph of right over wrong—at least not in this world. Instead, showing respect for the philosophy of Emmanuel Levinas, Pollefeyt appeals to "the face of the other," which, he believes, "inherently and continually challenges our human closedness." Above all, he thinks, Nazism preached and enacted a death-dealing closedness. Its obsession to eliminate everything that failed to conform to Nazi ideals testifies to that.

The past cannot be undone, any more than the nature of the future is guaranteed, but Pollefeyt suggests that post-Holocaust ethics may succeed or fail depending on its ability to call attention to the moral quality of the human face. Seen ethically, the face calls out for respect, help, and love. It beckons us to enact our humanity accordingly. For these reasons, it can make sense to say that the face is created in the image of God.

Didier Pollefeyt wants these sensibilities to govern post-Holocaust ethics. His view appeals to me, but because his essay got me thinking about Heinrich Himmler, the question I most want to ask him is this: What would it have taken to make "the face of the other" appeal to Himmler in the way that Pollefeyt wants it to appeal to us in post-Holocaust ethics? This challenge is one that post-Holocaust ethics must think about if it is to be successful. That claim is true not simply because the Holocaust could have been prevented if leaders like Himmler had seen the face of the other in a different light than he did. That claim is also true because Himmler could not have been the architect of genocide unless countless others—and not only Germans and their collaborators—were unmoved by human faces that reveal what cruelty, injustice, and killing do.

If Heinrich Himmler could have been moved by the face of the other, then plenty of other people might have been moved in better ways, too. In that case, even if Himmler might still have harbored murderous antisemitic thoughts, his speech at Poznan and the Holocaust it celebrated would not have taken place.

Notes

[1]My account of Himmler's speech is drawn from Michael Berenbaum, ed. *Witness to the Holocaust* (New York: HarperCollins, 1997), 172-80.

[2]See Richard Breitman, *The Architect of Genocide: Himmler and the Final Solution* (Hanover, NH: Brandeis University Press, 1991).

[3]Ibid., 242.

[4]Cited in Berenbaum, *Witness to the Holocaust*, 176.

[5]Breitman, *The Architect of Genocide*, 242.

[6]Elie Wiesel, "Exile and the Human Condition," in *Against Silence: The Voice and Vision of Elie Wiesel*, ed. Irving Abrahamson (New York: Holocaust Library, 1985), 1:183.

Pollefeyt's Response to Critiques

In his response to my essay, David Hirsch writes: "Auschwitz still has not yielded its secrets. But why should a Christian balk at mystery? For two millennia, Christian religions have based their existence on mystery: the three-personed God, the resurrection, and transubstantiation." Herein perhaps lies the biggest difference between Hirsch's approach and mine. In my view, Auschwitz is not a mystery, at least not in the profound sense of mystery that is at the heart of (Jewish or Christian) faith. In contrast to the mysteries of sacraments, incarnation, and resurrection, I see no divinity at work in Auschwitz. What I see in Auschwitz is simply the work of ordinary human beings and thus the radical negation of every kind of mystery in the religious sense of the word. I do not seek to make from Auschwitz a new kind of religion, some unique anti-religion, or even a new mystical foundation for post-Holocaust Jewish or Christian identity. Indeed, Hitler does not deserve that outcome. To use the concepts of Gabriel Marcel, for me as a Christian ethicist, Auschwitz is more a "problem," first and foremost a *Christian* problem, than a "mystery." Of course, we will never be able to explain the Holocaust fully, not because Auschwitz is a sacral mystery but because of the magnitude, complexity, and twisted quality of this human phenomenon. Therefore, I think we are in need of as many complementary paradigmatic approaches to the Holocaust as possible. Only then can we do justice, as much as is possible, to the extraordinary and finally inexplicable evil character of this event.

Post-Holocaust ethics will have its best chances to work in a pluralistic, multidisciplinary, interfaith setting. Ethicists need to listen to victims, scientists, and perpetrators, even if the ethical value of these perspectives is very different. Each of these viewpoints has its own contribution to offer, and *each* perspective also has its own limits: the perspective of the victims (first paradigm) because the victims are (were) understandably confined within a limited perspective formed by the brutality they experienced and their desire to communicate a (moral) message, which makes their interpretation selective; the scientific (second paradigm) because of its reductionistic methodology; the viewpoint of the perpetrators (third paradigm) because of its self-defensive character.

Roth's response asks what interpretative paradigm would best fit the life and career of Heinrich Himmler. Even in the case of the architect of Nazi genocide, I think that every paradigm has relevant things to say. Himmler's role as *Reichsführer* of the SS during the Second World War makes him, like Eichmann, very suitable for being characterized as "the evil genius of the Third Reich."[1] And I agree with Hirsch that the higher we climb in the Nazi hierarchy, the more the first paradigm is relevant (and the third paradigm less so). Nevertheless, it is well-known that Himmler became sick when he visited Auschwitz,[2] that he was obsessed by the *idée fixe* that the mass destruction had to be carried out quickly and soberly, and that he even gave instructions to punish perpetrators who found pleasure in torturing the victims.[3] These elements stand in clear contradiction to Patterson's diabolizing statement that the Nazis were selected on the basis of their willingness "to act in a monstrously evil manner." While Patterson is correct when he mentions that the executions happened as standard procedures in accord with Himmler's will, I take those factors as an argument in support of functionalism and the second paradigm. In that paradigm, one will also emphasize Himmler's "colorlessness." Historian Joachim Fest, for example, characterized Himmler as "utterly mediocre" and "indistinguishable from the commonplace by any special trait of character." Hannah Arendt described Himmler similarly in her *Origins of Totalitarianism*. In this approach, one will show, for example, how Himmler grew up in a very tense, paternalistic family structure.[4] The third paradigm will bring to light the ethical character of the person and acts of Himmler, whose motto was "my honor is called truth" (*Meine Ehre heißt Treue*). A classic example of the third paradigm is Himmler's speech to the SS in Poznan in October 1943, where he spoke about the morality of the SS.[5] In the third paradigm, one will take the moral framework seriously,[6] while in the first paradigm such ethical statements will be seen as moral hypocrisy, and in the second paradigm as the expression of an inability to think.

After studying Peter Haas's critique, I still believe there is a fundamental difference between the second and third paradigms. First, even though he takes functionalism into account—it is central in the second paradigm—I consider his approach to be primarily intentionalistic. The difference with the first paradigm, however, is that in Haas's view the Nazis were intentionally working towards a *good*, while in the first paradigm the Nazis are considered to be working toward evil for evil's sake. Nazism was a struggle for the good. The Nazis had intentions, in Haas's view *good* intentions (for them). Second, an important difference between the second paradigm (Arendt) and Haas's paradigmatic approach is that his anthropology is—in my view—not as optimistic as Arendt's but ultimately much more deterministic. In Haas's interpretation, I see no real possibility to escape the ethical framework in which people live. In Arendt's analysis, however, she holds Eichmann responsible for his behavior, because he had perverted the dialogue with himself. In Haas's theory, as I have argued in my response to his essay in this volume, I see no ground for such condemnation. The impact of the "Nazi ethic" was overwhelming, and there was no real possibility to escape once it was in power. In this sense, relativism is indeed the problem of the third paradigm but not of the second paradigm. If there is an ethical point of reference for criticizing Nazism in Haas's view, as is in Arendt's, then it would be completely inappropriate to speak, as he does, about Nazi *ethics*.

Roth's crucial question, of course, is which picture of Himmler, and of Nazism in general, is closest to reality. The first paradigm will (too) strongly identify evil act and actor. The second and third paradigms will (too) clearly separate evil act and actor. Thus, the principal question of post-Holocaust ethics is how to understand the complex relation between the object of evil (evil acts) and the subject of evil (evildoers). It is true, as Haas claims, that my approach becomes meta-normative here, introducing "openness" (which implies distance between act and actor) as a meta-value. The presupposition of my approach to post-Holocaust ethics is that every (normal) human being, in being *human*, is structurally capable of developing an openness in himself or herself toward the vulnerability of the other. Consequently, I begin with an optimistic (theological) anthropology: every human being is capable of experiencing good and evil, or even stronger, each person discovers himself or herself as ethical, as connected with the good, even before he or she has consciously chosen good or evil. This ethical capacity of human beings can be selectively neutralized by a modern society or manipulated by a (democratic or totalitarian) society, but even then the basic connection with the good remains, if only in a perverted way. This outlook implies that human beings cannot choose evil for evil's sake, or directly assault the Good as such, as Patterson claims. Only monsters can assault the Good. If human beings do (even monstrous) evil, they always try to do it in the name of one or another (particular or, at times, pseudo) good (for example, the *Volk*, *Lebensraum*, genetic purity). As perverted as it was, killing the Jews was *for the Nazis* not an assault on the Good as such, but an assault (thoroughly corrupted though it was) on Evil. For me, therefore, the Holocaust is not simply about immorality but particularly about the vulnerability and the manipulability of ethics. Ethics as an openness to the vulnerability of the other can so easily become a closed system of self-justification, invulnerable to the sufferings it produces.

In other words, evil always happens with a form of closedness, a moment wherein one makes oneself invulnerable or blind to the real other. This daily process is complex. It combines activity and passivity, wicked will and anxiety, indifference and bad faith, individual responsibility and collective power. The Nazi genocide embodied these elements. The perpetrators closed themselves off from the evil effects of their own acts. The *Einsatzgruppen*, for example, did so by drunkenness. Modern techniques (extermination camps) made the suffering of the victims more or less invisible. In this regard, Robert Jay Lifton rightly speaks about the phenomenon of "doubling." The case of Dr. Kremer, mentioned by David Hirsch as an illustration of monstrosity, is in my view a typical example of such "doubling." This medical officer of the SS in Auschwitz describes on the same page of his diary a *Sonderaktion* (killing operation) and the menu of his lunch. In doubling, the perpetrator builds a psychic screen between himself or herself and evil. Of course, the perpetrator always is (to a certain degree) responsible for the self-built screen and for the manipulative ethical argumentations one develops to establish and maintain the doubling. Underlying this position is the traditional notion of evil as corruption of the good. In doubling, the second self (doing evil) depends upon a first self (which is oriented toward the good). The second self receives its legitimation from the first self, while at the same time it manipulates and perverts the first self. As such, evil is always parasitic upon the good and cannot exist apart from it. Even if evil deceives and betrays that good, individually and collectively, it is never able to assault directly the Good as such.

This perspective also implies, in my view, that in theory nothing is finally capable of destroying completely and definitively a human being's orientation towards the Good, even if people (perpetrators) are very deeply doubled and closed. In this regard, Roth asks a crucial question: "Could Himmler see the face of the other in the Jew?" I would like to put forward the following hypothetical answer: if we could have put Himmler on a psychoanalyst's couch every week for a year during the war, searching in depth all his manipulations, his problematic education, his perverted post-Christian sexual life, his blind spots, his bad faith, his lust for power, and his self-deception, he could have possibly re-discovered his own vulnerability for the face of the Jewish other. A good starting point for such therapy would be the previously mentioned fact that he became ill visiting Auschwitz. This response would also be my answer to Haas's asking what argument could lead "the truly thoughtful and intelligent Nazi" to reconsider his or her commitments. I would argue that it is not a question of arguments but of a context (as in psychoanalysis) beyond a pure morality of condemnation, typical for Nazi ethics, and its imitations in diabolization. My point is precisely that a "truly thoughtful Nazi" simply did not, indeed could not, exist.

Haas argues that this appeal to openness is still within a paradigm of moral understanding. Even if I believe that this openness is not merely "our" paradigm but a universal human experience (recognized today by appeals to human rights), it is also true that this openness probably would have been completely powerless in confronting Nazism. Himmler would never have been prepared to open himself in psychotherapy, or in daily life, for the Jew. This realization points to what I would call a sometimes inescapable hermeneutical circle: for someone to become open already presupposes a form of openness. Theories of diabolization emphasize a version of this idea, for they would stress how the perpetrators lost their openness. The problem with diabolization, however, is that it forgets, with its very intentionalistic view, the genesis and the context of this closedness. It confuses ethics (*de facto* closedness) with anthropology (the possibility of openness) and is so sure about its diagnosis that it risks eliminating in advance, in principle and in general, the possibility of a change from closedness to openness.

Here Grob's most significant question is very relevant: "How can we be certain that being open to an other will result in the manifestation of ethics?" Since ethics is not a physical science, working with cause and effect, we can never be sure. We should not be naive in this regard: openness in itself does not automatically lead to ethics. Because openness is a necessary, but insufficient, condition for an ethics, openness can indeed be easily abused. Consequently, I speak about openness in a *qualified* way: we should not be open to every other, but only to "*positive* alterities." Otherwise, we would use a purely formal concept of openness and it could result in a "lazy tolerance" that would lend comfort, for example, to Holocaust deniers. As Ricoeur puts it: the intolerance of the other is the limit of my own tolerance. Or, in my own words I would say that the closedness of the other is the limit to my own openness for this other. This point brings me to the complex relation between power and ethics. "What if the Nazis had won?" Roth asks. The answer is that the possibility of openness would have been lost for a very long time (but not necessarily forever). In history, there can be no guaranteed eschatology of the Good (or of Evil).

Because of this vulnerability of ethics, I would not dare to say as confidently as Patterson that I myself would never be capable — under specific, pressing historical, social and individual circumstances — to work in the crematoria of an extermination camp. I do know, however, that there were people who did not become perpetrators but rescuers instead. I would not, however, follow Patterson in speaking of the Righteous Gentiles as "angelic" saviors. Just as the perpetrators were not demons, the rescuers were not angels. Both were human beings. The testimonies of most Righteous Gentiles make clear that just as the perpetrators did not choose *demonically* for pure Evil, the rescuers did not choose *heroically* for pure Good. They did small acts of daily goodness, in a complex constellation of courage and fear, altruism and egoism, choice and fate, decision and hesitation, circumstance and moral conviction. In this way, they created, step-by-step, a brilliant example of humanity. Study of the rescuers makes clear that post-Holocaust ethics must transcend the moralistic scheme of "saints and sinners." Post-Holocaust ethics should not focus primarily upon the demonic finality of Nazi cruelties, nor on the heroic resistance against it. First and foremost, it should deal with the complex genesis of good and evil, the daily steps that eventually lead to demonic or heroic acts, steps that ultimately bring each of us to be moral or immoral human beings.

Notes

[1] W. Frischauer, *Himmler: The Evil Genius of the Third Reich* (Boston: Beacon Press, 1953).

[2] See Herman Langbein, *Hommes et femmes à Auschwitz* (Paris: Fayard, 1975), 175.

[3] F. E. Katz, *Ordinary People and Extraordinary Evil* (New York: State University of New York Press, 1993), 35.

[4] H. Höhne, *Der Orden unter dem Totenkopf* (Doornik: Casterman, 1968), 35.

[5] F. Bayle, *Psychologie et éthique du national-socialisme: Etudes anthropologique des dirigeants S.S.* (Paris: Press Universitaires de France, 1953), 436: "Most of us know what it means to see a hundred corpses together, or five hundred, or a thousand. To have endured this, and to have remained decent, with some exceptions of human failure, has made us strong.…In general, we can say that we have carried out this difficult task for our people. And we have not known harm to our inner self, of our soul, of our character."

[6] J. Bernauer, " Nazi Ethics: On Heinrich Himmler and the Origins of New Moral Careers," in *Remembering for the Future*, ed. Yehuda Bauer et al. (Oxford: Pergamon Press, 1988), 2071-82.

CHAPTER SIX

Returning Home: Reflections on Post-Holocaust Ethics

John K. Roth

> ...Now we are returning home...
> —Calel Perechodnik, *Am I a Murderer?*

On August 20, 1942, a Polish Jew named Calel Perechodnik returned home. This fact is known because Perechodnik recorded it in the writing that he began to do on May 7, 1943. Sheltered at the time by a Polish woman in Warsaw, the 26-year-old engineer would spend the next 105 days producing a remarkable document that is at once a diary, memoir, and confession rooted in the Holocaust.

Shortly before Perechodnik died in 1944, he entrusted his reflections to a Polish friend. The manuscript survived, but it was forgotten and virtually unknown in the United States until Frank Fox's translation appeared in 1996.[1] Charged with ethical issues, Perechodnik's testament is of special significance because he was a Jewish ghetto policeman in Otwock, a Polish town near Warsaw. While that role was not his chosen profession, it was a part that he decided to play in February 1941—not knowing all that would soon be required of him.

Already the German occupiers of his native Poland had forced Perechodnik, his family, and millions of other Polish Jews into wretched ghettos. "Seeing that the war was not coming to an end and in order to be free from the roundup for labor camps" Perechodnik would write, "I entered the ranks of the Ghetto Polizei."[2]

When Calel Perechodnik returned home on August 20, 1942, he knew in ways that can scarcely be imagined how optimistic, mistaken, fateful, and deadly even his most realistic assumptions had been. His decision to join what the Germans called the *Ordnungsdienst* (Order Service) had not only required Perechodnik to assist them in the destruction of the European Jews but also implicated him, however unintentionally, in the deportation of his own wife and child to the gas chambers at Treblinka on August 19, 1942. Perechodnik's testament says that he returned home on August 20, but his words—expressing what his experience meant—indicate that "home" could never be a reality for him again.

What about the century, the world, that led Calel Perechodnik to the choices and consequences that were his? Are such times and places ones in which we feel—casually, comfortably, confidently—at home? Or does Calel Perechodnik's *Am I a Murderer?* make it impossible to return home without the company of profoundly disturbing questions that rightly make us wonder about our comfort and essentially interrupt our confidence as a new century begins, one that may prove even more devastating than the bloody twentieth?

The disturbing questions that Perechodnik's testament provokes can concentrate on him and his decisions. This essay, however, focuses its attention differently because it is too easy to cast blame on Perechodnik and thereby to miss the point that most deserves consideration: a genocidal Nazi state created the circumstances in which the intention was that all Jews, including Perechodnik, should die. By showing how the destruction process capitalized on a cunning that enticed and then required Jews to participate in the annihilation of their own people, Perechodnik's case serves best as a point of departure to reveal, first, how calculated and systematic the Holocaust turned out to be and, second, how far those facts reach to question some of our fondest assumptions about moral judgments and ethical norms. Thus, with the stage set by the multifaceted tragedy of Calel Perechodnik's case, reflect on some of the fundamental moral dilemmas that confront humankind, and especially us Americans, as we try to return home in a post-Holocaust world.

Calling their regime the Third Reich, Adolf Hitler and his Nazi Party ruled Germany from 1933 to 1945. The Holocaust happened during those years. It was Nazi Germany's planned total destruction of the European Jews and the actual murder of nearly six million of them, including about 1.5 million children under age fifteen. This genocidal campaign—the most systematic, bureaucratic, and unrelenting the world has seen—also destroyed millions of non-Jewish civilians. They included Roma and Sinti (Gypsies), Slavs, Jehovah's Witnesses, Freemasons, homosexuals, the mentally retarded, physically handicapped and insane. Those people, the Nazis believed, posed a threat to the Third Reich's racial purity that approached, though it could never equal, the one posed by Jews.

Nazi Germany's system of concentration camps, ghettos, murder squadrons, and killing centers took more than twelve million defenseless human lives. While not every Nazi victim was Jewish, the Nazi intent was to rid Europe, if not the world, of Jews. Hitler went far in meeting that goal. Vast numbers of the Jewish victims came from Poland—Calel Perechodnik and his family among them—where the German annihilation took ninety percent of that country's three million Jews. Located in that place, Auschwitz-Birkenau was the largest Nazi killing center. More than one million Jews were gassed there. Although Europe's Jews resisted the onslaught as best they could, by the time Germany surrendered in early May 1945, two-thirds of the European Jews—and about one-third of the Jews worldwide—were dead.

One of the most disturbing moral issues posed by the Holocaust is summed up in *The Cunning of History*, a short but hardly sweet book by Richard L. Rubenstein. It hits hard by contending that "the Holocaust bears witness to *the advance of civilization*."[3] To begin to see how that proposition bears on Calel Perechodnik's case and how that assertion is charged with ominous portents for the future as well, consider that in 1933, the year when Hitler took power in Germany, the Chicago World's Fair celebrated what its promoters optimistically acclaimed as "A Century of Progress." As *The Cunning of History* points out, the fair's theme was expressed in a slogan: "Science Explores; Technology Executes; Mankind Conforms."[4] Cast in those terms, the Holocaust not only bears witness to the tragically cunning and ironic elements of "progress" but also delivers a warning about what could—but ought not—lie ahead for humanity.

The "final solution" was symptomatic of the modern state's perennial temptation to destroy people who are regarded as undesirable, superfluous, or unwanted because of their religion, race, politics, ethnicity, or economic redundancy. The Nazis identified what they took to be a practical problem: the need to eliminate the Jews and other so-called racial inferiors from their midst. Then they moved to solve it. Consequently, the Holocaust did not result from spontaneous, irrational outbursts of random violence. Nor was the "final solution" a bizarre historical anomaly. It was instead a state-sponsored program of population riddance made possible by modern planning and the best technology available at the time.

Significantly the Holocaust did not occur until the mid-twentieth century, but conditions necessary, though not sufficient, to produce it were forming centuries before. Decisive in that process was Christian anti-Judaism and its demonization of the Jew. For example, Rubenstein appraises the Christian New Testament correctly in his *After Auschwitz* when he writes that "no other religion is as horribly defamed in the classic literature of a rival tradition as is Judaism."[5] The reason for that defamation was the Christian belief that the Jews were, as Rubenstein puts it, "the God-bearing and the God-murdering people *par excellence*."[6] Jesus, the incarnation of God according to Christian tradition, was one of the Jewish people, but the Christian telling of this story depicted the Jews as collectively responsible for his crucifixion and thus for rejecting God through deicide, the most heinous crime of all. Christian contempt for Jews was advanced further by the belief that the dispersion of the Jews from their traditional homeland after the Judeo-Roman War and the Fall of Jerusalem in 70 C.E.—and perhaps all of their subsequent misfortune—was God's punishment for their failure to see the light. The effect of this centuries-old tradition was, as Rubenstein says, "to cast them [the Jews] out of any common universe of moral obligation with the Christians among whom they were domiciled. In times of acute social stress, it had the practical effect of decriminalizing any assault visited upon them."[7] Building on a long history that went beyond religious to racist antisemitism, the assaults reached their zenith as Nazi Germany became a genocidal state.

When we think of the dilemmas that Calel Perechodnik and his family confronted in wartime Poland, it is crucial to understand that the Nazis' antisemitic racism eventually entailed a destruction process that required and received cooperation from every sector of German society. On the whole, moreover, the Nazi killers and those Germans who aided and abetted them directly—or indirectly as bystanders—were civilized people from a society that was scientifically advanced, technologically competent, culturally sophisticated, efficiently organized, and even religiously devout. Those people were, as Holocaust scholar Michael Berenbaum has cogently observed, "both ordinary and extraordinary, a cross section of the men and women of Germany, its allies, and their collaborators as well as the best and the brightest."[8]

Some Germans and members of populations allied with the Nazis resisted Hitler and would not belong in the following catalog, but they were still exceptions to prove the rule that there were, for example, pastors and priests who led their churches in welcoming Nazification and the segregation of Jews it entailed. In addition, teachers and writers helped to till the soil where Hitler's racist antisemitism took root. Their students and readers reaped the wasteful harvest. Lawyers drafted and judges enforced the laws that isolated Jews and set them up for the kill. Government and church personnel provided birth records to document who was Jewish and who was not. Other workers entered such information into state-of-the-art data processing machines. University administrators curtailed admissions for Jewish students and dismissed Jewish faculty members. Bureaucrats in the Finance Ministry handled confiscations of Jewish wealth and property. Postal officials delivered mail about definition and expropriation, denaturalization and deportation.

Driven by their biomedical visions, physicians were among the first to experiment with the gassing of "lives unworthy of life." Scientists performed research and tested their racial theories on those branded sub- or non-human by German science. Business executives found that Nazi concentration camps could provide cheap labor; they worked people to death, turning the Nazi motto, *Arbeit macht frei* (Work makes one free), into a mocking truth. Radio performers were joined by artists such as the gifted film director, Leni Riefenstahl, to broadcast and screen the polished propaganda that made Hitler's policies persuasive to so many. Railroad personnel drove the trains that transported Jews to death, while other officials took charge of the billing arrangements for this service. Factory workers modified trucks so that they became deadly gas vans; city policemen became members of squadrons that made mass murder of Jews their specialty. Meanwhile, stockholders made profits from firms that supplied Zyklon B to gas people and that built crematoriums to burn the corpses.

It is instructive to consider the crematorium builders in more detail when Richard Rubenstein argues that the Holocaust is symptomatic of an ironic advance of civilization, for his thesis gets telling support from "Engineers of Death," which is the title of a *New York Times* article that has reminded me of Rubenstein's contention ever since that newspaper account by Gerald Fleming came to my attention several years ago. A noted historian, Fleming has also written *Hitler and the Final Solution.* That important book tries to identify when the decision was made to destroy the European Jews by mass murder, a puzzle that persists because no written order by Hitler seems to exist. What occasioned Fleming's writing in the *New York Times*, however, was a Holocaust puzzle of a different kind.

Since the collapse of the Soviet Union at the end of the Cold War, scholars have had better access to historical documents in Moscow. Research about World War II and the Holocaust in particular has benefited from that accessibility. For some time, Fleming had been studying the Auschwitz Central Building Authority records that were captured by Soviet troops and stored in Soviet archives. In May 1993, his searching led him to File 17/9 of the Red Army's intelligence branch. Previously off limits to historians from the West, this file contained information about four senior engineers who had worked for a German firm named Topf und Söhne. It was known that these men had been arrested by the Soviets in 1946, but Western intelligence lost track of them after that.

Topf had been manufacturing cremation furnaces for civilian use since 1912. That fact was less than noteworthy, but the puzzle that eventually took Fleming to File 17/9 involved another piece of information that was much more significant. Nameplates on the crematorium furnaces in Nazi concentration camps at Buchenwald,

Dachau, Mauthausen, Gross-Rosen, and Birkenau (the main killing center at Auschwitz) showed that they, too, were Topf products.

At the war's end, Kurt Prüfer, a specialist in furnace construction
and one of Topf's senior engineers, had been interrogated by the
American Third Army. He persuaded his interrogators that the concentration camp crematoriums had existed for health reasons only.
The Americans released him. The Red Army, however, could document another story. Although German orders in late November 1944
called for the destruction of equipment and records that would im-
plicate Auschwitz-Birkenau as a death factory, the enterprise was simply too vast to cover up. When the Red Army liberated that place
two months later, the massive evidence included, in Fleming's words,
details about "the construction of the technology of mass death, complete with the precise costs of crematoriums and calculations of the
number of corpses each could incinerate in a day."[9] Well beyond
documenting the Red Army's arrest of Prüfer and three of his colleagues in Erfurt, Germany, on March 4, 1946, File 17/9 contained
transcripts of the revealing interviews that interrogators had conducted with Prüfer and his associates.

At Auschwitz-Birkenau the *Krema*, as they were sometimes called
in German, became full-fledged installations of mass death.[10] Especially given the constraints on wartime building projects, the construction of the four carefully-planned units at Birkenau took time.
Topf was only one of eleven civilian companies needed to produce
them. Utilizing prisoner labor as much as possible, the building began in the summer of 1942, but it was nearly a year before the last
facility was operational. Each included an undressing room, a gas
chamber, and a room containing Topf's incineration ovens. These
lethal places were designed to dispatch thousands of people per day.
Even so, Prüfer told his Red Army interrogators, "the [crematorium]
bricks were damaged after six months because the strain on the furnaces was colossal." Periodic malfunctions notwithstanding, the gassing and burning went on and on.

"From 1940 to 1944," Prüfer went on to tell his captors, "twenty
crematoriums for concentration camps were built under my direction." His work took him to Auschwitz five times; he knew that "innocent human beings were being liquidated" there. In addition to

excerpts from the Red Army's interviews with Prüfer, Fleming's article contains parts of the depositions taken from one of Prüfer's superiors, Fritz Sander, a crematorium ventilation specialist whose work for Topf took him to Auschwitz three times, often in tandem with Prüfer. In late 1942, Sander submitted plans to "improve" what was happening at Auschwitz-Birkenau. He envisioned a crematorium with even higher capacity than those already planned for installation there. To Sander's dismay, his project was not accepted. It would have used "the conveyer belt principle," he explained. "That is to say, the corpses must be brought to the incineration furnaces without interruption."

Apparently without remorse or apology, Sander admitted his knowledge of the mass murder at Auschwitz. "I was a German engineer and key member of the Topf works," he reasoned on March 7, 1946. "I saw it as my duty to apply my specialist knowledge in this way in order to help Germany win the war, just as an aircraft construction engineer builds airplanes in wartime, which are also connected with the destruction of human beings." Less than three weeks later, Sander died in Red Army custody, the victim of a heart attack. Having been sentenced to "25 years deprivation of liberty," Prüfer died of a brain hemorrhage on October 24, 1952.

As Fleming's "Engineers of Death" suggests, short of Germany's military defeat by the Allies, no other constraints—social or political, moral or religious—were sufficient to stop the "final solution." That fact led to Calel's Perechodnik's fateful decisions. It also led Richard Rubenstein to write *The Cunning of History*. In addition, and Perechodnik would probably join him if he could—that same fact made Rubenstein wonder about the truths that Thomas Jefferson taught Americans to hold "self-evident."

None of those truths is more crucial than the claim that persons are "endowed by their Creator with certain unalienable Rights." Those rights, Jefferson believed, are not merely legal privileges that people grant to each other as they please. Rather, his philosophy held, reason—rightly used—shows that such rights are "natural." Part and parcel of what is meant by *human* existence, they belong equally to all humanity and presumably cannot be violated with impunity. Nonetheless, the sense in which rights are unalienable—inviolable,

absolute, unassailable, inherent—is an elusive part of Jefferson's Declaration, for it also states that "to secure these rights, Governments
are instituted among Men." Apparently unalienable rights are not
invulnerable; but if they are not invulnerable, then in what way are
they unalienable?

One answer could be that what *is* and what *ought to be* are often
not the same, and reason can make the distinction. To speak of unalienable rights, therefore, is to speak of conditions of existence so
basic that they ought never to be abrogated. Persuasive though it
may be, such reasoning may still give too little comfort. As Calel
Perechodnik knew all-too-well, rights to life, liberty, and the pursuit
of happiness are qualified repeatedly. But even more radically,
Auschwitz questions the *functional* status of unalienable rights. In
Rubenstein's words, the Holocaust, genocide, and related instances
of state-sponsored population elimination suggest that "there are
absolutely no limits to the degradation and assault the managers and
technicians of violence can inflict upon men and women who lack
the power of effective resistance."[11]

True, nearly everyone says that certain rights must not be usurped.
Still, if those rights are violated completely and all too often with
impunity—and Perechodnik's cases shows that they can be and are—
how can they convincingly be called "natural" or "unalienable"? Is
that not one more idealistic illusion, another instance of how humanistic optimism obscures reality? Rubenstein's proposition is debatable—it should be on the agenda especially when we Americans
talk about ethics—but he contends that greater credibility is found
when one concludes that "*rights do not belong to men by nature.* To
the extent that men have rights, they have them only as members of
the polis, the political community....Outside of the polis there are
no inborn restraints on the human exercise of destructive power."[12]

A contemporary of Calel Perechodnik—albeit one who made
very different choices was an Austrian Jew named Hans Maier. Like
Perechodnik, Maier knew too well whereof Richard Rubenstein
speaks. Born on October 31, 1912, the only child of a Catholic mother
and a Jewish father, more than anything else he thought of himself
as Austrian, not least because his father's family had lived in that
country since the seventeenth century. Hans Maier, however, lived

in the twentieth century, and so it was that in the autumn of 1935 he studied a newspaper in a Viennese coffeehouse. The Nuremberg Laws had just been promulgated in Nazi Germany. Maier's reading made him see — unmistakably — the fatal interdependence of all human actions. Even if he did not think of himself as Jewish, the Nazis' definitions meant that the cunning of history had given him that identity nonetheless. By identifying him as a Jew, Maier would write later on, Nazi power made him "a dead man on leave, someone to be murdered, who only by chance was not yet where he properly belonged."[13]

When Nazi Germany occupied Austria in March 1938, Maier drew his conclusions. Fleeing his native land for Belgium, he joined the Resistance after that country fell to the Third Reich in 1940. Arrested by Nazi police in 1943, Maier was sent to Auschwitz and then to Bergen-Belsen where he was liberated in 1945. Eventually taking the name Jean Améry, by which he is remembered, this philosopher waited twenty years before breaking his silence about the Holocaust. When Améry did decide to write, the result was a series of remarkable essays about his experience. In English they appear in a volume entitled *At the Mind's Limits: Contemplations by a Survivor on Auschwitz and Its Realities*. One is simply entitled "Torture."

Torture drove Améry to the following observation: "The expectation of help, the certainty of help," he wrote, "is indeed one of the fundamental experiences of human beings." Thus, the gravest loss produced by the Holocaust, Améry went on to suggest, was that it destroyed what he called "trust in the world,…the certainty that by reason of written or unwritten social contracts the other person will spare me — more precisely stated, that he will respect my physical, and with it also my metaphysical, being."[14]

Jean Améry would join Calel Perechodnik and Richard Rubenstein to interrogate American affirmations about unalienable rights. "Every morning when I get up," Améry wrote, "I can read the Auschwitz number on my forearm…. Every day anew I lose my trust in the world….Declarations of human rights, democratic constitutions, the free world and the free press, nothing," he went on to say, "can again lull me into the slumber of security from which I awoke in 1935."[15]

Far from scorning the human dignity that those institutions claim to honor, Améry yearned for the right to live, which he equated with dignity itself. His experiences, however, taught him that "it is certainly true that dignity can be bestowed only by society, whether it be the dignity of some office, a professional or, very generally speaking, civil dignity; and the merely individual, subjective claim ('I am a human being and as such I have my dignity, no matter what you may do or say!') is an empty academic game, or madness."[16]

Lucidity, believed Améry, demanded the recognition of this reality, but lucidity did not end there. "What happened, happened," he wrote. "But *that* it happened cannot be so easily accepted."[17] So lucidity also entailed rebellion against power that would make anyone "a dead man on leave." Unfortunately, it must also be acknowledged that Améry's hopes for such protest were less than optimistic. On October 17, 1978, he took leave and became a dead man by his own hand.

Améry's testimony questions assumptions that have long been at the heart of American understandings. They include beliefs that the most basic human rights are a gift of God and that nature and reason testify to a universal moral structure which underwrites them. But what if we live in the time of the death of God? What if there is no God? What if nature is amoral? Granting that reason can make critical distinctions between what *is* and what *ought to be*, what if reason also insists that the most telling truth of all is that history is what G. W. F. Hegel, the nineteenth-century German philosopher, called it: a slaughter bench, a realm where unalienable rights are hardly worth the paper they are written on — unless political might ensures them.

Such questions have crossed American minds in the past, but in a post-Holocaust age they cross-examine American optimism more severely than before. For it is no longer clear that anything but human power does secure a person's rights, and, if rights depend on human power alone, then they may well be natural and unalienable in name only. In such circumstances, to call rights unalienable may still be a legitimate rhetorical device, perhaps buttressed by religious discourse, to muster consensus that certain privileges and prerogatives must not be taken away. No doubt the idea of unalienable rights functions — and will continue to do so — precisely in that way as an ingredient in American experience. But ideas do not necessarily correspond to facts any more than dreams do to waking life. It appears increasingly that rights are functionally unalienable—which may be what counts most in the long and short of it—only within a state that will successfully defend and honor them as such.

As an American who studies and teaches about the Holocaust, my current research on post-Holocaust ethics is driven by what I call "Rubenstein's Dilemma." Driven home by the powerful Holocaust oppression that ruined the lives of Calel Perechodnik, Jean Améry, and millions of others, this dilemma is important for every person and for every community, but it is especially provocative for us Americans, who have a tradition that speaks of "self-evident" truths about "unalienable rights" to life, liberty, and the pursuit of happiness.

The Holocaust's evil appears to be so overwhelming that it forms an ultimate refutation of moral relativism. No one, it seems, could encounter Auschwitz and deny that there is a fundamental and objective difference between right and wrong. Nevertheless, the "final solution" paradoxically calls into question the practical status of moral norms. Thus, the dilemma I have in mind is underscored by statements from *The Cunning of History* that warrant repeating. As Rubenstein assesses the situation, and the cases of Calel Perechodnik and Jean Améry come to mind, the Holocaust suggests that "there are absolutely no limits to the degradation and assault the managers and technicians of violence can inflict upon men and women who lack the power of effective resistance."[18] A key implication of that point of view, adds Rubenstein, is that "until ethical theorists and theologians are prepared to face without sentimentality the kind of action it is possible freely to perpetuate under conditions of utter respectability in an advanced, contemporary society, none of their assertions about the existence of moral norms will have much credibility."[19] Rubenstein knows, of course, that there are philosophical arguments to defend "a higher moral law" and ethical principles that hold persons and even nations morally responsible for their actions. Yet the Holocaust, he contends, sadly shows that there is "little or no penalty for their violation. And, norms that can be freely violated are as good as none at all."[20]

The answer to Rubenstein's dilemma, if there is one, will not be

found in some clinching intellectual argument or irrefutable philosophical analysis, for the best responses to this challenge are not that
easy or simple. Instead they involve sustained reflection on the memories people should share, the emotions we should express, the beliefs we should hold, the decisions we should make about how to
live after Auschwitz, and the questions that we ask about all of those
aspects of our experience, individually and collectively.

The Holocaust made Calel Perechodnik ask, "Am I a murderer?"
His confession answers yes. As we hear his answer, however, it should
settle nothing. Instead it should arouse us to soul searching and community building that resist as best we can every inclination and power
that make the best senses of returning home impossible. Some of the
steps, thought by no means all, that need to be taken in that direction
can be discerned by recalling one more set of Holocaust encounters.

About the time that Calel Perechodnik was writing his testament
in hiding and Jean Améry was enduring Auschwitz, Albert Camus, a
member of the French Resistance against Nazi Germany, was working on *The Plague*, which would become his most important novel.
Set in the Algerian city of Oran in the 1940s, the story chronicles
Dr. Bernard Rieux's battle against a deadly pestilence. As Pierre
Sauvage points out in his masterful film, *Weapons of the Spirit*, Camus
wrote *The Plague* while living in the vicinity of Le Chambon sur
Lignon, a mountain village in south-central France. Led by André
and Magda Trocmé, Le Chambon's Protestant pastor and his wife,
that place became a haven in Nazi-occupied Europe. Jews—some
five thousand—and other refugees found help there while the Holocaust raged around them.

Le Chambon did not become a Holocaust haven overnight. It
did so over time and partly because the Chambonnais had a tradition of bringing their religion to pointed public expression. Since
the sixteenth century, for example, Le Chambon has been predominantly Protestant, an anomaly in Catholic France. Many of the villagers are descendants of Huguenots who fled to that high plateau so
they could practice their Protestant Christianity without fear of punishment. But persecution persisted. Some people and pastors of Le
Chambon were hanged or burned at the stake for fidelity to the biblical principles that gave meaning to their lives.

Far from weakening their faith, such persecution — and the memory of it — strengthened the solidarity of the hardy Chambonnais. That solidarity manifested itself distinctively soon after Nazi Germany invaded France on May 12, 1940. Even before that plague arrived, André Trocmé had been preaching the simple lessons of the Christian gospel: peace, understanding, love. His was a message of nonviolence, but a nonviolence that rejected inaction and deplored complicity with injustice. André and Magda Trocmé's ways meant learning to read the signs of the times so that steps could be taken to get people out of harm's way. Those steps meant actively resisting evil when confronted by it. That meant remaining human in inhuman times. When the time came for the people of Le Chambon to resist the Nazi death machine, to act in solidarity and on behalf of others, the villagers — Protestant and Catholic alike — backed André Trocmé. Unlike so many other "Christians" during the Holocaust, they made their village an ark of hope in a sea of flames and ashes.

Le Chambon's resistance to the Holocaust started with small gestures — with Magda Trocmé, for example, opening her door and welcoming a German Jewish woman into her home. She and everyone else were aware of the danger, but that did not deter them. They regarded their acts of rescue as natural, as just the right thing to do. As Magda Trocmé said, "None of us thought that we were heroes. We were just people trying to do our best."[21] When Camus had Dr. Rieux conclude *The Plague* by observing that "there are more things to admire in men than to despise," the people of Le Chambon may well have been on his mind.[22]

In Camus's story, Rieux says that he compiled the chronicle "so that he should not be one of those who hold their peace but should bear witness in favor of those plague-stricken people; so that some memorial of the injustice and outrage done them might endure." Though the plague eventually left Oran, Dr. Rieux believed that there was nothing final about the victory. "The plague bacillus never dies or disappears for good," he says at the novel's end. The fight against "terror and its relentless onslaughts," concludes Dr. Rieux, must be "never ending."[23] Surely Jean Améry and Calel Perechodnik would agree.

Notes

[1]Calel Perechodnik, *Am I a Murderer? Testament of a Jewish Ghetto Policeman*, ed. and trans. Frank Fox (Boulder, CO: Westview Press, 1996).

[2]Ibid., 9.

[3]Richard L. Rubenstein, *The Cunning of History: The Holocaust and the American Future* (New York: Harper Torchbooks, 1987), 91.

[4]Ibid., 78.

[5]Richard L. Rubenstein, *After Auschwitz: History, Theology, and Contemporary Judaism*, 2d ed. (Baltimore: Johns Hopkins University Press, 1992), 131.

[6]Ibid., 131.

[7]Ibid., 132.

[8]Michael Berenbaum, *The World Must Know: The History of the Holocaust as Told in the United States Holocaust Memorial Museum*, with photographs edited by Arnold Kramer (Boston: Little, Brown and Company, 1993), 220.

[9]Gerald Fleming, "Engineers of Death," *New York Times*, 18 July 1993, E19. In my discussion of Fleming's findings, all the quotations are from this same source and page.

[10]Two especially significant works on Auschwitz are Yisrael Gutman and Michael Berenbaum, eds. *Anatomy of the Auschwitz Death Camp* (Washington, DC: United States Holocaust Memorial Museum and Bloomington: Indiana University Press, 1994) and Deborah Dwork and Robert Jan van Pelt, *Auschwitz: 1270 to the Present* (New York: W. W. Norton, 1996). In the context of this discussion, the following articles in *Anatomy of the Auschwitz Death Camp* are particularly relevant: Francisek Piper, "Gas Chambers and Crematoria," 157-82, and Jean-Claude Pressac with Robert-Jan Van Pelt, "The Machinery of Mass Murder at Auschwitz," 183-245. For further information about Kurt Prüfer, see *Auschwitz: 1270 to the Present*, especially 269-71.

[11]Rubenstein, *The Cunning of History*, 90.

[12]Ibid., 89.

[13]Jean Améry, *At the Mind's Limits: Contemplations by a Survivor on Auschwitz and Its Realities*, trans. Sidney Rosenfeld and Stella P. Rosenfeld (New York: Schocken Books, 1986), 86. The book was originally published in 1966.

[14]Ibid., 28.

[15]Ibid., 94-95.

[16]Ibid., 89.

[17]Ibid., xi.

[18]Rubenstein, *The Cunning of History*, 90.

[19]Ibid., 67.

[20]Ibid., 88.

[21]This account of Le Chambon draws on Carol Rittner and John K. Roth, eds., *Different Voices: Women and the Holocaust* (New York: Paragon House, 1993), 309-316.

[22]Albert Camus, *The Plague*, trans. Gilbert Stuart (New York: Vintage Books, 1991), 308.

[23]Ibid.

Critiques

Critique by Leonard Grob

Richard Rubenstein (as quoted by John Roth) is right on the mark when he points out that one lesson to be learned from the Holocaust is that "there are absolutely no limits to the degradation and assault the managers and technicians of violence can inflict upon men and women who lack the power of effective resistance." Yes, the Holocaust shatters conventional notions of the evil of which humans are capable. It leads us, as Roth suggests, to question in a radical fashion such basic concepts as the "unalienable" nature of human rights and a "universal moral structure" that underwrites them. Yet the Holocaust summons us, as well, to rethink conventional notions of human *goodness*: Rescue during the Holocaust, as manifest in the actions of the inhabitants of Le Chambon — also described by Roth — gives the lie to some of our deepest assumptions about goodness. We are often tempted to believe that altruism is only skin deep, that it is a surface mode of being, ultimately reducible to self-interest. The witness of those who risked their lives and the lives of their families to save Jews attests to a human goodness seemingly irreducible to any merely self-serving motives. By their own testimony, rescuers speak only of doing "what needed to be done": Amid their many different self-characterizations, rescuers are nearly united in attesting to the simple purity of their response to calls for help.

The Holocaust, then, provides examples which demand a fundamental reexamination of our ordinary understandings of *both good and evil*. This is not to say that the example of rescuers negates the claim, so clearly articulated by Roth, that the Holocaust challenges a basic belief in "unalienable" human rights. It is not a matter of attempting to find some balance between examples of new kinds of evil and new kinds of good effected during the Holocaust. Individual acts of evil or goodness constitute a world unto themselves: As Elie Wiesel reminds us, any place where oppression occurs becomes the center of the universe; at the same time, the Talmud proclaims that whoever saves a single soul, it is as if he had saved the whole world. Roth's discussion of Le Chambon does not—indeed, cannot—refute claims of new and terrifying forms of evil perpetrated during the Holocaust. As Roth argues, answers to Rubenstein's challenge "will not be found in some clinching intellectual argument or irrefutable philosophical analysis, for the best responses to this challenge are not that easy or simple. Instead they involve…the decisions we should make about how to live after Auschwitz." What the discussion of rescuers *can* do, in other words, is to remind us, in the face of the reality of the evil of the Holocaust, that there can no longer be "business as usual." Perpetrators have taught us the evil of which humans are capable; rescuers teach us not that humans are fundamentally good, but rather that human nature is essentially self-constituting, that humans are empowered to act in an infinite number of ways in response to the evil of the Holocaust.

But rescuers teach us more. They do not merely give us data for reflection on the nature of human nature. Rescuers are provocateurs, summoning us to respond to evil, sounding a call to action. Rescuers let us know that we have it within ourselves to help "repair the world." They do more than inform: In a post-Holocaust world, in a world in which traditional ethical norms have lost their credibility, their example beckons us to construct a life which has moral import. We are called to account for the moral dimension of our lives. I am in full agreement, then, with Roth's contention that any response to lessons Rubenstein draws from the Holocaust must take the form, among others, of "questions we must ask about all…aspects of our experience, individually and collectively." Rescuers urge upon us the task of asking such questions.

While it is certainly true, as Rubenstein (quoted by Roth) contends, that "until ethical theorists and theologians are prepared to face without sentimentality the kind of action it is possible freely to perpetuate under conditions of utter respectability…none of their assertions about the existence of moral norms will have much credibility," I am less convinced by further implications drawn from this claim. Rubenstein, according to Roth, goes on to argue that human rights may now depend on the play of *power*. Whether or not we possess what were formerly called *human* rights may now rest on the ability of states to defend these, or any other, rights on behalf of their citizens. This claim, in my view, does not necessarily follow from the rejection of the Jeffersonnian or other declarations concerning "unalienable" human rights. A fundamental rethinking of traditional moral assertions does not necessarily entail the notion that *power* alone can guarantee rights once thought to be "unalienable." To say that it is no longer "self-evident" that such rights belong to human-kind is not to say that human empowerment must inevitably be re-placed by power.

While it is true that traditional moral systems must be questioned in the light (one might better say "shadows") of the Holocaust, it may not follow, as Rubenstein, quoted by Roth, suggests, that "To the extent that men have rights, they have them only as members of the polis, the political community." Following in the tradition of Enlightenment thought, Jefferson has articulated a *proposition* about the human condition: It is in the nature of things, he tells us, that these rights are granted to the human being *qua* human. What must be called into question here is the notion of us humans "having" or "being granted" rights—or, indeed, being granted any*thing* whatso-ever. Humans are not fundamentally substances to which attributes can ultimately be given or withheld. Jefferson, like many other mor-alists, is mistaken in his belief that *propositions* about the moral con-dition of humans can be made. Following in the tradition of Jean-Paul Sartre and his fellow existential philosophers, I contend that we humans are more verb than noun, that we do not *have* a nature, but that we are a nature in question for ourselves. We are always in process, always making and remaking ourselves, morally speaking. Unlike the plant that bends in the wind, humans are beings the shape of whose existence is always in question for themselves. "How to be" is for us always an issue, a task rather than a given.

For Jefferson, human rights were granted "in the nature of things." That this nature of things has been challenged by the events of the Holocaust does not mean only that a mistaken attribution has oc-curred; rather, and more fundamentally, it is the act of attribution that is mistaken. As the contemporary philosophers Martin Buber and Emmanuel Levinas suggest, traditional static absolutes, such as the alleged self-evidence of "unalienable" rights belonging to humankind, are derivative from a "living absolute" of what may be called the "face-to-face" or "I-Thou" encounter between persons. Whether or not a human being possesses or fails to possess rights, in other words, cannot be determined by searching some alleged human nature for their presence or absence. Nor is it a foregone conclusion that such rights can only be granted by the power of states. For Buber, there exists an "inborn Thou," a fundamental predisposition to relate to a sacred other. For Levinas, I am born into a primordial "ethical relationship," with an other before whom I stand with responsibility—the ability-to-respond.

Yet what about these claims on the part of Buber and Levinas? Have we not simply replaced Jeffersonian ethics, based in natural law, with another set of attributions of moral qualities? I argue that this is not the case. When Buber and Levinas speak of a primordial or inborn relationship, they are not speaking about fixed characteristics belonging, as givens, to human nature understood as a substantive. Buber articulates an alternate creation tale: "In the beginning is relation," he tells us. In making this claim, Buber argues that *relation* is the primordial ground within which all of us exist. Although we may be "born to relate," however, there is no guarantee that the presence of an inborn Thou will eventuate in I-Thou encounters in which each party acknowledges the sacred nature of the personhood of the other. For Buber, the It-world—the ordinary world of instrumentality, of actions in which means lead to ends—"congeals," most often obscuring from our sight the primacy of the other as a Thou. Our task is to remain open to the possibility of encountering a Thou in our endeavor to realize ourselves as fully human.

For Levinas, the ontological primacy of our responsibility for the other person is also continually in danger of not being realized in practice. It is most often obscured by our desire to appropriate the other for our own ends, to see the other impersonally, as a means to an end beyond him- or herself. We are in constant danger of "totalizing" all that is, of subsuming the ultimately unsubsumable "face" of the other to categories of our own making. The primacy of relating to the sacred other is thus, for both Buber and Levinas, continually in need of actualization: We stand in need of a call, a summons to become who we most fundamentally are.

The Holocaust was an extraordinary moment in human history when impersonal, totalizing forces congealed so fully as to make expendable the members of an entire people. We must learn from the Holocaust to act so as to realize the relational potential in our humanity which Buber and Levinas have named. The actions of rescuers who risked all to stand steadfastly before the face of the Other—these actions constitute such a response to the Holocaust. We must strive to emulate these rescuers in the face of the evils of our own time and place. Roth addresses this point when he quotes Rieux in Camus's *The Plague* as saying that he composed the tale "so that he should not be one of those who hold their peace but should bear witness in favor of those plague-stricken people; so that some memorial of the injustice and outrage done them might endure."

Finally, then, I argue that we must ourselves create such a memorial to the six million Jews and millions of non-Jewish civilians murdered during the Holocaust. In so doing, we must not, as Roth quotes Rubenstein as suggesting, turn ultimately to the power of states as guarantors of our humanity. Rather, the witness of rescuers must call upon us to become (in an extended sense of this word) "rescuers" ourselves: In the face of the realizations brought home by the study of the Holocaust, we must rededicate our lives to standing before the face of the other, to remain open to the other as a Thou. As Roth suggests, our response to the challenges posed by Rubenstein lie in "the decisions we should make about how to live after Auschwitz." The teachings of the Holocaust are a call to action for the sake of *tikkun olam*, the repair of the world.

Critique by Peter Haas

John Roth makes a persuasive and moving case for what he calls
"Rubenstein's Dilemma." The "dilemma" is that we Americans have
built our lives on the deeply shared conviction that there are such
things as unalienable rights that belong to all people. The challenge
of Rubenstein's argument is that such rights have in fact been shown
to be alienable, if not altogether fictitious. People like Calel
Perechodnik who lived in a situation in which there was no state to
stand up for his rights simply did not have those rights. The dilemma
for Roth, I gather, is to find a way to continue to hold that such
unalienable rights exist in light of the fact that in the Holocaust they
were systematically suspended, ignored, or treated as if they did not
exist. Can I be said to have an unalienable right to X, if my access to
X rests on the legislative decision of some state?

The dilemma seems to lead to something like the two following
choices. On the one hand, we can simply acknowledge that such
rights do not exist, or do not exist any longer. That is, it may in fact
have been true at one point in Western history that people regarded
being human as including certain rights. This view is no longer part
of how we look at the world, and so such rights do not exist. We have
only those rights for which some state is willing to fight on our behalf and that is the end of that. Talk of unalienable rights in our
world is in a real sense meaningless. This of course means that at the
end of the day, there is nothing really that the Nazis did that was
objectively wrong. The Jews and others who were killed in the Holocaust had no right to life when they were executed, that right having been already revoked by the state upon which it would have
fallen to defend them. I suppose we could argue that the revocation
of such rights was not carried through appropriately according to the
"constitutional" requirements of the states in question. But this places
the "evil" of the Holocaust on an entirely different plane than that
in which it is usually discussed. The incredible acts of sustained
humiliation, brutality, and murder that occur thus reduce to a kind
of exercise in legalistic niceties.

If this reduction of Nazism to poorly conceived legislation is
unsatisfactory, then we are forced into the only other alternative

opened by "Rubenstein's Dilemma," namely, to insist that nonetheless such rights exist and furthermore exist unalienably, even if they are "vulnerable." On this view, for example, the rights to life, liberty and the pursuit of happiness remain "rights" the claim to which cannot be alienated, that is, taken away. To be sure, in actual fact these rights have been and are even today being violated all the time. The Holocaust is but the most systematic and sustained example of this. But, *contra* Rubenstein, this does not mean that the rights themselves are not there or are alienable. The rights are unalienably there, but have been violated or ignored. It is on this basis, at least in part, that we can look back and say that what the Nazis did was wrong.

The problem with this second view is that it is hard to see how in the modern world it is intellectually defensible. It has, to be sure, strong emotional appeal, but can we really ground the existence of rights in any firm knowledge of the cosmos or the human place in it? The answer would seem to be *no*. We can no longer call on the assumptions invoked in the past that there exists some supernatural "Good" or some essence of humanity that provides us at least in principle with some objective way of measuring right and wrong. These types of assumptions are simply not part of the intellectual possibilities open to us in the modern world. They were not destroyed by the Nazis, but have given way to some two centuries of philosophical inquiry. We no longer see human beings as standing at the center of cosmic concern, on a planet that forms the foundational core of the universe. If anything, modern science has relegated humanity to being the accidental evolutionary product of a rather nondescript planet in an average solar system at the edge of a rather pedestrian galaxy in a universe made of billions of similar galaxies. This is not to say that scientific progress is the ultimate cause of the Holocaust. It is to say that the assumptions upon which claims that there are "unalienable rights" can simply no longer be maintained.

Roth tries to address this dilemma. He notes, correctly in my view, that "the answer...will not be found in some clinching intellectual argument or irrefutable philosophical analysis." He then goes on to state, however, that the best responses "involve sustained reflection on the memories people should share, the decisions we should make about how to live after Auschwitz, and the questions that we ask about all of those aspects of our experience."

This proposed solution raises two questions in my mind. The first is why reflection on such issues should make a difference at all. That is, it is not clear to me what the connection might be between reflection and avoiding another Holocaust. Perhaps there is a sort of Kantian anthropology at work here that assumes that our reflections will lead to "objectively" good intentions and that our actions in turn will conform to such good intentions. The mechanism of transferring good reflection into good intention, and then good intention into good action, however, needs to be spelled out. It is hardly self-evident in the postmodern world.

The other question assumes that reflection can somehow be useful in shaping future policy. I cannot help but wonder what insures that future potential Nazis, upon reflection, will reach the conclusions we want them to. What if upon reflection they decide we should support racial warfare, that the memories people of their race should share are memories of victory and triumph, and so on. I wonder if one of the operative assumptions here is that the Holocaust occurred because its framers did not reflect enough, that they were ill-informed or uneducated. All the evidence that we have, however, suggests just the opposite. There were in fact many intellectuals, philosophers, and theologians among them, who did reflect on what was happening around them, who did understand what the Nazi persecution of the Jews and others was about, and who did nonetheless openly approve. So reflection itself is no guarantee that people will come to the "right" conclusion.

In the end, then, I am not sure that we have moved any closer to a solution to "Rubenstein's Dilemma." In fact I wonder if maybe the "Dilemma" itself can be said to be a misstatement of the problem. In the postmodern world, there is no way of positing in any objective, verifiable way that there are unalienable rights built into the cosmos. There is a dilemma here for us only because we Americans find ourselves wedded to an eighteenth-century Enlightenment concept that is out of date. The call posed by what probably needs more appropriately to be called the "Rubenstein Challenge" is simply to give up our eighteenth-century Romantic notion of "unalienable rights" and focus on what really counts, having state power ready to deploy in the defense of rights we want to insure that we enjoy. It could in fact be argued that it was precisely the failure of people to realize that there were no unalienable rights that prevented firmer action against Nazi atrocities from forming. Many well-intentioned people, working under the assumption that there were unalienable rights and that upon reflection sufficient people would realize and act upon this, may simply have assumed that the Nazi program would eventually fall apart. By assuming that there is a "dilemma" here rather than a challenge that calls us to abandon old world views, I wonder if we may simply be prolonging the final acceptance of the truth.

Critique by David Hirsch

In his "Reflections on Post-Holocaust Ethics," John Roth calls attention to one of the more puzzling paradoxes of Holocaust studies. Though the annihilation of the Jews and the liquidation of Jewishness as a culture took place almost exclusively on the European continent, it is in the United States that the study of the Holocaust has been most widely and effectively promulgated.

In 1933, Germany became an asylum run by the inmates, and by the end of 1941, the inmates were running not only Germany but almost all of Europe. In this inmate-ruled asylum, the two morally tainted characters singled out by Roth — Calel Perechodnik and Kurt Prüfer — lived and acted. A Jew, Perechodnik joined the Jewish police, where one of his duties was to herd other Jews into boxcars; ultimately, he wound up delivering his own wife and their two-year-old daughter to the train that he knew was taking them to their execution. Perechodnik was a fearful man who wanted desperately to survive, and as Roth notes, it is not for those of us sitting comfortably at our word processors to condemn him. At any rate, we could not condemn him more severely than he condemns himself.

Perechodnik, who describes himself, as "an engineer of agronomy" (*Am I a Murderer?*, xxi) writes with the clinical detachment of an architect drafting a blueprint, but as the translator notes, "His style is by turns mordant and sentimental, accusatory and self-pitying" (x). I assume the translator means self-accusatory. Perechodnik contrasts his own behavior with that of a fellow Jewish policeman, Willendorf, who when he saw what was happening to his family, threw away his armband and voluntarily joined his wife and family among the Jews being deported. Perechodnik confesses that he himself "did not have the courage [to] throw away my armband." "The example of the crowd," he adds, " took hold of me completely. I thought as did the others: Let it be one day later, even under force, even with shame. I couldn't do it a day earlier, by myself, voluntarily, with pride" (40).

Perechodnik cannot make the decision to die, as he himself sees it, with self-respect; he chooses, rather to live, even if only one more day, with a life-long burden of guilt and shame. To live one day longer, even in shame, Perechodnik was willing to look on as his wife and daughter were consigned to the death machine. He made no effort to rescue them, and couldn't bring himself to join them on the death train. Presumably, Primo Levi would have assigned this wretched soul to one of the murkier regions of the "the gray zone." In spite of his cowardice, Perechodnik would still qualify for the gray zone, albeit as "a valor-ruined man," as Melville once marvelously phrased it.

Not so, I believe, Kurt Prüfer, an "Aryan" engineer, who willingly participated in designing and enabling the construction of the crematoriums that became the last cog in the vast machine intended to liquidate human beings for the crime of having been born Jewish. Prüfer, like his superior, Fritz Sander, must remain outside the gray zone because, if for no other reason, they knew no remorse and felt no shame. Levi described this phenomenon of human robots among Germans who participated in the killing process in *The Re-Awakening*, and repeated the description in a later essay entitled, simply, "Shame." The Russian soldiers who liberated the camp, Levi writes, "did not greet us, nor smile; they seemed oppressed, not only by pity but also by a confused restraint which sealed their mouths, and kept their eyes fastened on the funereal scene. It was the same shame which we knew so well, which submerged us after the selections, and every time we had to witness or undergo an outrage: the shame that the Germans never knew...."[1] As we know from Raul Hilberg's meticulous documentation, it took thousands, perhaps millions, of workers and bureaucrats throughout Europe doing their jobs to put the "final solution" into effect, and none of them seems to have felt any shame.

Prüfer and Sander were higher in the technological hierarchy of killing than the accountants, railroad workers, and other functionaries who were more distant than they were from the actual annihilation process. Because they were highly skilled engineers, presumably trained to think clearly and objectively about problems in a real world, their behavior seems especially reprehensible.

Sander's explanation of his behavior echoes the excuses tendered by so many others. "I saw it as my duty," he testified, "to apply my specialist knowledge in this way in order to help Germany win the war, just as an aircraft construction engineer builds airplanes in wartime, which are also connected with the destruction of human beings" (see Roth's essay). Sander sees no difference between the wartime manufacture of weapons of destruction by powerful evenly matched military adversaries, as opposed to the manufacture of machines designed specifically for the purpose of incinerating non-combatant civilians.

The same bizarre logic used by Sander, Prüfer, and other ordinary Germans was employed by the greatest German philosopher of the twentieth century, Martin Heidegger, in his well-known declaration that "agriculture is now a mechanized food industry. As for its essence, it is the same thing as the manufacture of corpses in the gas chambers and extermination camps, the same thing as blockades and reduction of countries to famine, the same as the manufacture of hydrogen bombs."[2] How is it possible that Sander should have seen no difference between building airplanes for combat and constructing gas chambers to liquidate women and children; or that Heidegger should see no difference between "mechanized food industry" and "the manufacture of corpses"?

Both assertions bespeak an ethical denseness all the more shocking for being found in highly intelligent persons who were brought up in a Christian society and educated in the tradition of Western culture. Nor was this moral denseness limited to the great philosopher and the finely trained engineer. As Roth forcefully points out, "teachers and writers helped to till the soil where Hitler's racist antisemitism took root. Their students and readers [contributed].... Lawyers drafted and judges enforced the laws that...set [Jews] up for the kill. Government and church personnel..." cooperated, as did "university administrators,...bureaucrats in the Finance Ministry, postal officials, physicians, scientists, business executives, railroad personnel, factory workers," and many others.

Roth's meditation on the guilt-ridden Jewish policeman and the unrepentant "Engineers of Death" brings him to the thought that the insufficiency of "social, political, moral, [and] religious constraints [when it came to] stop[ping] the Final Solution...led Richard Rubenstein...to wonder about the truths that Thomas Jefferson taught Americans to hold 'self-evident.'" The Jeffersonian "truth" that appears most questionable to Rubenstein and Roth is "the claim that persons are 'endowed by their Creator with certain unalienable Rights.'" It seems, then, Rubenstein concludes, that "rights do not belong to men by nature. To the extent that men have rights, they have them only as members of the polis, the political community.... Outside of the polis there are no inborn restraints on the human exercise of destructive power" (Roth quotes from Rubenstein's *The Cunning of History*).

At first sight, Roth's juxtaposing the behaviors of Prüfer/Sander and Perechodnik to the doctrine of natural rights and the Declaration of Independence seems incongruous. And yet, for that very reason, it is a juxtaposition worth further exploration. As Americans, it is natural for Roth and myself to seek to understand the Holocaust from an American perspective. The Declaration was a distillation of the most sublime ideals of the Enlightenment, while Nazism was the very antithesis of the ideals of the Enlightenment. While Thomas Jefferson and the signers of the Declaration believed that "all men...are endowed by their Creator with certain unalienable Rights," they also recognized that those rights could be taken away, and they therefore added the clause, "...to secure these rights Governments are instituted among Men." Few in history have understood the dynamics of power more profoundly than the Founders, and few have expressed that understanding more nobly than the nineteenth-century American writer, Herman Melville.

Moby-Dick is, among other things, an epic of the tumultuous conflict between the Enlightenment ideals of liberty, equality, fraternity, on the one hand, and the Romantic worship of power and dominance, on the other. In a chapter entitled "Fast-Fish and Loose-Fish," Ishmael explains the practice of "waifing," that is, the practice of putting a mark of possession on a whale that has been "caught," so that the whaling ship may go in pursuit of other whales, while at the same time maintaining "ownership" of the waifed whale. The "code" of waifing is notable, as Ishmael puts it, for its "admirable brevity":

> I. A Fast-Fish belongs to the party fast to it.
> II. A Loose-Fish is fair game for anybody who can soonest catch it.

In a mock legal brief that follows, Melville proceeds to present a series of litigations and legal decisions which finally establish the "self-evident truth" that the principle of ownership of private property is based on raw power. Any property belongs to the party that can grab it and hold onto it. But living in the era of Emersonian idealism, Melville also perceived that material nature was a "symbol of spirit," and so he concludes his meditation on real property in the physical world with the rhetorical question that turns "real property" into a symbol of abstract values: "What are the Rights of Man and the Liberties of the World," Ishmael asks, "but Loose-Fish?" That is, human rights are unalienable only to the extent that any given human being has the power to hold onto them.

Roth cites Jean Améry's observation that "dignity can be bestowed only by society." The view of American nineteenth-century thinkers (and not just idealists), however, was that dignity was inherent in the human form, and what nondemocratic governments did was to take it away. Nazi rule was the complete antithesis of the ideal of democratic government. Though Nazi ideology glorified "Aryans," and reduced Jews to vermin, such an ideology was as destructive to the dignity of Aryans as of Jews. Ishmael, at one point, invokes the "just Spirit of Equality, which hast spread one royal mantle of humanity over all my kind! Bear me out in it, thou great democratic God!"

The Nazis were intent on destroying both the Judeo-Christian God and the progressive gains of the Enlightenment. They wanted to murder the "just Spirit of Equality, [the] great democratic God!" They believed that to achieve that end they would first have to exterminate the Jews. A literary critic has suggested parallels between the fictional Ahab and the historical Hitler. But here again, as in the case of the juxtaposition of the Declaration to the Nazi engineers of death and Perechodnik, the comparison seems incongruous. The Holocaust constitutes a rupture in Western history that renders such comparisons fruitless.

Had Perechodnik's "unalienable rights" been respected, he would most likely have achieved the blessed anonymity of an ordinary man, a human being neither remarkably good nor evil; at worst, a weak and selfish man.

But what about Sander and Prüfer? They were granted, not so

much "unalienable rights," as a special privilege. They were endowed by their Leader with the right to participate in the extermination of other human beings, and they took advantage of that right whole-heartedly. What is more, having done so, they seem to have felt neither guilt nor shame, neither remorse nor the need to repent. To discover such moral idiocy in men of intelligence and learning constitutes a rupture in the Western image of the human form that remains beyond comprehension.

Notes

[1]Primo Levi, *The Drowned and the Saved*, trans. Raymond Rosenthal (New York: Vintage, 1989), 72.

[2]From a speech Heidegger delivered in Bremen in 1949.

Critique by David Patterson

In his essay "Returning Home: Reflections on Post-Holocaust Ethics," John Roth raises several important issues and responds to those issues with insight and urgency. Taking Calel Perechodnik's book *Am I a Murderer?* as his example, Roth raises a question that is perhaps most decisive for modern humanity: is it possible to return home? Roth demonstrates his awareness of the relationship between the waxing of this question and the rise of civilization, particularly with respect to a civilization gone awry in Nazi Germany; for in Nazi Germany, as Roth points out, every quarter of science and industry—often considered keys to civilization—played a role in the extermination of the Jews. Roth also offers a good reply to Richard Rubenstein's insistence that "norms that can be freely violated are as good as none at all,"[1] suggesting—but not much more than suggesting—that the value of resisting evil does not rest on the prospects or pragmatics of an expected outcome. Indeed, the path of return is a path of resistance undertaken *in spite of* prospects for "success," a path that Rubenstein eliminates with his abrogation of the Covenant with God[2] and his insistence on measuring the value of the Good in strictly utilitarian terms.

My primary criticism of Roth is that he does not go far enough or deep enough in his response to these matters, at times overlooking decisive aspects of the issues he addresses. For example, in his consideration of Perechodnik's question "Am I a murderer?" Roth might examine more carefully the notion of *home* and what it has to do with murder, the Holocaust, and civilization—in short, what it has to do with good and evil. "'Good' is the movement in the direction of home," as Martin Buber once stated it.[3] As the most fundamental violation of the Good, murder most radically renders a person homeless. Thus Cain, the first murderer, was banished to the land of Nod, literally the land of "Wandering," condemned to a condition of homelessness. And what did he do there? He built a city, where people were divided into classes according to their vocations and where his descendent Lamech became a murderer: thus the advent of civilization.

Contrary to the wandering signified by Cain—and contrary to

the fundamentally antisemitic epithet "the Wandering Jew"—the Jew signifies the possibility for humanity to dwell in the world. Entering into the Covenant with God, Abraham was promised a dwelling place and was known for his ability to open up to others a place to dwell: according to legend, Abraham was an innkeeper. The movement of the Israelites from exile to homeland, moreover, was possible because they bore the Torah with them; as vessel of God's teachings and summons to humanity, the Torah makes it possible for humanity to have a home. For there is no home without holiness and no holiness without the Holy One. As an assault on the truth of the Torah, the Nazis' assault on the Jew entailed an assault on the sanctity of the home. Living in a camp, in a ghetto, or in hiding, every Jew in Nazi Europe was homeless. Indeed, a first step toward the extermination of Jewish souls prior to the extermination of Jewish bodies was to render the Jews homeless by moving them into a ghetto, a measure that had not only logistical and psychological implications but also metaphysical significance.

Roth, however, appears to be unaware of this metaphysical dimension of the annihilation of the Jews, noting only their "threat to the Third Reich's racial purity" and referring to the victims of the Nazis as "the Jews and other so-called racial inferiors." If, as both Roth and Rubenstein[4] maintain, the advance of civilization is an advance toward the Holocaust, it is because the advance of civilization comes in an eclipse of God and thus in a movement away from the Good, which is a movement away from home. In the modern, civilized world there is no place for the One known as the Place; hence, as His Chosen, the Jew, has no place; hence human being has no place. For the Jew is chosen to attest to the chosenness and the sanctity of every human being. *That* is what the Nazis slated for annihilation, what civilization cannot accommodate, and what Roth overlooks.

Roth does well to note the case of Fritz Sander, who justified his role in building the crematoria by invoking his duty "to help Germany win the war," but he fails to raise a critical question: the war against what? Certainly not against the Allies. Against what, then? Against the Jews and all that they signify, not just racially but, above all, metaphysically: the Nazis waged war against the holy, against the family, against the Good—in a word, against the home.

But there is more. In addition to signifying the sanctity of every human being, the Jews signify the Law.[5] The war against the Jews is a war against the Law, that is, against every form of constraint. Here Roth correctly points out that there were no moral or religious constraints that could put a stop to the "final solution" and that Calel Perechodnik himself was without constraint. What Roth does not point out is that this very absence of restraint—this absence or eclipse of the Law—is precisely what precludes any movement in the direction of home on the part of Perechodnik. For home is a place of constraints. It is not the place where I have my rights; it is the place where I meet my responsibility, where the other person is in a position higher than my own. That is why invoking such champions of human rights as Thomas Jefferson or turning to the notion of having rights by nature will not go far in the response to the evil of Nazism. Indeed, the Nazis understood themselves, as Aryans, to be endowed by nature with certain unalienable rights.

No, in the response to the evil of Nazism, we must consider what Nazism wanted to exterminate. The Nazis did not assail the dignity so much as the sanctity of human being, if dignity is understood as Jean Améry understood it, saying, "dignity can be bestowed only by society."[6] Roth cites this line from Améry without realizing that, in an important sense, it is perfectly consistent with Nazi thinking: if society alone bestows dignity, what is to prevent society or the *Volk* from bestowing dignity selectively? From a Jewish standpoint—that is, from the standpoint antithetical to Nazism and slated for elimination by Nazism—human dignity lies not in having rights or in the bestowals of society; rather human dignity consists of being commanded by God to meet certain responsibilities to our fellow human beings. Thus commanded, we are sanctified.

But "what if there is no God?" Roth is not afraid to ask. For a Jew, however, this is like asking, "What if the other human being does not matter?" or "What if there is no commandment to love?" For "God is the commandment of love," as Emmanuel Levinas points out. "God is the one who says that one must love the other."[7] And, as the example of the *Chasidei Umot HaOlam*—the Righteous Gentiles—of Le Chambon demonstrates, we have the commandment to love: not just loving actions, mind you, but the *demand* for loving actions, despite inclination, inconvenience, or danger. This commandment that precedes us, and not personal wishes or any history of persecution, is what accounts for the courageous actions of the people of Le Chambon. Indeed, the Nazis did not want to persecute the Jews—they wanted to murder them. And, inasmuch as "the glory of the Infinite reveals itself through what it is capable of doing in the witness,"[8] one beholds in the response of such rescuers not only an act of courage but a trace of the holy.

Does their response to the plight of the Jews amount to a moral deed and a testimony to human sanctity only because it worked? Do the many failed efforts to save more lives have less moral value because they were not successful? Are the people of Le Chambon counted among the *Chasidei Umot HaOlam* simply because they did not get caught? Certainly not. And yet Roth's concern with Rubenstein and "the practical status of moral norms" might lead us to think that he is ready to adopt such a position. Judging from his discussion of the people of Le Chambon, however, he is not ready to adopt such a position. For, as Roth shows, the people of Le Chambon were concerned not with the practical but with the moral, not with the useful but with the good, not with enjoying rights but with saving lives.

When faced with evil, the questions that confront us are not "Do moral norms have practical value?" or "Can moral norms be freely violated?" Rather, the questions are "Is it wrong?" and "What must be done?" For "to know God," Levinas has shown, "is to know what must be done,"[9] regardless of the outcome of our action. That is why to know God is to know the Good. And to know the Good is to know the way home.

Notes

[1]Richard L. Rubenstein, *The Cunning of History: The Holocaust and the American Future* (New York: Harper and Row, 1987), 88.

[2]See Richard L. Rubenstein, *After Auschwitz: Radical Theology and Contemporary Judaism* (Indianapolis: Bobbs-Merrill, 1966), 147, where he states, "I find it impossible to believe in the doctrine of the Chosen

People."

[3]Martin Buber, *Between Man and Man,* trans. Ronald Gregor Smith (New York: Macmillan, 1965), 78.

[4]See Rubenstein, *The Cunning of History,* 78.

[5]For a good discussion of this point, see the opening pages of Jean-François Lyotard, *Heidegger and "the jews,"* trans. Andreas Michel and Mark S. Roberts (Minneapolis: University of Minnesota Press, 1990).

[6]Jean Améry, *At the Mind's Limits: Contemplations by a Survivor on Auschwitz and Its Realities,* trans. Sidney Rosenfeld and Stella P. Rosenfeld (New York: Schocken, 1986), 89.

[7]Emmanuel Levinas, "The Paradox of Morality," in *The Provocation of Levinas: Rethinking the Other,* ed. Robert Bernasconi and David Wood (London: Routledge, 1988), 176-77.

[8]Emmanuel Levinas, *Ethics and Infinity,* trans. Richard A. Cohen (Pittsburgh: Duquesne University Press, 1985), 109.

[9]Emmanuel Levinas, *Difficult Freedom,* trans. Sean Hand (Baltimore: Johns Hopkins University Press, 1990), 17.

Critique by Didier Pollefeyt

John Roth's essay "Returning Home" confronts the most challenging of all contemporary moral questions: the problem of the foundation of ethics and the issue of moral relativism. At first glance, it might seem strange to raise the problem of moral relativism in the context of the Holocaust, because in confrontation with Nazi genocide, as Roth indicates, people spontaneously and immediately abandon any claims of ethical relativism and quasi-unanimously say: "This is evil!" Starting from this fact, it becomes difficult to explain how the Nazis could have unleashed such "unambiguous" evil and yet moral forces were unable to stop them. Roth rejects the popular idea of the Holocaust as the work of a group of extraordinarily evil monsters who did evil for evil's sake. Even if there were monsters among the Nazis, such an approach cannot explain how millions of ordinary Germans from every sector of German society participated in the Nazi genocide. It is implausible to argue that such a large and varied group of people suddenly set aside their moral conscience for more than a decade and then simply took it up again after the war, continuing their lives as if nothing had happened.

The explanation Roth wrestles with is much more challenging. Like Richard Rubenstein, he suggests that human beings have no rights that are universal or natural, the violation of which is self-evidently recognized by all human beings as objectively evil. For Rubenstein, Auschwitz reveals the powerlessness and bankruptcy of that optimistic morality. Accordingly, ethics after Auschwitz can no longer be based on beliefs in universal or divinely legitimized norms. Values can no longer be deduced by reason from God or nature; they are instead the creation of human beings. In a world where Auschwitz is a continual possibility, ethics in its classical sense has lost its credibility. It is merely a thin layer of varnish that provides no effective protection against humankind's destructive forces.

Rubenstein's analysis of the Holocaust is especially challenging for ethics. No student of post-Holocaust morality should ignore it. For Rubenstein, human beings have no "natural" rights, but only the rights that are guaranteed by a community that has the political power to protect those rights.[1] People without political rights are dispensable. After the "death of God" and the failure of objective morality, the community and its stories become the only power for determining what is good and evil. Accordingly, for example, if the narrative of a community defines Jews as subhuman—using old Christian anti-Judaism and new biomedical visions—then Jews may lose every right for protection. This "narrative" interpretation of good and evil brings Rubenstein to the disturbing conviction that in Auschwitz, there was, in a sense, not a single crime committed. The Nazis had violated no law since their victims were not protected by any law of the ruling community.

I think that Roth's answer to this challenge would not completely convince Rubenstein. Roth refers to the moral experience of indignation and condemnation everyone experiences in confrontation with the brutal facts of the Holocaust as a refutation of Rubenstein's relativism: "The Holocaust's evil…forms an ultimate falsification of moral relativism. No one, it seems, could encounter Auschwitz and deny that there is a fundamental and objective difference between right and wrong." In line with Rubenstein's framework, however, one could counterargue that "moral indignation" is likewise determined by the community of power wherein one lives. We feel ethical anger in confrontation with the Holocaust because we have been educated by our community in that way, because Auschwitz is so well integrated into our personal and collective master story. We then could analyze the powers at work in that master story and understand why, for example, the extermination of Indians has been much less an element of the American story than the Holocaust.

Rubenstein contends that moral outrage is yet another form of "false consciousness."[2] Even if the meaning of the moral indignation in facing the Holocaust would be "universally human," there are for Rubenstein too many situations where making oneself a (potential) victim, vulnerable to and dependent on moral intuition and ethical anger, would be irresponsible and dangerous. For Rubenstein, Jews have learned that their age-long nonviolent position as a minority in a predominantly Christian Europe did not provide them the moral respect they had hoped for and anticipated, based as it was on a belief in universal morality. Rather, they have only found deadly persecution. In confrontation with evil, Jews may no longer trust spontaneous moral outrage and universal ethical sensibility as foundational for ethics. In the same way, one could criticize Levinas's notion of the "appeal of the face" as merely the expression of the powerless desire to be respected, a powerlessness for which there is no place after Auschwitz because it guarantees nothing.

Are there other ways to falsify Rubenstein's relativism and power positivism than the "evidence" of moral outrage? I would argue that Rubenstein mistakenly confuses *fact* and *norm*. The Holocaust was indeed created in a relativistic and nihilistic Nazi spirit, but does this mean that it illustrates the excellence of this ideology? One needs to distinguish the (relativistic) categories that established Nazism from the ethical conclusions that can be deduced from a study of it. Does the unethical and murderous behavior of the Nazis discharge us of the obligation to act ethically and peacefully ourselves? Should we abandon ethics simply because the Nazis did so before us? In other words, the existence of Auschwitz does not make authentic moral actions impossible or insignificant after Auschwitz. As the French ethicist Tzvetan Todorov has indicated in *Face à l'extréme*, factuality and conviction do not always coincide.[3]

In fact, there are some remarkable analogies between the Nazi ideology and the conclusions of Rubenstein (for instance, his mystical paganism, his interpretation of nature, or the role of the community). Emil Fackenheim[4] even concludes that Rubenstein's approach unsuspectingly completes the work of Hitler.[5] For Fackenheim, if people begin to become desperate about ethics because of Hitler's monstrous deeds, then they ironically collaborate in the realization of Hitler's project: the destruction of morality itself. Nazism clearly and brutally illustrated the consequences of the divinization of the powers of the community. In devastating ways, Nazism showed how a powerful, sheltering community that lacks a transcendent point of reference can become unethical and murderous toward those (the Jew, the Gypsy, the incapacitated, or the Jehovah's Witness) who disturb the "safety" of the collective order. Nazism involved a closed narrative community that elevated itself to the *Ein und Alles* and tried to protect its own identity by any means necessary.

If we try to defend a narrative interpretation of good and evil, we risk delivering the world into the hands of a merciless, Nazi struggle for power once again. Is it true that the strongest (the most beautiful, the richest, the most powerful, or the most intelligent) really hold all rights to determine what is good and evil? Is this not precisely what the Nazis thought?

Roth nevertheless seeks to deal with Rubenstein's relativism through a kind of narrative ethics. Since the well-known study of the ethicist Philip Hallie,[6] the story of Le Chambon has become the paradigm of narrative ethics in Holocaust studies. Apparently following Hallie, Roth explains how the people of Le Chambon resisted Nazism in an extraordinary way through fidelity to "biblical principles" and the "simple lessons of the Christian gospel: peace, understanding, love." Still, this answer is problematic. As Roth explains elsewhere in his essay, anti-Judaism is also a part of the Christian story (as is violence against non-believers, women, and nature). One could counterargue that anti-Judaism is merely part of the *history* of Christendom, but not an essential element of the Christian message *as such*. Some biblical scholars, however, argue that anti-Judaism (e.g., supersessionism) is an intrinsic part of the Gospels.[7] But even if this last hypothesis were not correct, what criteria do we have in the shadow of Auschwitz that allow us to maintain that peace and love are essential part of the Christian story and anti-Judaism is a perversion of that story? Can we so easily separate the ethical essence of Christianity from its historical development? Are these principles ethical simply because they are biblical? Or are they rather biblical because they are ethical? The same questions can be raised concerning the biblical principle of peace. What does this "simple" lesson of the Gospel teach us about the question of the use of violence after Auschwitz: radical pacifism? proportionate violence? just war? In general, what are the criteria to evaluate and to apply a narrative in the post-Holocaust era, and to compare it with others?

A consistent ethical relativism finally becomes internally destructive. If all ethical argumentation is determined by the story from which one speaks, then that perspective is also colored by a particular story that is logically and historically relative. The question becomes whether there is no *form* of ethics that might transcend different stories and with which one can criticize one's own story, thereby escaping ethical relativism and falsifying Nazi definitions of good and evil. An answer to this question presupposes the identification of a number of values or characteristics that in some way surpass the particularity of different stories or traditions.

These values, however, can no longer be thought to be story-independent, objective characteristics. Concerning this point, Rubenstein is correct: Ethics will always be expressed in and supported (or not) by particular narrative communities. An essential task of ethics after Auschwitz is to identify ethical-religious and fundamental human experiences in different ethical traditions that transcend their original cultural and historical circumstances, and that can thereby have a liberating and humanizing meaning in other times and places. Because these kinds of values, traditions, or stories have proven to be transcultural and even transreligious, it is the task of the ethicist to make them understandable and communicable.[8] In this way, characteristics and criteria that enable criticism of ruling cultures, ideologies, and religions can emerge.

Roth's essay contains one such interesting characteristic: "to act in solidarity and on behalf of others." In his study of the Holocaust, Todorov has warned against a certain form of solidarity which is a notion that is not incompatible with Nazism.[9] In such kind of solidarity, I always automatically help those who are in my group and do not feel in the same way responsible for those who are not in my group. This kind of solidarity is for Todorov only a quantitative extension of the principle of self-interest. Egoism is replaced by "nousism" (egoism of the *nous*). This form of solidarity excludes the stranger, who will always be the victim of it. In the camps, the newcomers were frequently the victims of the solidarity of the group that was already formed and that feared losing its privileges. In that case, solidarity with one's group sometimes meant the death of others. It becomes a principle to defend the ruling group. Roth conversely defends a *very specific kind* of solidarity: not acting automatically on the basis of the nationality, language, job, or the religion of others, but solidarity "on behalf of others," a solidarity that is based only on their humanity. Here solidarity is no longer a principle in service of the closedness of the ruling group, but one that on the contrary questions the closedness of that group and breaks open the power of the ruling group. It is a criterion that comes from outside the group, a point of transcendence arriving from elsewhere. This point—beyond all human power—cannot be grounded itself, since every effort to make a picture of it, to grasp it by reason or by the narrative of one's community, would already be a violation of its transcendence.

I would argue that every human being *is capable of* experiencing the "difference" (Lyotard's *le différend*) between the powers of the ruling system and what questions that system (the other), between "being" (*être*) and "beyond being" (Levinas's *autrement qu'être*), between the immanent existence of mere survival and a transcendent otherness that provides a new orientation to our individual and collective lives. Here, I would argue—with Roth and against Rubenstein—that moral indignation *is* a refutation of relativism. Moral anger is an expression of the experienced difference between what is and what ought to be. Accordingly, Nazism was an extreme violation of this "difference" since it destroyed the possibility of experiencing this *différend* itself, not only in the lives of the perpetrators and bystanders, who made themselves the prisoners of a closed system, but also in the lives of the victims. This becomes extremely clear in the work of Jean Améry. As Roth notes, Améry's torture at the hands of the Nazis so imprisoned him in the narrow, closed limits of his tortured body that any perception of meaning became impossible. As Dagerman says about hunger, torture is "a form of irresponsibility, not only a physical condition but also a moral one, leaving very little room for long thoughts."[10]

Améry's work is not an argument for moral relativism, but rather for the *relativity* of ethics, in the sense that morality is dependent on some preconditions, such as a fundamental trust in reality. Extreme forms of pain, hunger, cold, or fear can affect this trust to such an extent that it becomes impossible to open oneself and one becomes (self-)enclosed by the immanence of survival needs. In such extreme cases of fear, especially among the prisoners of extermination camps, it is perfectly understandable that one can no longer think or act ethically and that one only sees one's neighbor as a threat to the protection or further development of one's own identity.

In a system where there is no trust, ethical behavior becomes impossible. That fact is also clear in the story of Calel Perechodnik's participation in the destruction of the European Jews as a member of the *Ordnungsdienst* in a Nazi ghetto. Roth rightly indicates the cunning of the Nazi system in requiring Jews to take part in their own annihilation. Jews such as Perechodnik constantly faced predicaments where they had to try to act "rationally" toward an enemy who espoused the most perverted logic. In such circumstances, where people could not even trust their own rationality, let alone that of their enemy, it was often impossible, as Perechodnik's case points out, to act ethically.

Ethical life is bound to some preconditions, such as basic trust. If these conditions are lost or destroyed, moral life becomes very difficult and even impossible. In the end, every person is vulnerable to finding oneself in a situation where the question "Am I a murderer?" becomes relevant. These extreme conditions, however, are not the norm. In normal human development, there is (given) a basic trust. As such, the Holocaust cannot really be the basis for building an ethics. The true identity of ethics will not reveal itself in such extreme circumstances, because humans are not made for such situations. Ethics after Auschwitz should bring to light the preconditions that make the experience of "difference" possible, and enter a critical dialogue with religious and political powers to guarantee the possibility of ethical life after Auschwitz. In this sense, power can serve or destroy ethics, but ethics can never be reduced to a battle of powers. Ethics should also criticize every ideological manipulation of moral indignation by political power. In the end, ethics after Auschwitz should reflect more profoundly on the basis of this basic trust. Herein we can seek to give a more theological (Jewish, Christian, Buddhist, for instance) or a more general human answer (for example, human rights) to the foundation of the universal human experience of ethical transcendence.

Notes

[1]Richard Rubenstein, *The Cunning of History: The Holocaust and the American Future* (New York: Harper and Row, 1978), 91.

[2]Richard Rubenstein, "Moral Outrage as False Consciousness," *Theory and Society* 9 (1980): 745-55.

[3]Tzvetan Todorov, *Face à l'extrême* (Paris: Seuil, 1991), 227.

[4]Emil Fackenheim, *To Mend the World: Foundations of Future Jewish Thought* (New York: Schocken Books, 1982).

[5]Even if this claim is an overstatement. See Richard L. Rubenstein, "Emil Fackenheim's Radical Monotheism," *Soundings* 57 (1974): 236-51 and especially 250: "I cannot believe that Fackenheim understands the bitter cruelty of the position he proclaims.... It is almost impossible to recall a single instance in the entire history of Judaism in which a religious thinker has so heartlessly condemned his co-religionist."

[6]Philip Hallie, *Lest Innocent Blood Be Shed: The Story of Le Chambon and How Good Happened There* (New York: Harper and Row, 1979).

[7]For this discussion, see George M. Smiga, *Pain and Polemic: Anti-Judaism in the Gospels* (New York: Paulist Press, 1992).

[8]See also the project of Darrell J. Fasching, *Narrative Theology after Auschwitz: From Alienation to Ethics* (Philadelphia: Fortress Press, 1992) and *The Ethical Challenge of Auschwitz and Hiroshima: Apocalypse or Utopia?* (Albany: State University of New York Press, 1993).

[9]Tzvetan Todorov, *Face à l'extrême*, 89-92.

[10]S. Dagerman, *Duitse herfst: Een naoorlogse reportage*, trans. K. Woudstra (Amsterdam: Meulenhoff, 1985), 15.

Roth's Response to Critiques

"Returning Home," my primary essay in this book, began with reflections about Calel Perechodnik, a Polish Jew not yet in his thirties who became a ghetto policeman, found himself implicated in the death of his wife and children when the Nazis deported them to Treblinka, and eventually managed to go into hiding, where he wrote his agonizing story before the Holocaust took his life, too. The writings he left behind include a poignant and disturbing document composed in Warsaw on October 23, 1943. Young Perechodnik's "Last Will and Testament" is a good departure point for my response to the thoughtful critiques my essay has received.

Almost apologetically, Perechodnik states "I am not a lawyer by profession, and so I cannot write a will that would be entirely in order, and I cannot in the present circumstances ask for help from the outside."[1] Explaining his "present circumstances," Perechodnik observes that, "as a result of the order of German authorities, I and my entire family, as well as all the Jews of Poland, have been sentenced to death."[2] This death sentence, he notes, has claimed almost all of his family, and thus Perechodnik's formal, documentary language is also an understated lamentation that records their fate as best he knows it. He has no personal property, Perechodnik goes on to say, but he is the legal heir to property left by his wife, Chana, and his father, Ussher. He makes clear what should be done with it. His last testament is a real will, prepared as carefully and executed as properly as Perechodnik knows how.

Nobody can say how much Perechodnik believed that anybody, let alone any legal system, government, or state, would care one whit about his will. Nevertheless — perhaps with irony and protest as much as hope, perhaps to resist despair by asserting his human dignity, or perhaps with none of those feelings — Perechodnik writes respectfully and specifically asks "the Polish court to make possible the execution of this will according to both the spirit of my wishes as well as the law involved."[3]

Perechodnik lists the property to which he is heir and designates those to whom he wants to leave it. Giving addresses and exact locations, he carefully explains that the property exists in Otwock, his home town. There is the movie house called "Oasis." There are two lots and two villas. The latter contain apartments.

The apartments were homes. Not just people but families—Jewish and Polish, members of Perechodnik's family, Perechodnik himself—returned to those family homes after work, school, or shopping, and after journeys that took them away but brought them back home again. After Perechodnik saw his wife and child deported to Treblinka in August 1942, he said that he returned home, but he did not return there—could not do so—because, as David Patterson underscores, the Holocaust destroyed not only Perechodnik's physical home, leaving him ghettoized, but senses of "home" that are even more precious and profound than the specific places and times without which those deeper senses of "home" cannot exist. By reflecting further on those senses of "home," I can respond here to some, though not all, of what I take to be the most important points that Patterson, Leonard Grob, Peter Haas, David Hirsch, and Didier Pollefeyt have made to my essay. In that order, I will focus briefly on one major theme from each of them.

"The Nazis," says Patterson, *"waged war against the holy, against the family, against the Good—in a word against the home."* Good critics make valuable contributions by drawing out themes and implications that are latent but undeveloped in a writer's initial statements. Patterson admirably plays that part for me. I am particularly grateful to him for calling to my attention Martin Buber's poignant and powerful idea that "'Good is the movement in the direction of home." Emphasizing that murder is "the most fundamental violation of the Good," Patterson urges me to go deeper in considering the "homelessness" that the Holocaust produced. As he interprets the Holocaust, its significance is profoundly metaphysical, and the "homelessness" it produced is the result of an arrogant *assault*—a word Patterson uses often—against God and Goodness themselves. Buttressed by his detailing of the particularity of the Nazis' assault on the Jewish people and religious traditions, Patterson's points are well taken. At the same time, they need to be reconsidered in relation to some of the points in my essay that cause difficulties for his perspective.

If we think about the most fundamental human needs and about the most important human values, *home* looms large. *Home* means shelter and safety, care and love. It has much to do with the senses of identity, meaning, and purpose that govern our lives, because *home* involves our closest relationships with other people and provides key motivations and reasons for the work we do. Not all particular homes fit that description, which sometimes leads us to speak of "broken homes," a condition that no one chooses as good. Unfortunately, the Holocaust and the devastating world war that provided "cover" for it did more than break homes. It ruined them—physically and metaphysically—because the Nazi assault, driven by a debased yearning for an exclusively German homeland, was so successful in destroying the *trust* on which *home* depends.

The senses of *home* that we identify most with goodness depend on stability, fidelity, communal ties, mutual respect, law, a shared ethical responsibility, and, for some but not all persons, religious faith. Phrases about *home*—for example, "going home" or "being at home" or even "leaving home"—reflect those elements. The Holocaust, as Jean Améry said, destroyed trust in the world. It showed that without sufficient defense, violent powers can leave people bereft of home, if those powers leave their victims alive at all. True, human resilience may act remarkably to rebuild senses of *home* in the ruins but never without a residue of distrust that is metaphysical and perhaps religious as well as political.

Patterson's analysis of the metaphysics of the Holocaust's destructiveness is more persuasive than his remedy for it. One way or another, his remedy involves knowing God, which is precisely what many will find impossible to do when they honestly confront the Holocaust's devastation. If Patterson's call for a return to God, which he takes to be essential for "returning home," is answered, the response will often be made *in spite of* history not because of it. His call's appeal would be stronger if the evidence in its favor were greater, and that is why my essay raised so strongly the issue of results or what I called the functional status of morality.

Patterson is correct, but only up to a point, when he questions, for example, whether failed efforts to save lives during the Holocaust have less moral value because they were unsuccessful. More than he seems to accept, my essay is an argument that results do matter. Granted, outcomes alone do not determine the moral value of intentions. Nor does disobedience eliminate the ethical content of injunctions against murder. But outcomes do affect trust in the impact of good intentions, and results do affect belief in the authority of ethical injunctions as well as the credibility of God's reality and presence in history. Post-Holocaust ethics must be concerned with outcomes. Seeking ways to "return home," it must emphasize not only good intentions that persist *in spite of* history but also how to achieve results that increase the trust on which our best senses of *home* depend.

"To say that it is no longer 'self-evident' that [unalienable] rights belong to humankind," Leonard Grob reminds me, *"is not to say that human empowerment must inevitably be replaced by power."* Grob's comment reflects on the fact that my essay focuses on the relationship between *might* and *right*. I hope it is clear that I reject the proposition that might *makes* right. In my view, what is good, just, and true is not determined by human pronouncement, let alone by the political power of a state. But if might does not make right, relationships between right and might still remain, and they are as important as they are complex.

Consider why Calel Perechodnik was unable to return home. He could not do so because Nazi power prevented him from doing so. I think that no ultimately sustainable reasons—judgments that could stand full critical scrutiny—could be found to justify that Nazi power, but nevertheless Perechodnik could not return home. Might did not make right in that case, but might had much to do with the functional status of right. The same point can be seen in relationships such as the following: A law that is not obeyed may still be a law, but its functional status depends on obedience and credible sanctions against disobedience. An injunction that is not heeded lacks credibility. When Nazi Germany unleashed the Holocaust, the force of the injunction "Thou shalt not murder" was impugned just to the degree that millions of Jews were slaughtered before the violence of a world war crushed the Third Reich. If God is not acknowledged, God's existence is not necessarily eliminated, but God's authority is curtailed. And if God's authority lacks credibility, then the nature of God's existence is affected, too.

Our senses of moral and religious authority have been weakened by the accumulated ruins of history and the depersonalized advances of "civilization" that are taking us from a bloody twentieth century into an even more problematic twenty-first. A moral spirit and religious commitment that have the courage to persist *in spite of* humankind's self-inflicted destructiveness remain essential, but it is a question how effective those dispositions can be in a world where power, and especially the power of governments, stands at the heart of that matter. As genocide scholar and statistician R. J. Rummel says, "Power kills; absolute Power kills absolutely," a statement that his chillingly titled book, *Death by Government*, supports as follows:

> In total, during the first 88 years of this [twentieth] century, almost 170 million men, women, and children have been shot, beaten, tortured, knifed, burned, starved, frozen, crushed, or worked to death; buried alive, drowned, hung, bombed, or killed in any other of the myriad ways governments have inflicted death on unarmed, helpless citizens and foreigners. The dead could conceivably be nearly 360 million people. It is as though our species has been devastated by a modern Black Plague. And indeed it has, but a plague of Power, not germs.[4]

Grob is correct: power, at least in its political form, would be a poor and even deadly substitute for what he calls "human empowerment." But that "human empowerment" must find ways to affect "the powers that be" so that their tendencies to lay waste to human life are checked. To do that, post-Holocaust ethics will need to draw on every resource it can find: appeals to human rights, emphases on "the face of the other," calls for "a return to God" of the sort that David Patterson stresses, respect and honor for people who save lives and resist tyranny, and attention to the Holocaust's warnings, to name only a few. Those efforts will need to be accompanied by efforts that build these concerns into our educational, religious, business, and political institutions. Steps in those directions will be steps on the way home.

Peter Haas wonders if one of my "operative assumptions" is that "the Holocaust occurred because its framers did not reflect enough." He also suggests that I may be clinging to views about human rights that involve an outmoded world view. Correctly, he understands that reflection can lead in many directions, including those that produced the Holocaust. Such outcomes, Haas also perceives, undermine the credibility of views that bank on reality's ultimate moral rationality.

Haas challenges me to give up convictions that, in his judgment, are no longer persuasive in a post-Holocaust situation. While I agree with much of his analysis, I do not accept all of his conclusions. Contrary to Haas, I do believe that better reflection would have kept the Nazis from unleashing the Holocaust. That proposition cuts more than one way historically, for better reflection could have prevented the Nazis from coming to power in the first place, just as it might conceivably have led the Nazis themselves to stop short of doing their worst. Everything, of course, hinges on what "better reflection" means. At the same time, we ought not to make that understanding more difficult than it is. The reflection I have in mind is driven by a persistent questioning that features the question "Why?" Such reflection is skeptical, especially at the points where human judgment wants to move to the conclusion that inquiry has reached its end and that "decisive action"—for example, a "final solution"—is necessary. The Nazis inquired, but not long or well enough. Had they resisted their yearnings for certainty and finality, their confidence that they were right, and especially their "knowing" that destiny, truth, or simply superior physical power were on their side—*Gott mit uns*—the Holocaust would not have happened.

As for human rights, Haas is right in thinking that some human hopes have been dashed. It is unlikely, for instance, that humankind will ever reach full agreement about one world view that will "ground" belief in such rights. But it does not follow that appeals to human rights are dashed as well. If people feel the need to "ground" appeals to human rights, a variety of options—philosophical and religious—may remain credible even if they will not be universally accepted. More importantly, there may be considerable agreement—especially after the Holocaust—about what the functional interpretation of human rights ought to be. Here, too, there will not be universal agreement, but the Holocaust itself has had an important impact in helping to clarify what ought not to happen to human beings. If we think about what ought not to happen to human beings, moreover, we may find considerable agreement about what ought to happen. Calel Perechodnik ought not to have been prevented from returning home—in all the best senses of *home*—and if that is true, then what ought to have happened (again in all the best senses of that phrase) is not so far to find.

"*But what about Sander and Prüfer?*" David Hirsch wants to know. Those Nazis designed and built the crematoriums at Auschwitz. "*They were granted, not so much 'unalienable rights,' as a special privilege. They were endowed by their Leader with the right to participate in the extermination of other human beings,*" Hirsch notes, "*and they took advantage of that right wholeheartedly.*" While he wonders why Sander and Prüfer could not see the wrong they did, Hirsch helpfully directs attention to Ishmael's reflection on "Fast-Fish and Loose-Fish" in Herman Melville's American classic *Moby-Dick*. Ishmael's reflection, Hirsch tells us, suggests that "the principle of ownership of private property is based on raw power. Any property belongs to the party that can grab it and hold on to it." Ishmael, however, resists such logic and appeals to the "just Spirit of Equality," which points toward what Hirsch calls a dignity "inherent in the human form." Then, in a most interesting Melvillian line, Ishmael says, "Bear me out in it, thou great democratic God!"

Ishmael *says*, I wrote above, but *says* could be replaced by more hearty and moving verbs—such as Ishmael *pleas, protests, yearns, laments,* even *prays*. Nazism and its Holocaust were an assault on the values that Americans and all people hold most dear when we are at our best. But these values are as fragile as they are precious, as precarious as they are fundamental. Each and every one of us needs *home*. If we think about that fact, we will find more to unite us than to divide us. Nevertheless those realizations are so difficult to implement in our fractured world that versions of Ishmael's words about the "just Spirit of Equality"—"Bear me out in it, thou great democratic God!"—deserve to be a crucial element in post-Holocaust ethics, for they express one of those cries of the heart that make us human and keep us focused on the right ways to return home.

"*An essential task of ethics after Auschwitz,*" Didier Pollefeyt has said to me, "*is to identify religious and fundamental human experiences in different ethical traditions that transcend their cultural and historical circumstances, and that can thereby have a liberating and humanizing meaning in other times and places."* Pollefeyt wrote those words partly to criticize what he takes to be my over-reliance on narratives and stories as a basis for post-Holocaust ethics. My essay does appeal to narrative, but I do recognize that those appeals have limitations because stories may be too particular and who tells them — and what stories are told — may be provincial, too nationalistic, exclusivistic, or subject to propagandistic controls. So as I acknowledge Pollefeyt's criticism, I also embrace a version of the combination of philosophical pluralism and transcendence expressed in the passage I have quoted here from his critique.

As I have already stated, I want to draw on any and all resources that would have helped Calel Perechodnik from becoming homeless. Philosophical theories, religious convictions, educational policies, political strategies — all of those and more can be important in that regard. Stories have their part to play as well because through their particularity they communicate universal and transcendent values more accessibly and persuasively than any other form of human communication.

If I may speak personally once more, Albert Camus's novel, *The Plague,* left a lasting moral mark on me when I read it as a college student. For good or ill, it did much to inform my moral outlook precisely because there were notes of universality and even transcendence in the details of Camus's story about resistance against evil. Furthermore, hearing the story of Le Chambon did much to revitalize my Christian commitment, partly because that story helped me to rediscover how the particularity of one's commitment is essential for underscoring the universal importance of saving people from harm's way. Still further, reading Perechodnik's diary narrative, including his "Last Will and Testimony," left me with mixed feelings — sadness, anger, rage — that produce in me a version of what the Christian New Testament calls "hunger and thirst for righteousness," a disposition not restricted to one tradition but expressible in and through many traditions. These realizations and passions, I know, are not sufficient to change or even to mend the world, but without them homelessness — physical and metaphysical — will not diminish. Thus post-Holocaust ethics must keep wrestling with Calel Perchodnik's story and its disturbing question, "Am I a murderer?"

Notes

[1]Calel Perechodnik, *Am I a Murderer?: Testament of a Jewish Policeman*, ed. and trans. Frank Fox (Boulder, CO: Westview, 1996), 211.

[2]Ibid., 209.

[3]Ibid., 211.

[4]R. J. Rummel, *Death by Government* (New Brunswick, NJ: Transaction Publishers, 1997), 1, 9. *Democide* is the term Rummel coined to refer to genocide and government mass murder. If one adds together the human cost of democide and war, he concludes, "Power has killed over 203 million people in this [twentieth] century" (13).

POSTSCRIPT

Post-Holocaust Ethics and the Future

John K. Roth

Printed on one of this book's first pages, a statement by Holocaust survivor Elie Wiesel is its governing epigraph. Asserting that "the Holocaust demands interrogation and calls everything into question," Wiesel adds that "traditional ideas and acquired values, philosophical systems and social theories—all must be revised in the shadow of Birkenau." Noting that "moralists, theologians and scholars," among others, are reflecting on the Holocaust with those principles in mind, he observes that "not to do so would mean to live a lie."[1] The perspectives, critiques, and responses in this book have followed Wiesel's lead. The contributors hope that these reflections will help their readers to do the same.

With that hope in mind, this postscript sums up the book's findings. It does so by providing two sets of six statements—one statement, both times, from each contributor. Individually and, more important, collectively, these statements respond to the following questions: What does this book say about the Holocaust? What does this book say about ethics after Auschwitz?

Reflecting the book's dialogue format, this summary's point is not that it should speak for every reader. Other summaries, emphasizing different points, are not only possible but needed. Meanwhile the points highlighted here, or perhaps in any similar summary, achieve their greatest depth not in isolated individuality but in relationship to each other. Their interplay modifies, corrects, and amplifies the individual statements and thereby emphasizes an interdependence that makes these themes, questions, and outlooks more sensitive and keeps them open for further inquiry.

What Does This Book Say about the Holocaust?

Leonard Grob: The Western philosophic tradition, when confronted by the Holocaust, has not merely been found wanting of a radical ethical analysis; in its totalizing intent, it has also provided the fertile ground upon which a holocaust can more easily take shape. Unless or until philosophy radically rethinks its vocation, it will neither prove able to respond to the Nazi Holocaust of the past, nor will it prove to be a force helping to combat the threat of potential holocausts in the future.

Peter Haas: The Nazis were simply able to convince Germans that killing Jews and other racial enemies was the most scientific, and therefore the most advanced, strategy available to them to solve their problems. At a time when other more conventional policies were failing and when people were disposed to place great store in science and technology, these features of the Nazi ethic proved irresistible to many, especially among the intelligentsia. All that was necessary was to suppress any outside source of critique.

David Hirsch: The Nazis wanted to uproot two thousand years of Judeo-Christian ethics, and to achieve this goal they believed that they first had to exterminate the people who introduced the "Thou shalt nots" into Western culture. It does not matter that the Jews of the 1930s and 1940s were not necessarily identical with the Israelites who first gave the world the "Thou shalt nots." The point is that the Nazis believed it, and therefore launched a campaign to exterminate the carriers of the virus of Judeo-Christianity. What is truly remarkable is that masses of European Christians joined in the campaign.

David Patterson: From the time of Cain, the murder of God has been undertaken through the murder of people. Rashi, the great eleventh-century commentator on Torah and Talmud, writes, "Whoever attacks Israel is as though he attacks the Holy One." This connection between God and Israel and the assault on both is attested to in many Holocaust diaries, including the *Vittel Diary* of Yitzhak Katzenelson, the Warsaw ghetto diary kept by Emmanuel Ringelblum, and the chronicle of the Vilna ghetto recorded by Zelig

Kalmanovitch. In these and many other testimonies we discover the uniqueness of the Holocaust: it is an attack not only on human beings but on the Holy One who sanctifies humanity. This singularity manifests itself in the calculated destruction not only of Jewish bodies but of Jewish souls and Jewish prayers, of Jewish texts and traditions, of synagogues and cemeteries. It manifests itself in a murder of God that follows in the wake of Nietzsche's assertion that God is dead.

Didier Pollefeyt: Because it had no respect for alterity, and it required the eradication of everything that could not be reduced to the closed system with its extreme good-evil polarities, Nazism was a politics without an ethic. Misappropriating ethics and God for the ideological ends of its own ("good") group, Nazism was an idolatrous effort that radicalized itself and eliminated everything that did not conform.

John Roth: The Holocaust's evil appears to be so overwhelming that it forms an ultimate refutation of moral relativism. No one, it seems, could encounter Auschwitz and deny that there is a fundamental and objective difference between right and wrong. Nevertheless, the "final solution" paradoxically calls into question the practical status of moral norms. As Richard Rubenstein assesses the situation, and the cases of Calel Perechodnik and Jean Améry come to mind as well, the Holocaust suggests that "there are absolutely no limits to the degradation and assault the managers and technicians of violence can inflict upon men and women who lack the power of effective resistance."

What Does This Book Say about Ethics after Auschwitz?

Leonard Grob: Philosophical reflection, like all activity of the mind, must be carried out before the face of the Other. That is to say, reflection must, at its core, be ethical: it must never forget that the Other is inviolable. Ethics, we recall, is an optics. The way we must "see" in philosophy—indeed, in all modes of thought—is to obey the injunction: "Thou shalt not kill," where "killing" refers to any form of violation of another.

Peter Haas: What happened in Nazi Germany stands as a stark historical example of what can happen when the human, and thus inherently flawed, intellectual enterprise of science is allowed to become the unchallenged and unchallengeable source of human values.

David Hirsch: Would the Holocaust not have been rendered impossible if all Christians had done nothing more than obey the commandments they had, in theory, already accepted as Christians: "Thou shalt not kill....Thou shalt not steal....Thou shalt not covet thy neighbor's house,...nor any thing that is thy neighbor's"?

David Patterson: When faced with evil, the questions that confront us are not "Do moral norms have practical value?" or "Can moral norms be freely violated?" Rather, the questions are "Is it wrong?" and "What must be done?" For "to know God," Levinas has shown, "is to know what must be done," regardless of the outcome of our action. That is why to know God is to know the Good. And to know the Good is to know the way home.

Didier Pollefeyt: The basic structure of ethics after Auschwitz should be openness to the vulnerability of the other. This criterion can be an efficacious touchstone for testing every ethical system after Auschwitz: Is it open for (positive) alterity, growth, discussion, questioning, hesitation, falsification, new challenges, for the vulnerability of the weakest?

John Roth: The Nazis sought a "final solution," the very thing that self-corrective inquiry rejects and must actively oppose because solutions of that kind are antithetical to the spirit of inquiry. Practiced in its most profoundly rational way, inquiry is a deeply moral act, one of the most important for post-Holocaust ethics to defend, teach, and respect. Such inquiry calls us to account and saves us from destructive arrogance. It does so by asking: Is our judgment true? Are our policies good? How do we know? Can we find better ways to act?

* * *

On October 9, 1943, Calel Perechodnik, the former Jewish ghetto policeman, made one of the final entries in his diary. "The course of my family's downfall," he wrote, "nears its end." Yet "only two months ago," he recalled, "it seemed to me that maybe, God be willing, good people would help and the Perechodniks would somehow 'smuggle' themselves through life."

Perechodnik wondered in October how he could have held that hope. He responded by noting that two months earlier his father—whose "first-rate Aryan appearance" included legal registration and a ration card—was still alive and able to help him and his mother, who were "hidden in a good place." Rumor indicated, moreover, that "the war must be reaching an end." There were "reasons, then, to be in good spirits." In October, however, Perechodnik's pen moved on to say that "it seems this is a delusion."[2] As Perechodnik wrote in October 1943, his father was dead and his own death was closer than Nazi Germany's defeat. He was right—his August reasons for good spirits were a delusion.

Calel Perechodnik's post-Holocaust readers surely know that neither he nor his reasons ought to have suffered that fate. That fact points to the note on which this book should end and with which ethics after Auschwitz should always begin. If we want to know whether we are on the right or wrong track, individually or collectively, we can hold ourselves responsible by asking: Would action like mine, would policies like ours, have tended to help or harm the Holocaust's victims? For post-Holocaust ethics and the future, helping or harming those most in need measures the difference between right and wrong.

Notes

[1]See Elie Wiesel's foreword to Harry James Cargas, *Shadows of Auschwitz: A Christian Response to the Holocaust* (New York, Crossroad, 1990), ix.

[2]Calel Perechodnik, *Am I a Murderer?: Testament of a Jewish Ghetto Policeman*, trans. John Fox (Boulder, CO: Westview Press, 1996), 195.

Select Bibliography

Abrahamson, Irving, ed. *Against Silence: The Voice and Vision of Elie Wiesel*. 3 vols. New York: Holocaust Library, 1985.

Améry, Jean. *At the Mind's Limits: Contemplations by a Survivor on Auschwitz and Its Realities*. Translated by Sidney Rosenfeld and Stella P. Rosenfeld. New York: Schocken, 1986.

Arendt, Hannah. *Eichmann in Jerusalem: A Report on the Banality of Evil*. New York: Penguin Books, 1983.

_____. *The Life of the Mind*. London: Secker and Warburg, 1978.

Bauer, Yehuda. *A History of the Holocaust*. New York: Franklin Watts, 1982.

_____. et al., eds. *Remembering for the Future*. Oxford: Pergamon Press, 1988.

Bauman, Zygmunt. *Modernity and the Holocaust*. Ithaca, NY: Cornell University Press, 1989.

Bayle, F. *Psychologie et éthique du national-socialisme: Etudes anthropologiques des dirigeants S. S.* Paris: Presse Universitaire de France, 1953.

Berenbaum, Michael, ed. *Witness to the Holocaust*. New York: HarperCollins, 1997.

Berenbaum, Michael. *The World Must Know: The History of the Holocaust as Told in the United States Holocaust Memorial Museum*. Boston: Little, Brown, 1993.

Bernasconi, Robert, and David Wood, eds. *The Provocation of Levinas: Rethinking the Other*. London: Routledge, 1988.

Bernstein, Richard J. *Hannah Arendt and the Jewish Question*. Cambridge: MIT Press, 1996.

Bezwinska, Jadwiga, and Danuta Czech, eds. *KL Auschwitz as Seen by the SS*. New York: H. Fertig, 1972.

Blanchot, M., T. Delhomme, and J. Derrida. *Textes pour Emmanuel Levinas*. Paris: Place, 1980.

Bohr, Niels. *Atomic Theory and the Description of Nature*. Cambridge: Cambridge University Press, 1934.

Borowski, Tadeusz. *This Way for the Gas, Ladies and Gentlemen*. Translated by Barbara Vedder. New York: Penguin Books, 1977.

Bourdieu, Pierre. *The Political Ontology of Martin Heidegger*. Translated by Peter Collier. Stanford, CA: Stanford University Press, 1991.

Brietman, Richard. *The Architect of Genocide: Himmler and the Final Solution*. Hanover, NH: Brandeis University Press, 1991.

Browning, Christopher. *Fateful Months*. New York: Holmes and Meier, 1985.

Buber, Martin. *Between Man and Man*. Translated by Ronald Gregor Smith. New York: Macmillan, 1965.

Bull, H., ed. *The Challenge of the Third Reich*. Oxford: Clarendon Press, 1986.

Burggraeve, Roger. *From Self-development to Solidarity: An Ethical Reading of Human Desire in Its Socio-Political Relevance According to Emmanuel Levinas*. Leuven: Peeters, 1985.

Burggraeve, Roger, and Didier Pollefeyt. *Ethiek als intimiteit met God?: Christelijke ethiek in gesprek met joodse denkers*. Kampen: Kok, 1998.

Camus, Albert. *The Plague*. Translated by Gilbert Stuart. New York: Vintage Books, 1991.

Cargas, Harry James. *Shadows of Auschwitz: A Christian Response to the Holocaust*. New York: Crossroad, 1990.

Cassirer, Ernst. *Kant's Life and Thought*. Translated by James Haden. New Haven: Yale University Press, 1981.

Cohen, E. A. *Human Behavior in the Concentration Camp*. Translated by H. M. Braaksma. London: Free Association Books, 1988.

Cohen, Richard A., ed. *Face to Face with Levinas*. Albany: SUNY Press, 1986.

Colijn, G. J., and Marcia L. Littell, eds. *Confronting the Holocaust: A Mandate for the 21st Century?* Lanham, MD.: University Press of America, 1997.

Crollius, A. R., ed. *Good and Evil after Auschwitz: Ethical Implications for Today*. Rome: Gregorian University Press, 1998.

Dagerman, S. *Duitse herfst: Een naaoorlogse reportage.* Translated by K. Woudstra. Amsterdam: Meulenhoff, 1985.

Derrida, Jacques. *De l'esprit.* Paris: Éditions Galilee, 1987.

Donat, Alexander. *The Holocaust Kingdom.* New York: Holocaust Library, 1978.

Dribben, Judith. *And Some Shall Live.* Jerusalem: Keter Books, 1969.

Dwork, Deborah, and Robert Jan van Pelt. *Auschwitz: 1270 to the Present.* New York: W. W. Norton, 1996.

Ehrenburg, Ilya, and Vasily Grossman, eds. *The Black Book.* Translated by John Glad and James S. Levine. New York: Holocaust Library, 1981.

Ettinger, Elzbieta. *Hannah Arendt/Martin Heidegger.* New Haven: Yale University Press, 1995.

Fackenheim, Emil. *Encounters between Judaism and Modern Philosophy.* New York: Basic Books, 1993.

_____. *The Jewish Return into History.* New York: Schocken, 1978.

_____. *To Mend the World: Foundations of Future Jewish Thought.* New York: Schocken, 1982.

_____. *What Is Judaism?* New York: Macmillan, 1987.

Fasching, Darrell J. *The Ethical Challenge of Auschwitz and Hiroshima: Apocalypse or Utopia?* Albany: SUNY Press, 1993.

_____. *Narrative Theology after Auschwitz: From Alienation to Ethics.* Philadelphia: Fortress Press, 1992.

Fleck, Ludwig. *Genesis and Development of a Scientific Fact.* Edited by Thaddeus Trenn and Robert Merton. Chicago: University of Chicago Press, 1979.

Friedman, Carl. *Nightfather.* Translated by Arnold and Erica Pomerans. New York: Persea Books, 1994.

Friedman, Philip. *Roads to Extinction.* New York: Jewish Publication Society, 1980.

Frischhaurer, W. *Himmler: The Evil Genius of the Third Reich.* Boston: Beacon Press, 1953.

Furet, François., ed. *L'allemagne Nazie et le génocide juif.* Paris: Gallimard, 1985.

Ginsburgh, Yitzchak. *The Alef-Beit.* Northvale, NJ: Aronson, 1991.

Goldhagen, Daniel. *Hitler's Willing Executioners: Ordinary Germans and the Holocaust.* New York: Knopf, 1996.

Gutman, Yisrael, and Michael Berenbaum, eds. *Anatomy of the Auschwitz Death Camp.* Washington, DC: United States Holocaust Memorial Museum and Bloomington: Indiana University Press, 1994.

Haas, Peter J. *Morality after Auschwitz: The Radical Challenge of the Nazi Ethic.* Philadelphia: Fortress Press, 1988.

Hallie, Philip P. *Lest Innocent Blood Be Shed: The Story of the Village of Le Chambon and How Goodness Happened There.* New York: Harper and Row, 1979.

Hand, Sean, ed. *The Levinas Reader.* Oxford: Basil Blackwell, 1989.

Hauerwas, Stanley, R. Bondi, and David B. Burrell. *Truthfulness and Tragedy: Further Investigations in Christian Ethics.* Notre Dame, IN: University of Notre Dame Press, 1977.

Hayes, Peter. *Industry and Ideology: I. G. Farben in the Nazi Era.* Cambridge: Cambridge University Press, 1993.

_____., ed. *Lessons and Legacies: The Meaning of the Holocaust in a Changing World.* Evanston, IL: Northwestern University Press, 1991.

Hegel, G. W. F. *Early Theological Writings.* Translated by T. M. Knox. Chicago: University of Chicago Press, 1948.

_____. *The Life of Jesus* in *Three Essays, 1793-1795.* Translated by Peter Fuss and John Dobbins. Notre Dame, IN: University of Notre Dame Press, 1984.

Heidegger, Martin. *Introduction to Metaphysics.* Translated by R. Mannheim. New York: Doubleday, 1961.

_____. *Kant and the Problem of Metaphysics.* Translated by J. S. Churchill. Bloomington: Indiana University Press, 1962.

_____. *Nietzsche.* Translated by David Krell. San Francisco: Harper, 1979.

_____. *Sein und Zeit.* Tübingen: Max Niemeyer, 1963.

_____. *Vom Wesen des Grundes.* Frankfurt am Main: Klosterman, 1965.

Herzberg, Abel. *Kroniek der jodenvervolgingen.* Amsterdam: Meulenhoff, 1978.

Hilberg, Raul. *The Destruction of the European Jews.* Revised and definitive edition. 3 vols. New York: Holmes and Meier, 1985.

Hirsch, David H. *The Deconstruction of Literature: Criticism after*

Auschwitz. Hanover, NH: University Press of New England, 1991.

Hirschfeld, G., and L. Kettemacker, eds. *Der "Führerstaat": Mythos und Realität. Studien zur Struktur und Politik des Dritten Reiches*. Stuttgart: Klett-Cotta, 1981.

Höhne, Heinz. *The Order of the Death's Head: The Story of Hitler's SS*. Translated by Richard Barry. New York: Ballantine Books, 1971.

Huberband, Shimon. *Kiddush Hashem*. Translated by D. E. Fishman. Hoboken, NJ: Ktav, 1987.

Jankélévitch, Vladimir. *L'impréscriptible: Pardonner? Dans l'honneur et la dignité*. Paris: Seuil, 1986.

Jonas, Hans. *The Phenomenon of Life*. New York: Harper and Row, 1966.

Kafka, Franz. *The Judgment and In the Penal Colony*. London: Penguin Books, 1995.

Kahane, David. *Lvov Ghetto Diary*. Translated by J. Michalowicz. Amherst: University of Massachusetts Press, 1990.

Kahler, Erich. *The Tower and the Abyss*. New York: George Braziller, 1957.

Kant, Immanuel. *The Conflict of the Faculties*. Translated by Mary J. Gregor. New York: Abaris, 1979.

_____. *Critique of Practical Reason*. Translated by Lewis White Beck. New York: Macmillan, 1985.

_____. *Critique of Pure Reason*. 2d ed. Translated by Norman Kemp Smith. New York: The Modern Library, 1965.

_____. *Groundwork of the Metaphysic of Morals*. Translated by H. J. Paton. New York: Harper and Row, 1964.

Kaplan, Chaim. *The Warsaw Diary of Chaim A. Kaplan*. Translated by A. I. Katsh. New York: Collier, 1973.

Katz, F. E. *Ordinary People and Extraordinary Evil*. Albany: SUNY Press, 1993.

Katznelson, Yitzhak. *Vittel Diary*. Translated by Myer Cohen. Tel Aviv: Hakibbutz Hameuchad, 1972.

Klieger, B. *Le chemin que nous avons fait*. Translated by Noah. Brussels: Editions Beka, 1947.

Kren, George M., and M. Rappoport. *The Holocaust and the Crisis of Human Behavior*. New York: Holmes and Meier, 1980.

Kuhn, Thomas. *The Structure of Scientific Revolutions*. Chicago: University of Chicago Press, 1970.

Küng, Hans. *Judaism*. London: SCM, 1992.

Lacoue-Labarthe, Philippe. *La Fiction du politique*. Paris: Christian Bourgeois, 1987.

Langbein, Herman. *Hommes et femmes à Auschwitz*. Paris: Fayard, 1975.

Langer, Lawrence L. *Holocaust Testimonies: The Ruins of Memory*. New Haven: Yale University Press, 1991.

Lanzmann, Claude. *Shoah: An Oral History of the Holocaust*. New York: Pantheon, 1985.

Levi, Primo. *The Drowned and the Saved*. Translated by Raymond Rosenthal. New York: Vintage Books, 1989.

_____. *Survival in Auschwitz: The Nazi Assault on Humanity*. Translated by Stuart Woolf. New York: Collier, 1976.

Levinas, Emmanuel. *Collected Philosophical Papers*. Translated by Alphonso Lingis. Dordrecht: Martinus Nijhoff, 1987.

_____. *De l'existence à l'existant*. Paris: Fontaine, 1947.

_____. *Difficult Freedom: Essays on Judaism*. Translated by Sean Hand. Baltimore: Johns Hopkins University Press, 1990.

_____. *Ethics and Infinity: Conversations with Philippe Nemo*. Translated by Richard A. Cohen. Pittsburgh: Duquesne University Press, 1985.

_____. *Nine Talmudic Readings*. Translated by Annette Aronowicz. Bloomington: Indiana University Press, 1990.

_____. *Noms propres*. Montpellier: Fata Morgana, 1976.

_____. *Time and the Other*. Translated by Richard A. Cohen. Pittsburgh: Duquesne University Press, 1987.

_____. *Totality and Infinity: An Essay on Exteriority*. Translated by Alphonso Lingis. Pittsburgh: Duquesne University Press, 1969.

_____. *Transcendance et Intelligibilité, suivi d'un entretien*. Geneva: Labor et Fides, 1984.

Littell, Marcia L., E. Geldbach, and G. J. Colijn, eds. *The Holocaust: Remembering for the Future II*. Stamford, CT: Vista InterMedia Corporation, 1996.

Lyotard, Jean-François. *Heidegger and "the jews"*. Translated by A. Michel and M. S. Roberts. Minneapolis: University of Minnesota Press, 1990.

Matthiessen, F. O. *American Renaissance*. New York: Oxford University Press, 1941.

Milchman, Alan, and Alan Rosenberg, eds. *Martin Heidegger and the Holocaust*. Atlantic Highlands, NJ: Humanities Press, 1996.

Neske, Gunther, and Emil Kettering, eds. *Martin Heidegger and National Socialism*. Translated by Lisa Harries. New York: Paragon House, 1990.

Newman, Louis I., ed. and trans. *The Hasidic Anthology*. New York: Schocken, 1963.

Nietzsche, Friedrich. *Thus Spoke Zarathustra*. Translated by Walter Kaufmann. New York: Penguin Books, 1978.

Nyiszli, Miklos. *Auschwitz: A Doctor's Eyewitness Account*. Translated by Tibere Kramer and Richard Seaver. New York: Arcade Publishing, 1986.

Ofstad, Harald. *Our Contempt for Weakness: Nazi Norms and Values— and Our Own*. Gothenburg: Almquist and Wiksell, 1989.

Perechodnik, Calel. *Am I a Murderer?: Testament of a Jewish Policeman*. Edited and translated by Frank Fox. Boulder, CO: Westview, 1996.

Poirié, François. *Emmanuel Levinas: Qui êtes-vous?* Lyon: La Manifacture, 1986.

Quinn, Patrick F. *The French Face of Edgar Poe*. Carbondale: Southern Illinois University Press, 1957

Rashi. *Commentary on the Torah*. Translated by M. Rosenbaum and A. M. Silverman. Jerusalem: Silverman Family, 1972.

Rebhun, Joseph. *Crisis of Morality and Reaction to the Holocaust*. Claremont, CA: OR Publishing, 1998.

Ricoeur, Paul. *Philosophie de la volonté: Finitude et culpabilité I: L'homme faillible*. Paris: Aubier-Montaigne, 1960.

Ringelblum, Emmanuel. *Notes from the Warsaw Ghetto*. Edited and translated by Jacob Sloan. New York: Schocken, 1974.

Rittner, Carol, and John K. Roth, eds., *Different Voices: Women and the Holocaust*. New York: Paragon House, 1993.

Rockmore, Tom. *On Heidegger's Nazism and Philosophy*. Berkeley: University of California Press, 1992.

Rockmore, Tom, and Joseph Margolis, eds. *The Heidegger Case: On Philosophy and Politics*. Philadelphia: Temple University Press, 1992.

Rose, Paul Lawrence. *German Question/Jewish Question*. Princeton: Princeton University Press, 1990.

Rosenbaum, Alan S., ed. *Is the Holocaust Unique?: Perspectives on Comparative Genocide*. Boulder, CO: Westview, 1996.

Rosenbaum, Ron. *Explaining Hitler: The Search for the Origins of His Evil*. New York: Random House, 1998.

Rosenberg, Alan, and Gerald E. Myers, eds. *Echoes from the Holocaust: Philosophical Reflections on a Dark Time*. Philadelphia: Temple University Press, 1988.

Rosenblum, Nancy L., ed. *Liberalism and the Moral Life*. Cambridge: Harvard University Press, 1989.

Roth, John K., and Michael Berenbaum, eds. *Holocaust: Religious and Philosophical Implications*. New York: Paragon House, 1989.

Rubenstein, Richard L. *After Auschwitz: History, Theology, and Contemporary Judaism*. 2d ed. Baltimore: Johns Hopkins University Press, 1992.

_____. *The Cunning of History: The Holocaust and the American Future*. New York: Harper and Row, 1987.

Rubenstein, Richard L., and John K. Roth. *Approaches to Auschwitz: The Holocaust and Its Legacy*. Atlanta: John Knox Press, 1987.

Rummel, R. J. *Death by Government*. New Brunswick, NJ: Transaction Publishers, 1997.

Sartre, Jean-Paul. *Being and Nothingness*. Translated by Hazel Barnes. New York: Pocket Books, 1956.

Schilpp, Paul A. *Albert Einstein: Philosopher-Scientist*. New York: Harper and Row, 1959.

Schleunes, Karl A. *The Twisted Road to Auschwitz: Nazi Policy toward German Jews 1933-1939*. Champaign: University of Illinois Press, 1970.

Semprun, Jorge. *Literature or Life*. Translated by Linda Coverdale. New York: Penguin Books, 1998.

Sluga, Hans. *Heidegger's Crisis*. Cambridge: Harvard University Press, 1993.

Smiga, George. *Pain and Polemic: Anti-Judaism in the Gospels*. New York: Paulist Press, 1992.

Staub, Ervin. *The Roots of Evil: The Origins of Genocide and Other Group Violence*. Cambridge: Cambridge University Press, 1989.

Steiner, George. *In Bluebeard's Castle: Some Notes toward a Redefinition of Culture*. London: Faber and Faber, 1971.

Tarrow, Susan, ed. *Reason and Light: Essays on Primo Levi*. Ithaca, NY: Cornell University Press, 1990.

Todorov, Tzvetan. *Facing the Extreme*. New York: Henry Holt, 1995.

Von der Dunk, H. W. *Voorbij de verboden drempel: De Shoah in ons geschiedbeeld*. Amsterdam: Prometheus, 1991.

Wiesel, Elie. *Legends of Our Time*. New York: Avon, 1968.

_____. *Night*. Translated by Stella Rodway. New York: Bantam, 1986.

_____. *One Generation After*. Translated by Lily Edelman. New York: Random House, 1970.

Wolin, Richard. *The Politics of Being*. New York: Columbia University Press, 1990.

Wundt, Max. *Deutsche Weltanschauung*. Munich: J. F. Lehmans, 1926.

Wyschogrod, Edith. *Spirit in Ashes*. New Haven: Yale University Press, 1985.

Zylberberg, Michael. *A Warsaw Diary*. Translated by M. Zylberberg. London: Valentine, Mitchell, 1969.

Index